Which Evidence-Based Practice Should I Use?

A Social Worker's Handbook for Decision Making

WHICH EVIDENCE-BASED PRACTICE SHOULD I USE?

A Social Worker's Handbook for Decision Making

Rose Wong

cognella®

SAN DIEGO

Bassim Hamadeh, CEO and Publisher
Amy Smith, Senior Project Editor
Alia Bales, Production Editor
Emely Villavicencio, Senior Graphic Designer
Stephanie Kohl, Licensing Coordinator
Kim Scott, Interior Designer
Natalie Piccotti, Director of Marketing
Kassie Graves, Senior Vice President of Editorial
Jamie Giganti, Director of Academic Publishing

Cover Image: Copyright © 2019 iStockphoto LP/Govindanmarudhai.

Printed in the United States of America.

3970 Sorrento Valley Blvd., Ste. 500, San Diego, CA 92121

BRIEF CONTENTS

DETAILED CONTENTS

PREFACE

This book is intended to teach the original evidence-based practice (EBP) model to social work and mental health students and practitioners. The EBP model, originating in the field of medicine, is a framework that guides the professional in the selection of evidence-based practices for individual clients. It is a process framework in which the practitioner obtains and integrates information from three components—*the best available evidence*; *clinical expertise*; and *the client's characteristics*, *values*, *and preferences*—to support the choice of an intervention for a client. Social work educators have long recognized the model's usefulness for advancing the profession and argued for the model's consistency with social work values and ethics, yet there has not been a significant attempt to operationalize the teaching of this model.

As a practitioner and teacher, I agree that the model is useful and that it can be consistent with social work values and ethics if it is applied with a critical frame of mind. Hence, I aim to teach students and practitioners how to apply the model from a critical stance—one that pursues both what is helpful to clients and a relationship with research that is deliberate and intentional. This critical stance is needed because much of the evidence base has not been generated with the values or viewpoints of minority and vulnerable populations in mind. This stance is also needed because, at the same time, there is a wealth of evidence from the fields of social and behavioral intervention science that *can be* very beneficial to individuals and communities from minority and vulnerable backgrounds, if the practices can be chosen and applied with clinical expertise and the needs and views of the client in the forefront.

In this handbook, I teach students how to access the intervention literature, how to consume it critically, what the research endeavor represents and who it excludes, how to engage with and rely on the expertise of our own practitioner community, how to carefully consider the client's views and wishes, what it means to be culturally responsive in choosing research-based practices, and, finally, how to think about and give value to participatory and emic research and other community-based sources of knowledge. I teach many of these pieces by borrowing from scholars and clinical experts, whom I acknowledge. I employ problem-based learning and case method approaches, which respectively emphasize developing autonomous information-gathering and decision-making processes and resolving real-life case dilemmas within their contextual nuances. Using these didactic approaches, this handbook guides the student to learn the criteria, skills, and tools for considering each component and to apply them to select an EBP for a real client.

This book comes out of teaching micro practice and research courses to master of social work (MSW) students in public and private universities in northern California, where there is strong population diversity. Arriving at my first faculty position, I was asked to teach students how to find and choose EBPs for a real client. This is the book's origin, with added inspiration from my background in using community-based and emic research approaches to develop mental health outreach and assessment tools for the Chinese American immigrant community.

How to Use This Book

This handbook, applying a case method approach, accompanies the student through the process of choosing an EBP for a real client and writing a case paper about the client that articulates the student's steps and reasoning. In support of this assignment, each chapter provides knowledge and skills that support completing one or more sections of the case paper. By the end of seven chapters, the student has assimilated the three components of the EBP model and completed a full case paper. The appendices contain the full case paper instructions and two full sample papers, for clients Laura and Eddie.

Within each chapter is an ordered mix of *Brief Lectures*, *Discussions*, *Activities*, and *Case Studies*. These should also be covered sequentially, because each component solidifies or *builds* on the previous. At the end of the chapters are *Case Paper Tasks*. A *case paper task* entails doing the work related to and writing a section of the case paper, such as gathering and analyzing needed information and writing about it. To illustrate each case paper task, the papers on Laura and Eddie are broken down and presented across the chapters, with examples of weaker and stronger content and writing for each task.

Brief Lectures provide conceptual frameworks and knowledge relevant to applying each of the three components of decision-making from a critical standpoint. Within brief lectures, *Reflection Questions* are provided for students' self-reflection as they read or for discussions in the classroom. Answers are not provided. *Critical Thinking* markers alert students to pay attention to important issues as they learn more or begin to apply their knowledge. *Tips* give students easy ways to recognize something when they apply the knowledge or skill in the future. *Quick Activities* entail a variety of brief tasks that assist in learning the idea being presented. *Notes* generally provide a peripheral or related point of information.

Discussions consist of questions asked to students according to a Socratic or dialogic learning approach. Students should jot down their answers and explanations and share their answers in class, or the questions can be used entirely for small and large group discussions in the classroom. How students have answered these discussion questions in the past are found in the *Answers* section at the end of each chapter. The answers demonstrate a process of reasoning. Students should resist glancing at the answers until they have thought through the questions. They should also read the answers critically, noting which they agree or disagree with and why.

Activities are varied. They range from answering true/false questions to conducting a database search. Answers are provided either within the activity or in the *Answers* section at the end of each chapter.

Case Studies for Laura and Eddie are introduced in Chapter 1. The cases are discussed across the seven chapters to illustrate how to complete and write each section of the case paper.

Evidence-Based Practice in Social Work
How to Decide What to Use

I n this chapter, we will discuss what is evidence-based practice (EBP) and its role in social work. After considering whether and how EBP could be useful for social work, we will design a decision-making model for choosing suitable interventions from the research literature for our clients. We will also discuss two cases and begin to apply the model.

> ## DISCUSSION 1.1 What Is Evidence-Based Practice?

Jot down at least several ideas for each question below.

1. What is "evidence-based" practice?
2. What should it be for it to be useful to your work as a social worker?
3. What are your requirements to determine whether what researchers produce is useful to you?

See how students answered on page 26.

DISCUSSION 1.2 How Do You Decide What to Use?

Jot down at least several ideas for each question below.

1. If an intervention has good evidence of its effectiveness, does that always mean you can use it with your client? How do you decide?
2. What are the reasons not to use an EBP for a particular client?
3. What are your implied values at play for each of these reasons?

See how students answered on page 30.

★ **ACTIVITY 1.1 Create Your Own Decision-Making Model**

Instructions

1. Create a model for how a social worker can decide whether to use interventions presented in the research literature.

   ·

   TIP Consider students' comments from Discussion 1.2. Group the ideas into main factors that you would want to consider and gather information on when deciding which of the EBPs found in the literature to select for a specific client.

   ·

2. Draw a diagram of your model.
3. Does your model capture fellow students' and your own ideas and requirements?

   Stop! Do not move on until you've done the above!

4. View the original EBP model in Figure 1.1. Compare it with your model. How do the models compare?

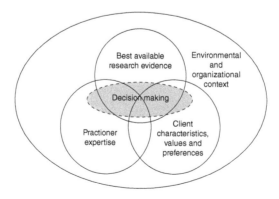

FIGURE 1.1 Original Evidence-Based Practice Model

BRIEF LECTURE 1.1

The Original EBP Model

Evidence-based practice (EBP) is a process of mutual decision-making between clinician and client that aims to select an intervention by considering three areas of information: (1) best research evidence, (2) clinical expertise, and (3) client characteristics, culture, and preferences. Referred to as the "original EBP model," this framework, first introduced in the field of medicine (Sackett et al., 1997), has been promoted in other human service fields, from psychology and education to criminal justice. Figure 1.1 shows the original EBP model. The sourcebook for EBP, *Evidence-Based Medicine (EBM): How to Practice and Teach EBM?* (Sackett et al., 1997; Straus et al., 2010; Straus et al., 2018), provides the following definition:

> Evidence-based medicine (EBM) requires the integration of the best research evidence with our clinical expertise and our patient's unique values and circumstances. ... When these three elements are integrated, clinicians and patients form a diagnostic and therapeutic alliance which optimizes clinical outcomes and quality of life. (Straus et al., 2010, p. 1)

The sourcebook further explains each component of information:

1. By **best research evidence** we mean clinically relevant research, sometimes from the basic sciences of medicine, but especially from patient-centered clinical research into ... the efficacy and safety of therapeutic, rehabilitative and preventive strategies.
2. By **clinical expertise** we mean the ability to use our clinical skills and past experience to rapidly identify each patient's unique health state and diagnosis, his or her individual risks and benefits of potential interventions/exposures/diagnostic tests, and his or her personal values and expectations. Moreover, clinical expertise is required to integrate evidence with patient values and circumstances.
3. By **patient values** we mean the unique preferences, concerns, and expectations that each patient brings to a clinical encounter and that must be integrated into shared clinical decisions if they are to serve the patient. (Straus et al., 2018, p. 1)

In clinical psychology, the American Psychological Association (APA) introduced to the interpretation of the EBP model an emphasis on cultural sensitivity, referring to EBP as "the integration of the best available research with clinical expertise in the context of patient characteristics, culture and preferences" (APA Presidential Task Force on Evidence-Based Practice, 2006, p. 273). Psychologists

Derald Wing Sue and David Sue (2013), pushing this emphasis further, placed the "individual" aspect, with culture a part of this, as the starting point of EBP altogether and the "individualizing of therapy" as its endpoint:

> The search for the "best research evidence" *begins* with a comprehensive understanding of the client's background and problem and goes on to consider which therapeutic approach is most likely to provide the best outcome. In other words, the selection of intervention occurs *only after* individual characteristics, such as cultural background and values and preferences, are assessed. This allows for the individualizing of therapy with strong consideration given to client background and characteristics. (p. 332, emphasis in original)

According to this view of EBP, using one's *clinical expertise* requires conducting a comprehensive and culturally sensitive assessment of the client and selecting and adapting treatments in a manner that is respectful of the client's worldview, values, and preferences. Clinical expertise also involves working collaboratively with the client to develop goals and treatment strategies that are mutually agreeable. The clinician's role is thus to gather information on *client characteristics, culture, and preferences*, which include age and life stage, sociocultural factors (e.g., gender, sexual orientation, ethnicity, disability), environmental stressors (e.g., unemployment, racism, recent life events), and personal goals of treatment and treatment preferences. With regard to the *best research evidence*, Sue and Sue (2013) emphasize the application of a broad definition of evidence—specifically, that evidence should come not only from randomized controlled trials but also interventions delivered in naturalistic settings, qualitative studies, and systematic case studies, among other research designs.

• •

NOTE   In this book, the term EBP is used to refer to both the original decision-making model, described in this brief lecture, and to the evidence-based interventions or treatments themselves.

• •

Reflection Questions

1. Does the original EBP model foresee the needs of ethnic minorities and other diverse populations? If so, how does it do so? What steps in decision-making could help to ensure this?
2. Will social work practitioners need to obtain outside consultation and training on the treatments available in the research literature in order to select interventions for specific clients? What kinds of consultation and training may be useful?

ACTIVITY 1.2 What Are Our Ethical Responsibilities?

Instructions

1. Obtain a list of ethical standards from the NASW *Code of Ethics*. You can view the *Code of Ethics* online at https://www.socialworkers.org/About/Ethics/Code-of-Ethics/Code-of-Ethics-English.
2. Mark all of the ethical principles that are relevant to EBP decision-making. For each principle you identify, explain how it is relevant.
3. Is the ethical standard in line with your own values? Why or why not?
4. Do you see any problems with having predefined ethical principles and standards that social workers must always apply strictly?

See how students answered step 2 on page 34.

BRIEF LECTURE 1.2

EBP in Social Work: History and Controversy

The EBP movement is the latest attempt to improve the integration of practice and research. The debate over the role of research in social work dates back to the 1960s and early 1970s, when early studies on social casework revealed its unclear effectiveness, spurring debate on the usefulness of available findings and whether practice decisions should be based on research (Fischer, 1973). Fischer, in a seminal review of social casework in 1973, nevertheless had already presumed an inseparable linkage of professional competencies with science: "The issue of effectiveness of practice always must be of paramount concern to the profession and cannot be brushed aside ... the professional values of commitment to the scientific method and the desire to promote capably the wellbeing of our clients demands such a stance" (p. 5). He noted, however, the importance of professional judgment in handling the uncertainties inherent in scientific knowledge: "But caseworkers do have to act, even in the face of such discouraging evidence ... Making judgments in the face of uncertainty of knowledge has long been a characteristic of most of the helping professions" (p. 18).

Both the National Association of Social Workers (NASW) and Council of Social Work Education (CSWE) in the past two decades have emphasized the centrality of research in professional responsibilities and competence, charging social workers both with using empirically based knowledge ethically to inform practice and with contributing to knowledge. NASW introduced its professional charge clearly in the 1996 *Code of Ethics*, which contained a section on evaluation and research responsibilities. Specifically, social workers are to "critically examine and keep current with emerging knowledge relevant to social work and fully use evaluation and research evidence in their professional practice," and furthermore, they should also "promote and facilitate evaluation and research to contribute to the development of knowledge" (NASW, 1996 Section 5.02[c]). In contrast, the earlier 1979 *Code of Ethics* had only stated more vaguely that the social worker should base practice on "recognized knowledge" and "share research knowledge and practice wisdom with colleagues" (NASW, 1979, Section V.O.3).

CSWE presented an educational charge in its 2015 accreditation standards (CSWE Commission on Accreditation, 2015) that not only addressed using and contributing to research knowledge but for the first time proposed a leadership role for social workers, who would "translate" evidence and create a "science of social work," with emphasis on culture and ethics. More specifically, social workers are to "use and translate research evidence to inform and improve practice, policy, and service delivery." They are also to "understand quantitative and qualitative research methods and their respective roles in advancing a science of social work ... know the principles of logic, scientific inquiry, and culturally informed and ethical approaches to building knowledge ... [and] use practice experience and theory to inform scientific inquiry and research" (CSWE Commission on Accreditation, 2015, Competency 4, p. 8). While similar educational objectives had first appeared in the 2008 standards, they did not mention the social worker's role of translating evidence and did not promote a science proper to social work, with cultural and ethical emphases (CSWE Commission on Accreditation, 2008). Earlier accreditation standards were even more limited, promoting only students' general consumption of research and ability to generate knowledge for practice by systematic evaluation of their own practice (CSWE Commission on Accreditation, 1984, 2003).

While EBP represents the latest attempt to integrate research with practice in social work, it is important to note one earlier such attempt, the *empirical clinical practice model* promoted from the late 1970s through the late 1990s (Jenson, 2005). The objective of this model, referred to commonly as *single-case evaluation*, was to teach students how to use single-case designs to evaluate the effectiveness of practice with their own individual clients. In the 1980s, most graduate schools of social work taught single-case evaluation to meet accreditation standards. However, interest in the model waned by the end of the century, as students trained in it were largely not using it in their practice (Mullen et al., 2005). Contextual reasons for its decline included practitioners' lack of agency support and resources to conduct evaluations, heavy caseloads, clients who do not remain in treatment very long (Tolson, 1990; Gerdes et al., 1996), and the inconclusive results commonly found when conducting single-case evaluations (Rubin & Knox, 1996). Methodological reasons included practitioners' difficulties with analysis of ambiguous data patterns and lack of opportunity to replicate the intervention with the same client or across clients to draw stronger conclusions (Rubin & Knox, 1996; see also Barlow et al., 1984). Eventually, without widespread use, educators began to emphasize other content areas in their research curriculum.

Even with clear professional and educational mandates, the fate of the EBP movement has at times appeared similar to that of the empirical clinical practice model. However, EBP, although waxing and waning in popularity, appears to be here to stay, due to circumstances not at play during the era of the empirical clinical practice model. Specifically, these circumstances include policies and growing social service funding mandates requiring agencies to increase their use of EBPs; the ongoing and rapid adoption of EBP in other human services fields; and the insurance industry's requirement of cost-effective, evidenced-based mental health care. Yet, in spite of these circumstances, EBP also does not appear to be taking root strongly in social work, as it remains the object of heated debate in search of a clear role and manner of implementation.

With this introduction, questions that arise are "Why do social workers resist EBP?" and "What is the nature of the debate against and for EBP?" Let's review seven issues, noting the arguments by both skeptics and proponents of EBP.

1. ***EBP is not feasible in real practice due to time constraints, insufficient resources, and organizational culture.*** Skeptics argue that organizational policies, which typically value productivity over quality, do not provide practitioners enough time and resources to carry out the EBP process. Many practitioners do not have access to internet resources for conducting literature searches, and they often lack the ability to critically appraise the evidence base and feel overwhelmed by the EBP process (Dulcan, 2005; Bilsker & Goldner, 2004). Older, more experienced practitioners often have been trained in only one or two main treatment approaches that are not the ones supported by the best evidence (Nelson et al., 2006), and they discourage the use of EBPs in which they lack training and expertise (Dulcan, 2005; Mullen & Bacon, 2004). Also, organizational cultures lack norms that promote achievement, innovation, staff development, and positive relationships and mutual support among staff, all of which would contribute to positive attitudes toward the adoption of EBP (Aarons & Sawitzky, 2006).

In response to these observations, proponents of EBP argue that practitioners, having little time and resources, can rely on practice guidelines that summarize empirically based best practices, rather than having to search for and appraise the research literature themselves (Mullen & Streiner, 2004). Proponents, however, do caution that reliance on sources such as systematic reviews and books that identify evidence-based interventions involves risks, because these sources are unable to respond quickly to new evidence as it emerges (Dulcan, 2005). Also, such reliance conflicts with the EBP philosophy, because it involves dependence on authority and reduces critical thinking regarding the quality of the research and clients' idiosyncratic needs (Gibbs & Gambrill, 2002). Overall, proponents nevertheless acknowledge that time and resource constraints are an unresolved obstacle to EBP (Mullen & Streiner, 2004). They also propose that organizational culture and leadership behaviors that value EBP, if addressed, could positively influence the uptake of EBP in organizations (Greenhalgh et al., 2004).

2. ***EBP is a top-down approach that disregards clinical expertise and ignores the client.*** Skeptics argue that EBP, in forcing the practitioner to use interventions designated as evidenced-based, promotes a cookbook approach to practice wherein cost-cutting is the main motivator, rather than clients' best interests (Mullen & Streiner, 2004). EBP thus undermines clinical knowledge, takes away flexibility in treatment delivery, and disregards the therapeutic relationship and the client as an individual. Skeptics also argue that it is natural that clinicians place higher value on lessons learned from their own clinical experience rather than on research (Dozois, 2013).

Proponents of EBP assert that skeptics misunderstand EBP completely. EBP is not top-down. They also caution, however, that practitioners should not view EBP as a bottom-up approach, where they only use the evidence to support their idiosyncratic practice decisions (Mullen, 2004). Practitioners, rather, need to understand that EBP relies heavily on their expertise in making clinical decisions and negotiating the best option for a client. In EBP, neither the client's individuality nor the practitioner's expertise is diminished. Instead, they are the key to effective treatment. The practitioner's role is to select and deliver a treatment with adaptations for the particular client. To achieve this, the practitioner must build a therapeutic relationship that allows for very careful assessment of the client's values and preferences and engagement in mutual decision-making. Proponents suggest that a next step, as a field, is to find effective ways to promote practitioners' understanding and acceptance of EBP, rather than attributing the slow update of EBP as a failure of practitioners (Gellis & Reid, 2004).

3. ***There is not enough evidence.*** Skeptics argue that there is simply not enough research evidence in many areas of social work practice. Proponents assert that practitioners can still use the best available evidence but need to proceed cautiously, such as by evaluating outcomes for their clients using the single-case evaluation design (Mullen & Streiner, 2004). Proponents acknowledge, nevertheless, that there is still a lack of effective approaches for translating research evidence into social work practice, which makes EBP difficult to understand and accept.

4. ***EBP is not applicable to real clients, because it is based on evidence from randomized controlled trials with limited external validity.*** Opponents argue that treatments judged to be effective in manipulated conditions do not generalize to the real world. The available evidence comes mostly from studies conducted in experimental conditions, which often take place in large hospitals and clinics rather than in community agencies. In these controlled-outcome studies, there are generally narrow eligibility requirements for participation that exclude the types of clients whom social workers typically serve. Social work clients have multiple problems and diagnoses, and many clients do not carry a formal diagnosis that fits the best research evidence (Messer, 2006). Diagnoses that are targeted in the research also do not capture the various unique concerns for which social work clients seek help (Webb, 2001). Westen (2006) observed that virtually all randomized controlled trials (RCTs) conducted in the previous several decades were limited to clients who met DSM-IV thresholds for single disorders and noted that such homogeneous eligibility requirements were requirements for obtaining research funding. This lack of systematic data on comorbidity makes it difficult to ascertain what types of clients are more or less likely to benefit from the interventions. As an example, in a meta-analysis of psychotherapies for PTSD, many studies did not provide information on comorbidities, did not distinguish among types of trauma, and lacked follow-up data beyond six months (Bradley et al., 2005). Evidence from these studies are not suited for social work clients who have severe and multiple traumas, such as repeated physical or sexual abuse during childhood and comorbid conditions, which means they may need longer term treatments and are vulnerable to experiencing a return

of symptoms (Bradley et al., 2005). Additionally, real-world clients drop out of treatment and attend services inconsistently (Nelson et al., 2006). The strict treatment protocols used in RCTs are not suited for them. Given the low relevance of available evidence, opponents argue that weight must be given to evidence derived from other research designs, such as anecdotal case reports, clinical descriptions, qualitative studies, uncontrolled pre-test-post-test studies, and client satisfaction surveys. In general, the evidence hierarchy must be de-emphasized because the noncritical elevation of the quantitative research paradigm as the gold standard for practice-oriented research is harmful (Westen, 2006).

Proponents of EBP assert that there is a misunderstanding of EBP. When higher levels of evidence from RCTs are not available, evidence at or near the bottom of the evidence hierarchy can and should be used to guide practice. However, it also becomes dangerous to think that any study conducted with clients produces the same quality of evidence regardless of the study design (Shlonsky & Gibbs, 2004). To define "evidence" in ways that ignore the evidence hierarchy goes completely against making practice more evidence-based (Howard et al., 2003). If the field were to not use EBPs, the alternative would be to use unstudied procedures based only on clinical memory, ignoring systematic observations of how often and for whom they work (Mullen & Streiner, 2004). What practitioners need is help with viewing the research literature as relevant to their practice. This can be achieved by developing effective approaches for translating research evidence into social work practice (Wike et al., 2014) and promoting implementation research, which is testing an EBP in the real world of community practice to determine whether and why it is effective or ineffective, due to the treatment itself or problems of implementing the treatment in the field (Proctor et al., 2011).

5. ***EBP perpetrates racism and discrimination due to not including minorities and using mainstream models of illness and treatment.*** Opponents of EBP argue that many EBPs have limited generalizability to racial and ethnic minority communities because study samples have favored the mainstream population, and the diagnostic definitions applied and theoretical models tested have been limited to mainstream conceptualizations of illness and treatment (Sue and Zane, 2006). Essentially, the interventions and problems addressed are defined by those in power, not by the people from the diverse minority communities made object of the interventions. Additionally, because most of the available evidence comes

from Western models based on positivistic approaches that are diag-
nostically driven to treat problems identified through empirical studies,
intervention approaches reported to be effective may not be appropriate
for the context or cultural concerns of clients. There has also been little
interest in studying whether EBPs effective for the mainstream population are effective among minority groups, due to the overemphasis
on internal, as opposed to external, validity in intervention research
(Sue, 1999). Overall, the current approach to evidence building devalues
clients' cultures, because those receiving the EBPs did not define the
problem being treated and the method of treating it. Different cultures
have approaches to treatment that have not been studied, which makes
EBP-based therapy useless. EBP also does not deal with problems like
acculturation stress, lives ruled by oppression and state violence, and
other problems that are congruent with the cultural lives of clients. With
these considerations, and even though mental health disparities and the
acute gap between research and practice for minorities have received
some recognition, there is a lack of research on minority clients that
satisfies rigorous research criteria. Assessments and interventions should
be culturally based or tailored for use with culturally diverse populations
if EBP is to be successful.

Proponents of EBP suggest that EBPs can be used with any client, even
if the client's diversity group has not been included in the study samples,
as long as the practitioner carefully monitors outcomes. Also, a practitioner may modify the EBP by incorporating culturally based models
of illness to meet clients' needs. To reduce racism and discrimination,
proponents also advocate for methodological pluralism, integrating emic
or bottom-up community-based research approaches that include cultural and community beliefs and circumstances. They contend that more
inclusive intervention strategies can be attained by studying culturally
based interventions developed from an emic approach and comparing
them with their traditional Western counterparts.

6. ***Social workers lack the knowledge, skills, and training to effectively apply
   research knowledge to their work with clients.*** Skeptics of EBP note that
   scientific knowledge cannot be adequately disseminated and properly
   applied because social work practitioners lack the skills for appraising
   studies and applying findings to practice (Bledsoe-Mansori et al., 2013).
   They have difficulties understanding research methods and statistics,
   differentiating useful versus misleading studies, and determining the

appropriateness of findings to their practice question (Gray et al., 2013). In the work context, practitioners often have not had the time and resources to obtain the training needed to deliver the EBPs found in the literature. In the educational context, faculty members resist incorporating EBP content in their classrooms due to the lack of time, resources, and competing academic pressures (Bledsoe et al., 2013; Bellamy et al., 2006).

In response to these challenges, proponents of EBP recognize, as a first step, the need for systematic and widespread trainings in the EBP process, coupled with ongoing consultation and supervision for practitioners as they implement the process (Fixsen et al., 2005). In the work setting, training and supervision for the delivery of EBPs should be made available. In the educational setting, schools of social work must assume a leadership role in preparing students for EBP by incorporating a strong and explicit EBP-focused curriculum.

7. ***EBP is an unethical preoccupation with positivistic methods that excludes other forms of knowledge.*** Skeptics of EBP argue that the steady and increasing emphasis on quantitative research methods as the dominant paradigm for social work practice, to the exclusion of other paradigms, is unethical. This positivistic emphasis started with the doubt cast on the effectiveness of casework in the late 1960s and early 1970s, and is marked today by the consistent call for outcome research and the critique of those who teach practices and theory that lack an empirical basis. The argument that all practice teaching should be grounded in empiricism rather than theory, or that EBP should be considered over other forms of knowledge and knowledge generation, favors the use of certain techniques like cognitive-behavioral approaches, which have been studied more extensively (Goldstein, 2007). Skeptics emphasize that empiricism should not be taken too far. Abandoning the profession's repertoire of theories, models and interventions, and community-based knowledge not only leads to the erosion of professional expertise (Munro, 2002) but also fundamentally disrespects diversity and self-determination. Students need to assess clients as person-in-environment, consider diverse sources of knowledge, and provide interventions according to clients' unique perspectives and life circumstances. The EBP framework restricts social work to a narrow ends-means rationality, such that only certain forms of knowledge and action are considered legitimate (Webb, 2001). Social workers engage in a reflexive and comprehensive process

of understanding and not a certainty-based decision-making process based on objective evidence.

Proponents of EBP argue that skeptics misunderstand EBP, focusing again on the key roles of practice wisdom and client preferences in the EBP model. Skeptics wrongly view EBP as refuting practice experience, taking away from clients' power to define their problems, and ignoring the client's social and environmental context. Appraising the evidence regarding the likely effects of an intervention and sharing this information with the client engages clients in an informed consent process. In this way, the EBP process is client-centered (Gambrill, 2005). Skeptics also wrongly believe that they must only diagnose a client with formal mental health criteria and seek and use empirically tested interventions and that EBP requires the existence of RCTs, meta-analyses, or systematic reviews. In the EBP process, when there are no experimental findings, the practitioner may seek out quasi-experimental and pre-experimental studies. A minority of practitioners know that EBP is a process that includes locating and appraising evidence as a part of practice decisions (Rubin & Parrish, 2007). This misconception may be due to the earlier empirically supported treatment (EST) initiative of the 1990s, which relied heavily on evidence. In the EST initiative, researchers decided how much evidence was necessary to consider a treatment "empirically supported" and developed lists of ESTs for use by professionals. EBP, in contrast, is not a list of treatments but a holistic approach to practice that explicitly incorporates nonscientific considerations into decision-making. EBP is thus ethical and does not dehumanize.

Proponents of EBP also portray skeptics as defending the status quo, while skeptics claim that EBP is authoritarian due to its reliance on science (Gambrill 2005; Gibbs & Gambrill, 2002; Mullen & Streiner, 2004). Proponents instead describe traditional social work practice as authoritarian when it relies only on published or spoken case studies (Zayas et al., 2011) and uses practice models based on the authority of one's supervisor or favorite theorist (Gambrill, 1999). It is because of such authoritarian traditions that practitioners today reject EBPs with strict definitions of therapist roles and timing and sequence of techniques. The original intent of EBP was to place lower value on such authority by training the practitioner to be an independent decision-maker (Guyatt et al., 1992). However, proponents recognize that the majority of the literature on EBP has not stressed the autonomy that is emphasized in the original EBP model.

Reflection Questions

1. Which of the above issues do you find the most troublesome? Why are they troublesome?
2. Do you fall more on the side of the skeptics or the proponents of EBP? And why?
3. Aside from research evidence, what other forms or sources of knowledge could be important for practice decisions? *(Be creative and inclusive!)*
4. Does the EBP model foresee the inclusion of these other forms of knowledge? If so, how? If not, how could it do so more explicitly?
5. Does EBP account for the models of health and illness, values, beliefs, and life circumstances of racial/ethnic minorities and other diverse populations? If so, how? If not, how would you change or enhance the model to ensure this?
6. Would it be acceptable to not consider research evidence in your social work practice (i.e., not even review or use any EBPs)?

⌘   Case Study: Laura

Laura, age 15, was born in a rural town in Mexico. Her father left for the U.S. for economic reasons as an undocumented immigrant when Laura was 3 and her younger brother, Miguel, was 6 months old. About two years after her father left, Laura's mother learned that he had remarried and started another family in the U.S. One year later, when Laura was 7, her mother immigrated to the U.S. without documents, leaving Laura and Miguel to be raised by their maternal grandparents in a home with other extended relatives. When Laura was 14, her mother had saved enough money working as a nanny to reunite Laura and Miguel with her near Sacramento, California. Laura's mother had had no contact with their father, who lived in Reno, Nevada, with his second wife and their two children.

Laura had suffered much from the separations with her parents and the loss of her father. Her grandparents, while they provided a stable home and instrumental care, were unable to provide the affection, attention, and sense of security that Laura needed as a young child. Her grandparents worked long hours, and Laura had full responsibility for Miguel's care. In addition, the extended relatives in the home never fully included Laura and her brother in their lives. Laura's life with them entailed fending and standing up for herself and her younger brother. Laura longed for her mother and grew tougher and tougher, holding inside intense fear, sadness, and anger by the time she was about to immigrate.

Upon arriving in the U.S., Laura had to adjust to a new school as a ninth grader, make new friends, and learn a new language. Her new school was strong academically but had fewer students who were immigrants and people of color. Laura's adaptation occurred slowly and with many difficulties. She felt very upset when teachers and other students did not understand her English. She mistrusted her peers, who rejected and bullied her, making fun of her accent, simple clothes, and messy hair and poor self-care. At age 15, at the start of her sophomore year, she began to externalize her anger. She lashed back verbally at teachers for picking on her when her work was submitted late or of poor quality and began to engage in physical altercations with peers. She also experienced much sadness and isolation. Not only was she not connected to her school due to her slow adaptation, but she was also not connected to her mother, who worked as a nanny for two families and had not tried much to reconnect with her.

At home, Laura had a close and strong relationship with her younger brother, whom she had essentially raised. However, she harbored a strong sense of burden and resentment because she had full responsibility for his care. She dedicated herself to helping him with his homework and all other needs every afternoon and evening until her mother returned home late at night. In the relationship with her mother, neither Laura nor her mother had spoken about the separation trauma that Laura experienced due to the mother's migration to the U.S. The possible impact for Laura of the loss of her father and the seven-year separation from her mother on her acting-out behaviors, mistrust, and difficulties with forming relationships with school peers had not been explored. Laura had never expressed to her mother how frightening and difficult it was when her mother left, nor the distress and desperation she was feeling in her new home and school life in the U.S. Laura's mother, similarly, had never spoken about the trauma of leaving her children behind.

Laura's social environment in the U.S. was empty and without support compared with what she was accustomed to in Mexico. In Mexico, she was always surrounded by immediate and extended family members in her grandparents' home, even if the relatives were rarely inclusive. In the U.S., although she had a few extended cousins and other relatives in the Bay Area, she did not see them regularly or build connections with them. She also had not made friendships at school due to her own avoidance and distrust. As a result, Laura was very isolated, without social supports and outlets. Additionally, being from a small rural town in Mexico, Laura and her mother were unaccustomed to talking openly about Laura's mental health symptoms due to the stigma of mental illness.

Considering Laura's home, school, and social environments, Laura did not feel grounded and comfortable with herself. She had not developed a strong sense of self, and she had few mirroring and supportive resources to support her development and ability to bridge to a new life and build a sense of stability and well-being in the U.S.

Laura's strengths were succeeding in school, although her homework was sometimes late and she struggled with English; attending school regularly; having a good relationship with her brother; maintaining contact with her grandmother and friends in Mexico; and being very talented at making handicrafts, because of having produced handmade decorations for parties and events when she lived in Mexico. Laura also had fairly strong insight and cognitive and emotional awareness of her and her mother's difficulties.

⌘   **Case Study: Eddie**
....

Eddie is a 39-year-old African American heterosexual male who moved from rural Mississippi to a low-income neighborhood with a high crime rate in downtown Los Angeles one year ago. Eddie is seeking help for his emotional dysregulation and explosive behaviors. As a child, Eddie experienced extreme poverty, physical abuse, and rape. His early life included living in a van for several years, suffering his mother's severe physical abuse, and being raped by a worker in a mental health hospital when he was age 9.

Since his teenage years, Eddie has been hospitalized at least a dozen times for psychiatric episodes, including rage. He has a history of violence involving fighting due to being aggravated, including "grabbing a nurse" and telling her, "I will kill you." Eddie has had numerous surgeries from a fall injury while work-ing in construction when he was 22 years old. He has rods and screws and an electric stimulator implanted in his back. He has difficulty standing or sitting for longer than 15 minutes. He experiences chronic suicidal ideation, although with no suicide plan due to his chronic pain, for which he practices responsible daily cannabis therapy.

Eddie arrived to the intake appointment well-groomed and casually dressed. His attitude was friendly and cooperative. He appeared oriented to person, place, time, and situation. He reported his mood as "feeling good, feeling chill." His affect was calm, and when he spoke, he had a smile on his face. His thought process was logical and linear, his thought content was normal, and he exhibited normal speech rate, volume, and tone. He appeared to have good insight and judgment. His cognition was within normal limits. His memory appeared to be in excellent condition. He had persistent thoughts of suicidal ideation, either going to Colorado Street to jump off or jumping in front of a bus. He endorsed auditory hallucinations and denied visual hallucinations. He abstains from all substance use except for cannabis for pain management.

Eddie endorsed the following symptoms, which support his diagnoses of post-traumatic stress, major depressive, bipolar, and intermittent explosive disorders:

- Emotional symptoms: emotional dysregulation, trouble controlling emotions, excessive fear and anxiety around other people, strong will, irritability, negative attitude, and mood swings from extremely happy to severely depressed
- Cognitive symptoms: auditory hallucinations, very good memory, short temper and irritability affecting good insight at times, attention-deficit issues, impaired judgment, distractibility, poor concentration, and decreased goal-directed activity
- Behavioral symptoms: short temper outbursts, fits of rage, avoidance of other people, normally not leaving room unless he has an appointment, and threatening to harm others when triggered by others
- Physiological symptoms: chronic pain caused by the back injury

Eddie's current problems include difficulty getting out of his single room occupancy (SRO) apartment and isolating, with his thinking focused on thoughts such as "I don't want to get triggered by those thugs," and "It's better to stay in." These thoughts make him feel angry and fearful that he may act out, which then lead to feeling more isolated, so that he stays home playing video games, smoking cannabis, and avoiding others. Another problem is financial. After paying rent each month, he is left with only $175. He has a difficult time managing his money, while feeling the added pressure of needing to give money to his four children, at least for special occasions. He feels guilty that he cannot give them more monetarily, with thoughts that he is a "worthless dad" and "a loser," especially after squandering a very large settlement from the construction accident he suffered. He was also turned down for Social Security Disability Insurance (SSDI).

Eddie maintains the core beliefs of "I am worthless, I am no good, and I am unlovable," which can be traced back to his childhood experiences. As a child, he thought, "Something must be wrong with me to be experiencing all this negativity in my life." This belief continued, and he began to get more and more angry over time; he has therefore had to keep a check on his underlying anger for most of his life. He often acted out violently, which landed him in prison twice. The first time was for an aggressive assault in which he pulled out a machine gun on a police officer. The second time was for violating parole. Eddie frequently reports that he most definitely does not ever want to go back to prison, which helps him keep tabs on his poor impulse control. Fortunately, his overriding good insight and vigilance have kept him out of jail for the last five years.

Eddie copes with his fits of anger and feelings of agitation by isolating. He is highly cognizant that he needs to avoid triggering situations that would cause him to act out violently toward others. He is also coping currently by seeking help to vent and process his traumas and to learn ways to control his anger and acting out. Another means of coping and important source of support for Eddie are his strong traditional Southern morals and values, which were instilled by his mother and the cultural norms and mores of the region where he grew up, of which he speaks frequently.

Eddie's main source of internal support is his relationships and love for his children and grandchild. He wants more than anything to be a good influence and role model for them. However, his attitude and assumption are that he will never be accepted and loved no matter what he does, which lead him to discounting and keeping himself from accepting the love and admiration shown by his children and grandchild. He also deals with his children's mother, who "poisons the minds of my kids about me." Fortunately, her family has a positive view of Eddie, so that his children, who reside in Mississippi, do not get only a one-sided story. He continues to build strong emotional bonds with them, and this connection ultimately keeps him from making plans to commit suicide to end the chronic pain, which he experiences every day.

 ACTIVITY 1.3   **Conceptualize the Case Paper Assignment**

Instructions

1. Jot down the steps you would take for choosing an intervention for a specific client using the original EBP model. (You are essentially designing the case paper assignment.)

. . . .

   TIP   For each of the three components, consider the main pieces of information you would need to gather and how you would use that information to decide on an intervention.

. . . .

Stop! Do not go on until you've done the above.

2. Read the assignment instructions in Appendix 1 and compare your steps with the steps in the instructions. How did your steps match up with the instructions?

 ACTIVITY 1.4 Share a Brief Case Description of a Client
In-Class Activity

Instructions

1. Identify a real client whom you will use or might use for the case paper assignment. It is best to use a current client. If that is not possible, you may use a former client whom you know well.
2. Prepare a 3-minute case presentation to share in a small group or with your class. Use Laura's and Eddie's case studies above as examples, but your case presentations can be less detailed.
3. Include some or all of the following information, taking care to not reveal identifying information of real clients:

    a. Client name (use pseudonym)

    b. Sociodemographic characteristics (age, gender, race/ethnicity, SES, immigration background, marital status, birthplace, living situation)

    c. Cultural background, including client's identification with specific diversity groups (e.g., LGBTQ)

    d. Developmental phase, needs, and history

    e. Presenting problem (what client is asking help for)

    f. Mental health problems and history, including DSM diagnoses

    g. Health problems and history

    h. Coping behaviors/style, attachment style, or other psychological characteristics

    i. Strengths (individual, family, and community)

    j. Social supports (family, community, professionals, and others)

    k. Current or past environmental stressors

⌘   **Case Paper Task 1.1**

Write the *Introduction* Section

Instructions: Write the *Introduction* of your case paper assignment. You will need to have identified the current or past client who will serve as your case for this paper. Note that this section does not require subheadings.

Case Paper Instructions:

1. INTRODUCTION (2–3 paragraphs, 2 points)

   a. *Purpose of the Paper.* State that the purpose is to find and evaluate the appropriateness and usefulness of three different interventions for a client using an evidence-based practice decision-making model that considers the following: (a) research evidence, (b) clinical expertise, and (c) client characteristics, culture, and preferences. (*2–3 sentences, ½ point*)

   b. *Identification of Client, Clinician, and Setting.* Identify the client, you and your role, and the service setting, including any restrictions on types of interventions that can be considered given service/time limits, insurance, or other factors. (*1 paragraph, 1 point*)

   c. *Paper Content.* State the content sections that will be covered in the paper. (*1–2 sentences, ½ point*)

Laura's Example

Needs Strengthening

Introduction

This paper will consider three interventions for my client at the Meadowview Community Center. I will choose one of them by reviewing research articles and finding one that fits my client's mental health problems. My client, Laura, is 15. I am her counselor and case manager. Her high school offers group and individual therapy. This paper will discuss Laura's background and evaluate three interventions for her issues. It will also include a treatment plan.

How would you improve the above? Is the required content incorporated?

Well-Written

As you read the example below, note the important pieces of information covered that were omitted from the above paragraph.

Introduction

The purpose of this paper is to evaluate three evidence-based interventions to determine which intervention will work best for the presenting client. The interventions evaluated are Cognitive Behavioral Therapy for Adolescents (CBT-A), Mindfulness-Based Stress Reduction (MBSR), and Interpersonal Psychotherapy for Depressed Adolescents (IPT-A). The decision of the best intervention for the client will be based on available research evidence, clinical expertise, and the specific characteristics and needs of the client while encompassing their culture.

My client, Laura (pseudonym), age 15, attends a public high school where I am a school-based counselor. As an MSW student, I intern at Meadowview Community Center (MCC), a community-based social services agency with school-based programs in numerous high schools. My role is to provide mental health interventions, case management, and psycho-education and to assist in creating environments that support students' academic success. I help monitor students' grades and attendance; contact caregivers and provide resources for families; and work closely with teachers and administrators to provide assistance and consultation for student success. MCC operates on a brief, eight-session therapy model so that the needs of more students can be met throughout the school year. This model is also intended to foster independence for the individual. When additional support is needed, a longer duration of services is permitted, such as ongoing case management for foster youth and homeless youth and families.

This paper will describe the client's cultural and socioeconomic background and views of their presenting problems, goals, preferences, and desired forms of help. As further background, it will include a case conceptualization and identification of appropriate forms of treatment and treatment goals. Next, this paper will describe and assess the three evidence-based interventions. Finally, it will identify the best evidence-based intervention for this unique client and explain how it will be implemented in this particular setting.

Eddie's Example

As you read the below example, assess whether it provides an effective introduction to the paper and whether you like the writing style better than Laura's example.

Well-Written

Introduction

The purpose of this paper is to identify and evaluate the usefulness and appropriateness of three different evidence-based practices (EBPs) for a therapy client using a decision-making model that considers research evidence, clinical expertise, and client characteristics, culture, and preferences. The client's profile, background, and treatment goals will be discussed, and then three EBPs will be reviewed, concluding with the rationale for the intervention with the best fit for the client and a proposed treatment plan using that EBP.

The client, whom I call "Eddie," is a 39-year-old heterosexual African American male who lives in a single room occupancy (SRO) apartment in a low-income, high crime neighborhood in downtown Los Angeles. Eddie self-referred to Mission Community Clinic (MCC) to address his experiences of severe emotional dysregulation and explosive behaviors. MCC provides services to low-income and homeless residents of Los Angeles. As a mental health intern at MCC, I conduct intakes, provide therapy under supervision, refer clients to the on-site case manager for housing referrals, and generally advocate for clients. The three EBPs that I will consider for Eddie are Cognitive Behavioral Therapy (CBT), Prolonged Exposure Therapy (PET), and Cognitive Processing Therapy (CPT).

⌘   ## Case Paper Task 1.2

....

Write the *Client Profile* Section

Instructions: Write the *Client Profile* section of your case paper assignment.

Case Paper Instructions:

1. *CLIENT PROFILE (2–3 paragraphs, 3 points)*

    a. *Social and Cultural Background.* Provide a brief description of your client's socio-demographic and cultural background. (*1 paragraph, 1 point*)

    b. *Developmental, Psychological, and Environmental Background.* Provide information on your client's developmental phase, needs, and history; DSM provisional diagnoses; relevant psychological characteristics (e.g., defenses, coping skills, attachment style); strengths (individual, family, and community); and current or past environmental stressors. (*1–2 paragraphs, 2 points*)

Laura's Example

Needs Strengthening

Client Profile

Social and Cultural Background

Laura is a 15-year-old Latina female in the 10th grade who was born in Mexico. She and her younger brother moved to the U.S. one year ago to live with their mother. Her mother cares for the children by herself. They are low-income and do not see their father because the mother does not want the contact, even though he lives only a few hours away.

Developmental, Psychological, and Environmental Background

Laura has multiple losses: her father, her mother, and family in Mexico who raised her and her brother. Due to reaching her teenage years and her immigration experience, she acts out and keeps to herself to cope. She has depression and anxiety. Her younger brother is her strength, as he is the only person she is close with. Her school and neighborhood are both stressful. In terms of developmental models, her next stage is to build an intimate relationship.

How would you improve the above? Is some of the required content omitted? Is a developmental and strengths approach reflected?

Well-Written

As you read the following example, note the important pieces of information covered that were omitted from the above paragraphs.

Client Profile

Social and Cultural Background

Laura is a 15-year-old Latina female in the 10th grade. She was born and grew up in a small town in rural Mexico and immigrated to the U.S. at the age of 14. She lives in a suburb of Sacramento, California, with her younger brother, age 11, and her mother, age 42. Laura's father migrated to the U.S. when Laura was 3 years old, followed by her mother's migration when Laura was 7 years old. Laura and her brother lived with her maternal grandparents until they joined their mother in the U.S. Before and after coming to the U.S., Laura has been her brother's primary caregiver. Laura has had almost no contact with her father, who remarried and started a new family within 2 years of settling in the U.S. He lives with his new family in Reno, Nevada. Laura is semi-fluent in English and fluent in Spanish. Laura's mother, who works for two families as a nanny, is the family's single provider.

Developmental, Psychological, and Environmental Background

Acquiring a sense of identity and defining her role in life are important to Laura as an adolescent in Erikson's psychosocial stage of identity vs. role confusion. Laura is trying to experience and define her sense of self and her future, but she requires supportive resources and grounding at home and school for this to occur. She has struggled with developing trusting relationships with those outside her home, especially peers, teachers, and administrators. From an attachment perspective, Laura's working model of relationships is one of mistrust and insecure-anxious avoidance due to the separations from her father and mother as a young child, her grandparents' inattentiveness, and her current lack of emotional and social support. She copes by acting out and keeping to herself. She has exhibited defiant behaviors in the classroom and begun to engage in physical fights as a result of being bullied and being unable to manage her anger. She exhibits some symptoms of depression and anxiety, but not enough to indicate major depression or generalized anxiety. Her provisional DSM-5 diagnosis is Mood Disorder, Not Otherwise Specified.

Laura's individual strengths include her excellent insight and cognitive and emotional awareness, her desire to grow, and her openness to receiving therapy and other interventions. Laura's home environment is also an important strength. Laura's mother is very supportive of Laura, although the mother works two jobs, with only most Sundays off. Laura has a close relationship with her younger brother, and the family has relatives in the San Francisco Bay Area. The school setting, however, is an environmental stressor. Laura's being bullied,

(continued)

acting out, avoidance, and lack of friendships, along with having no mental health and academic counselors until recently, contribute to a very stressful and unsupportive environment. Laura has struggled academically due to the unfriendly classroom environments with negative attitudes from peers and teachers. Also, because she does not live near the school, she must take the bus to her school. She has expressed that she feels isolated in her neighborhood. She does not feel connected to the school, because she must leave immediately after school to get home to care for her younger brother.

Eddie's Example

Well-Written

As you read, think about which writing example, Laura's or Eddie's, you like more.

Client Profile

Social and Cultural Background

Eddie was born and raised in Columbia, Mississippi, and moved to Los Angeles 6 months ago. Eddie suffered severe physical abuse by his mother and grew up in extreme poverty (e.g., his family lived for several years in a van when he was a child). When he was 9 years old, a worker raped him while he was admitted to a psychiatric hospital. Without a high school education, he worked in construction until he was severely injured on the job at age 22. Eddie holds dear to him and uses as his lens on the world the strong traditional Southern morals and values instilled by his physically abusive mother. He also maintains strong Southern cultural norms and mores from the region where he grew up. Eddie has four children and one grandchild, all residing in Mississippi. Currently, Eddie does not have the capacity to work due to his severe chronic pain and his sometimes debilitating mental health diagnoses. His chronic pain causes him to readily assert chronic suicidal ideation with no plan.

Developmental, Psychological, and Environmental Background

Eddie is diagnosed with Major Depressive Disorder (single episode, unspecified), Bipolar Disorder, Post-Traumatic Stress Disorder (chronic), and Intermittent Explosive Disorder. Living in a new city, especially a high crime and drug use neighborhood, has exacerbated his various symptoms and behaviors. While these symptoms and behaviors were present before his move, he was more easily able to keep his emotions in check, because he was not living in a congested urban area with neighbors on the other side of his walls. Eddie's difficulties with impulse control and behaving violently toward others previously led to two prison terms. Eddie copes by isolating and keeping himself out of harm's way when he is feeling agitated, for his own and others' safety and to avoid returning to prison. He is highly cognizant that he needs to avoid triggering situations. Eddie's early history, including extreme poverty, physical abuse, and rape, led to core beliefs of worthlessness and being unlovable and to stronger and stronger anger over time as adulthood life stressors impacted him. Eddie's strengths include his overriding good insight and vigilance, which have kept him out of jail for the last five years; his traditional Southern morals and values; and his strong focus on his children. Also, his children's mother's family maintain a positive view of Eddie, even though their mother does not, which allows him to build strong bonds with his children and provides him with a reason for living.

 ACTIVITY 1.5 Formulate a Search Question for a Client

Instructions

1. A search question focuses your information needs and points you in the direction of studies that are potentially relevant to your client's problems and treatment needs.
2. Formulate a question that will guide your search of the literature for potentially useful interventions for your client. The client can be the one you are using for your case paper assignment or any client, if you have not yet decided on a client for the case paper.
3. See the below examples of search questions for Laura and Eddie.

Examples
LAURA
Imprecise Search Question

What intervention works for Mexican-American teenagers who act out and have problems with peers?

The above question provides few specifics on what the intervention(s) needs to address and for whom (i.e., it leaves out the real client). How could you improve this question? Note how the below question is more precise. It provides more information for the literature search.

Well-Formulated Search Question

What evidence-based interventions are available for managing anger and externalizing behaviors, reducing depression and self-isolation, and building relationships at school for a 15-year-old bicultural and bilingual Mexican-American adolescent girl living in a supportive home environment with her single mother and younger sibling?

EDDIE
Well-Formulated Search Question
What evidenced-based interventions are available for managing anxiety and anger, building healthy coping skills, and processing traumas and negative self-beliefs for an African American adult with strong Southern cultural values and excellent cognitive awareness, who is new to living in a tense urban environment?

ANSWERS

Discussion 1.1 Answers   **What Is Evidence-Based Practice?**

How Students Answered

1. **What is "evidence-based" practice?**

    a. It's using a certain technique, such as motivational interviewing (MI), and looking at the results. It's doing research to obtain evidence to back up the claim that the technique is helpful to clients.

    b. It's the idea that there should be numbers and data that support or negate whether the intervention works.

    c. EBP is having what we do come from the research.

    d. It's data that's been gathered to find out which intervention is better for a certain population, such as older adults or teenagers, and for a certain problem, such as substance use or behavioral issues. The EBP has to be related to the population and the problem. For example, I wouldn't want to use MI with a child if that research hasn't been done.

    e. EBPs are therapies that have a proven track record of improving people's quality of life. But if the client doesn't want it, you have to go along with what the client wants. It isn't like you have a cold and we can use insulin or vitamin C or you can do exercise. We can also just check back in a week to see how you feel about this cold. To me, that's what evidence-based practice is. It's not about forcing anyone to do anything. You explain to them that some people have had success on vitamin C, but if your religion tells you to never take vitamin C, then we're going to try to do exercise or find other ways to build your immunity. We use whatever's beneficial and what the client wants.

f. Making our own interventions and testing them could be interesting and dangerous. That's what EBP is. They have the money to go out and do the research. They get funding. What's funded is the "good idea," but we may have a million ideas and not get funded. Does it mean those interventions are not a good idea?

2. **What should evidence-based practice be for it to be useful to your work as a social worker?**

   a. EBPs should be consumer-friendly tools that are accessible and meaningful [to our clients and us].

   b. EBP should help me figure out what to use with my clients, what would be successful for them, and what would make their symptoms decrease.

   c. An EBP should work in different contexts, such as when a person has this or that problem. It should be flexible.

   d. The intervention can't be so complicated that you can't use it for other populations. The EBP should be easily replicated.

   e. We should be able to tweak interventions even when they are evidence-based. For example, you're certified in CBT, you've learned it well, and then you tweak it, and it works. Your clients tell you it's helping their mood and their relationships. You shouldn't have to follow the book, but use your own judgment.

   f. I'd look for an EBP that has worked in the field.

   g. We should be able to look and find research for a certain condition or client problem and for a specific population. For example, if I have a young child with anger, I should be able to find an intervention on anger for young children.

   h. The studies should tell us what the condition looks like, what the intervention consists of, and that it works therapeutically. [In other words,] we should be able to see results in real time.

   i. The results provided on the interventions should be concrete, so that you can actually apply and implement the interventions.

j. I don't want just a research article, but instead, information on how to apply the intervention.

k. I'd look for an intervention where they address relationships among people and the research considers all different systems in the environment.

l. We want interventions that have been well criticized and for which the contraindications are well-defined, because we have to deal with the fears that we could harm the client.

m. The research supporting the intervention should have been done with the cultural group I'm working with if I'm going to consider that evidence. And it's not just relevant to cultural identity groups, but also gender, class, race, and other identity factors.

n. There should be a high rate of success in many communities based on race/ethnicity, SES, and everything else.

o. Research is supposed to be narrow and specific. If one study leaves a group out, then another study should be done that includes that population. A lot of research needs to be done so all populations are covered.

p. Bottom-up research is needed for certain populations that are excluded from research, [where] you have to figure out language access and cultural issues. This is different from top-down research, like when you use an existing theory or body of knowledge.

q. The research should be done over a period of time; it should be longitudinal, maybe five or ten years, to be more certain it's useful.

r. We want recent and updated research, studies that keep going into the future and are not done once and for all.

s. We should be aware of changes. EBP shouldn't be stagnant. New research should be done in new ways and to get new evidence.

t. The evidence shouldn't be stuck. It should be dynamic. Times are changing. It isn't one-size-fits-all. It isn't like we did it, found it, and that's it. For example, it's different now because the landscape isn't the Obama years. We have to be updated with [what works and what's needed in] the current moment.

u. To be useful to me, it depends what my client wants. I want interventions that match what they want.

v. It depends on money and time. You have to [be able to] find experts who know the intervention [and can train and supervise you].

w. We should be able to give the intervention even if we don't get all the training the researchers define.

3. **What are your requirements to determine whether what researchers produce is useful to you?**

a. The researchers should have looked very closely at the problem.

b. Because social work is about the person-in-environment, seeing how the intervention works in the environment, such as how different systems levels impact the intervention, would be interesting. I don't think this is usually done.

c. The research should be done with different populations, including with my client's population.

d. I would use interventions that have more evidence for my [racial/ ethnic or other] population of interest.

e. They should have been used [or researched] in many communities. The communities we want to use the intervention with should also be included in the sample.

f. We can't take an intervention and use it with Native Americans if the researchers never considered cultural impacts. They shouldn't take a theory and assume it's applicable to everybody.

g. There should be research on people with comorbid conditions [like our clients have].

h. It should be based on a substantial amount of data. There should be repeated studies. It should be reliable.

i. They should use good methods, such as randomized controlled trials.

j. There should always be qualitative studies and case studies about the intervention so we learn the nuances of how it works and how people react to it, including people from all different cultures.

k. I'd make sure the studies are from peer-reviewed journals.

l.   Social work is focused on a strengths and empowerment perspective, so research and interventions should be too. Research should focus on interventions that build a person's strengths and their community's strengths, and not only treat the person's symptoms.

Discussion 1.2 Answers   **How Do You Decide What to Use?**

How Students Answered

1. **If an intervention has good evidence on its effectiveness, does that mean you can use it with your client? How do you decide?**

     a.   It has to be appropriate to their specific characteristics, such as age.

     b.   We should look at the client's population and characteristics. We have to take into consideration different contexts and needs for each population.

     c.   You need to make sure the intervention is culturally appropriate and sensitive and considers intersectionality. For example, if you have a male who is in his 70s and Asian, you would need to consider all these characteristics and how they intersect.

     d.   I'd ask my clients what they have already tried. What has worked and not worked?

     e.   I would consider the client's goals of treatment, history and background, strengths, and diagnosis.

     f.   You have to look very closely at their problem. It's not just that they have PTSD, but what is this PTSD looking like for them?

     g.   We want to know how the client tells their narrative about what's going on for them. Does the intervention fit with this?

     h.   If you have a transition-age youth with substance use problems and they've been to inpatient treatment and say they didn't like it, you have to figure out what's going to work for them now. You have to work closely with the case manager to know their history.

     i.   We are treating people individually. What does the client want? We can explain the available interventions and ask them. They may have certain experiences or biases and may not accept the EBPs we propose.

j.   You can't necessarily use EBPs with your client. The client must trust you first. Then, what you recommend will be acceptable.

k.   If an intervention works for the majority, it doesn't mean it works for the one specific individual. We have to be very careful about what we choose.

l.   Just because an intervention's been shown to work in schools in other cities [doesn't mean it will in our specific situation;] we still have to work with each individual client [and also consider where they live and go to school] to assess whether it's a good fit.

m.   When you give an intervention, you're getting the client's input. With the input, you're able to customize the intervention. You could have an intervention developed for folks with mental health problems in urban areas, but you use it in a rural area by getting people's input and tailoring it.

n.   There should be priorities established regarding what and when to use something. There's an order of operations. You may do trauma processing later but give other types of needed supports first.

o.   It isn't just about the quality of the research evidence. We should consider the practicality of the intervention [for the person], such as doing MI first and then CBT.

p.   I would use interventions that I'm strong in, that I'm good at delivering.

q.   Find out if your supervisor knows the technique. Then they can help you [learn] to do it.

r.   You should consult with your supervisor and coworkers who've worked with the population. See what they think about the interventions.

s.   You go to your peers to find out what's been helpful for the cultural population you're going to serve.

t.   You've been working in the field for 20 years. You're bringing this into your decisions.

u.   The agency has to permit the intervention. You can't just do something you find out of the blue.

v.   It has to be cost-effective.

2.   **What are the reasons not to use an EBP for a particular client?**

a.   Even if there is good evidence, your client may not want it. It depends on whether the client accepts the treatment or not.

b.   The client's risk factors and safety concerns need to be met first when choosing an intervention. For example, the person lives in a high-crime area and is a substance user.

c.   The client has to be ready for it. They need to make some changes in their life, but they are not ready. They're in precontemplation.

d.   [I might not use an EBP because] we need to be able to engage with the client and sometimes humanize the situation because they've been through trauma. We have to meet them where they're at.

e.   We may not have any help to learn how to conduct the intervention.

f.   It depends on agency rules and money and time issues, what's allowed and what's possible.

g.   I wouldn't use interventions that don't align with my belief system. For example, I feel at home with psychodynamic therapies.

h.   My instinct keeps me from using a lot of evidenced-based practices because I have experience that what I've been doing with the kids I see works, but if it's not working, then I will reach out to the research.

i.   There are biases from the researchers and therapists [in developing the EBPs]. You expect that the low-income groups will take whatever [interventions] they are offered, but they may not be willing or capable of participating. Certain groups will respond differently.

j.   [Many EBPs are biased.] They are from a deficit approach. It's a form of bias to say, "What's wrong with you?"

k.   The DSM [which many EBPs and the research evidence are based on] is not necessary to everyone or applicable to all cultures. There's cultural bias. [Our clients] may not answer the [research instrument] questions or think about their problem in this way.

l.   Gender needs to be considered. [Women and people with different gender identities] don't answer the same things on questionnaires, so the research [evidence] may not be applicable to them.

m. For minority clients, they don't know how interventions based on mainstream theories are going to be effective. They don't know what theories they are based on. Is it even broken down for them to understand? They don't have the trust to ask about them when they reach out for said services. These [EBPs] are there, but they're applicable to people who know about it and are going to use it.

n. I'd ask how a social justice framework comes into the decision-making.

3. **What are your implied values at play for the reasons you provided?**

a. We value cultural humility and cultural knowledge and competency. We have respect for different cultures. We don't want to make people use EBPs that don't respect their culture. It's not only about our own competence but about valuing diversity and inclusion and the dignity of every person.

b. One of the values in social work is people's self-determination. We can only help them if they want, even if we offer them five EBPs. We only use what the client wants. This has to do with the value of human dignity and worth.

c. We want to focus on the clients' strengths and hopes for the future when we decide on an intervention—not only on the deficits.

d. I take the lens of social justice. Who's not being respected? How much bias and prejudice are there? Social workers challenge injustice. A lot of research has been done with White males and not in minority communities. It's also our own integrity at play if we ignore the biases represented in the evidence.

e. A body of knowledge is produced at universities, but a lot of the time this is not practice [knowledge]. When they apply it on the ground, it doesn't work. Research is very American-centered. There's work in the third world that's important. It's about how you define research and how you apply it. Practice should inform theory. This is valuing social justice.

f. Another social justice issue is asking how we want to participate in research. For example, people say it's a myth that drug abusers want drug treatment. They say for the treatment to work, the drug abusers have to want it. You can't say that if the EBP doesn't work, it's because the people weren't ready for it. The researchers just don't want to be stuck saying the interventions aren't working.

What Are Our Ethical Responsibilities?

How Students Answered

Which social work ethical principles and standards, as listed in the NASW *Code of Ethics*, are relevant to EBP decision-making? How is each relevant?

a.   *Social Justice: We strive to ensure access to services and resources, equal opportunity, and clients' participation in decision-making.* This relates to EBP because existing research evidence is often not based on minority samples and because we may be forcing EBPs onto minority clients without them knowing about the big picture.

b.   *Dignity and Worth of the Person: We're aware of individual differences and diversity and treat people respectfully, helping them to identify their goals and build their capacity to address their own needs.* You don't want to make clients feel like another statistic. We have to make their experience humanizing. You want to be genuine. You want to tailor the intervention toward them. You shouldn't even use the EBP if it doesn't meet their goals.

c.   *Importance of Human Relationships: We engage people as partners in promoting clients' well-being.* We have to give our clients clear information about the EBPs, such as how they work and don't work, before just using them. We also have to get social workers and other professionals on board to fight for equal amounts of research and good research for minority communities.

d.   *Integrity: We behave in a trustworthy manner, acting honestly and responsibly, including promoting ethical practices in our organizations.* We have to be honest with our clients about EBPs. We have to make sure our agencies use interventions, with or without evidence backing them, that are culturally sensitive and based on what our clients want.

e.   *Commitment to Clients (Standard 1.01): Our clients' interests and well-being are primary.* When deciding on EBPs to offer clients, we need to think about their well-being rather than our own needs or our organization's benefit. We should also promote research that is relevant to our clients' communities and viewpoints. We need the system to adapt to them.

f. *Self-Determination (Standard 1.02). We promote clients' right to self-determination.* We don't assume they should get the EBPs we know. Our job is to give clients information and the opportunity to decide. Do they want to do this, even if you told them this intervention will help their problem? Do they want this kind of help?

g. *Informed Consent (Standard 1.03).* We should tell clients the purpose, risks, and limits of services, as well as reasonable alternatives. We need to tell people if there's a little or a lot of evidence on the intervention. We also should be honest that some of the ideas and methods in the intervention may be unusual, and we're not sure if they're helpful. We should always talk about alternatives in a thoughtful manner.

h. *Competence towards Clients (Standard 1.04).* We are responsible for providing services within the boundaries of our training and professional experience and only provide new intervention techniques after appropriate training and supervision. You need to be well trained in the intervention, if it's possible. For example, with CBT or MI, you need to understand the concept and know what you want with the implementation, and then you can get the outcome you want.

i. *Cultural Awareness and Social Diversity (Standard 1.05).* We provide services that are sensitive to clients' cultures and the differences among people. Since most EBPs don't have extensive evidence based on diverse samples, this means we may have to tweak the interventions and monitor ourselves as to whether they are helping our clients. Overall, there should be more research that looks at concepts of illness and healing from different cultural viewpoints.

j. *Conflicts of Interest (Standard 1.06).* We should inform clients when a conflict of interest arises and resolve the issue in a way that makes their interests primary. There are agencies that require their staff to use an EBP and have clients' outcome data used in the evaluation study too. This can be driven by the agency's need for funding, but the EBP may not meet every client's needs and goals, and our clients may not want to be part of an evaluation.

k. *Consultation (Standard 2.05).* We seek the advice of colleagues to promote the best interests of our clients. We can ask colleagues who know our client's culture and the EBP we want, not use it whether they recommend it or not. It's a critical decision to offer an EBP to someone, so it's important to draw on the available expertise. You also need to have a clinical supervisor who's checking your work when you use an EBP with a client.

l.   *Continuing Education and Staff Development (Standard 3.08).* Agencies should provide continuing education for their staff on emerging knowledge related to social work practice. To help us become competent in the new EBPs, it makes sense there should be resources for training and supervising us to use them.

m. *Commitment to Employers (Standard 3.09).* We should improve the effectiveness of the services of our employing agencies. We should not let them interfere with our ethical practice of social work. This means we should take a stand on both providing and not providing certain EBPs after evaluating the EBPs with our clients.

n.   *Competence as Professionals (Standard 4.01).* We should critically examine and keep current with emerging knowledge and the literature related to social work and participate in continuing education relevant to practice. It's part of our job to read the research and get trained in new evidenced-based techniques.

o.   *Discrimination (Standard 4.02).* We should not practice, condone, facilitate, or collaborate with any form of discrimination. We may be discriminating if we use EBPs blindly, such as without asking who funded the research and whether it fits my client's worldview and what intervention they want. We need to protect our clients. Also, many EBPs don't take a strengths perspective. EBP is based on a pathology perspective. I tell my client, "Your strength is how you view your illness. I should see your strengths. You're not a ball of putty or playdough." Why not use only a strengths-perspective therapy? We know that the therapeutic alliance is important for healing.

p.   *Dishonesty, Fraud, and Deception (4.04).* We should not participate in dishonesty or deception. You need to make your client aware you've never done MI before, for example, that you're learning on your own from a book. "I've done a little bit of self-training, and I want to try it on you now." Or tell them that you think this EBP can help you, but it hasn't been researched with many people with your ethnic and language background. We need to tell people if there's a little or a lot of evidence on the intervention.

q. *Misrepresentation (Standard 4.06).* We should not misrepresent our services and expected treatment outcomes or our professional credentials to clients. If you're not trained in it, then you shouldn't say you are a CBT therapist. That's lying. You also shouldn't tell your client they're going to get fantastic results when you're not sure. But whatever works is good, even if you're not well trained in CBT and you use it and you evaluate to show that your clients benefit a lot from working with you.

r. *Integrity of the Profession (Standard 5.01).* We should promote high standards of practice, improve the integrity of our profession through research and thoughtful criticism, and dedicate time to promoting the competence of the profession and contribute to the social work knowledge base and literature. This means we should take leadership in developing EBPs for social work populations, including a push for developing ones that are culturally relevant and not going along with evidence that's not relevant.

s. *Evaluation and Research (Standard 5.02).* We should monitor practice interventions and fully use evaluation and research evidence in our professional practice. This means we can do our own evaluations with clients on the interventions we use. It could be EBPs or not. We can add to the knowledge base by doing small evaluations ourselves. Whatever works is good, and you use it, and your clients benefit a lot from working with you.

REFERENCES

The Original EBP Model

American Psychological Association Presidential Task Force on Evidence-Based Practice. (2006). Evidence-based practice in psychology. *American Psychologist, 61*(4), 271–285.

Sackett, D. L., Richardson, W. S., Rosenberg, W. M., & Haynes, R. B. (1997). *Evidence-based medicine: How to practice and teach EBM.* Churchill Livingstone.

Straus, S. E., Glasziou, P., Richardson, W. S., & Haynes, R. B. (2018). *Evidence-based medicine: How to practice and teach EBM* (5th ed.). Elsevier.

Straus, S. E., Richardson, W. S., Glasziou, P., & Haynes, R. B. (2010). *Evidence-based Medicine: How to practice and teach it* (4th ed.). Churchill Livingstone Elsevier.

Sue, D. W., & Sue, D. (2013). *Counseling the culturally diverse: Theory and practice* (6th ed.). John Wiley & Sons.

EBP in Social Work: History and Controversy

Aarons, G. A., & Sawitzky, A. C. (2006). Organizational culture and climate and mental health provider attitudes toward evidence-based practice. *Psychological Services, 3*(1), 61–72.

Barlow, D. H., Hayes, S. C., & Nelson, R. M. (1984). *The scientist practitioner: Research and accountability in clinical and educational settings.* Pergamon.

Bellamy, J. L., Bledsoe, S. E., & Traube, D. E. (2006). The current state of evidence-based practice in social work: A review of the literature and qualitative analysis of expert interviews. *Journal of Evidence-Based Social Work, 3*(1), 23–48.

Bilsker, D., & Goldner, E. (2004). Teaching evidence-based practice: Overcoming barriers. *Brief Treatment and Crisis Intervention, 4*(3), 271–275.

Bledsoe-Mansori, S. E., Manuel, J. I., Bellamy, J. L., Fang, L., Dinata, E., & Mullen, E. J. (2013). Implementing evidence-based practice: Practitioner assessment of an agency-based training program. *Journal of Evidence-Based Social Work, 10*(2), 73–90.

Bradley, R., Greene, J., Russ, E., Dutra, L., & Westen, D. (2005). A multidimensional meta-analysis of psychotherapy for PTSD. *American Journal of Psychiatry, 162*(2), 214–227.

Council on Social Work Education Commission on Accreditation. (1984). *Handbook of accreditation standards and procedures (revised July 1984).* Council on Social Work Education.

Council on Social Work Education Commission on Accreditation. (2003). *Educational policy and accreditation standards (5th ed.).* Council on Social Work Education.

Council on Social Work Education Commission on Accreditation. (2008). *2008 Educational policy and accreditation standards.* Council on Social Work Education.

Council on Social Work Education Commission on Accreditation. (2015). *2015 Educational policy and accreditation standards.* Council on Social Work Education.

Dozois, D. J. A. (2013). Psychological treatments: Putting evidence into practice and practice into evidence. *Canadian Psychology, 54*(1), 1–11.

Dulcan, M. K. (2005). Practitioner perspectives on evidence-based practice. *Child Adolescent Psychiatric Clinics of North America, 14*(2), 225–240.

Fischer, J. (1973). Is casework effective? A review. *Social Work, 18*(1), 5–20.

Fixsen, D. L., Naoom, S. F., Blase, K. A., Friedman, R. M., & Wallace, F. (2005). *Implementation research: A synthesis of the literature.* University of South Florida, Louis de la Parte Florida Mental Health Institute, The National Implementation Research Network.

Gambrill, E. D. (1999). Evidence-based practice: An alternative to authority-based practice. *Families in Society: The Journal of Contemporary Social Services, 80*(4), 341–350.

Gambrill, E. D. (2005). Critical thinking, evidence-based practice, and mental health. In S. A. Kirk (Ed.), *Mental Disorders in the Social Environment: Critical Perspectives* (pp. 247–269). Columbia University Press.

Gellis, Z. D., & Reid, W. J. (2004). Strengthening evidence-based practice. *Brief Treatment and Crisis Intervention, 4*(2), 155–165.

Gerdes, K., Edmonds, R. M., Haslam, D. R., & McCartney, T. (1996). A statewide survey of licensed clinical social workers' use of practice evaluation procedures. *Research on Social Work Practice, 6*(1), 27–39.

Gibbs, L., & Gambrill, E. D. (2002). Evidence-based practice: Counterarguments to objections. *Research on Social Work Practice, 12*(3), 452–476. doi:10.1177/1049731502012003007

Goldstein, E. (2007). Social work education and clinical learning: Yesterday, today, and tomorrow. *Clinical Social Work Journal, 35*(1), 15–23.

Gray, M., Joy, E., Plath, D., & Webb, S. A. (2013). What supports and impedes evidence-based practice implementation. A survey of Australian social workers. *Research on Social Work Practice, 23,* 157–166.

Greenhalgh, T., Robert, G., MacFarlane, F., Bate, P. & Kyriakidou, O. (2004). Diffusion of innovations in service organizations: Systematic review and recommendations. *The Milbank Quarterly, 82*(4), 581–629.

Guyatt, G., Cairns, J., Churchill, D., Cook, D., Haynes, B., Hirsh, J., Irvine, J., Levine, M., Levine, M., Nishikawa, J., Sackett, D., Brill-Edwards, P., Gerstein, H., Gibson, J., Jaeschke, R., Kerigan, A., Neville, A., Panju, A., Detsky, A., … Tugwell, P. (1992). Evidence-based medicine: A new approach to teaching the practice of medicine. *Journal of the American Medical Association, 268*(17), 2420–2425.

Howard, M. O., McMillen, C. J., & Pollio, D. E. (2003). Teaching evidence-based practice: Toward a new paradigm for social work education. *Research on Social Work Practice, 13*(2), 234–259. doi:10.1177/1049731502250404

Jenson, J. M. (2005). Connecting science to intervention: Advances, challenges, and the promise of evidence-based practice. *Social Work Research, 29*(3), 131–135.

Messer, S. B. (2006). Patient values and preferences. In J. C. Norcross, L. E. Beutler, & R. F. Levant (Eds.), *Evidence-based practices in mental health: Debate and dialogue on the fundamental questions* (pp. 31–40). American Psychological Association.

Mullen, E. J. (2004). Facilitating practitioner use of evidence-based practice. In A. R. Roberts & K. R. Yeager (Eds.), *Evidence-based practice manual: Research and outcome measures in health and human services* (pp. 205–210). Oxford University Press.

Mullen, E. J., & Bacon, W. (2004). Implementation of practice guidelines and evidence-based treatment: A survey of psychiatrists, psychologists, and social workers. In A. R. Roberts & K. R. Yeager (eds.), *Evidence-based practice manual: Research and outcome measures in health and human services* (pp. 210–218). Oxford University Press.

Mullen, E. J., Shlonsky, A., Bledsoe, S. E. & Bellamy, J. L. (2005). From concept to implementation: Challenges facing evidence-based social work. *Evidence & Policy: A Journal of Research Debate and Practice, 1*(1), 61–84.

Mullen, E. J., & Streiner, D. L. (2004). The evidence for and against evidence-based practice. *Brief Treatment and Crisis Intervention, 4*(2), 111–121.

Munro, W. (2002). The role of theory in social work research: A further contribution to the debate. *Journal of Social Work Education, 38*(3), 461–470.

National Association of Social Workers. (1979). *NASW Code of ethics (Guide to the everyday professional conduct of social workers).*

National Association of Social Workers. (1996). *NASW Code of ethics (Guide to the everyday professional conduct of social workers).*

National Association of Social Workers. (2015). *NASW Code of ethics (Guide to the everyday professional conduct of social workers).*

Nelson, T. D., Steele, R. G., and Mize, J. A. (2006). Practitioner attitudes toward evidence-based practice: Themes and challenges. *Administration and Policy in Mental Health, 33*(3), 398–409.

Proctor, E., Silmere, H., Raghavan, R., Hovmand, P., Aarons, G., Bunger, A. C., Griffey, R. T., & Hensley, M. (2011). Outcomes for implementation research: Conceptual distinctions, measurement challenges, and research agenda. *Administration and Policy in Mental Health, 36,* 24–34.

Rubin, A., & Knox, K. S. (1996). Data analysis problems in single-case evaluation: Issues for research on social work practice. *Research on Social Work Practice, 6*(1), 40–65.

Rubin, A., & Parrish, D. (2007). Challenges to the future of evidence-based practice in social work education. *Journal of Social Work Education, 43*(3), 405–428. doi:10.5175/JSWE.2007.200600612

Shlonsky, A., & Gibbs, L. (2004). Will the real evidence-based practice please stand up? Teaching the process of evidence-based practice to the helping professions. *Brief Treatment and Crisis Intervention, 4*(2), 137–153.

Sue, S. (1999). Science, ethnicity, and bias: Where have we gone wrong? *American Psychologist, 54*(12), 1070–1077.

Sue, S., & Zane, N. (2006). Ethnic minority populations have been neglected by evidence-based practices. In J. C. Norcross, L. E. Beutler, & R. F. Levant (Eds.), *Evidence-based practices in mental health: Debate and dialogue on the fundamental questions* (pp. 329–337). American Psychological Association.

Tolson, E.R. (1990). Synthesis: Why don't practitioners use single-subject designs? in L. Videka-Sherman and W.J. Reid (eds.), *Advances in clinical social work research* (pp. 58–64). NASW Press.

Webb, S. A. (2001). Some considerations on the validity of evidence-based practice in social work. *British Journal of Social Work, 31*(1), 57–79.

Westen, D. I. (2006). Are research patients and clinical trials representative of clinical practice? In J. C. Norcross, L. E. Beutler, & R. F. Levant (Eds.), *Evidence-based practices in mental health: Debate and dialogue on the fundamental questions* (pp. 161–175). American Psychological Association.

Wike, T. L., Bledsoe, S. E., Manuel, J. I., Despard, M., Johnson, L. V., Bellamy, J. L., & Killian-Farrell, C. (2014). Evidence-based practice in social work: Challenges and opportunities for clinicians and organizations. *Clinical Social Work Journal, 42*(2), 161–170.

Zayas, L. H., Drake, B., & Jonson-Reid, M. (2011). Overrating or dismissing the value of evidence-based practice: Consequences for clinical practice. *Clinical Social Work Journal, 39*(4), 400–405.

RESOURCES

The Original EBP Model

"Evidence-based Practice for Social Work," University of Michigan Library website.

> The website introduces the original EBP model and steps in its usage (Ask, Acquire, Appraise, Apply & Analyze/Adjust).

> https://guides.lib.umich.edu/EBP-Research

"Nursing: Evidence-Based Practice—What is EBP?" Daemen Library website.

> The website provides a brief and clear introduction to the EBP model, including a 4-minute video and links to EBP guides and tutorials.

> https://libguides.daemen.edu/EBP

Thoma, A., & Eaves, F. F. (2015). A brief history of evidence-based medicine (EBM) and the contributions of Dr. David Sackett. *Aesthetic Surgery Journal, 35*(8).

> The website listed below provides a free PDF download of this article, which provides a history of EBM and brief biography of Dr. David Sackett.

> https://academic.oup.com/asj/article/35/8/NP261/251339

"A Brief History of Evidence-based Practice," Evidence-based Optometry website.

> The website provides a brief discussion of EBP history and the role of EBP for eye care.

> https://www.eboptometry.com/content/optometry/article/brief-history-evidence-based-practice-0

"Evidence Based Practice (EBP)," *Physiopedia* website.

> The website provides a brief discussion of definition, steps and problems with EBP, and links to many training resources, including videos and websites, especially related to physiotherapy and medicine.

> https://www.physio-pedia.com/Evidence_Based_Practice_(EBP)

EBP in Social Work: History and Controversy

"Evidence-based Practice: NASW Practice Snapshot," National Association of Social Workers website.

> The website provides an overview of issues in the incorporation of EBP into mental health practice.

https://www.socialworkers.org/News/Research-Data/Social-Work-Policy-Research/Evidence-Based-Practice

Farley, A. J., Feaster, D., Schapmire, T. J., D'Ambrosio, J. G., Bruce, L., Oak, C. S., & Sar, B. K. (2009). The challenges of implementing evidence based practice: Ethical considerations in practice, education, policy, and research. *Social Work and Society Online Journal*, *7*(2).

This is a very nice overview article about what is EBP and the levels of implementation challenges, from training needs to organization policies.

https://ejournals.bib.uni-wuppertal.de/index.php/sws/article/view/76

Sackett, D. L., Rosenberg, W. M., Gray, J. A., Haynes, R. B., & Richardson, W. S. (1996). Evidence based medicine: What it is and what it isn't. *British Medical Journal*, *312*, 71–72.

The authors of this brief article promote an accurate understanding of the new evidence based medicine model at a time when the model faced negative reactions.

https://www.ncbi.nlm.nih.gov/pmc/articles/PMC2349778/

Satterfield, J. M., Spring, B., Brownson, R. C., Mullen, E. J., Newhouse, R. P., Walker, B. B., & Whitlock, E. P. (2009). Toward a transdisciplinary model of evidence-based practice. *Millbank Quarterly 87*(2), 368–390.

The article discusses core challenges in EBP by comparing EBP models across the disciplines of medicine, nursing, psychology, social work, and public health, including the evolution of the evidence-based medicine model with three circles.

https://www.ncbi.nlm.nih.gov/pmc/articles/PMC2698591/

Surface, D. (2009). Understanding evidence-based practice in behavioral health. *Social Work Today*, *9*(4), 22.

The article provides a good overview of the confusion over what EBP is, difficulties in putting EBP into practice, and reasons for resistance to EBP.

https://www.socialworktoday.com/archive/072009p22.shtml

Credit

Beginning with the Client's View

This chapter covers the client characteristics, culture, and preferences component of the EBP model. The EBP process begins with the client component, because it is client information obtained through careful assessment that drives the search for potentially useful EBPs. In this chapter, we will discuss the importance of cultural humility and our ethical responsibilities toward clients. We will also learn a framework for taking into consideration, when choosing an EBP, a client's view of their problem, acceptable means of resolution, and desired outcomes.

BRIEF LECTURE 2.1

Cultural Humility and Mental Health Disparities

Understanding cultural humility and disparities in the use of mental health services is important to EBP decision making for several reasons. First, taking a culturally humble standpoint is key to being able to establish a therapeutic alliance and conduct a comprehensive assessment, which includes gaining information on cultural and community influences on the client's preferences and values. Cultural humility is also a basic ingredient in a process of credibility (Sue & Zane, 1987), as covered in Brief Lecture 2.2, that ensures a thorough and culturally sensitive assessment, which is necessary for finding and selecting the right EBP. Second, cultural humility and mental health disparities are intimately linked, because clients' perceptions and experiences of poor cultural humility impact their access to care, including poor care initiation and early drop out. Being able to gain knowledge of the client's cultural background by showing a culturally humble stance will help in assessing the cultural fit of available EBPs and modifying the chosen one so that it will be accepted rather than rejected. Third, knowledge of the solutions advanced for reducing disparities, which center on developing community-based, family-based, and culturally oriented services, will be important for assessing what is the "best evidence" for a client, especially because most EBPs currently are individual-centered and do not come from the communities and cultures of the diverse clients served by social workers. Let's begin with an overview of cultural humility.

Cultural Humility

Cultural humility is maintaining a willingness to suspend what we think we know about a client and their culture. We are learners when it comes to understanding another's experience. Cultural humility is a process of self-reflection to understand personal and systemic biases and to develop respectful processes and relationships based on mutual trust. It is a means of recognizing and redressing power imbalances in the provider-patient relationship at the individual and institutional levels. It is a patient-centered approach to care in which culture and cultural difference are made salient rather than ignored. To practice cultural humility, the practitioner becomes aware especially of the negative influences of their own culture and cultural assumptions. Such awareness comes from the practitioner's commitment to examining their patterns of unintentional and intentional homophobia, racism, classism, and other "-isms." Institutionally, cultural humility involves systematic, planned steps and goals that support appreciation and respect for diversity and inclusion of culture and communities in the provision of care.

Tervalon and Murray-Garcia (1998) developed the construct of cultural humility in the context of healthcare and physician training. Below are the four components of their framework with slight adaptations for a social work context.

1. ***Lifelong learning and critical self-reflection.*** Understanding and putting aside our biases is a lifelong process involving ongoing critical self-reflection. To practice cultural humility, we need to learn to manage the feelings of superiority, confusion, and alienation that can occur when

cultural difference arises, and to stay open-minded when clients talk about identity or oppression in ways that heighten our anxiety. This emphasis on self-awareness does not discount the importance of gaining knowledge about cultural health care practices and beliefs and the histories of cultural groups. Rather, cultural humility is avoiding the false security of such knowledge and building our flexibility so we can assess anew the cultural aspects of each client's experiences. This component of cultural humility also entails systematic use of consultation with colleagues and community members who have expertise with the cultures of our clients.

2. ***Recognizing and challenging power imbalances through client-focused interviewing and care.*** Practicing cultural humility involves applying a client-focused and language-focused interviewing process. This involves allowing clients to ask questions and set the work agenda. It also requires treating clients from every cultural group equally when providing information on their conditions, giving positive and reinforcing comments, and allowing them time to speak. The practitioner also learns to use a less controlling and less authoritative style of communication so that the client can experience enough openness to be able to communicate aspects of culture and other needs and preferences.

3. ***Community-based care and advocacy.*** Cultural humility entails taking responsibility for implementing a community- and population-based approach to health promotion, illness prevention, and treatment that considers well-being holistically and addresses social determinants of health. This involves the practitioner's and organization's immersion in nonpaternalistic and respectful working relationships with community members and organizations, as well as letting the focus of expertise reside in the community rather than inside the agency or the Western medical model. The goal of cultural humility at the community level is identifying, believing in, and building on the strengths and healing practices of communities. This involves advocacy for changes in policies and practices of community and health organizations so that cultural healing practices and ways of understanding illness can be recognized and incorporated.

4. ***Institutional or organizational accountability.*** Self-reflection and self-critique are also required at the institutional level to ensure that policies and the institution's mission support inclusion and respectful consideration of cultural difference. Institutional processes that obstruct cultural humility are identified and addressed systematically. For example,

staff and administrators should come to represent diverse cultural groups based on an explicit hiring plan. Language interpretation by professionals (rather than reliance on clients' family members) is always made available. An ongoing cultural humility curricular plan is established. Institutional accountability, finally, also includes deliberate development of collaborative relationships and partnerships with the community that are respectful and mutually beneficial.

First Nations Health Authority

The First Nations Health Authority (FNHA) in British Columbia, Canada, emphasizes cultural safety together with cultural humility. Cultural safety is presented as an end result of a process of cultural humility and an element of higher quality care: "Cultural safety is an outcome based on respectful engagement that recognizes and strives to address power imbalances inherent in the health care system. It results in an environment free of racism and discrimination, where people feel safe receiving care" (FNHA, 2020). It is indigenous people who determine whether cultural safety has been achieved. A graphic illustration, "Leading a Framework for Cultural Safety & Humility for First Nations in BC," describes this framework (Bradd, 2016). The following practical tips and a call to action for providers are given in an FNHA webinar (Peters & McDonald, 2017):

- Be open when clients request cultural or alternative healing as part of their care. Be supportive, not dismissing. Have open conversations about what success looks like for your client.
- Collaborate with local Traditional Practitioners to offer holistic care.
- Learn and implement ways to integrate traditional wellness and healing into Western medicine.
- Support traditional wellness by protecting and enhancing family and community knowledge; finding appropriate healers/elders; revitalizing teachings; preserving traditional foods and medicines, mentoring, and guides; and promoting safety and accountability.
- Participate in cultural events and gatherings in the community.
- Include cultural and spiritual activities in your [and your organization's] annual plans.

Reflection Questions

1. How do you know if you are practicing cultural humility? How do you know that you are not working in a way that leads your client to terminate treatment prematurely?
2. Think about a client who is from a minority background and a background different from your own. Can you identify a prejudice or stereotype that you have had to manage mentally to not let it get in the way of working with the client respectfully?
3. How can cultural humility help you in your process of selecting an EBP for a client? How might it impact your selection of the EBPs that you will consider?

Mental Health Disparities

The literature on the delivery of mental health services has consistently drawn attention to inadequacies in the provision of services for racial and ethnic minority populations in the U.S. The 2015 report "Racial/Ethnic Differences in Mental Health Service Use among Adults" by the Substance Abuse and Mental Health Services Administration (SAMHSA) showed that White adults, in the past year, used mental health services (16.6%) more than American Indian or Alaska Native (15.6%), Black (8.6%), Hispanic (7.3%), and Asian (4.9%) adults. Similar patterns are observed for the likelihood of using a prescription psychiatric medication and for use of outpatient mental health services in the past year. Disparities in the use of services occur both in initiation of mental health care and in continuity of care (i.e., early dropout) (Snowden & Yamada, 2005). Compared with the majority population, racial and ethnic minority groups are more likely to delay initial treatment contact after first onset of mental disorders (Wang et al., 2005), and more likely to receive lower quality of care (Alegría et al., 2008). They are also less likely to use community mental health services and more likely to use inpatient hospitalization and emergency services (Samnaliev et al., 2009).

The reasons that racial and ethnic minorities are underserved include the lack of therapists with language skills, clinicians' stereotypes against ethnic clients, and discrimination. As a result of therapists' being unfamiliar with the cultural backgrounds of ethnic minority groups, they do not provide culturally appropriate forms of treatment, and ethnic minority clients find the services offered to be strange and unhelpful. The need to appreciate the cultural values of Black, Native American, Asian, and Hispanic/Latinx cultural groups has long been emphasized.

For several decades, researchers have been producing small pieces of evidence to argue the role of provider discrimination, prejudice, and cultural insensitivity in mental health disparities and the need to address these factors not only individually but institutionally. And only recently have there been publicly funded attempts to do so. We will gain an overview of provider-patient care issues related to culture through a seminal Institute of Medicine report and of how disparities can be reduced in community and culturally based programs through the California Reducing Disparities Project (CRDP; California Pan-Ethnic Health Network, 2018).

Institute of Medicine

An Institute of Medicine report, *Unequal Treatment: Confronting Racial and Ethnic Disparities in Healthcare*, provided an incisive review of the role of discrimination and cultural difference in disparities and health care quality (Smedley et al., 2003). The authors concluded, as background, that minorities with the same incomes, insurance coverage, access to care, health status, and medical conditions as Whites received less and poorer health care. In their search for factors that could explain disparities were patient-level factors and clinical care appropriateness. Patient-level factors viewed as contributing to lower quality and intensity of care included: (a) a historical legacy of mistrust of physicians and health care institutions; (b) minorities' negative experiences of real or perceived discrimination; and (c) experiences of subtle, subjective mistreatment in health care settings. The authors cautioned against explaining disparities with patient preferences, a recognized patient-level factor, without considering the impact of racial discrimination on the patient's expression of preferences for treatment.

Clinical care appropriateness factors, viewed as producing discriminatory patterns of care, included two mechanisms. The first was a provider's conscious and unconscious prejudice and stereotyping about the behavior and health of minorities. Such bias and stereotypes impact the provider's subjective perception, which leads to uncertainty and ambiguity when choosing from multiple treatment options, which themselves already have uncertainties. The second was greater clinical uncertainty when interacting with minority patients. Clinicians' perception of clinical signs and symptoms is sometimes incomplete when working with minority patients, and the patient's input also becomes subject to ambiguity and misunderstanding. Given that patients' experiences and reporting of symptoms and help-seeking behaviors vary greatly, the subjectivity and incompleteness of clinical perception leaves room for professional judgment and action. With these uncertainties and faced with multiple therapeutic options, providers' decision making also becomes ambiguous. A final factor pointing to the importance of cultural understanding was the racial and ethnic match between patient and provider; patients who were not matched rated their visits as less participatory and experienced lower satisfaction.

This Institute of Medicine report included other factors occurring outside of the clinical encounter. Institutional factors included how institutional and policy forces are geared toward promoting cost-effective and efficient care in a way that disproportionately affects minority patients. The provider is also impacted in their interpretation and choice of an intervention by financial incentives, the legal environment, and cultural influences.

California Reducing Disparities Project

The CRDP Strategic Plan (California Pan-Ethnic Health Network, 2018) is a culmination of five years of research and planning by a broad partnership of community organizations. The plan's objective is to address mental health disparities based on assessments of the mental health needs of five underserved populations: African American, Latinx, Native American, Asian and Pacific Islander, and LGBTQ. CRDP, funded with the passage of Proposition 63, the Mental Health Services Act, in 2004, represents an unprecedented attempt to allow minority communities to conduct on-the-ground research and plan how to address disparities for their own communities. A key theme of the strategic plan is that mental health providers will learn cultural competence skills and provide culturally tailored and community-based interventions. In the current phase of CRDP, selected community organizations across the state are implementing and evaluating community-based mental health prevention and intervention programs, which if shown to be effective will later be disseminated.

Below are some of the key strategies and actions proposed in the strategic plan aimed at more effectively reaching individuals and communities:

- Use currently available community assets to form the foundation of a community-based system of services that can meet the needs of the diverse communities.
- Reduce disparities and improve well-being by linking individuals to communities to build their resiliency. Such linkage will help individuals to better handle and reduce the risks of stress and mental illness associated with experiences of discrimination, which lead to feelings of invalidation, negation, dehumanization, disregard, and disenfranchisement, faced by minorities.

- Build community resiliency by having families, friends, churches, schools, and community groups work together to strengthen individuals and communities.
- Include family involvement in treatment and recovery to address rejection by family and faith communities (especially for LGBTQ youth and young adults).
- Develop innovative programs that fuse cultural activities with mental health services and programs to integrate individuals into cultural practices where they will feel accepted and affirmed (especially for LGBTQ services).
- Enhance school-based mental health and faith-based programs to fill the mental health needs of the unserved, underserved, and inappropriately served.

Reflection Questions

4. As a social work practitioner, how would you weave together traditional wellness and mainstream health concepts and methods? Can you give an example? Think about a Western-based psychotherapy that you know, its aims and methods, and how you might integrate that with a traditional wellness practice for a client.

5. In light of the problem of disparities and the need for but low availability of community-based interventions and programs (such as those proposed by CRDP), do you go ahead and use EBPs that are one-on-one (client-therapist focused) because strong evidence for these exist? How do you best help your client and the community?

6. If you find two EBPs that were evaluated in RCTs in university medical centers and a third EBP developed and evaluated in the community with a small sample using pre- and post-tests but no comparison group, which would you choose for your client? Assume that (a) all three EBPs address your client's problem areas, (b) the two RCTs included a very small number of participants from your client's diversity group, and (c) the entire sample of the community-based EBP consisted of people from your client's diversity group.

> BRIEF LECTURE 2.2

Credibility and Gift Giving

Stanley Sue and Nolan Zane in 1987 wrote "The Role of Culture and Cultural Techniques in Psychotherapy: A Critique and Reformulation" to present a framework for culturally responsive psychotherapy with ethnic minority populations. Their reformulation was in response to the lack of helpfulness in reducing dropout rates of the recommendation that psychotherapists know the client's culture and apply specific cultural techniques. Their framework assists in EBP decision making because it focuses on two processes, credibility and gift giving, that can guide the practitioner in choosing the best EBP and applying it sensitively. This brief lecture summarizes their argument, as laid out in the article, starting with their critiques of historical efforts to increase the effectiveness of psychotherapy for ethnic minorities.

Critique of the Concept of Match or Fit

The concept of match or fit guided early attempts to increase effectiveness. Treatments provided would need to match the cultural values and experiences of clients. Changes in the mental health system were implemented based on this concept. Mental health services hired bilingual/bicultural personnel and provided training and continuing education on cultural groups and ethnic issues. Health systems introduced ethnic-specific mental health centers and created units within mental hospitals that specialized in an ethnic population. Some communities also created multiservice centers where mental health treatment was offered together with other services so that clients could avoid the social stigma of mental illness. Sue and Zane (1987) critiqued this concept of match or fit:

> Is it not impossible to gain sufficient knowledge of the different ethnic groups? If traditional forms of treatment should be modified, does this mean that ... psychoanalysis, gestalt therapy, humanistic approaches and behavior modification are inappropriate? In what ways should therapy be modified? If match is important, should not therapists be ethnically similar to their clients? The notion of match brings forth a whole host of problems and issues. (p. 39)

Sue and Zane also noted the practical difficulties with achieving the system changes. For instance, graduate programs would not be admitting enough Spanish-speaking students to fill the ranks, and degree programs did already offer courses in ethnicity and cultural diversity.

Critique of Emphasis on Learning and Applying Cultural Knowledge and Values

Sue and Zane especially critiqued the recommendation to gain knowledge of the client's culture and apply cultural values in therapy. For example, Hispanic Americans were described as valuing linearity, role-structured rather than egalitarian relationships, and a present-focused orientation in therapy (Szapocznik, Santisteban, Kurtines, Hervis, & Spencer, 1982, as cited in Sue & Zane, 1987, p. 37). Therapists working with Black Americans would need to understand the group's cultural traditions of group identification and collectivity, spirituality, and a flexible concept of time, along with reactions to racial oppression (Nobles, 1980, as cited in Sue & Zane, 1987, p. 38). Sue and Zane observed the frequent inappropriate application of cultural knowledge. They described a case presentation of a fourth-generation Chinese American in which the intern applied knowledge of Chinese culture in a literal and stereotypic fashion. They concluded:

> The point is that in working with ethnic-minority groups, no knowledge of their culture is detrimental; however, even with this knowledge, its application and relevance cannot always be assumed because of individual differences among members of a particular ethnic group. (p. 38–39)

Critique of Applying Culture-Specific Techniques

Investigators next developed and recommended ethnic-specific intervention techniques, rather than being satisfied with advocating cultural sensitivity and knowledge of the backgrounds of clients. As an example, therapists who work with Asian Americans should be directive, providing structure and guidance, rather than nondirective, because Asian Americans are more familiar with structured relationships (Atkinson, Maruyama, & Matsui, 1978, as cited in Sue & Zane, 1987, p. 39). Filipino Americans expect an authoritative rather than egalitarian therapist role, and therapists should avoid approaches involving introspection, interpersonal feelings, and communication (Ponce, 1974, as cited in Sue & Zane, 1987, p. 39). With Hispanics, therapists should reframe the client's problems as medical issues to lower resistance to therapy (Meadow, 1982, as cited in Sue & Zane, 1987, p. 39). In this fashion, recommendations of cultural techniques for ethnic groups also appeared.

Sue and Zane, with this development, showed that cultural knowledge and technique-oriented approaches were distal (or distant) from the goal of treatment, because neither is linked to processes that result in effective therapy.

> Therapists assume that [cultural knowledge] enables them to more accurately understand and assess clients and to develop treatment strategies that result in positive outcomes. In actuality, therapists' knowledge of the culture of clients is quite distal to therapeutic outcomes, in the sense that the knowledge must be transformed into concrete operations or strategies. This is why recommendations for knowledge of culture are necessary but not sufficient for effective treatment. (p. 39)

Regarding techniques on how to conduct therapy with ethnic minority clients, Sue and Zane reasoned that these were used to make therapy less foreign to clients and support clients' beliefs that their therapists understood them. Just like knowledge of a client's cultural background, cultural techniques were intended to support the therapist in assessing, understanding, and facilitating change. If this is so, the end goal of such strategies is to enhance the credibility of therapists and therapies. With this reasoning, it is not the techniques or tactics that necessarily facilitate positive outcomes, but it is the enhancement of credibility that does (see Figure 2.1, replicated from Sue & Zane, 1987, p. 40). With this background, Sue and Zane presented two basic processes, credibility and giving, which are not new to psychology but are important for working with ethnic minority clients.

Process of Credibility: Ascribed and Achieved Credibility

"Credibility refers to the client's perception of the therapist as an effective and trustworthy helper" (Sue & Zane, 1987, p. 40). Credibility is an expectancy of benefit from treatment or a belief in the therapist and the methods of treatment. There are two forms of credibility. The first is ascribed credibility, the position or role that others assign. This may be based on age, gender, expertise, or other factors. A older male physician would have higher ascribed status than a young female social work intern, especially in some cultures more than others. The second is achieved credibility, gained through the therapist's skills and actions—what the therapist does to earn the client's trust and hope. Actions that contribute to achieved credibility are diverse, including, for example, providing empathic understanding and accurate assessment. These forms of credibility may contribute to effectiveness. The lack of ascribed credibility may contribute to underuse (or under-initiation) of mental health treatment; people do not believe that practitioners have what it takes to help them. The lack of achieved credibility may contribute to premature termination. To be effective, credibility and a therapeutic alliance must be formed within a few sessions.

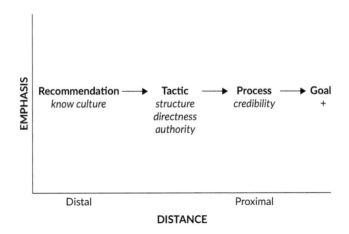

FIGURE 2.1 Relationship Between Therapeutic Emphasis and Distance from the Goal of Treatment

Achieved credibility can be examined in three areas where cultural issues are important:

1. **Conceptualization of the problem:** The problem is conceptualized in a manner congruent with the client's belief systems. Therapists convey an understanding of the causes of the problem in a way that is not antagonistic to the client's understanding.
2. **Means for problem resolution:** The therapist does not require the client to respond in a way that is culturally incompatible or unacceptable (e.g., asking an Asian client to directly express anger to her father in family therapy).
3. **Goals of treatment:** The definitions of the goals of treatment are concordant (e.g., the therapist does not pursue facilitating deep insight, which would only make the client very uncomfortable).

Achieving congruence with the client across these areas enhances credibility. When incongruence occurs, the therapist can try to restore credibility by showing the validity of their viewpoint. Incongruities also signal the need to review the treatment strategy and any misunderstandings related to desired outcomes, means of resolution, and problem conceptualization. Cultural knowledge can help in achieving credibility, because knowing the client's cultural values assists with assessing credibility across the three areas. At the same time, focusing on the process of credibility helps therapists to not confuse the values of the client's ethnic group with those of the client. Enhancing credibility remains the focal point.

Process of Gift Giving

"Giving is the client's perception that something was received from the therapeutic encounter. The client has received a 'gift' of some sort from the therapist" (Sue & Zane, 1987, p. 40). Gift giving is attaining some form of meaningful gain early in therapy, even in the first session. Clients need to feel a direct benefit from treatment soon after the start of treatment. Sue and Zane call this benefit a "gift" because gift giving is a ritual in interpersonal relationships among Asians. Gift giving builds achieved credibility as well as addresses skepticism toward Western treatments and contributes to reducing dropout. In response to clients' anxiety and uncertainty about therapy, therapists often raise expectations of benefits by explaining how therapy works, but this is not enough. Gift giving shows clients the relationship between work in therapy and alleviation of problems. Gifts vary and depend on what can be helpful to the client. Examples include providing cognitive clarity to a client in a confusing or crisis situation, normalizing thoughts and feelings and placing them in context, or alleviating negative emotions for a client who is depressed or anxious.

Reflection Questions

1. How are cultural humility and the processes of achieving credibility and gift giving related?
2. How can aiming for congruence with your client's view on problem conceptualization, means of problem resolution, and goals of treatment be helpful when choosing from among different EBPs from the literature for a client? How could it help you to choose or eliminate EBPs that, for example, are reported to be effective for depression?

 ACTIVITY 2.1 **Share a Client's Views Related to Culture**
In-Class Activity (Small Groups)

Instructions

1. Think about a client whose views regarding their problem conceptualization, means of problem resolution, and/or goals of treatment were different from your own. This could be your case paper client or another client or a friend or family member.

2. Jot down and try to address: (a) a brief background of your client and the service setting; (b) the areas in which your views differ from your client's, noting especially culturally based differences; (c) any difficulties you experienced in understanding and accepting their views; and (d) how you dealt with the differences.

3. Share your client case with your group.

Examples

I. Asian Senior

I visited an Asian senior facility for my diversity research paper. I was able to sit in on an individual therapy session. The facility's population are seniors struggling with dementia and depression. What I found really interesting is that the words or phrases *depression*, *mentally ill*, and *sick* were never used, and it was intentional. Moreover, rather than emphasize any emotional component during therapy, there was an emphasis on *overthinking*. For instance, instead of naming the client's emotions, the therapist would say, "You are thinking wrong. You are thinking too much." I think there is a significance in this distinction. In Chinese culture, especially with most elderly who immigrated, they do not believe in or want to admit that mental illness exists. There is also resistance to acknowledging feelings in the presence of others. The therapist told the senior that her overthinking and feelings would inconvenience the family.

While we, from a Western perspective, may not all agree that the suppression of feelings is healthy, I think that in this particular therapeutic relationship, it was helpful for the therapist to communicate with the patient in the way that he did. I feel that if he had taken an approach that forced her to confront her feelings, it would cause her to question her identity. His therapeutic communication was action-oriented and direct. The client had grown depressed because she felt that her old age stripped her of her roles and discredited her past achievements. The therapist advised her on what she needed to do to benefit the family. This was a culturally sensitive approach, because I think in Asian culture, especially if the person is older, they are especially motivated by hearing direct actions and the benefits that would contribute to the family. It taps on a collectivist mindset.

Tying together the cultural aspects, *overthinking* and role loss were the patient's problem—conceptualization rather than depression or emotional imbalance. An action-oriented or direct approach was the means of problem resolution, rather than confronting feelings. Finally, the culturally congruent goal was to take action that would benefit the family and restore her family role.

II. Seventh-Grade Girl

My client is a mixed-race (Black dad, White mom) seventh-grade girl who has very low self-worth. She lives in deep poverty. Both parents had learning difficulties as children and didn't graduate from high school. I work with her as a school-based counselor. Understanding her situation for me has mostly revolved around recognizing [social] class and the cutting effects of entrenched poverty. The family has food insecurity and challenges maintaining cleanliness in the home. My client reports poor hygiene. She sees her dad navigate and work street culture. Her mom has government assistance and mostly educated her daughter in a White culture of "respectability." My client's skills in self-advocacy are very limited. Her dad would like her to get her hair done. In our sessions, we navigate her understanding of their cultures and backgrounds. We explore how she has found a balance and how, within their family unit, they have created their own. However, she must understand both parents as unique individuals, and she has chosen to take and leave parts of both their characters and cultures as her own. I do my best to follow and understand her journey as she becomes her own person. To conceptualize the client's views, the therapist should understand the client's belief system. That's what I've tried to do at every moment.

III. 56-Year-Old African American Man

My client is an African American male, My client is an African American male in his mid-fifties. He has lived in this particular supportive housing residence for over 15 years. From the very first time the case manager introduced him to me, we have had a relationship that is not what I'm used to in therapist-client relationships. What I think is happening, and I've spoken about this with my supervisor, is that some part of my client understands that he is meeting with me for therapy sessions. But another part of him has the opinion that anyone who goes to therapy must be weak or is failing at life somehow. As a result of this ambivalence, my client claims we are not meeting for therapy but just visiting. Given the part of him that doesn't see himself as having any problem, he conceptualizes our interactions as a "visit," while I call it therapy. We "visit" every Monday at 2:00 p.m. for one hour and talk about his life and where he finds joy, what his childhood was like, and the values he bases his life on and more. One of our conversations covered his sharing with me how many African Americans don't think going to therapy is a normal activity, and I shared with him that many of my White friends talk openly about going to therapy and don't think a thing of it. This conversation was an eye-opener for me. It helped me understand that we were examples of two diverse cultures coming together. The way I approach these sessions with him is to remember to follow his lead, to keep my questions focused on the topics at hand, and to not introduce usual therapeutic language.

IV. South Asian Domestic Violence Survivor

I have previously worked with South Asian DV survivors. Women who are emigrants from India have several challenges to leaving an abusive relationship, aside from seeking safety. Often there is fear of the shame that will come to their family back in India and of a real possibility of being alone for the rest of their lives if they leave the abusive relationship. Arranged marriages are still very common, and being divorced often means you will remain single for the rest of your life. Although I am a South Asian woman who was born in India, my lens is more Western and very liberal. Working with these women, I had to approach them with an understanding of the cultural considerations, especially the idea that leaving an abusive relationship may be even more harmful. Working within their conceptualization of the problem, we didn't make the focus of our meetings about leaving but about building their self-esteem and resilience.

V. Older Chinese Woman

I worked with an older Chinese woman as her case manager. As we worked together longer, I saw that she seemed depressed and was rather isolated. After an incident where she expressed suicidal ideation, I had to address this issue with my supervisor and the client. She refused to see a mental health provider because she told me, "Chinese people don't talk to other people about these problems." In her own conceptualization, she did not think there was a problem or that traditional therapy or psychiatry would help. To the client, the main problem for her was her health as an epileptic. She feared going out on her own, since she could have a seizure, and felt that most Chinese people did not understand her condition. Her goals were to go back to her old doctor, get back on the medications she found helpful, and have someone to advocate with her in medical settings, while also having a companion to go out into the community with her. This changed my perceptive that therapy or traditional mental health treatment is the best option for clients who are depressed and isolated.

VI. High School Student

I provided counseling services to a high school student of Middle Eastern descent. He wanted to focus on the goal to strengthen his cultural identity. He was kicked out of his family home for having a tumultuous relationship with his father and was left homeless. He began living with the family of a classmate who was White American. He was required to attend weekly Catholic church services while staying with this family and became distant from his identity. The goal during therapy that was expressed and cultivated was to develop his cultural identity and link him to services that would allow him to practice his religious beliefs, as well as obtain cultural wealth. The goal of treatment with this student was completely rooted in a cultural standpoint, which required me not only to research knowledge of the culture but also have the student divulge his cultural beliefs and values with me. Obtaining pertinent information from him about his cultural identity allowed him to own his culture again. This, in turn, built trust and hope within him.

VII. Refugee from Iraq

I worked with refugees that had just arrived in the U.S. One client was a single man from Iraq. We had been working together toward goals that we had mutually come up with, but after several weeks, he brought up the importance of community and finding people who shared his culture. While I had been supporting him to get his basic needs met, I had failed to see an aspect that was just as essential to him. Once I recognized this, I was able to connect him with other Iraqi refugees in the city who had come through the program. The client was able to form a community with people who had a better understanding of his situation and background and provided him a different form of support than I could give.

❯ DISCUSSION 2.1 How Do I Choose an EBP? There's So Much to Consider!

Sue and Zane argue that the practices of ethnic matching of clinician and client, using culture-specific techniques, or applying the values of the client's ethnic group can turn out to be unhelpful. They argue that working to achieve credibility will be more directly helpful to reaching the goal of treatment.

1. Do you agree with Sue and Zane's framework?
2. In Sue and Zane's framework, how does culture come into play in the treatment? Can a treatment be completely free of culture? How do you decide when and how culture comes into play?
3. Are Sue and Zane saying that we can use Western-based treatments with ethnic minorities? How do we decide?
4. Does this mean it is *not important* and *not necessary* to develop a community system of care, build community resilience, and integrate mental health and community services?

5. Does this mean we do not have to worry about the underlying issues of cultural bias with controlled experiments that apply mainstream constructs and samples—how reductionist they are and how they exclude other ways of perceiving and knowing, nonexperts, and other properties and factors?

See how students answered on page 65.

 ACTIVITY 2.2 **Test Your Understanding of the Chapter**

Answer the following true or false questions. Provide an explanation of your answer.

1. Social workers' lack of cultural humility likely contributes to clients' early termination or dropout from treatment, which contributes to disparities in access to care for minority groups.

2. Through social work practice experience across many years with clients from different diversity groups, a social worker will naturally develop cultural humility. When one does not yet have much practice experience, it is important to devote time to learning historical and cultural facts about clients' cultural groups.

3. One aspect of practicing cultural humility is challenging power imbalances in the provider-client relationship, such as the provider giving careful attention to treating every client, whatever the client's cultural group, equally.

4. Cultural humility at the institutional level includes the deliberate development of respectful and mutually beneficial relationships and partnerships with communities.

5. Two aspects of mental health disparities are minority populations receiving lower quality of care and delaying the initiation of mental health care after the onset of a mental illness.

6. Disparities in mental health services utilization is wholly due to minority patients' preferences that do not match the types of treatments and to the race or ethnicity of the service providers offered to them, even though they may claim experiences of discrimination and mistreatment by their providers.

7. Culturally tailored and community-based mental health interventions will likely not contribute to reducing mental health disparities, and resources should not be wasted in these areas.

8. According to Sue and Zane, cultural knowledge and technique-oriented approaches are distal to therapeutic outcomes, because they must be transformed into concrete operations and strategies and be linked to processes that result in effective therapy.

9. Ascribed credibility is a client's expectancy of benefit from treatment because the therapist has carefully selected an EBP that matches the client's views and preferences about their problem, the means for resolution, and goals of treatment.

10. A mental health clinician can achieve credibility in many ways. The client needs to perceive that something helpful occurred in the client-provider encounter, especially early in therapy.

See the answers on page 70.

⌘ Case Paper Task 2.1

Write the *Client's Conceptualization* Section

Instructions: Write the *Client's Conceptualization* section of your case paper assignment.

Case Paper Instructions:

Client's Conceptualization (3–4 paragraphs, 5 points)

a. *Problem Conceptualization.* State your client's understanding of their presenting problem, including causes and impact. (*1–2 paragraphs, 2 points*)

b. *Treatment Goals and Appropriate Forms of Treatment.* Formulate meaningful and measurable goals for your client and identify form(s) of treatment that would be acceptable and helpful considering your client's background, preferences, and culture. Address both micro-level (individual and family) and mezzo-level (school, work, and community) goals and interventions, even though the EBPs you review are micro-level interventions. (*2 paragraphs, 3 points*)

Laura's Example

Needs Strengthening

Client's Conceptualization

Laura is a teenager who has issues of acting out in high school. Her problem may be long-term, because she has incorporated negative coping skills. She cannot control her anger and isolates. Her mother is unsupportive because she works two jobs and has no time for Laura. Laura's autonomy is important; she needs to build her independence from her mother. Laura has made no friends. She is depressed and anxious. Her provisional diagnosis is Mood Disorder, Not Otherwise Specified.

Teachers and administrators reported that Laura has problems controlling her anger, gets into fights, and disrupts the classroom at least once or twice a day. They requested individual and group counseling for Laura to reduce her number of fights, disruptions, and suspensions. The goal of treatment is for Laura to control her anger and get in trouble less. Individual therapy is the choice of treatment approach for Laura.

How could you strengthen the above? Are Laura's views of her problems, goals of treatment, and preferred forms of treatment described?

Well-Written

As you read the below example, reflect on what makes the description richer in terms of client information and the client's viewpoints that are useful for defining treatment goals and finding appropriate interventions.

Client's Conceptualization

Problem Conceptualization

Laura reports that she has problems controlling her anger, especially with other students, teachers, and administrators. She says she feels anxious when there are any possible interactions and confrontations with others. She also reports that she is sad, lonely, has problems trusting peers and adults, and does not feel connected to school or to her mother. Laura would like to work on managing her anger and to learn how to develop trusting relationships, including making friends and being closer to her mother. She would like to participate in individual therapy to vent about her experiences, explore the reasons for these problems, and come up with possible solutions. She is open to involving and learning to talk with her mother. She also expressed interest in academic counseling and planning for college. She recognizes that addressing the separation traumas that occurred will be helpful to her but is not ready to connect with her father.

Treatment Goals and Appropriate Forms of Treatment

The treatment goals are to decrease instances of anger escalation, decrease symptoms of depression, establish meaningful relationships with others, and build the relationship with her mother, including processing the attachment traumas. The treatment outcomes will be measured by recording all instances in which the client has had altercations with others as a result of anger, client's report of number and severity of depression symptoms at each session, and client's record-keeping of positive social interactions with peers and adults. Individual and family psychotherapy will be beneficial in treating the client in the micro level. Also, gaining the support and involvement of the client's mother on the client's goals and planned interventions and building an active alliance with the family will be an important component of treatment. At the mezzo level, the intervention is to provide case management that ensures linkages and supportive resources that promote academic success and personal and social development.

(continued)

Eddie's Example

Well-Written

Does the below problem conceptualization reflect Eddie's viewpoints rather than the social worker's? Are the treatment goals meaningful to Eddie? Are they measurable, and do they address micro, mezzo, and macro levels?

Problem Conceptualization

Eddie sought therapy at MCC to address his feelings of severe emotional dysregulation and explosive behaviors, especially when in situations where he feels stressed and attacked. He also wants to address his use of video games and smoking cannabis as his sole coping strategies after recently relocating to an urban, high-crime neighborhood from rural Mississippi. His goals are to address the negative symptoms of his PTSD by learning healthier and varied coping skills to feel less angry, to talk about his past traumas, and to continue to foster healthier relationships and strengthen the emotional bonds with his children and grandchild after being estranged for years. Eddie declared, "I want to enjoy my life." He is interested in exploring San Francisco, increasing his social activities, and reducing his isolation in his small SRO. He is open to different types of therapies and activity groups.

Treatment Goals and Appropriate Forms of Treatment

Individual and group therapy and social groups would be appropriate types of intervention for achieving the following treatment goals defined with Eddie that support promoting his ability to regulate his emotions and behaviors in the short- and long-term:

a. Learn strategies for managing anxiety and regulating emotions and behaviors, such as practicing mindfulness and breathing exercises, visiting serene places, and avoiding potentially triggering situations like certain bus lines;

b. Learn healthy coping skills to replace smoking cannabis and playing video games;

c. Join and participate in community support networks that affirm him and promote his ability to manage anxiety and regulate emotions;

d. Increase social activities (see sf.freecheap.com), including leaving his tense neighborhood, visiting scenic areas of Los Angeles creating new hobbies, and participating in the photography group therapy at MCC;

e. Increase positive social contacts with children and grandchild;

f. Process past life experiences with a therapist, especially processing traumas so he can view them in their proper place; and

g. Learn to challenge long-held negative core beliefs and assumptions that are maladaptive and no longer serve him.

ANSWERS

Discussion 2.1 Answers   **How Do I Choose an EBP? There's So Much to Consider!**

How Students Answered

Sue and Zane argue that the practices of ethnic matching of clinician and client, using culture-specific techniques, or applying the values of the client's ethnic group can turn out to be unhelpful. They argue that working to achieve credibility will be more directly helpful to reaching the goal of treatment.

1. **What are your thoughts on Sue and Zane's framework?**

   a. [It gives me] slimy feelings, manipulating clients into believing credibility through cultural match, techniques, and values. It's an enterprise based on human suffering. Therapists should [instead] observe and validate cultural values and individual values. They should guide healing and self-recovery! No one wants a therapist who's ignorant to personal and systemic struggles. We are ambassadors for our people. Yes, I agreed with all [their ideas of] striking a balance of our cultures and our individuality.

   b. I know I wouldn't want a therapist who sees me as a queer Chinese American ambassador for the people, but I also wouldn't want a therapist who is ignorant to my personal and systemic struggles either. The framework was ultimately extremely helpful to consider in my own practices, in terms of how I can balance understanding one's cultural context while holding space for them to have their own meaningful and sometimes contradictory values, experiences, and desires in session.

   c. I found the point about being culturally sensitive as a means to establish credibility extremely interesting. Though I understood the idea that cultural techniques cannot be the sole intervention for an effective practice, I hadn't thought about the deeper benefit that comes from having these cultural knowledges.

   d. I appreciated learning about both parts of the model, credibility and gift giving. I think a lot about how I am perceived by my clients in my internship, particularly when opening services, and it's valuable to know that credibility with clients can be built through actions and skills that communicate understanding and alliance. In particular, I found the notion of gift giving interesting, as it is absolutely aligned with what many of us do when entering a new space or culture; we bring a token of our appreciation and welcome. To me, in my case management work, I have typically thought about this as a way of achieving "buy in," in that I want my clients to see that the time they spend engaging with me will be quickly beneficial in some tangible way.

e.   I would imagine that it takes a fair amount of skill to assess a client and provide a "gift" within the first couple of sessions. This underscores the importance of developing assessment skills, since that is the basis of our knowledge of clients. Without being able to conduct an appropriate and thorough assessment, a clinician would have little to go off of for providing a gift within therapy or increasing credibility.

f.   The model speaks to the concepts of cultural relevance and cultural humility rather than cultural competence as key approaches for therapists. Their model of credibility stood out to me particularly. Essentially, these three congruencies between client and therapist mean that the therapist respects and believes the client's reality, is not claiming a superior understanding of the client's life than the client themselves, and trusts the client to direct their own process. Being aware of these congruencies goes a long way in reframing the therapist's position as facilitator rather than the expert who is going to "fix" the client. I see my clients as entirely capable of growing and healing themselves with the right support and resources. This framework puts words to how I think about therapeutic work. It allows for a client's dignity and self-determination.

g.   I believe deeply in the use of general cultural training and education to better serve ethnic groups. Ethnic-specific health care creates a safer space and the most culturally responsive services. If I were in a macro health care role, I would advocate having ethnic-specific health care centers.

h.   Gift giving is an interesting way to put it. I agree with the sentiment, that the therapist must make an effort to make positive strides early on and build that therapeutic bond. Gift giving almost implies that the client doesn't deserve to be told positive aspects of their progress or life experience, but that you have appeared to bless them with your gifts. Using this approach, they already were a whole person when they walked in.

i. The power of a match is intriguing to me. As a queer clinician, I find my most impactful and deepest work to be with LGBTQ clients. However, as a White clinician, I don't feel that same energy with a White client.

2. **In Sue and Zane's framework, how does culture come into play in the treatment? Can a treatment be completely free of culture? How do you decide when and how culture comes into play?**

a. Sue and Zane say culture comes into play in the assessment of the three areas: problem conceptualization, means of problem resolution, and goals of treatment.

b. I see it as what the client says about each area—the content. For example, for problem conceptualization, the client is completely distressed because he sees himself as failing to fulfill his family duties as the male provider. He's unable to keep a job. He's not doing the higher status work he did in Malaysia. Also, his wife is the one earning the money with a regular job.

c. An example for means of problem resolution for someone who is African American is that she says she wants to include her spirituality, talking about it and practicing it and involving her church community and resources in the treatment.

d. I would choose EBPs that fit how the client sees the three areas. The EBP has to target the client's goals, it has to match the client's means of resolution, and it definitely has to fit how she or he sees what the problem is. This is [determined] through the search question.

e. I think a treatment can't be completely free of culture. Even if the ethnic minority client never talks about their culture and works with you for a year, you're still using the culture behind the therapy method. For example, you might be using psychodynamic or cognitive-behavioral techniques. Those definitely have Western assumptions.

f. Treatment can be free of the client's culture if the client never brings anything up explicitly. It's also disrespectful to insist a client give cultural information when they don't want to or don't have any to give. This would not be practicing cultural humility.

g. I agree that to practice cultural humility, it's up to the client when culture comes into play. It should be incorporated when she or he brings something up.

h. If the client doesn't communicate any culture-based preferences in the assessment, and we're already using CBT or something else, the cultural issues can still come up as goals, as ways of working through a problem, and these should be respected and incorporated.

3. **Are Sue and Zane saying that we can use Western-based treatments with ethnic minorities? How do we decide?**

a. Yes, they are. But I would say that the Western-based treatment has to fit the client's goals, means, and view of the problem. Otherwise, we would not be gaining more credibility, and the client might drop out.

b. It's fine to use Western-based treatments, but we should tell the client how they work, how problems are resolved, what kind of goals are targeted—like is it insight or concrete problem-solving—and then let the client confirm they want this.

c. What I liked about Sue and Zane's approach is that they let us know it is okay. We don't have to not use psychodynamic or motivational interviewing with someone who's not at all acculturated to the U.S., as long as it supports credibility and is gift giving. The lesson for me of their article is to focus on what the client really needs to help them, right away and ongoing. It's about culture but not about culture.

d. I think we have to decide extremely carefully. There are still all those other problems we learned about—ethnocentrism, reductionism, and epistemic violence. We have to decide more broadly, take a look at everything that's available, and maybe use the CBT but work with the community too.

4. **Does this mean it is not *important* and *not necessary* to develop a community system of care, build community resilience, and integrate mental health and community services?**

a. No, it doesn't mean it's not important. We have to develop a community system of care. People in social work who work with minority communities know that's what's needed. The research is very slow to catch up, and the resources to do so will be even slower.

b.   If we don't support the creation of new community practices, like the CRDP ones, then ethnocentrism will always dominate.

c.   We can't continue to give these one-on-one clinic-based services to everyone. We leave out a lot of people. A lot of people won't get help at all, and for those who do, we may not be helping them in the best way if we don't set up more options based on what communities see as necessary.

d.   I think it's important to see that Sue and Zane didn't say "Western therapies for everyone" and no more cultural techniques! There should be and are Native American indigenous therapies and services that involve the community.

e.   If we look at the client holistically, conduct a holistic assessment that includes needs at all levels, micro, mezzo, and macro, and all facets of life that the client needs support for, we will easily see that community care and building the communities' capacity should be given the emphasis.

f.   I agree. We can't get lost in using only the current, available EBPs because that's what there is that's been researched. We can't forget the social justice questions.

5.   **Does this mean we do not have to worry about the underlying issues of cultural bias with controlled experiments that apply mainstream constructs and samples—how reductionist they are and how they exclude other ways of perceiving and knowing, nonexperts, and other properties and factors?**

a.   We have to worry about all of these issues all the time, even when choosing an EBP for one client. The problem is that there are a lot of EBPs coming from controlled experiments, and we know they have the highest grade of evidence, but all of that is about internal validity. Social workers look at external validity and exclusion. That's our job.

b.   From the last chapter, we learn that a lot of people can be left out of these tightly controlled experimental studies. That is a huge issue that shouldn't be ignored, along with the other ones that are also hidden.

c.   I don't know if it's practice-informed research or social justice–informed research that's needed, but we have to do it in a way that's inclusive, and we have to advocate funding and policies that allow community building and community interventions to grow.

d. I agree, and it shouldn't just be done through implementation studies on Western treatments created at a high level. The research should start down low in the community, with an exchange of knowledge among experts from all sides.

e. We always have to remember that DBT, CBT, ACT, Mindfulness-Based Stress Reduction, and other treatments come from certain value frameworks. They are evaluated and made available, but we always have to help our clients as whole people, and they will need more than what one of these common evidence-based treatments can give them. We have to keep our vision on what each EBP can provide and not provide.

Activity 2.2 Answers **Test Your Understanding of the Chapter**

Answers: 1. True, 2. False, 3. True, 4. True, 5. True, 6. False, 7. False, 8. True, 9. False, 10. True.

REFERENCES

Cultural Humility and Mental Health Disparities

Alegría, M., Chatterji, P., Wells, K., Cao, Z., Chen, C., Takeuchi, D., Jackson, J., & Meng, X.-L. (2008). Disparity in depression treatment among racial and ethnic minority populations in the United States. *Psychiatric Services*, *59*(11), 1264–1272.

Bradd, S. (2016). Leading a framework for cultural safety and humility for First Nations in B.C. [graphic illustration]. FNHA. http://www.fnha.ca/PublishingImages/wellness/cultural-humility/FNHA-Cultural-Safety-and-Humility-Graphic-Sam-Bradd.jpg

California Pan-Ethnic Health Network. (2018). *California Reducing Disparities Project: Strategic plan to reduce mental health disparities*. Project Administrator: Office of Health Equity, California Department of Public Health. https://cpehn.org/page/california-reducing-disparities-project

First Nations Health Authority. (2020). *Cultural Safety & Humility*. www.fnha.ca/wellness/cultural-humility

Peters, V., & McDonald, S. (2017), *Webinar 11: Leading with culture in First Nations community contexts.* https://www.youtube.com/watch?v=N_LpTXiTqCI

Samnaliev, M., McGovern, M. P., & Clark, R. E. (2009). Racial/ethnic disparities in mental health treatment in six Medicaid programs. *Journal of Health Care for the Poor and Underserved, 20*(1), 165–176.

Smedley, B. D., Stith, A. Y., & Nelson, A. R. (2003). *Unequal treatment: Confronting racial and ethnic disparities in healthcare.* Institute of Medicine, National Academies Press.

Snowden, L., & Yamada, A. (2005). Cultural differences in access to care. *Annual Review of Clinical Psychology, 1*(1), 143–166.

Substance Abuse and Mental Health Services Administration. (2015). Racial/ethnic differences in mental health service use among adults. HHS Publication No. SMA-15-4906. https://www.samhsa.gov/data/sites/default/files/MHServicesUseAmongAdults/MHServicesUseAmongAdults.pdf

Sue, S., & Zane, N. (1987). The role of culture and cultural techniques in psychotherapy: A critique and reformulation. *American Psychologist, 42*(1), 37–45. https://www.pathways2promise.org/wp-content/uploads/2017/01/The-Role-of-Culture-and-Cultural-Techniques-in-Psychotherapy-1.pdf

Tervalon, M., & Murray-Garcia, J. (1998). Cultural humility versus cultural competence: A critical distinction in defining physician training outcomes in multicultural education. *Journal of Health Care for the Poor and Underserved, 9*(2), 117–125.

Wang, P. S., Berglund, P., Olfson, M., Pincus, H. A., Wells, K. B., & Kessler, R. C. (2005). Failure and delay in initial treatment contact after first onset of mental disorders in the national comorbidity survey replication. *Archives of General Psychiatry, 62*(6), 603–613.

RESOURCES

Cultural Humility and Mental Health Disparities

FNHA offers excellent online cultural safety and cultural humility webinars and instructional materials

www.fnha.ca/wellness/cultural-humility

Centers for Disease Control and Prevention. (2016). Strategies for reducing health disparities: Selected CDC-sponsored interventions. *Morbidity and Mortality Weekly Report 65*(1), Supplement.

https://www.cdc.gov/mmwr/volumes/65/su/pdfs/su6501.pdf

"Strategies for Reducing Health Disparities," Centers for Disease Control and Prevention website.

Learn about projects such as the "Traditional Foods Project" for American Indian and Alaska Natives" and "Best Practices for HIV Prevention," including a "Couples HIV Intervention Program (CHIP)" for transgender women and their primary cisgender male partners.

https://www.cdc.gov/minorityhealth/strategies2016/index.html

Credibility and Gift Giving

Daya, R. (2001). Changing the face of multicultural counselling with principles of change. *Canadian Journal of Counselling, 35*(1), 49–62.

This article discusses Sue and Zane's (1987) gift giving and achieving credibility as principles of change in a common-factors approach that supports successful multicultural counseling. The article provides a thorough review of different perspectives that have formed multicultural counseling.

https://files.eric.ed.gov/fulltext/EJ622698.pdf

Nagayama Hall, G. C., Kim-Mozeleski, J. E., Zane, N. W., Sato, H., Huang, E. R., Tuan, M., & Ibaraki, A. Y. (2019). Cultural adaptations of psychotherapy: Therapists' applications of conceptual models with Asians and Asian Americans. *Asian American Journal of Psychology, 10*(1), 68–78.

The public access article presents an overview of how psychotherapies have been culturally adapted for 30 years and qualitative findings on how therapists have applied adaptation strategies for Asians and Asian Americans in the U.S. vs. Japan, including Sue & Zane's (1987) model of credibility and gift giving.

https://www.ncbi.nlm.nih.gov/pmc/articles/PMC6402600

Credit

CHAPTER 3

Accessing Research on Interventions

This chapter supports the best-evidence component of the EBP model. It focuses on strategies to find the most relevant studies to evaluate—where and how to search for the articles and reports on interventions to consider for your client. Students will learn about types of articles and reports, databases and resources for finding EBPs, and how to conduct searches that are effective for EBP decision-making.

BRIEF LECTURE 3.1

Understanding the Literature: Primary vs. Secondary Studies

To search the available literature thoroughly and effectively, practitioners need to know about the different types of scholarly and professional literature where intervention research can be found. They also need to know the research lingo that is used and the advantages and disadvantages of each type of research literature. The two main types are primary and secondary research articles. Primary articles are original scientific reports, where the authors are reporting on a study they themselves conducted. Primary studies are also referred to as empirical studies, where *empirical* means systematically observing and experiencing to gain knowledge using quantitative and/or qualitative methods. Primary (or empirical or original) articles typically include an introduction containing a literature review and sections on methods, results, discussion, and references. Primary articles are usually published in academic or scholarly journals, but they may also be research reports published online or in paper format by nonprofit and community-based organizations, governmental agencies, and other entities. When they are published in academic journals, they are often peer-reviewed, which means experts in the field evaluate them before they are accepted for publication. This is generally not the case when the pieces are research reports published by nonprofit organizations, such as foundations or public agencies. Graduate theses and dissertations are also sources of original or primary research, but they are not peer-reviewed unless the author one day submits their work for publication in a peer-reviewed scholarly journal. Additionally, dissertations that report original empirical research typically contain very comprehensive, long, and useful literature reviews, which articles published in academic journals do not.

In contrast, secondary articles about interventions summarize or interpret original research. These articles synthesize, analyze, interpret, and evaluate primary studies. They provide a commentary on and discussion of evidence. Secondary pieces include systematic reviews, meta-analyses, literature reviews, and books. The authors of secondary articles will gather, analyze, and summarize original research conducted by others that is often already published. Secondary sources are useful to practitioners because they are usually easy to read and provide an overview of a topic. Furthermore, the listed references are an important resource for finding useful primary research articles. Let's now become familiar with the different forms of literature and the research jargon used within each category, with an eye on the utility of these different forms for EBP decision-making.

Primary Research Articles
Academic Journal Articles and Reports

Academic or scholarly journals are one of the practitioner's main resources for locating intervention research. A journal, like a magazine, is a collection of articles that is published regularly throughout the year in print or online formats. Researchers write and submit articles to academic journals to be read by other researchers, faculty, and professionals. Academic organizations or publishing companies are generally the publishers of academic journals. These journal articles always include full citations for sources and use a scholarly or technical language. A citation is a reference to a published or unpublished source that the author discusses in the article. Having citations is in itself a hallmark of academic research articles because the study needs to be situated within the context of the studies that preceded it. In other words, authors cite previous researchers' work to show how they are extending or filling a gap in the research. "Peer-reviewed" or "refereed" academic journals have an editorial board of subject experts who evaluate submitted articles with the help of outside *peer reviewers* before accepting the article, or *manuscript*, for publication. Whether an article is accepted for publication depends on the significance of the research—whether it makes a significant contribution to the discipline. Articles that are peer-reviewed suggest a certain level of rigor and are commonly viewed as higher quality. Not every academic and scholarly journal, however, is peer-reviewed. If it is peer-reviewed, the journal's website will have an editorial statement or section with instructions to authors that describes a peer-review process. Databases also often allow you to limit your search to peer-reviewed articles.

Original research may also be reported orally at professional meetings, seminars, symposia, and workshops. These oral reports may be based on previously written published reports or become the content for a future written report. Conference organizers sometimes select a small number of reports and publish them as "conference proceedings."

To find interventions for a client, practitioners will need to identify and evaluate original research articles themselves. The main source of primary research is academic journals, although these journals also publish literature reviews, meta-analyses, and systematic reviews, which are secondary research. Again, an article is considered original research if the authors are reporting on a study they themselves conducted. For example, I, as the author, have submitted an article about a study I did, wherein I designed the study and collected and analyzed data. In the article, I describe my research question and hypothesis (if any), purpose of the study, research methods, and results or findings. I also provide a literature review (with many citations) that situates my study within a specific area of research, and I discuss the possible implications of my study's findings. In contrast, if I wrote an article containing descriptions of other researchers' studies and their findings, published or not, my piece would not be original research.

• •

NOTE Primary research technically refers to a study that uses *primary data,* which is new or fresh data collected by the researcher. When a researcher uses data collected previously by someone else, the research is called *secondary research* because it employs *secondary data* and involves a *secondary data analysis* or *secondary analysis of existing data.*

• •

Journal articles are available to those who subscribe to the journal or an academic database that includes the journal. University libraries, educational and other nonprofit organizations and consortia, and individuals are common subscribers. An emerging resource for practitioners is scholarly journals that provide *open access*, which means free online distribution of articles. The Directory of Open Access Journals (DOAJ; https://doaj.org) is a free database of open-access journals in all disciplines worldwide that contains articles in English, Spanish, and other languages. Searching the DOAJ database under "psychology" journals for "intervention" and "therapy" resulted in identifying the following article titles in several English-language open-access journals:

- Bunge, E. L., Williamson, R. E., Cano, M., Leykin, Y., & Muñoz, R. F. (2016). Mood management effects of brief unsupported internet interventions. *Internet Interventions*, 5, 36–43. https://doi.org/10.1016/j.invent.2016.06.001 (This study explored the effects on depression, anxiety, mood, confidence, and motivation of an internet-based single-interaction intervention.)
- Dopp, R. R., Mooney, A. J., Armitage, R., & King, C. (2012). Exercise for adolescents with depressive disorders: A feasibility study. *Depression Research and Treatment*, 2012, 9 pages. https://doi.org/10.1155/2012/257472.
- González-Bueso, V., Santamaría, J. J., Fernández, D., Merino, L., Montero, E., Jiménez-Murcia, S., del Pino-Gutiérrez, A., & Ribas, J. (2018). Internet gaming disorder in adolescents: Personality, psychopathology and evaluation of a psychological intervention combined with parent psychoeducation. *Frontiers in Psychology*, 9, Article 787. https://doi.org/10.3389/fpsyg.2018.00787

TIP 1   DOAJ is a good resource for identifying interesting open-access journals, which can then be accessed directly rather than through DOAJ. Knowing about open-access resources is especially important when one does not have access to academic databases.

TIP 2   Another useful online resource is www.sciencedaily.org. This site provides summaries of research articles published in peer-reviewed journals. Trained science journalists write these summaries. Check out the "Mind and Brain," "Health and Medicine," and "Society/Education" pages. It is best to avoid articles in the popular media, because they are often incomplete or inaccurate.

Nonacademic and Non-Peer-Reviewed Original Research Reports

Academic or scholarly journals are the main source, but not the only source, of primary or original scientific reports. Practitioners can also consider studies conducted or sponsored by foundations, other nonprofit entities, and governmental agencies, which are generally not submitted to academic journals for publication. These studies are often not RCTs but are studies conducted in the natural setting of the community, with more diverse samples. While such nonacademic original research reports are relatively rare compared to the abundance of peer-reviewed research articles found in academic journals, they should not be neglected, since they have stronger external validity. (Remember that external validity refers to the generalizability of a study's findings to real-world populations and settings.)

An example of non-peer-reviewed, community-based research is the California Department of Public Health's California Reducing Disparities Project (CRDP), which aims to evaluate the effectiveness of "community-defined evidence projects," which are community practices for preventing or reducing the severity of mental illness. CRDP created a procedure (which they call "templates") for evaluating community-defined practices, including their cultural relevance and indicators of effectiveness, in the current phase of the project.

- Read about CRDP here: https://www.cdph.ca.gov/Programs/OHE/Pages/CRDP.aspx
- Browse a sample report, the *Asian Pacific Islander Population Report: In Our Own Words* (2013), which identifies over 50 promising community practices used by API communities across California. In the appendices, you can see the templates for evaluating community practices. http://crdp.pacificclinics.org/resources/crdp/document/crdp-api-population-report-our-own-words
- Download population reports for LGBTQQ, Native American, Latinx, and Black communities here: https://cpehn.org/page/california-reducing-disparities-project

Secondary Research Articles
Systematic Review
We first discussed systematic reviews in Chapter 2 (pages xx-xx). To support health care and human services professionals' ease of consumption of the clinical literature, the Campbell Collaboration's clinical teams search and analyze the clinical research literature and write the reviews for us. Again, systematic reviews are careful, comprehensive summaries of what the available evidence says about an intervention's effectiveness or about the various interventions available for a certain condition. Their purpose is to examine all available single studies for the practitioner, which makes them good starting points for EBP decision-making.

If you base your practice decision solely on a systematic review, however, you skip the step of analyzing the quality of the available evidence yourself, including, most importantly, the validity and applicability of the evidence to your client's characteristics. A good strategy is to use the systematic review, if one exists for your client's condition and goals, to gain an overview and then read through the review's reference list to identify a few research articles that sound relevant to your client, which you will then obtain and analyze in detail. Systematic reviews are not limited to those produced by the Campbell Collaboration. Diverse working groups and groups of researchers and professionals also conduct systematic reviews covering a wide range of topics. Here are some titles of systematic reviews not conducted by the Campbell Collaboration. Note that "systematic review" is always in the title.

- Marshall, K. J., Fowler, D. N., Walters, M. L., & Doreson, A. B. (2018). Interventions that address intimate partner violence and HIV among women: A systematic review. *AIDS and Behavior, 22*(10), 3244–3263.
- Weissman, J., Kanamori, M., Dévieux, J. G., Trepka, M. J., & De La Rosa, M. (2017). HIV risk reduction interventions among substance-abusing reproductive-age women: A systematic review. *AIDS Education and Prevention, 29*(2), 121–140.
- Slobodin, O., & de Jong, J. M. (2015). Family interventions in traumatized immigrants and refugees: A systematic review. *Transcultural Psychiatry, 52*(6), 723–742. doi:10.1177/1363461515588855
- Chapman, R. L., Buckley, L., Sheehan, M., & Shochet, I. (2013). School-based programs for increasing connectedness and reducing risk behavior: A systematic review. *Educational Psychology Review, 25*(1), 95–114. doi:10.1007/s10648-013-9216-4

Governmental organizations also provide reviews of interventions in specialty areas, although these reviews are not conducted with the same rigorous procedure as systematic reviews; however, they have the same purpose of identifying and recommending current EBPs, like the Cochrane Collaboration. The National Child Traumatic Stress Network (NCTSN) provides reviews of this nature. NCTSN, with the goal of developing interventions and resource materials for professionals, is administered by the Substance Abuse and Mental Health Services Administration and coordinated by the UCLA-Duke University National Center for Child Traumatic Stress. As an example, NCTSN recommends several treatments, one of which is "Integrative Treatment of Complex Trauma for Adolescents" (ITCT). The organization provides a short list of original research articles about ITCT and how and where to obtain treatment materials and training. One of these original research articles is given here:

- Lanktree, C. B., Briere, J., Godbout, N., Hodges, M., Chen, K., Trimm, L., Adams, B., Maida, C. A., & Freed, W. (2012). Treating multi-traumatized, socially-marginalized children: Results of a naturalistic treatment outcome study. *Journal of Aggression, Maltreatment & Trauma, 21,* 813–828.

  "[ITCT] was developed as a specialized treatment that is empirically informed, culturally sensitive, extendable beyond the short term, and customized to the specific social and psychological issues of each child. This article examines the potential effectiveness of ITCT in assisting 151 traumatized children living in an economically deprived environment." (Abstract excerpt, p. 813)

Meta-Analysis

We first discussed meta-analysis in Chapter 2 (pages xx-xx). Meta-analyses combine the results of multiple studies, usually RCTs, using sophisticated quantitative analysis methods. While meta-analyses cover a broad range of topics, it is not difficult to find a meta-analysis of an intervention that has been well studied, especially using experimental methods. While RCTs represent the highest level of evidence, choosing an intervention for a client based only on a meta-analytic study of RCTs may turn out to be limiting, especially if the samples in the included RCTs excluded people with the racial/ethnic or cultural characteristics of your client. Furthermore, RCTs are commonly not conducted in community-based study sites, which means their effectiveness in a community setting is unknown. Like systematic reviews, a good strategy is to find the meta-analysis, if one exists for the condition and goals of your client, to gain an overview of the available evidence and then read through the reference list to identify a few articles that sound relevant to your client, which you will analyze yourself.

Meta-analyses, which analyze prepublished data from other researchers' investigations, are not original research, although some argue that they are because the author has formulated and answered their own hypotheses and generated new knowledge using others' data. Below are some sample titles of meta-analyses. Note that the word "meta-analysis" is always in the title.

- Ferguson, L. M., & Wormith, J. S. (2013). A meta-analysis of moral reconation therapy. *International Journal of Offender Therapy and Comparative Criminology, 57*(9), 1076–1106.
- Dijkstra, S., Creemers, H. E., Asscher, J. J., Dekovic, M., & Stams, G. J. J. M. (2016). The effectiveness of family group conferencing in youth care: A meta-analysis. *Child Abuse & Neglect, 62,* 100–110.

- Van Andel, H. W. H., Grietens, H., Strijker, J., Van der Gaag, R. J., & Knorth, E. J. (2014). Searching for effective interventions for foster children under stress: A meta-analysis. *Child and Family Social Work, 19*(2), 149–155.
- Panos, P. T., Jackson, J. W., Hasan, O., & Panos, A. (2014). Meta-analysis and systematic review assessing the efficacy of dialectical behavior therapy (DBT). *Research on Social Work Practice, 24*(2), 213–223.

Literature Review

We first mentioned literature reviews in Chapter 2 (pages xx-xx). Literature reviews summarize current knowledge, including research findings on a particular topic. Unlike systematic reviews, which guide clinical practice, literature reviews cover a very broad range of topics and disciplines. It is possible to find some that cover social and mental health problem areas and interventions. Unlike systematic reviews and meta-analyses, however, literature reviews are not focused primarily on summarizing the results of RCTs, since their underlying aim is not to highlight an intervention based on best evidence but to summarize the range of available findings from studies with diverse research designs. Even when it is not possible to find a literature review on interventions for a client's problem areas, literature reviews are an important source of background information for working with a client. Consider the following titles. Note that the words "review" and "literature" are almost always in the title.

- Peled, E. (1997). Intervention with children of battered women: A review of current literature. *Children and Youth Services Review, 19*(4), 277–299.
- Bruder, C., & Kroese, B. S. (2005). The efficacy of interventions designed to prevent and protect people with intellectual disabilities from sexual abuse: A review of the literature. *The Journal of Adult Protection, 7*(2), 13–27.
- Gelman, C. R. (2003). Psychodynamic treatment of Latinos: A critical review of the theoretical literature and practice outcome research. *Psychoanalytic Social Work, 10*(2), 79–102.
- Stepteau-Watson, D. (2014). Dating violence, young African American males, and risk and protective factors: A review of the literature. *Journal of Human Behavior in the Social Environment, 24*(6), 694–701.
- Sen, S., Nguyen, H. D., Kim, S. Y., & Aguilar, J. (2017). HIV knowledge, risk behavior, stigma, and their impact on HIV testing among Asian American and Pacific Islanders: A review of literature. *Social Work in Public Health, 32*(1), 11–29.

CRITICAL THINKING

How can the above literature reviews support your work with a client, even when they are not reviews of interventions? How can they help you to avoid "confirmation bias," which is selecting only studies that confirm your view of the right treatment for the client?

· ·

TIP   Recent systematic reviews, meta-analyses, literature reviews, and dissertations are good starting points for gaining an overview of the literature for a problem area and can be sources from which specific intervention research articles can be identified for closer analysis. "Recent" would be within the past 5–7 years, or a little longer, depending on the topic. Always find and read these to gain important background information about your client's population and problem areas.

· ·

 ACTIVITY 3.1   Test Your Understanding of the Types of Research Literature

Answer the following true or false questions. Provide an explanation of your answer.

1. Articles that appear in academic journals are all peer-reviewed, because the articles are written for peers, which typically include university faculty and researchers.

2. Primary research is the first study to answer a specific research question, as opposed to subsequent studies that replicate the first or primary study.

3. Original research refers to authors who report on the study they themselves conducted. The research article or report describes how the study was conducted and its findings, as well as discusses the implications of the findings.

4. A meta-analysis is a higher level analysis using statistical procedures to integrate the quantitative results of many independent studies.

5. Secondary research refers to articles in which the authors summarize and interpret other researchers' studies.

6. Open-access articles are always reports of RCTs.

7. Teams of clinicians collaborate to prepare literature reviews, which answer defined questions in the social, behavioral, educational, and health arenas,

with the purpose of helping professionals to choose interventions for specific conditions or problems based on current evidence.

8. Systematic reviews summarize the research literature on a wide variety of topics, such as the risk factors associated with a social problem, illness etiologies, and theories.

9. Systematic reviews, literature reviews, and meta-analysis articles will have a list of references that is worth reviewing to pick out original research articles to consider for a client.

10. Academic journals are the main but not the only source of original research reports.

See the answers on page 102.

> **DISCUSSION 3.1** What Are the Advantages of the Different Types of Research Literature for EBP Decision-Making?

Jot down at least several ideas for each question below. Provide an explanation for your answers.

1. Why would a practitioner want to examine original research articles when there are secondary research articles that summarize the evidence?
    - Think about what information you hope to find in an original article that would help you to decide if the intervention is suited for your client.
    - Think also about what might be lost or excluded from a secondary article, such as a systematic review or meta-analysis.

2. How is a systematic review more suited than a meta-analysis for initially identifying possible interventions for a particular client?
    - Read through the sample titles of systematic reviews and meta-analyses in the brief lecture above and think about how they are different from one another.

3. How might a literature review be useful in helping a particular client, especially understanding their problem areas and choosing an appropriate intervention?
    - Read through the sample titles of literature reviews in the brief lecture above and think about how some of them could be used to support decision-making for a client.

See how students answered on page 102.

BRIEF LECTURE 3.2

Databases and Resources for Finding EBPs

In order to identify potential EBPs for a client, it is important to know how to access the research literature. There are two main ways. The first way is to access the literature through scholarly databases that index many journals from a field or a set of related fields. The managers of the database purposely include or exclude journals, making these databases closed, or limited by their choice of journals. Scholarly databases useful for EBP are *PsycINFO*, *Social Services Abstracts*, *CINAHL*, *PubMed* (or *MEDLINE*), and *Education Research Complete*. These databases, commonly available through university libraries, contain reports of empirical research, as well as literature reviews, systematic reviews, meta-analyses, book reviews, and editorials. Another useful database is *ProQuest Dissertations & Theses Global: The Humanities and Social Sciences Collection*. Also, *EBSCOhost* and *ProQuest* are online platforms that allow the user to search multiple databases simultaneously; these platforms are large databases that encompass the smaller databases.

The second way to access literature is with Google Scholar, a search engine. Google Scholar is populated by publishers directly rather than being managed by a team who decides which journals to include or exclude. It searches resources from academic publishers, universities, and academic repositories. Using a built-in algorithm, Google Scholar creates an expansive academic universe by adding to its index any piece that looks like an academic article, research report, thesis, working paper, or book chapter. It adds thousands of new articles every day. Different from the scholarly databases, each search on Google Scholar can give different results due to new sources being added and sources being lost (such as when an article is removed from a university repository). This is why Google Scholar is not a permanent database like, for example, PsychINFO, where a defined search will always bring up the same articles, given that documents once indexed are never removed.

The remainder of this brief lecture introduces the scholarly databases, with a demonstration of their overlap, and provides a few resources for systematic reviews in mental health.

Scholarly Databases
PsycINFO

This database indexes journals in the behavioral and social sciences. As a psychology database, it is very useful for finding research on mental health and psychological therapies.

Social Services Abstracts

This database indexes journals in fields relevant to EBP, including community development, crisis intervention, evaluation research, the family and social welfare, gerontology, poverty and homelessness, support groups/networks, violence, abuse and neglect, and welfare services. This database, compared to PsychINFO, provides a broader reach into a range of social services–related interventions.

Education Research Complete

This database covers research related to all areas of education. It is designed for educators and administrators.

CINAHL

CINAHL is the Current Index to Nursing and Allied Health Literature. This database indexes journals in nursing, biomedicine, alternative/complementary medicine, consumer health, and other allied health disciplines.

As an example of articles that may be of interest to EBP decision-making in CINAHL, a search of "trauma" in the Title field and "Latin* AND therapy OR treatment OR intervention" in the Abstract field returned 22 items, two of which are copied below. Among the two journals cited below, *Child & Adolescent Social Work Journal* is also indexed in Social Services Abstracts, PsychINFO, and Education Research Complete, and *Psychological Trauma: Theory, Research, Practice & Policy is* also indexed in PsychINFO.

- Ferreira, R., & Allison, A. (2017). Implementing Cognitive Behavioral Intervention for Trauma in Schools (CBITS) with Latino youth. *Child & Adolescent Social Work Journal, 34*(2), 181–189. doi:10.1007/s10560-016-0486-9

    This article describes an effective school-based intervention, the Cognitive Behavioral Intervention for Trauma in Schools (CBITS), studied in Spanish-speaking middle school students in New Orleans.

- Hoskins, D., Duncan, L. G., Moskowitz, J. T., & Ordóñez, A. E. (2018). Positive Adaptations for Trauma and Healing (PATH), a pilot study of group therapy with Latino youth. *Psychological Trauma: Theory, Research, Practice & Policy, 10*(2), 163–172. doi:10.1037/tra0000285

    This article describes a new culturally adapted, manualized 10-session group treatment for Latino youth and their caregivers, Positive Adaptations for Trauma and Healing (PATH), with positive outcomes regarding depression symptoms and externalizing and internalizing behaviors.

PubMed (MEDLINE)

PubMed comprises biomedical literature from the U.S. National Library of Medicine's MEDLINE database, as well as life science journals and online books. MEDLINE indexes journal articles in biomedicine and health and related fields that are important to clinical care and research. Although MEDLINE is a health care database that indexes primarily medical journals, it is also a good source for psychological interventions. PubMed is free to the public and provides links to some free full-text articles. The PubMed website is https://www.ncbi.nlm.nih.gov/pubmed.

As an example, a search of "African American AND depression" in the Title field and "intervention" in the Title/Abstract field returned 29 items, two of which are copied below. Among the two journals cited below, *Journal of Evidence-Based Social Work* is also indexed by Social Services Abstracts and Education Research Complete, but not PsychINFO. *Preventive Medicine* is indexed by Education Research Complete, but neither Social Services Abstracts nor PsychINFO.

- Wahab, S., Trimble, J., Mejia, A., Mitchell, S. R., Thomas, M. J., Timmons, V., Waters, A. S., Raymaker, D., & Nicolaidis, C. (2014). Motivational interviewing at the intersections of depression and intimate partner violence among African American women. *Journal of Evidence-Based Social Work, 11*(3), 291–303.

  This article describes the design, using a community-based participatory research approach, of a culturally tailored, multifaceted intervention using motivational interviewing and case management to reduce depression among African American survivors of intimate partner violence.

- Duffy, S., Brown, T. M., Katsonga-Phiri, T., Bouris, A., Grant, K. E., & Keenan, K. (2016), Development of an empirically based preventive intervention for depression in preadolescent African American girls. *Preventive Science, 17*(4), 503–512. doi:10.1007/s11121-016-0634-7

  This article describes the development and pilot RCT of a new preventive intervention for depression in African American girls living in urban poverty. The intervention targets suppression of negative emotion, lack of assertiveness with peers, memory for positive emotion, active coping, and family connection.

EBSCOhost

This online platform allows the user to search multiple databases simultaneously. For EBP searches, the user can click a checkbox to include CINAHL, Education Research Complete, and PsychINFO, rather than searching each individually.

ProQuest

This online platform, like EBSCOhost, allows the user to search multiple databases. The user can choose to include Social Services Abstracts, PsychINFO, and MEDLINE.

PQDT Global

ProQuest Dissertations & Theses Global: The Humanities and Social Sciences Collection provides comprehensive historic coverage of dissertations and theses from North American universities and includes research from universities worldwide. Finding a dissertation on a topic of interest for a client or client's cultural group is like discovering a "gold mine," as the dissertation will have an extensive reference list from which to draw.

As an example, a search of "African American AND trauma" in the Title field and "intervention OR therapy OR treatment" in the Keywords field returned five items, two of which are copied below.

- Worthen, B. L. (2016). Utilizing spiritual gifts for the treatment of complex bereavement in African American survivors of traumatic death circumstances (Publication No. 10183640) [Doctoral dissertation, Azusa Pacific University]. ProQuest Dissertations & Theses Global: The Humanities and Social Sciences Collection.

  This dissertation study includes a case study that demonstrates how the gifts of the Holy Spirit, with prayer and medication, can be incorporated into a therapy session as an adjunctive treatment model in the promotion of holistic treatment outcomes.

- Gibbs, S. (2013). Evaluating the treatment effectiveness of an integrated trauma focused model on African-American children suffering from trauma symptoms (Publication No. 3600762) [Doctoral dissertation, The Chicago School of Professional Psychology]. ProQuest Dissertations & Theses Global: The Humanities and Social Sciences Collection.

  This dissertation study examined the effectiveness of integrating trauma-focused art therapy (TF-ART), trauma-focused cognitive behavioral therapy (TF-CBT), and Afrocentric psychocentric (ACP) interventions into guidelines for treating African American children.

 ACTIVITY   If you have access to the above research databases through a library, access each database one by one and conduct a few searches, including the sample searches described above, to become acquainted with what they can provide.

Resources for Systematic Reviews

Three main resources for finding systematic reviews are *The Campbell Collaboration*, *SAMHSA's Evidence-Based Practices Resources Center*, and an online journal from the United Kingdom called *Evidence-Based Mental Health*. The Campbell Collaboration was discussed earlier in Chapter 3 (pp. 77–78).

SAMHSA's Evidence-Based Practices Resource Center

SAMHSA's EBP Resource Center, a website released in 2018 (https://www.samhsa.gov/ebp-resource-center), provides research-based practice resources for clinicians, policy makers, and community members. The SAMHSA publications, drawing on the literature and knowledge of experts, describe evidence-based and promising practices for a specific population and problem area and includes a literature review. Users can search by "Issues, Conditions and Disorders" (e.g., "Serious Emotional Disturbances," "Suicide," or "Substance Abuse"), "Publication Primary Audience" (e.g., "Practitioner/Professional" or "General Public"), "Population Group" (e.g., "Young Adults," "Inmates," or "Foster Care Children"), and "Format" (e.g., "Guidelines or Manual," "Report," or "Kit").

"Guidelines or Manual" includes best-practice guidelines for the prevention and treatment of substance use and mental disorders developed to assist service providers and administrators in improving their services. These are typically titled or referred to as *Guides*, *Treatment Improvement Protocols (TIPs)*, *Kits*, and *Toolkits*. Toolkits provide everything needed to choose an EBP and implement it in an agency. Most toolkits have a component called "The Evidence" or "Selecting Evidence-Based Practices," with information on available interventions and the cost and amount of training needed. However, not every toolkit provides a literature review of interventions, but rather only a list of references, including of interventions and reviews of interventions.

Let's try some searches to survey the Resource Center's publications. First, on the website's "Publications" tab, a search for TIPs shows over 300 results, and a search for Toolkits returns over 100 results. Second, let's conduct a few searches and sample the available publications.

SEARCH 1

Conducting a search on "Practitioner/Professional" under "Publication Primary Audience" and "Homeless" in the main Search box returned (on April 25, 2020) over 120 publications, the first of which was: "TIP 55: Behavioral Health Services for People Who Are Homeless" (November 2015, Publication ID SMA15-4734), containing a main document of 249 pages and a literature review of 191 pages called "TIP 55 Lit Review." In the literature review document, there is a review of "Behavioral Health Interventions" on pages XX–XX. It reviews Motivational Interviewing, Community-Based Intensive Case Management Services and Treatment, Critical Time Intervention, Assertive Community Treatment, Interventions to Improve Social and/or Family Support, Integrated Treatment for Co-Occurring Disorders, and Trauma-Informed and Trauma-Specific Services, among other interventions. Learning about the state and quality of the evidence for each intervention through the review and identifying individual research articles to read closely would contribute to selecting an EBP for a homeless client.

SEARCH 2

Conducting a search on "Practitioner/Professional" under "Publication Primary Audience," with "disruptive behavior" in the main Search box, and "children" under "Population Group" returned (on April 25, 2020) 14 publications, one of which was "TIP 39: Substance Abuse Treatment and Family Therapy" (October 2015, Publication ID SMA15-4219). This guide introduces substance use disorder treatment and family therapy, including models for integrating the two approaches and a discussion of cultural competence, considerations for specific populations, and guidelines for assessing violence. A long bibliography, including the empirical research used to develop the guidelines, is in Appendix A, which begins on page 307. Some of these bibliographic references may be of interventional or observational studies, which can help inform the choice of an EBP for a specific client.

SEARCH 3

Conducting a search on "Practitioner/Professional" under "Publication Primary Audience" with "psychoeducation" in the main Search box returned (on April 25, 2020) over 50 publications, the first of which was "Family Psychoeducation Evidence-Based Practices (EBP) Kit" (March 2010, Publication ID SMA09-4422), which offers EBPs for developing family psychoeducation programs. One of the 10 documents in this kit is called "Family Psychoeducation: The Evidence," a

42-page document with the first 10 pages summarizing the research literature, followed by a bibliography and references. This summary was not conducted by the kit's authors, who used the following review from a peer-reviewed journal. Both this publication and the review article it employed are old, but they may be useful for providing the history of best practices for family psychoeducation.

- Dixon, L., McFarlane, W. R., Lefley, H., Lucksted, A., Cohen, M., Falloon, I., Mueser, K., Miklowitz, D., Solomon, P., & Sondheimer, D. (2001). Evidence-based practices for services to families of people with psychiatric disabilities. *Psychiatric Services, 52(7)*, 903–910.

ACTIVITY   Go to SAMSHA's EBP Resource Center. Find and read a guideline or manual on a topic of interest to you personally or for a client. Download the PDF, browse the therapeutic recommendations, and locate the bibliography or reference list. As you read, evaluate whether the guidelines are useful and culturally sensitive for a specific diversity group that you have in mind.

Evidence-Based Mental Health

This online journal from the United Kingdom is indexed in PubMed. It provides free and paid summary articles, which are essentially literature reviews, relevant to psychiatrists and psychologists drawn from international medical journals. These summary articles consist of brief expert commentaries focusing on the studies' key findings and implications for clinical practice. However, the journal does not focus on only clinical or intervention reviews but also publishes original research articles, editorials, and commentaries. To search for reviews, go to https://ebmh.bmj.com, click on "Advanced Search," fill in your search terms under "Authors, Keywords," and check the box "Review Articles" under "Include Only."

- Hussain, H., Dubicka, B., & Wilkinson, P. (2018). Recent developments in the treatment of major depressive disorder in children and adolescents. *Evidence-Based Mental Health, 21(3)*, 101–106. (Found by searching "major depressive disorder" under Title and "children" under Abstract or Title.)

  This clinical review identifies and discusses the relative effectiveness of CBT, interpersonal therapy, and family-focused approaches and the uncertainty that treatment with both antidepressants and psychological therapy is better than treatment with a psychological therapy alone.

- Baruch, N., Burgess, J., Pillai, M., & Allan, C. L. (2019). Treatment for depression comorbid with dementia. *Evidence-Based Mental Health*, *21*(4), 167–171. (Found by searching "dementia" under Abstract or Title and "depression" under Full Text or Abstract or Title.)

  This article reviews RCTs of antidepressants, which do not show significant improvement in depressive symptoms in patients with comorbid dementia; reasons for the unclear role of antidepressants; and the state of current research on the effectiveness of individual psychological interventions, structured sleep hygiene programs, exercise, arts interventions, music therapy, electroconvulsive therapy, and neurostimulation techniques.

- Aggarwal, S., & Patton, G. (2018). Engaging families in the management of adolescent self-harm. *Evidence-Based Mental Health*, *21*(1), 16–22. (Found by searching "suicide" under Abstract or Title and "adolescents" under Full Text or Abstract or Title.)

  This review article, based on mostly low-quality evidence from 10 RCTs and two non-randomized-controlled trials in high-income countries, found that brief interventions did not reduce adolescent self-harm. However, intermediate-level interventions, such as Resourceful Adolescent Parent Program, Safe Alternatives for Teens and Youth Program, and attachment-based family treatment reduced suicidal behavior, attempts, and ideation, and intensive therapies such as Dialectical Behavior Therapy and mentalization-based therapy reduced suicidal ideation and self-harm.

BRIEF LECTURE 3.3

An Efficient Search: Gold Mining and Citation Cycling

For EBP decision-making, the goal of a literature search is to identify interventions that could be relevant to a particular client. For an intervention to be relevant, ideally the study should have included participants from our client's racial/ethnic group and the outcomes (or treatment goals) of interest to our client. This is consistent with the applying the client characteristics, values, and preferences component of the EBP model and finding research that has strong external validity that can be generalized to the client's community. However, regarding the best evidence component of the model, it is also important to locate research that has strong internal validity, which means finding interventions with the higher levels of evidence, such as those tested in RCTs, or at least quasi-experimental studies.

An efficient, time-saving search strategy that addresses especially the client component of the EBP model starts with locating one article, reading it to see if it applies, and if it applies using citation cycling (looking at the research of those who cited the article) to find other articles. The strategy is to repeat this process—find an article, read it, and citation cycle—until enough interventions and articles are found. This strategy allows the practitioner to identify and become connected with researchers who are experts on a certain community and problem area and to create a meaningful relationship with the research community. For example, a practitioner working in the area of trauma treatment among Native American communities could become acquainted with and follow the small network of researchers specialized in this area. This strategy involves "mining for gold" because the objective is to find a golden resource, be it one article that leads to others or a recent dissertation, systematic review, or meta-analysis that provides a rich overview of interventions for a given problem area and a list of references from which to pull a good article or two. The search strategy steps are as follows:

1. Define the search terms: List the terms to search related to racial/ethnic group, age, conditions or problem areas, desired outcomes, and other factors important to the client and service setting (e.g., time limits, individual versus group therapy, etc.).

2. Mine for gold: Search the scholarly databases or Google Scholar using the defined search terms to find a recent dissertation, systematic review, or meta-analysis, from which you will pull one empirical article to read closely.

3. Mine for gold: If no recent dissertation, systematic review, or meta-analysis exists, search the scholarly databases or Google Scholar for one empirical article to read closely.

4. Evaluate the article: Read the article and judge whether it is useful to your client; search for another article if the first article does not apply.

5. Citation cycle: With an article that applies, citation cycle using Google Scholar to locate other articles and identify researchers of interest; search and browse the work of these researchers.

6. Evaluate the article(s): Read the article(s) found via citation cycling and evaluate them.

7. Repeat this process: Find an article, read and evaluate, and citation cycle until you are satisfied with the number of interventions and articles or have exhausted search possibilities.

8. Reflect on possible biases in your search strategy: Are you looking only for articles that support your preferred approach? Are you including studies that provide negative or weaker positive findings?

The above strategy focuses on entering into a conversation with an interrelated group of scholars whose work is relevant to a client's cultural population rather than on finding the "perfect search." This means spending much more time using the research than searching for it. The goal is to quickly pick one article to use and, if it is useful, expand from that article. The initial database search should take only 10 minutes; a successful search would be finding a set of up to 50 titles to browse and from which to choose one piece to read.

To address the best evidence component of the EBP model, the following ninth step can be added to the search strategy.

9. Search for RCTs and studies on the mainstream population: For the interventions identified in the above process, search for RCTs and other research on these interventions conducted with mainstream samples to gauge if the interventions have a high level of evidence generally (i.e., outside the racial/ethnic/cultural group of your client).

· ·

TIP Students may be tempted to search for hours until they find the number of required articles for their assignment, without having read any article along the way. This can be frustrating and could lead to finding research with a superficial or poor fit to the client's cultural background and specific problems. It also avoids engaging with researchers more closely, and these researchers may be the ones who are dedicated to sensitive and innovative research with a minority or under-studied population.

· ·

 ACTIVITY 3.2   Defining Your Search and Conducting an Initial Search

Instructions

1. Define your search for a particular client by developing a table with the following row headings: racial/cultural group, age group, problem areas, interventions, and other considerations, such as time limits and other important factors to keep in mind. Most of the information with which to complete the table is in the search question, such as the one you wrote for a client in Activity 1.4.

2. As you define the search, note broader and more specific search terms and alternative terms for finding relevant articles.

· ·

TIP How broad or narrow your terms are will depend on the amount of research done on a specific group and problem area. For example, searching for "Hmong immigrants" and "hopelessness" will be too narrow, while searching for "Southeast Asian immigrants" and "depression" will lead to more hits. A good rule of thumb is to aim for a search that gives up to 50 hits.

· ·

3. Conduct an initial search to find one or two articles to read and evaluate closely.

Examples

Laura

Search Question

"What evidence-based interventions are available for managing anger and externalizing behaviors, reducing depression and self-isolation, and building relationships at school, for a 17-year-old bicultural and bilingual Mexican American adolescent girl living in a supportive home environment with her single mother and sibling?"

Search Definition

Racial/ethnic group	• **Latinx** • Bilingual or Spanish-speaking • Mexican American
Age group	• **Adolescent or teenager** • Older adolescent or older teenager
Problem areas	• **Anger management** • Externalizing or acting-out behaviors • **Depression** • Social isolation • **Peer relationships or social skills**
Interventions	• **Therapy or intervention or treatment** • Individual therapy • Family therapy • Social skills group

Other considerations	<ul><li>School-based therapies</li><li>Brief therapies</li><li>Therapies that make use of supportive home environment</li><li>Immigrant mother and single-parent home</li><li>Bicultural client</li></ul>

Prioritizing Search Terms

- An initial search could focus on the bolded terms. They are Laura's main characteristics and issues defined in broader terms.
- For racial/ethnic group, finding studies on Spanish-speaking teens is important, but these may be rare. You can search "Latin*" to locate potential studies, which you will read to check for inclusion of Spanish speakers.
- For problem areas, "anger management" and "externalizing or acting-out behaviors" are related problem areas, just as "depression" and "social isolation" are related, such that a search of one may turn up interventions that address both. However, "anger management" and "depression" are more commonly treated as distinct problem areas with distinct interventions, so you may want to search each individually.
- "Peer relationships" stands out alone; if finding treatments that specifically address building "peer relationships" (or "social skills") is important, you should conduct a search on this term rather than leaving it out. You can also search for a "social skills group" intervention.

. . . .

TIP Do not spend too much time working out the perfect set of terms for your initial search, because no such perfect set exists. Start with the broader terms and problem area(s) that will return the most hits. Your goal is to quickly find an article to read, which will lead to others.

. . . .

Conducting an Initial Search

The following search produced 31 hits using EBSCOhost with CINAHL, PsychINFO, and Educational Research Complete databases included.

Abstract: Latin* AND (adolescent or teen*) AND depression OR anger

AND

Title: intervention or treatment or therapy

Browsing the 31 titles, the following two potentially relevant articles appeared, but there were no hits related to "anger management." The top article is for close reading and evaluation. The bottom article, with an intervention that targets trauma and depression, is for browsing and using its reference list to find other articles.

- Mufson, L., Yanes-Lukin, P., & Anderson, G. (2015). A pilot study of Brief IPT-A delivered in primary care. *General Hospital Psychiatry, 37*(5), 481–484.

  This study examined the effectiveness of a brief version of Interpersonal Psychotherapy for Depressed Adolescents (BIPT-A), which includes parent participation, in low-income Latinx adolescents treated in an urban pediatric primary care clinic.

- Ferreira, R., & Allison, A. (2017). Implementing Cognitive Behavioral Intervention for Trauma in Schools (CBITS) with Latino Youth. *Child & Adolescent Social Work Journal, 34*(2), 181–189.

  This study examined the effectiveness of Cognitive Behavioral Intervention for Trauma in Schools (CBITS), a school-based intervention, with Spanish-speaking, Latinx youth with symptoms of trauma and depression.

Conducting a Follow-Up Search

Given Laura's need for an anger management intervention, leaving out "Latin*" and "depression" returned 71 hits. Limiting these search results to only dissertations narrowed the hits to 15. However, these 15 dissertations were focused on boys, younger children, or other populations or were outdated (more than 10 years old).

Title: (therapy or treatment or intervention) AND anger*

AND

Abstract: adult*

Limiting the 71 hits to only academic journals narrowed the hits to 15, from which two relevant articles were found. The first article is a better piece to read and evaluate. The second article is 14 years old and was published by authors from England.

- Cole, R. L. (2008). A systematic review of cognitive-behavioural interventions for adolescents with anger-related difficulties. *Educational and Child Psychology, 25*(1), 27–47.

  This review included 14 empirical studies, focusing on summarizing short- versus long-term effects and issues of methodological quality.

- Sukhodolsky, D. G., Kassinove, H., & Gorman, B. S. (2004). Cognitive-behavioral therapy for anger in children and adolescents: A meta-analysis. *Aggression and Violent Behavior, 9*(3), 247–269.

  This meta-analysis included 21 published and 19 unpublished reports. It compared skills training and multimodal treatments for reducing aggressive behavior and improving social skills, as well as problem-solving treatments for reducing subjective anger experiences.

Eddie

Search Question

What evidenced-based interventions are available for managing anxiety and anger, building healthy coping skills, and processing traumas and negative self-beliefs for my client, who is an African American adult with strong Southern cultural values and excellent cognitive awareness and is new to living in a tense urban environment?

Search Definition

Racial/ethnic group	• **African American or Black**		
Age group	• **Adult**		
Problem areas	• **Anger management**		
	• **Anxiety**		
	• Coping skills		
	• **Trauma**		
	• Negative self-beliefs (or depression)		
Interventions	• Therapy or intervention or treatment		
	• Cognitive Behavioral Therapy		
Other considerations	• Southern cultural values		
	• Cognitive focus		
	• New resident in tense urban environment		

Prioritizing Search Terms

- An initial search could focus on one or more of Eddie's problem areas.
- For problem areas, "negative self-beliefs" may be considered, in a cognitive framework, as an aspect of depression for the purpose of finding relevant interventions. Researchers generally treat "anger management," "anxiety," and "trauma" as distinct problems with distinct treatments, even though they are closely intertwined in Eddie's case.

- Eddie specifically emphasizes the need for better coping skills, but building coping skills is an aspect of treatment for the other problem areas. It can be left out of the search but kept in mind as a treatment goal and outcome.
- For interventions, given Eddie's strong cognitive abilities, searching specifically for cognitive therapies is called for, whether as a search term or while browsing through hits from a broader search.

Conducting an Initial Search

The following first search produced 28 hits using EBSCOhost with CINAHL, PsychINFO, and Educational Research Complete databases included.

Title: (African* or Black*) AND (therapy or treatment or intervention) AND (depress* or anxi* or anger*)

AND

Abstract: adult*

Browsing the 28 titles, no article had the word "anger" in its title, and two articles had "anxiety" in their titles but were not relevant. The following two potentially relevant articles on depression appeared. The top one is for close reading and evaluation. The bottom is for browsing to see if the intervention addresses negative self-beliefs and coping and for using its reference list to find other articles.

- Gregory, V. L., Jr. (2016). Cognitive-behavioral therapy for depressive symptoms in persons of African descent: A meta-analysis. *Journal of Social Service Research, 42*(1), 113–129.

    This meta-analysis evaluated the size of effect of CBT in persons of African descent with depressive symptoms.

- Ward, E. C., & Brown, R. L. (2015). A culturally adapted depression intervention for African American adults experiencing depression: Oh Happy Day. *American Journal of Orthopsychiatry, 85*(1), 11–22.

    The article reports on two pilot studies examining the effects of the Oh Happy Day Class (OHDC), a 12-week, culturally specific cognitive behavioral group counseling intervention, in reducing symptoms of major depressive disorder.

Conducting a Follow-Up Search

The following search left out "African American" and focused on "anger" alone. It returned 72 hits.

Title: (therapy or treatment or intervention) AND anger*

AND

Abstract: adult*

Limiting the search to only dissertations resulted in eight dissertations, of which the following was relevant and recent.

- Plambeck, K. L. (2016). Acceptance and Commitment Therapy (ACT) treatment groups targeting the reduction of problematic anger-related behaviors and psychological inflexibility in incarcerated men: A pilot study. Dissertation Abstracts International: Section B: The Sciences and Engineering. ProQuest Information & Learning.

  This study examined the effectiveness of an 8-week ACT group treatment for problematic anger in incarcerated men.

Limiting the search to only academic journals resulted in 61 hits, from which the following article on incarcerated males was found. Browsing the titles showed that much anger management research has been conducted among people with intellectual disabilities, substance use problems, children, and other defined populations. Among these were a couple of articles of potential interest.

- Fuller, J. R., DiGiuseppe, R., O'Leary, S., Fountain, T., & Lang, C. (2010). An open trial of a comprehensive anger treatment program on an outpatient sample. *Behavioural and Cognitive Psychotherapy, 38*(4), 485–490.

  This pilot study examined a 16-session treatment among outpatient adults with psychiatric disorders. It involved skills training, relaxation, cognitive restructuring, and other cognitive techniques.

- Vannoy, S. D., & Hoyt, W. T. (2004). Evaluation of an anger therapy intervention for incarcerated adult males. *Journal of Offender Rehabilitation, 39*(2), 39–57.

  This study examines an anger therapy using cognitive-behavioral approaches and practices from Buddhist psychology.

ACTIVITY 3.3 **Practicing Citation Cycling**

Instructions

1. Using Google Scholar, type in the reference information for an article that you evaluated as being relevant for your client.

2. When the search result appears for your article, click on "Cited by #" to see the list of articles that cited your article. Browse these to identify more articles and authors of interest.

3. When you find a relevant title and abstract, click on "Related Articles" to browse another list, and so on.

4. For authors that appear to be specialized on your population and topic of interest, you can also search Google Scholar or academic databases to browse all of their work.

Example

Laura

- Searching for Mufson's (2015) "A pilot study of BRIEF IPT-A delivered in primary care" showed that the article was "Cited by 5."
- Clicking on "Cited by 5" led to three articles of interest:
  - Hooper, L. M., Mier-Chairez, J., Mugoya, G. C. T., & Arellano, B. (2016). Depressive symptoms, assessment, and treatment in Latino/a adolescents: A brief review. *Current Psychiatry Reviews*, *12*(2), 150–162.
  - Mychailyszyn, M. P., & Elson, D. M. (2018). Working through the blues: A meta-analysis on Interpersonal Psychotherapy for depressed adolescents (IPT-A). *Children & Youth Services Review*, *87*, 123–129.
  - Mufson, L., Rynn, M., Yanes-Lukin, P., Choo, T. H., Soren, K., Stewart, E., & Wall, M. (2018). Stepped care interpersonal psychotherapy treatment for depressed adolescents: A pilot study in pediatric clinics. *Administration and Policy in Mental Health and Mental Health Services Research*, *45*(3), 417–431.
- Browsing the above meta-analysis shows other works by Laura Mufson on Interpersonal Psychotherapy for Latinx adolescents.
- Clicking on "Related Articles" under Mufson et al.'s (2018) "Stepped Care ..." article shows the following paper by Mufson and other colleagues on the importance of cultural competence in working with Latinx teens:

    o   Mufson, L., Yanes-Lukin, P., Gunlicks-Stoessel, M., & Wickramaratne, P. (2014). Cultural competency and its effect on treatment outcome of IPT-A in school-based health clinics. *American Journal of Psychotherapy, 68*(4), 417–442.

⌘   **Case Paper Task 3.1**

Find Three Different EBPs to Consider for Your Client and Write the *Description of Intervention* for Each

Instructions: The case paper assignment requires that you find and consider three different EBPs for your client. Start by creating your search question, and then use the search methods described in this chapter to find two empirical research articles for each of the three EBPs. The articles will contain descriptions of the interventions studied, which you can use to write the *Description of Intervention* section for each EBP. You can obtain additional information about the interventions from the internet or other articles and books if needed.

Below are examples of the *Description of Intervention* for the first of three EBPs from Laura's and Eddie's case papers. You can see other examples in the full case papers in Appendix B (p. 311) and Appendix C (p. 323).

Case Paper Instructions:

Review of EBP #1 (6–7 paragraphs, 9 points)
This section is based on your review of two empirical research articles and other information found online, in print, and through interviews. (Note that the components of this section will be discussed over the next several chapters. The first component is the description of the intervention.)

Description of Intervention: Provide information on length of intervention, theoretical foundation, components and activities involved, problem or diagnostic areas or population for which it is suited, and anything else important to give a brief but thorough overview of the intervention. (*1–2 paragraphs, 1 point*)

Laura's Example

Needs Strengthening
Cognitive Behavioral Therapy for Adolescents (CBT-A) can be used for a variety of issues. It is based on a model of the relationship of thoughts, emotions, and behaviors. It is an adult modality but can be used with children. It is a brief therapy. For work with teens, it helps them to build their independence so they can view their core beliefs with perspective and not let their lives be driven by the core beliefs, which are formed in childhood but are not always true.

How could you strengthen the above? Are there missing details? Are Laura's views of her problem(s), her goals of treatment, and her preferred form(s) of treatment described?

Well-Written

As you read the below example, reflect on what makes the below description richer in terms of client information and the client's viewpoints that are useful for defining treatment goals and finding appropriate interventions.

EBP #1: Cognitive Behavioral Therapy for Adolescents

Description of Intervention

Cognitive Behavioral Therapy for Adolescents (CBT-A) is an adaptation of Aaron Beck's cognitive behavioral therapy for adults but modified for the psychological development of adolescents. It can be applied for depression, anxiety, and adjustment issues. In CBT, the client learns to become aware of their automatic thoughts that occur in stressful situations and the relationship of thoughts, emotions, and behaviors. By questioning the validity of the automatic thoughts, as well as the inaccurate core beliefs underlying everyday thoughts, the client can reduce the associated negative emotional states and behaviors. The role of the cognitive behavioral therapist for adolescents is to use examples given by the client that help explain the cognitive behavioral model. Also, CBT-A focuses on helping the client to gain independence and nurture trusting relationships with others by developing problem-solving and healthy coping skills. In the adolescent model for cognitive behavioral therapy, the clients are not expected to do extensive homework, such as logging automatic thoughts. However, the therapist uses the 12–16 sessions to develop skills in recognizing thoughts and affects.

Eddie's Example

Well-Written

As you read the below example, reflect on whether the description gives you a nice quick overview of the intervention. Do you understand the theory behind the therapy and what treatment entails for the client?

Review of EBP #1: Prolonged Exposure Therapy

Description of Intervention

Prolonged Exposure Therapy (PET) is based on emotional processing theory (EPT; Foa & Kozak, 1986). In EPT, it is the avoidance of processing the trauma memory and not the trauma memory itself that prevents the emotional processing of trauma and symptomatic relief from PTSD. EPT posits that two dysfunctional beliefs may be created: (a) the world is completely dangerous (e.g., "It is dangerous to be alone"), and (b) one's self is totally incompetent (e.g., "I can't handle any stress" and "My PTSD symptoms mean that I am going crazy") (p. 62). Most PTSD survivors correct these mistaken beliefs through daily activities, but those who systematically avoid trauma-related thoughts and activities do not get the chance to challenge and correct these erroneous beliefs, leaving the trauma memory undisturbed. Due to systematic avoidance, the habituation achieved by challenging erroneous beliefs through repeated and prolonged exposure to traumatic events does not occur. In these cases, EPT asserts that effective psychological intervention is required to remedy the two inaccurate conclusions of the world—its overwhelming danger and the inability to cope with that danger (Foa, 2011).

Following the EPT hypothesis, PET involves systematic confrontation of the trauma memories by having patients repeatedly retell the trauma (Foa, 2011). PET consists of 10–12 90-minute sessions and four main modules: psychoeducation, breathing retraining, imaginal exposure, and in vivo exposure. The imaginal exposure component consists of repeating, reconsidering, and recounting the initial trauma aloud. The in vivo ("real life") component is repeated exposure to the trauma activators. These two activities are immediately followed by a discussion of the revisiting experience, known as the processing phase. By concurrently disconfirming the erroneous beliefs that underlie PTSD, the memory is restructured.

ANSWERS

Activity 3.1 Answers   **Test Your Understanding of the Types of Research Literature**
Answers: 1. False, 2. False, 3. True, 4. True, 5. True, 6. False, 7. False, 8. False, 9. True, 10. True.

Discussion 3.1 Answers   **What Are the Advantages of the Different Types of Research Literature for EBP Decision-Making?**

How Students Answered

1. **Why would a practitioner want to examine original research articles when there are secondary research articles that summarize the evidence?**

   a.   The secondary articles might not be focused on the racial or ethnic group of my client. I would ideally want to read articles that cover my client's racial or ethnic group. For example, a systematic review might conclude that CBT is effective for depression in general, but I would want to see articles where CBT was used with Latinx immigrants.

   b.   I want to read about the intervention, especially if it was adapted for my client's culture. I also want to know if they used the intervention in the type of agency where I work. I'm not sure if summary articles have this information.

c. The secondary articles may not discuss interventions for the specific problems and goals that my client has. For example, I have a Latina teen client who wants to work on how she copes with stress as a new immigrant, or I have an African American college student who wants to better handle stress related to discrimination with peers and teachers. I want to see if there are articles on these specific problem areas, and not just on depression or PTSD.

d. Any kind of summary would lose the diversity. You only see the average, like the intervention was effective for a lot of people, but this is the average person. The original article might say who are the people it didn't work so well for.

2. **How is a systematic review better suited than a meta-analysis for initially identifying possible interventions for a particular client?**

a. The meta-analysis titles look like they are generally about one specific intervention, such as moral reconation therapy, family group conferencing, or dialectic behavior therapy. If I want to see the overall effectiveness of one of these, the meta-analysis would be useful.

b. If meta-analyses are generally about combining the results of all the RCTs done on a certain therapy, it would be limiting to look at these, because I'd miss out on therapies where there are not yet many RCTs. On the other hand, it'd be useful to see which therapies have had a lot of RCTs done on them too.

c. A systematic review is better suited than a meta-analysis because systematic reviews survey and present different interventions that have been studied for a problem area and a population. It can be broader than a meta-analysis.

d. I would definitely search for both systematic reviews and meta-analyses if I want to see what's been studied and is available for my client. I could use the reference lists from both to pick out original research articles that sound like they apply to my client's cultural population and problem areas.

3. **How might a literature review be useful to helping a particular client, especially understanding their problem areas and choosing an appropriate intervention?**

   a. Peled, E. (1997). Intervention with children of battered women: A review of current literature. *Children and Youth Services Review, 19*(4), 277–299.

   If my child client has a mom who is a victim of interpersonal violence, this literature review, I expect, would tell me about all the different types of interventions that are available. It would be useful for identifying a few from its list of references, which I would then find original research on.

   b. Gelman, C. R. (2003). Psychodynamic treatment of Latinos: A critical review of the theoretical literature and practice outcome research. *Psychoanalytic Social Work, 10*(2), 79–102.

   I'm not sure what the title means by "theoretical literature," but it'd be interesting to see what outcomes are found and if the outcomes are meaningful to my client's situation. It's nice there's an article just on Latinos. This can't be common. Reading this might help me know if psychodynamic therapy is useful and how it might be useful. If it sounds useful, I could consider using it with my client.

   c. Stepteau-Watson, D. (2014). Dating violence, young African American males, and risk and protective factors: A review of the literature. *Journal of Human Behavior in the Social Environment, 24*(6), 694–701.

   If my client is a young Black man who has been involved with dating violence, this article might tell me what to work on and what to address with my client. First, it would tell me areas—the risk and protective factors—that I should be aware of and could assess in my client. This literature review doesn't tell me what interventions to use, but it might give a lot of important background for choosing an intervention.

   d. Sen, S., Nguyen, H. D., Kim, S. Y., & Aguilar, J. (2017). HIV knowledge, risk behavior, stigma, and their impact on HIV testing among Asian American and Pacific Islanders: A review of literature. *Social Work in Public Health, 32*(1), 11–29.

I'd read this for sure if my client is an API adult at risk for HIV. The article might give me a lot of knowledge on what the client might be going through or what he's dealing with culturally. It's a starting point, even though I'd listen to my client for his own story. If I can understand my client thoroughly, this helps to find the right intervention.

RESOURCES

Understanding the Literature: Primary vs. Secondary Studies

McCrocklin, S. (2018, October 4). *Primary vs. secondary research.* GeoPoll.

> The article provides an excellent basic description and diagram differentiating primary versus secondary research.
>
> https://www.geopoll.com/blog/primary-vs-secondary-research

Market Research Guy. (2020, July 7). *Primary vs. secondary market research: What's the difference?* My Market Research Methods.

> This webpage provides two tables comparing and contrasting primary vs. secondary research. Although the article is focused on the field of marketing, the clear explanations are useful.
>
> https://www.mymarketresearchmethods.com/primary-secondary-market-research-difference

Formplus Blog. (2020, April 23). *Primary vs secondary research methods: 15 key differences*

> This webpage provides detailed definitions and a practical explanation of advantages of each, including feasibility, data recency, and examples.
>
> https://www.formpl.us/blog/primary-secondary-research

Databases and Resources for Finding EBPs

Evidence-Based Behavioral Practice. (2018). *Searching for the evidence.*

> This website provides many links to useful secondary reviews of evidence and practice guidelines for mental and behavioral health practice, as well as describing primary research literature databases (e.g., PubMed, PsychINFO, and CINAHL).
>
> https://ebbp.org/resources/searchevidence

Simmons University Library. (n.d.) *Open access social work resources: Databases & online resources.*

> This website provides links to numerous databases of EBPs for social work, including an EBP Substance Abuse Database and the California Evidence-Based Clearinghouse for Child Welfare.
>
> https://simmons.libguides.com/c.php?g=830722&p=5964570

PEW Trusts. (2020, September 11). *Results First Clearinghouse Database for social policy programs.*

> The online searchable database brings together information on social policy programs from nine national clearinghouses allowing easy access to a spectrum of programs.
>
> https://www.pewtrusts.org/en/research-and-analysis/data-visualizations/2015/results-first-clearinghouse-database

An Efficient Search: Gold Mining and Citation Cycling

Herrlich, K. (2020). *Top ten search tips.* Northeastern University Library.

> This webpage covers basic search methods, including basics such as when to use "AND" (called a Boolean operator) and "*" and tips on how to research like a detective.
>
> https://library.northeastern.edu/get-help/research-tutorials/effective-database-searches/top-ten-search-tips

Benedictine University Library. (2020, September 11). *General library research tutorial: Module 4: Searching a database.*

> This webpage provides a good explanation of differences between using library databases versus the internet and how to search library databases by using keywords, subjects, phrases, Boolean operators, and more.
>
> https://researchguides.ben.edu/general-research/searching

Kent State University Library. (2020, July 29). *NURS 70630: Research methods for evidence-based practice: Basic search strategies.*

> This website provides step-by-step directions on how to search for EBPs. It includes basic search steps and search strategy worksheets. Overall, reading through the site makes a good tutorial.
>
> https://libguides.library.kent.edu/c.php?g=723350&p=5160509

CHAPTER 4

Best Evidence

How Research Designs Form a Hierarchy of Evidence

This chapter covers the best-evidence component of the EBP model. We will review basic interventional research designs and learn how a study's design contributes to the quality of the evidence that it produces. We will also learn how to classify studies using a hierarchy of evidence, with the "best" evidence at the top.

> ### DISCUSSION 4.1 Is There Such a Thing as "Good" Versus "Bad" Evidence?

Jot down at least several ideas for each question below. Provide an explanation for your answers.

1. What makes "good" evidence?

   •••

   NOTE *Evidence* is another word for the findings of a study. It could also refer to the set of findings from multiple studies on an intervention, as in the phrase, "There is strong evidence for the effectiveness of Dialectical Behavior Therapy."

   •••

2. Can there be "stronger" or "weaker" evidence related to how a study is designed (i.e., without considering who was sampled)?

3.   Have you heard of *levels of evidence* or a *hierarchy* of evidence? What might this mean?

See how students answered on page 143.

BRIEF LECTURE 4.1

Understanding Research Quality: Internal and External Validity

In this brief lecture, we will review the research concepts of internal and external validity, which are essential to understanding the design of studies and the linkage of study design with quality of evidence. Given our task in EBP decision-making of finding and considering interventions with the 'best evidence' for our clients, our role as clinical experts includes evaluating how the evidence was derived in order to judge whether the evidence is strong (or credible) and useful (or applicable) to our clients. We will learn that the strength (or credibility) of the evidence depends on the study's internal validity, and the usefulness (or applicability) of the evidence depends on the study's external validity.

Internal Validity

Internal validity describes designing an intervention study in a way that makes it possible to infer (or conclude) causality between the intervention and the observed outcomes. We want to design the study so that we can be as certain as possible that the observed outcomes result from the intervention rather than from other factors, called *confounding variables*. For instance, we want to be able to conclude that the depression intervention caused the reduction in depression symptoms rather than something else, such as improvements in the patients' physical health over time, another treatment happening simultaneously, or a variety of other imaginable factors. In research language, a study has *high internal validity* when, because of its design, it allows causal inferences to be made. You can think of *internal* validity as being about the *internal* design of the study—how well the study was set up, such that we can believe in its results.

What contributes to high internal validity in an intervention study? To achieve high internal validity, researchers need to reduce threats to the internal validity of a study. Reducing threats to internal validity means reducing the factors that can get in the way of being sure that the intervention was responsible for the outcomes. There are many possible threats, which you can review in a research textbook, but an important one is *selection* or *sampling bias*. How were people selected into the study? Was the sample biased in such a way that the mental health of the participants receiving the new intervention could be improving due to other factors, personal or environmental, and not due to the intervention? For instance, were study participants receiving the parenting intervention selected from the parents who eagerly volunteered and signed up first, so that it was their higher motivation that contributed to the positive outcomes? The parents' level of motivation is a confounding variable; it confounds or gets in the way of knowing whether the intervention indeed *caused* the positive results.

How then does a researcher design a study to reduce selection bias and other threats to internal validity? Three basic design elements are used to deal with threats to internal validity. They are using pre- and posttests, introducing a (nonequivalent) comparison group, and introducing a control group using a random assignment procedure. A good way to strengthen internal validity is to administer a pretest and posttest to see if there is any improvement after the intervention takes place. A stronger method would be to introduce a comparison group in order to see if there is a difference between those who received the intervention (the *intervention group*) and those who did not (the *comparison group*). An even stronger but more costly approach is to randomly assign participants to an experimental group and a control group and then compare outcome scores before and after the intervention is administered to the experimental group. We will review each of these three design elements closely.

Before doing so, however, let's introduce research design notation, which helps to understand the level of experimentation and the design's ability to protect against threats to validity. The notations are R for random assignment, X for the intervention, and O for the observation (or pretests and posttests). Using these symbols, how would you describe each of the below designs? Are there pre- and posttests? How many? Is there a control or comparison group?

$$O_1 \quad X \quad O_2$$

In the above study, there is one pretest, one intervention, and one posttest. The numbers indicate the number and order of the observations. There is neither a control nor comparison group. In other words, there is one whole sample, rather than subsamples, that receives the single intervention. The first observation, O_1, is sometimes referred to as the *baseline* level. By comparing the scores at O_1 and O_2, we determine whether the sample improved, became worse, or stayed the same. For example, if the sample's mean depression score dropped from 18 to 10, then there was arguably an improvement resulting from the intervention.

$$O_1 \quad X \quad O_2 \quad O_3$$

In the above study, there is one pretest, one intervention, and two posttests. The final observation, or posttest O_3, is a follow-up assessment, such as one given at six months after the intervention to assess whether the benefits obtained at O_2, right after the intervention concluded, were sustained. For example, if the sample's mean depression score dropped from 18 to 10, but six months later, at O_3, the mean score is 15, then the benefits were not sustained, making it hard to conclude that the intervention was effective in general or in the long run.

$$R \quad X \quad O$$
$$R \qquad O$$

In the above study, there is no pretest, only a posttest. The R signifies random assignment into two groups (or subsamples), with each row representing one group. The top row is the intervention or experimental group. The bottom row is the control group. This is a *posttest-only control group design*. The design avoids a potential effect where participants improve their scores at retest because the process of testing itself enhances performance. It may also avoid the social desirability effect of answering that one has improved from treatment, given that one is socially expected to report an improvement. If the intervention group has a mean depression score of 10 after the intervention, at O, compared with the control group's score of 16, the researcher has some justification for inferring causality.

$$O_1 \quad X_A \quad O_2$$
$$O_1 \quad X_B \quad O_2$$
$$O_1 \qquad O_2$$

In the above study, two different interventions are compared with each other and with no intervention. This is an *alternative treatment design*. The group in the top row received intervention A. The middle-row group received intervention B. The third-row group is the comparison group, which received no intervention or treatment. Given the absence of an R, random assignment of participants into the three groups did not occur, making this a comparison study rather than an RCT. Can you imagine some possible mean scores at O_1 and O_2 to show that X_A was the superior treatment? With this introduction to experimental design notation, let's turn to the three design elements that strengthen internal validity.

Strengthening Internal Validity with a Control Group

One way to strengthen internal validity is to design the study with two similar groups so that the outcomes of the groups can be compared fairly. *How does the researcher ensure similar groups?* The sure way is to randomly assign participants, so that each group, for example, will likely have participants who are rich and poor, motivated and nonmotivated, and other characteristics both known and unknown to the researcher. In research language, random assignment ensures that confounding variables are "controlled for" (but not eliminated), because there will be equality or equal distribution of characteristics between the two groups. When using random assignment, the study design is called an experimental design, and the study is referred to as a randomized controlled trial (RCT), which is the classic or "gold standard" in experimental design. The group that receives the intervention is the experimental or intervention group. The other is the control group, which receives no intervention, or "treatment as usual." Below is the notation for an RCT. The RCT has the highest level of internal validity; it deals with selection bias and other threats to validity. Note how this design has stronger internal validity than the posttest-only control group design, because this design has pretests at O_1. The pretests serve to confirm that the two randomized groups are indeed similar if their scores turn out to be similar, such as both groups showing a mean depression score of 18.

$$R \quad O_1 \quad X \quad O_2$$
$$R \quad O_1 \quad \quad O_2$$

How is having two similar groups helpful? When the two groups are alike, we have more confidence that nothing but the intervention caused the outcomes. Random assignment thus avoids selection biases by controlling for factors at play such as level of motivation. With random assignment, every parent has an equal chance to be in each group. As a result, the motivated parents will be split between the two groups rather than stacked in the intervention group because they eagerly signed up to try the new intervention first. In this way, parents' level of motivation and other factors are controlled for and will no longer be confounders. Although RCTs are ideal, it is often not possible, especially in community settings, due to their high cost. When random assignment is unfeasible, researchers conduct quasi-experiments by creating or finding a suitable comparison group, a group that is as similar as possible to the intervention group.

Strengthening Internal Validity with a Comparison Group

There are many ways to create or find a comparison group. For instance, a study could have the sample comprise elderly patients in two skilled nursing facilities. The researcher would find two facilities located in similar neighborhoods with patients from similar socioeconomic and racial/ethnic backgrounds. All of the patients in one facility would receive the new stress-reduction intervention. This is the intervention group. All of the patients in the second facility would receive treatment as usual. This is the comparison group. If we find that stress is reduced in the intervention group but not the comparison group by a significant amount, then we can confidently conclude that the intervention led to the improvements. Of course, if the stress level did not decrease in either group, then the intervention was ineffective. Below is the study design notation. It is the same as the RCT notation, except without the Rs, since there was no random assignment. This is technically a *nonequivalent comparison group design* (or simply *comparison group design*), where the pretests serve to demonstrate the similarity of the two groups (e.g., both groups are shown to be very depressed, with mean scores of 18). The design is referred to as quasi-experimental for having a (nonequivalent) comparison group.

$$O_1 \quad X \quad O_2$$
$$O_1 \qquad \ \ O_2$$

Without a comparison group, we would be less certain that the intervention was responsible for the reduced stress. Again, this is because something not accounted for in the study may have contributed to the decrease in stress level. For example, facilities improvements occurring just before the intervention led to the reduced stress, or the intervention group had many more participants with more years of education, or more with a human services background with exposure to stress reduction skills when they were working adults. (Note that even though both control and comparison groups serve the purpose of making comparisons, the term *control group* is reserved for RCTs. Also, random assignment must be involved for the design to be *experimental*.) Below is the notation for a pre-post study without a comparison group. This is called a *one-group pretest-posttest design*, a *preexperimental design* with low internal validity due to the lack of accounting for possible influential factors via a comparison or control group.

$$O_1 \quad X \quad O_2$$

Without a comparison group, even if the mean depression score dropped from 18 to 10, we cannot make a strong inference that the decrease was due to the intervention. Perhaps it was due to the natural healing that occurs with the passage of time, or external circumstances such as receiving another social services program at the same time as the intervention. Incorporating a comparison group helps to rule out these other possible influences. As an example, observations that would be supportive of causal inference would be both groups showing a baseline mean score of 18 (which confirms that the two groups are similar), the intervention group dropping to 10, and the comparison group staying at a high level of depression at 16.

Which would better strengthen internal validity, designing a study with a control or comparison group? With a comparison group, there could still be the problem of the intervention and comparison groups being dissimilar. For example, the patients in the facility that made up the intervention group may have more education and more regular visits from family members than those in the comparison group. These factors, *education* and *social support*, may have contributed to the stress reduction, which puts into question the effectiveness of the intervention. Perhaps the intervention is only effective for those with more education. Or perhaps it was social support rather than the intervention that caused the positive outcomes. In other words, there is some uncertainty about how effective the intervention is. An RCT, in contrast, eliminates selection or sampling bias, a significant threat to the internal validity of a study, by ensuring that the two groups are as similar as possible via a random assignment procedure. A study with a comparison group, even when participants between the groups appear similar, may not reduce the threat of selection or sampling bias as well as an RCT. However, when it is not possible to randomize, the next best design element is to include a comparison group. Researchers sometimes go to great lengths to show that their comparison and intervention groups are similar across different characteristics, but the doubts always persist.

CRITICAL THINKING

As you read more studies, pay attention to how researchers show that their intervention and comparison groups have similar characteristics. Think also about participant characteristics not considered and not measured by the researchers that lead you to feel unsure about the believability of the study's results.

Strengthening Internal Validity with Pretests and Posttests

Another way to strengthen internal validity is to design the study using pretests and posttests, which allow the researcher to gather information on each partici-pant across time. Pretests are given to gather information on how the participant is faring at baseline before the intervention. Posttests, commonly the same instru-ment(s) used in the pretests, are given to assess for any improvements during and after the intervention. Both experimental and quasi-experimental studies, using control and comparison groups, respectively, nearly always include pre- and posttests in their designs. *Can you reason why this is so?* Pre- and posttests are used to observe and quantify the outcome of interest over time, with the hope of improvements in the targeted outcome variables. For example, if we want to show reduced stress or improved parenting skills, we need to measure the levels of stress and skills before and after the interventions. Without pre- and posttests, there would be no quantitative measures for evaluating differences and levels of differences between groups.

Can giving a pre- and posttest strengthen internal validity even when the study design uses no control or comparison group? Yes. While having a control or compar-ison group lets us know that one group improved over the other, having pre- and posttests lets us know that the sample improved over time. This is a very important piece of information when comparing two groups is unfeasible. Also, pre- and posttests allow the researcher to quantify the amount of change or improvement that occurred for the sample. It lets us know how much of a reduction in stress or increase in parenting skills was achieved. Compare the below two designs. The left is a *one-shot case study*. The right is a *one-group pretest-posttest design*. The latter allows us to document an improvement and quantify the amount of improvement. Nevertheless, the former can still provide some information if the mean score observed is compared with mean scores observed in other studies (e.g., we know from past studies that 10 is a mild depression score).

$$X \quad O \qquad \text{vs.} \qquad O_1 \quad X \quad O_2$$

While pre- and posttests are useful in and of themselves, coupling this design element with a comparison or control group strengthens internal validity much more. Using pre- and posttests without a comparison or control group is a *pre-experimental design*. A researcher may pilot an intervention with this design with the intention of introducing a comparison or control group in a future study.

How does giving multiple pretests strengthen internal validity? With multiple pretests, the researcher wants to establish that the participants are not already showing improvements before the intervention starts. That is, the researcher wants to show that no other factors are at play in the participants' improvements. For example, in the skilled nursing facility, the researcher may observe that stress levels are already going down three, two, and one week before the intervention, as in the below diagram.

$$O_1 \quad O_2 \quad O_3 \quad X \quad O_4$$

The researcher may try to identify the reasons for the unexpected decreases occurring prior to the intervention. For example, perhaps it is facilities improvements taking place or recently added social activities that are contributing to the preintervention improvements, leaving the interpretation of the impact of the intervention uncertain. (Ask yourself how adding a comparison group may be helpful to this researcher to tease out the effect from the intervention.) Imagine another example where two pretests are given before providing treatment to victims of recent trauma. This allows the researcher to be more certain about participants' baseline level of trauma. If trauma symptoms are already decreasing before the intervention starts, the researcher must question what other factors are at play. For instance, the decreases may be due to *statistical regression*, another threat to internal validity. This threat occurs when participants enter a study because they have *extreme scores*, such as those seeking help for trauma symptoms when their symptoms are being experienced as severe. Even without the intervention, this group would improve over time. Also, the extreme scores may include many who happened to score very high the day of the assessment, but actually they are not at that high level; their scores will statistically regress to their true score. The idea is that scores will not stay at their extreme, and they can only go down.

How does giving multiple posttests strengthen internal validity? With multiple posttests, the researcher wants to establish that improvements attributed to the intervention are maintained over time after treatment has ended. Imagine a depression treatment that leads to a reduction in symptom scores right after the treatment ends. If one, three, and six months later, the low symptom scores are sustained, then the researcher may be justified in concluding that the treatment had a longer term effectiveness. The notation below represents this design.

$$O_1 \quad X \quad O_2 \quad O_3 \quad O_4 \quad O_5$$

In research language, the researcher can also more strongly infer that the intervention caused the positive outcomes. If the symptom scores instead go back up across the postintervention months, then the researcher cannot say the treatment has a long-term impact and would be less certain in drawing conclusions about the treatment's overall effectiveness. Finally, what would it mean if symptom scores decrease over the many months after the intervention ends? If this happens, the researcher would again be alerted that other factors, and not the intervention, could be contributing to the improvements.

Which is better, giving a single pre- and posttest or multiple pre- and posttests? Collecting more data points gives the researcher more certainty about the stability of the baseline and the follow-up scores. Two pretests showing high symptom levels would clearly establish the participants' poor state and rule out the possibility that other factors, like maturity or healing with the passage of time, were already causing improvements before the intervention began. Two posttests showing low symptom levels would indicate that the improvements were not a fluke and that the intervention has a sustained impact. With a study design involving the collection of multiple data points, it is possible to make a stronger inference that the positive effects were caused by the intervention. Below is such a design. It is called a *simple time-series design*.

$$O_1 \quad O_2 \quad O_3 \quad O_4 \quad X \quad O_5 \quad O_6 \quad O_7 \quad O_8$$

More pre- and posttests also help to rule out other factors that are also influencing changes in the outcomes being measured. It is especially helpful when it is not possible to have a comparison group. But researchers often do not have the financial support or time to collect data at multiple points in time.

How is using both pre- and posttests and a control or comparison group together the best study design? An example will illustrate this point. Imagine a study in a middle school where two classrooms of students make up the sample. One classroom will be the intervention group, receiving a 4-week discrimination awareness curriculum. The other classroom will be the comparison group, holding classes as usual. We will give the youth in both classrooms three pretests and three posttests that assess their awareness of discriminatory behaviors. The design notation is below.

$$O_1 \quad O_2 \quad O_3 \quad X \quad O_4 \quad O_5 \quad O_6$$
$$O_1 \quad O_2 \quad O_3 \quad \quad O_4 \quad O_5 \quad O_6$$

RECAP

Do you understand the following basic points on internal validity?

···

- A study design that has strong internal validity is important because it allows the researcher to confidently infer that the intervention led to the observed outcomes.

- An RCT has the strongest internal validity because it uses random assignment of participants into two equivalent groups, the experimental or intervention group and a control group.

- Random assignment reduces selection or sampling bias by giving each participant an equal chance of being in each group, rendering the groups similar (or equivalent) in composition (as much as possible).

- When comparing an intervention group with a comparison group, it is important that the groups have similar characteristics, so we know that differences in outcomes are due to the intervention and not to a characteristic present in only one of the groups.

- Pre- and posttests are an integral part of experimental, quasi-experimental, and preexperimental research because they allow quantitative comparisons across time and/or between groups, which helps to pinpoint whether outcomes are actually from the intervention rather than the effects of extraneous variables.

- Using multiple pre- and posttests strengthens internal validity more than using a single pre- and posttest.

- The strongest design is to combine pre- and posttests with a comparison or control group, whichever is feasible in terms of the study setting and costs.

- When it is not possible to have a control group, incorporating a comparison group and testing across time (giving pretests and posttests to both groups) strengthens internal validity.

- When it is not possible to have either a control or comparison group, using multiple pre- and posttests strengthens a study's internal validity by establishing a clear baseline before an intervention begins and showing stable postintervention outcomes.

- Internal validity is related to the design of the study. It is one facet of the quality of the evidence. External validity is another.

Comparing the pretest results between the classrooms, we find that levels of awareness are slightly increasing over time, but this is happening in both classrooms. *The pretests thus function, importantly, to help establish that the groups are similar; their baseline levels are the same.* Comparing the posttest results, we find that the intervention group has a very strong improvement in level of awareness compared to the pretest levels, and the improved level of awareness continues to increase slightly across the remaining two posttest measures. In comparison, we find that the comparison group did not experience a big jump in awareness like the intervention group, but it did continue to have slight increases in level of awareness across the three posttest measures. *Having a comparison group thus helps to establish the impact of the intervention even when there are changes occurring across time.* This example illustrates how collecting outcome measures across time and using a comparison (or control) group allows the researcher to make a stronger inference than using only one of these design elements alone. It is called a "multiple time-series design," which adds time series analysis to the nonequivalent comparison groups design.

External Validity

External validity refers to the extent to which we can generalize a study's findings to populations and settings beyond those studied. *Generalizing* a study's findings means that the findings can be extended to another setting (i.e., another population, place, and time), especially the "real world" setting of social work. Given that every study is conducted within a specific sample and setting, we would expect an intervention to be effective for people and settings similar to those studied, but the intervention's effectiveness would be uncertain for people and settings different from those studied.

As critical consumers of research, what question would we want to ask regarding every intervention study that we read? We would ask, "Are the findings of this study valid for the person, place, and time in which I intend to use it?" or "Given who was studied, where the study took place, and when it took place, will the intervention work equally well for the person or people for whom I now need an intervention?" As examples, we would ask:

- Will a discrimination awareness curriculum, evaluated among low-income minority youth in an urban middle school, be effective among middle-income minority youth in a suburban middle school?
- Will a depression intervention offered to older adults with depression in a primary care clinic in a large hospital be effective when provided to

older adults with comorbid depression and substance use disorder in a social services organization in the community?

- Will an interpersonal therapy intervention tested in English-speaking Latinx Americans in a primary care clinic be effective in Spanish-speaking Latinx American immigrants in a prison?
- Will an intervention tested in 2007 be as effective in 2018?

Evaluating whether a study's findings can be generalized will require assessing whether the study sample and setting are similar to the people and setting where one wants to use the intervention in question. You may think of external validity as being about the expected effectiveness of an intervention to people and situations in the *external* or outside real world.

What can researchers do to strengthen external validity? They can conduct the studies in the types of community clinics and organizations where they intend the intervention to be used one day. They can include in their study people from diverse backgrounds, such as minority racial/ethnic groups, people with comorbid conditions, LGBTQ groups, and different age groups, whom they expect to be the end users of the intervention. From this discussion, we can see that external validity is a key requirement for us as consumers of research and that ultimately we would want the interventions to be tested with clients and settings like those of our clients.

RECAP

Do you understand the following basic points on external validity?

....

- A study's external validity depends on who was studied and where they were studied, and to whom and where we would like to apply the intervention.

- A study's external validity is strong if there is a good match between who was studied and where they were studied and to whom and where we would like to apply the intervention.

- To strengthen external validity, as a researcher, you would include in your sample the population for whom you would like the findings (or intervention) to be valid and conduct your study in the type of setting where you would like the findings (or intervention) to be valid.

Reflection Question

1. Is internal or external validity more important when judging a study's findings and trying to decide whether to use the intervention with your client? Explain your answer.

BRIEF LECTURE 4.2

Review of Study Designs

In this brief lecture, we will review study designs used in interventional and observational studies, focusing on designs used in the types of studies we will read and evaluate in choosing interventions for our clients. Interventional and observational studies have very different designs, and they serve different purposes in the larger evidence-based practice endeavor. Let's first distinguish between interventional and observational research, and then we will turn to the eight study designs most important for evidence-based practice decision-making.

Interventional and Observational Research

Interventional Studies

In interventional research, the researcher assigns participants to specific interventions so they can evaluate the effects of the interventions on outcomes of interest. In essence, the researcher conducts an experiment to show that those who receive an intervention, whether a treatment or preventive measure, will show positive outcomes compared with another group who did not receive the intervention. These studies are the experimental, quasi-experimental, and pre-experimental studies just reviewed. Interventional studies generate knowledge about specific practices that may be useful for our clients. They are the ones we commonly read to find interventions for our clients.

CRITICAL THINKING

As you read interventional studies, pay attention to the types of interventions being tested. Who decides what gets studied? Are interventions commonly used within minority ethnic communities represented in the literature? Is the literature biased in any way?

Observational Studies

In observational research, the researcher observes natural relationships between individual and environmental factors and outcomes. They neither assign participants to different groups nor give or withhold interventions, as in interventional studies. The researcher does not manipulate but only observes. Observational investigations have three purposes: to explore, to describe, and to explain a phenomenon. This is why they are called, respectively, *exploratory*, *descriptive*, and *explanatory* studies. These three research aims can be thought of as sequential. Exploratory research lays the groundwork for future research by looking at new topics or new angles on old topics. Descriptive research, the next step, is used to gain more knowledge on the newly explored topics. It describes what is happening in more detail, expanding our understanding and providing information on *what* is happening and *how* it is happening. It uncovers information about a population and phenomenon and negative outcomes that are occurring. Finally, explanatory research attempts to understand cause and effect, explaining what is going on or *why* something is happening. It focuses on cause and effect and generates information about the specific factors that contribute to or cause the condition. For an observational study to be labeled explanatory, it should collect data on many different variables in order to control statistically for alternative causes of the outcome under study.

Observational studies, overall, have an important role in supporting the development of evidence-based practices, because they point us to aspects of a condition that require our attention, including who needs help, why an intervention should be developed, and what contributing factors the intervention should address. A few specific observational designs, however, have an important role in providing more direct information about useful interventions for our clients. These are *cohort*, *case control*, and *case study* or *case report* investigations. These can be thought of as explanatory research, because they try to link how an intervention caused certain desired outcomes. We will review these designs below.

CRITICAL THINKING

As you read observational studies, pay attention to the researchers' choice of what is observed. Did their choice of variables or instruments restrict or determine the findings produced by the study? What else would you have wanted to observe that was omitted?

ACTIVITY   Do Activity 4.1 now to practice identifying interventional and observational studies by their titles and abstracts.

Eight Study Designs Important for EBP

We turn now to eight study designs that are important to evidence-based practice decision-making. These are the ones that we will read the most in searching for interventions for our clients. Among interventional designs, we will review RCT, comparison group, and pre-post study designs. Among observational designs, we will use cohort, case control, and case study or case report designs. Finally, we will discuss two types of evaluative summaries of intervention research, meta-analytic studies and systematic reviews.

NOTE   Interventional and observational studies are *primary sources* of evidence, because authors are reporting on new or original research that they themselves conducted. Meta-analyses and systematic reviews are *secondary sources* of evidence, because they summarize and analyze findings and data from other authors' original research.

1. Randomized Controlled Trial (Experimental Design)

In an RCT, study participants are randomly assigned to one of two groups, an intervention or experiment group and a control group. Those assigned to the intervention group will receive the intervention. Those assigned to the control group will receive "treatment as usual" or no intervention. An RCT, called an experimental design, is the best study design for achieving high internal validity (which is being able to attribute the outcomes to the intervention) due to using random assignment to limit sampling bias. With random assignment, the groups will have the best chance of being similar. For instance, we could randomly assign the 50 parents coming to our center for domestic violence counseling into two groups. The experiment group will receive a parenting support intervention, and both groups will take pre- and posttests. With the pretest, we can confirm that the two groups are indeed similar if their scores are similar. With the posttest, we expect to find that the parents in the experiment group show better well-being than the control group parents. This contrasts with giving the intervention to the 25 parents who are the clients of one of the two case managers in our agency or are the first to sign up for the intervention. Again, random allocation lets us be the most certain that it was the intervention and not something else that led to the positive outcomes.

Several additional design elements can be used to strengthen an RCT. One is blinding, which can be imposed on the research team or study participants.

To blind the research team, we would not let the person who administers the outcome instruments (called an *outcome assessor*) know the participants' group status. That is, the outcome assessor is blinded from knowing know whether the participant received the intervention. The aim is to promote more accurate assessment and to reduce bias. For this to work, the outcome assessor and the clinician who provides the intervention could not be the same person. To blind the study participant, we would not let the participants know whether they are in the intervention or control group, that is, whether they are receiving the innovative treatment or treatment as usual, respectively. Again, not knowing is expected to promote more accurate responses to the outcome instruments.

A second design element to strengthen an RCT is to reduce dropout rates by providing large enough incentive payments or by shortening the study duration. Addressing dropout is important, because when many participants drop out, results based on only those who remain in the study can be erroneous. When dropout rates in intervention and control (or comparison) groups are both high, or when there are differential dropout rates between the two groups, the data will likely be biased. Imagine if 20% of participants in the intervention group and 10% of participants in the control group dropped out of the study. Is it possible that those who dropped out of the intervention were the ones who found the intervention to be unhelpful or not meaningful? Or perhaps they did not continue sessions due to logistical or financial reasons and are people facing more stressors? If this were so, results based on data collected from the remaining 80% of the intervention group would be biased, possibly in favor of overstating the intervention's effectiveness.

A third design element that strengthens an RCT is to account for dropout by using an intention-to-treat (ITT) analysis. In ITT analysis, every participant who was randomly assigned to a group will be included in the final data analysis, even those who withdrew from the study, were noncompliant, only attended two of its ten sessions, or did not complete all the required post-tests leading to missing outcome data. How would the study results be biased or inaccurate if, for reasons such as these, 15% of participants were excluded from the data? What if the data left out those for whom the intervention was not a good fit or ineffective, leaving in those for whom the intervention worked well? Such omissions would lead to erroneous findings about the intervention's effectiveness. ITT analysis, using the full sample size that started the study, supports unbiased and more conservative results by accounting for every participant who started the study. There are many ITT analysis methods, but one common approach is to estimate the outcomes of the lost participants in different ways, so that they can be included in the statistical analysis.

• •

TIP   The words *randomized controlled trial* are often in the article's title, as in "Treating Sexually Abused Children: 1 Year Follow-Up of a Randomized Controlled Trial" (Cohen et al., 2005).

• •

2. Comparison Group Study (Quasi-Experimental Design)

In a typical comparison group study, participants are either placed in two groups, or two naturally occurring groups are identified: an intervention group that receives the intervention and a comparison group that receives no treatment or treatment as usual. The difference between this design and an RCT is that study participants are not assigned randomly. This is why comparison group studies are referred to as quasi-experimental or nonrandomized trials. Just like RCTs, pre- and posttests are given so that outcomes can be compared to see if the intervention group has more positive outcomes than the comparison group. However, because study participants are not randomly assigned to the two groups, there is less certainty that the two groups are alike. Without complete certainty that the two groups are alike, attributing the improvements to the intervention is less certain than in an RCT, because those in the intervention group may have a characteristic unique to their group (e.g., they were parents with higher motivation or skilled nursing facility patients with previous exposure to stress reduction concepts).

3. Pre-Post Study Without a Comparison/ Control Group (Preexperimental Design)

In a pre-post study, the outcome of interest is measured before and after an intervention is given, and there is neither a control nor comparison group. Multiple pretests and posttests can also be given rather than just one of each. This study design is called preexperimental or nonexperimental interventional design. An example is to administer a depression symptom scale before providing a one-on-one intervention for depression and administering the scale again after the intervention. Because we observe the study participant's state before and after the intervention, we have some support for attributing the decrease in symptoms to the intervention. However, with this design, it is still possible that other factors contributed to the improvements. For example, what if most of the participants were also in a support group during the same period that they were receiving the intervention? Or the participants were naturally healing over time without any influence of the intervention? To strengthen the ability to attribute improvements to the intervention, we can add a comparison or control group to the pre-post study, as discussed in the earlier designs. Then it would be possible to say that participants who received the intervention improved both across time and in comparison with another group who did not receive the intervention.

4. Cohort Study (Observational Design)

In a cohort study, a sample is drawn from people who have the same condition and/or receive a specific intervention. They are followed over time and are compared with a group not affected by the condition or not receiving the intervention. Cohort studies are longitudinal studies, because people are followed prospectively (i.e., into the future). It is an observational study where outcome data is collected across time and the interventions are not manipulated, as in experimental and quasi-experimental studies. Cohort studies are useful for evaluating treatments in broader populations in real-world settings. They have an advantage over RCTs because they can account for the adverse events that take place in real-world settings. For cohort studies to represent diverse populations, large community-ty-based, multicenter studies are most useful.

A cohort study is a good design for investigating whether a system of care can deliver good clinical outcomes in routine practice. An example is to collect data on anxiety from 2,000 consecutive patients referred to a set of outpatient mental health clinics. The data collected across time includes a score on an anxiety scale and the anxiety treatments received, including types, methods, and length of treatments. Pre- and posttreatment anxiety levels are calculated. Remission and recovery rates for those who completed treatment and who dropped out are calculated. The results of the study can be compared with results from experimental and quasi-experimental studies of the same treatment. In a cohort study, separate samples are drawn at pretest and at posttest. It is possible that that not all the people selected in the pretest sample will be selected in the posttest sample. If only people selected in the pretest are measured in the posttest, this would be a panel study.

5. Case Control Study (Observational Design)

In a case control study, people who have a condition (cases) are compared with people who do not have the condition (controls). Case control studies are observational studies where we look back retrospectively (i.e., into the past) to compare how frequently those in each group were exposed to a certain risk factor or intervention. No interventions are manipulated, as in experimental and quasi-experimental studies. The aim of case control studies is to identify possible causal associations between risk factors and adverse outcomes, such as the association between cigarette smoke and lung cancer. Case control studies are always quantitative, even though they may have a qualitative component. However, case control studies have also been used to assess the effectiveness of interventions. This study design is particularly useful for assessing rare outcomes, such as the intended and unintended effects of treatment or a program. It is also useful when RCTs are not feasible cost-wise. With their quantitative nature and focus on causal relationships, case control studies have an explanatory purpose.

An example of a case control study is to identify 100 cases each of children with and without inflicted traumatic brain injury (TBI). The cases and controls can be matched for socioeconomic class, race/ethnicity, previous contact with child welfare services, and other factors, so that the two groups are similar. Data collection consists of observing retrospectively whether the children and their parents had exposure to a program to prevent inflicted TBI, which involved receiving a pamphlet followed by verbal explanation by a social worker. With this data, it is possible to calculate and compare the odds (or chances) of being a case and to control whether the parent has received the preventive intervention. If the odds (or chances) of being a case are lower for families that received the intervention, then there is evidence of the intervention's effectiveness.

6. Case Study or Case Report (Observational Design)

In a case study (or case report), a clinician provides a treatment to one or several clients and reports on the outcomes. Case studies are often qualitative studies in which the clinician describes the intervention and its effects on a client, without using symptom scales. The aim of case studies is to gain an in-depth understanding of how an intervention led to positive effects and the nature of these effects in one or several individuals. (These studies are sometimes referred to as studies about a treatment's *mechanism of change*.) Another use of the case study is to pilot a new or adapted intervention. A case study is viewed as providing less certainty about an intervention's effectiveness for several reasons. First, the sample size is very small. Second, there was no control or comparison group to show that those who received the intervention improved more. Third, the clinician and client(s), not being blinded to who has and has not received the treatment, may be biased toward reporting positive outcomes.

An example of a case study is for a clinician to provide cognitive behavioral therapy (CBT) for depression to two Farsi-speaking immigrant clients. In the case report, the clinician will discuss the nature and severity of depressive symptoms that each client experienced before the treatment, how each responded to the different treatment techniques, what treatment and other factors might have contributed to symptom and other improvements, and any adaptations to the treatment that were necessary. Such a study might support the development of a culturally adapted CBT for depression or other clinicians' use of CBT for Farsi speakers.

7. Meta-Analysis

A meta-analysis is a statistical analysis that combines the results of multiple studies. Statistical approaches are used to obtain a pooled estimate or weighted average from the results of the individual studies. In conducting a meta-analysis, the researcher must decide how to search for studies, the criteria for including studies, how to deal with incomplete data, and how to analyze it. Most meta-analyses are of RCTs. A benefit of meta-analysis is being able to aggregate information that is available from many quantitative studies on a specific intervention. As an example, a meta-analysis may be conducted on a dozen RCTs of Cognitive Behavioral Therapy (CBT) for depression. Statistical methods will be used to combine the quantitative results to provide an overall result on the effectiveness of CBT for depression.

• •

TIP The words *meta-analysis* or *meta-analytic study* are always in the article's title.

• •

8. Systematic Review

A systematic review is a literature review prepared by a collaborative team of clinical and methodological experts that applies a structured methodology to find, analyze, and synthesize multiple studies related to a particular problem. The objective of a systematic review is to answer a focused clinical question through an exhaustive review and summary of current literature that fits prespecified criteria for inclusion. Systematic reviews may be quantitative or qualitative, with different structured methods available for combining evidence. Qualitative reviews synthesize qualitative and quantitative evidence to address questions on aspects other than effectiveness. Quantitative reviews use meta-analytic statistical techniques to combine results from the included studies. The type of systematic review most relevant to evidence-based social work practice is the intervention review. Other systematic reviews of interest to social workers focus on research methods, diagnostic test accuracy, and prognosis.

What are the steps in conducting a systematic review? Here are the steps: (a) formulating a study question; (b) performing a thorough search of the literature for relevant papers, including naming the databases and citation indexes that will be searched; (c) checking whether each study, by looking at its title and abstract, fits predetermined eligibility criteria; (d) defining review procedures, such as how many people will review each article and what to do in case of disagreements; (e) appraising methodological quality and risk of bias in each study (f) analyzing data and conducting meta-analyses; and (g) presenting and interpreting results.

Systematic reviews do the work of finding and assessing intervention studies for us by providing comprehensive and unbiased information on a clinical topic.

They are touted as an important tool for promoting evidence-based practice. Systematic reviews are not recommendations about what practitioners should use or not use but are careful summaries of what the research evidence says about the intervention's effectiveness. Systematic reviews came about in the biomedical field with the dramatic increase in published studies, which made it impractical for a clinician to track down and review all available primary studies. Clinicians also needed to draw from multiple studies to guide their decisions, as well as assistance with reconciling studies that provided conflicting answers to the same question. Systematic reviews are viewed as an improvement over their predecessor, narrative reviews. In narrative reviews, experts gave only a broad overview of research about a particular condition or treatment and did not typically use an explicit process for gathering evidence to support the review's statements. Readers often did not know which recommendations were based on the author's clinical experience, the breadth of the literature included, or why some studies were given more emphasis than others. Furthermore, quantitative summaries of the included studies were often absent.

· ·

NOTE   Systematic reviews are not the same as literature reviews. Literature reviews summarize current knowledge, including substantive findings on a particular topic. Literature reviews can cover diverse topics, including interventions or assessment methods for particular social or mental health problem areas. Literature reviews are similar to narrative reviews due to having a less rigorous procedure with regard to the literature search criteria, eligibility criteria, review procedures, and so on. Titles of literature reviews always contain the word *review*, such as "Adolescents in Residential and Inpatient Treatment: A Review of the Outcome Literature" (Bettman & Jasperson, 2009).

· ·

The Campbell Collaboration produces and promotes the use of systematic reviews relevant to social work and mental health, with online libraries available to the public. Its Social Welfare Coordinating Group produces reviews in fields related to social care. In January of 2018, there were 102 reviews in this group. Let's look at two examples.

In the first example, the study question is, "What is the effect of Mindfulness-Based Stress Reduction (MBSR) on health, quality of life, and social functioning in adults?" The intervention review that answers this question is "Mindfulness-Based Stress Reduction (MBSR) for Improving Health, Quality of Life and Social Functioning in Adults: A Systematic Review and Meta-Analysis" (de Vibe et al., 2017). This review identified 101 RCTs, with a total of 8,135 participants, using the protocol-based MBSR intervention developed by John Kabat-Zinn (1990). Now find this review on the Campbell Collaboration website: https://

www.campbellcollaboration.org/library/mindfulness-stress-reduction-for-adults. html. Read "About This Systematic Review," and then download and read the Plain Language Summary (2 pages) and Abstract (2 pages). You can also browse the Protocol on how the systematic review was conducted (25 pages) and the Review itself (267 pages).

In the second example, the study question is, "Are psychosocial interventions targeting children exposed to IPV effective at promoting well-being, including mental and behavioral health, other development, and school-based functioning?" A related question of interest is, "Are interventions with certain characteristics, such as modality (e.g., individual, family-based), theoretical approach (cognitive-behavioral, interpersonal), and type of setting (e.g., shelter, outpatient clinic), more effective in promoting well-being among children exposed to IPV?" These questions are answered in a systematic review called "Effectiveness of Interventions to Promote Well-Being Among Children Exposed to Intimate Partner Violence: A Systematic Review" (Latzman et al., 2019). This review is very different from the first example in several ways. First, it did not include only RCTs but assessed studies using both experimental and quasi-experimental designs where the aim was promotion of well-being following a child's exposure to IPV. It also excluded pre-post designs without any comparison group and studies presenting only qualitative data. Second, it did not review the literature on one specific protocol-based intervention but searched the literature for different available interventions for a specific problem. Those included were interventions that provided a variety of psychosocial services to the exposed child, as long as they emphasized psychological and/or social factors rather than biological ones. Third, given the objective of reviewing interventions for children exposed to IPV, this systematic review excluded studies where results for exposed children were not reported, even if, potentially, participants included exposed children, as in interventions designed for children exposed to trauma as more broadly defined. You can download and browse the Protocol (19 pages) at www.campbellcollaboration.org/library/children-partner-violence.html.

Reflection Questions

1. What would a social worker in search of an intervention for their client find useful about a systematic review?
2. Why might the social worker also, however, want to read certain studies firsthand rather than rely on a systematic review?

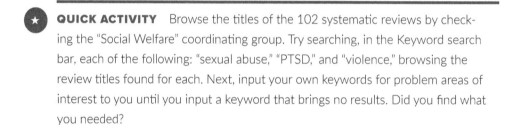

QUICK ACTIVITY   Browse the titles of the 102 systematic reviews by checking the "Social Welfare" coordinating group. Try searching, in the Keyword search bar, each of the following: "sexual abuse," "PTSD," and "violence," browsing the review titles found for each. Next, input your own keywords for problem areas of interest to you until you input a keyword that brings no results. Did you find what you needed?

ACTIVITY 4.1   Identify Study Designs from Titles and Abstracts

Instructions

1.   The title and an excerpt from the abstract are provided for 13 studies. For each, identify the following:

   - Is the study interventional or observational?
   - If interventional, is it an RCT, comparison study, or pre-post study?
   - If observational, is it exploratory, descriptive, or explanatory? Also, is it a cohort study, case control study, or case study/case report?

   . . . .

   TIPS   Try completing this exercise by reading only the title, and then read the excerpt to refine your answers. There is no right answer. Certain interventional studies are also observational, and certain observational studies are also interventional. Remember that our aim is to understand what the study is claiming based on seeing how it was designed!

   . . . .

2.   After you have identified the study designs, read the titles again and pick out the six that provide you with information on the effectiveness of an intervention. These are the studies that may be useful when choosing an intervention for a client.
3.   Optional. Pick one study that is not about the effectiveness of an intervention and think about whether and how it could support the development of a new intervention.

Study Titles and Abstract Excerpts

1. "Collaborative Care Management of Late-Life Depression in the Primary Care Setting: A Randomized Controlled Trial" (Unützer et al., 2002)

   Patients were randomly assigned to the IMPACT intervention (n = 906) or to usual care (n = 895) (p. 2836).

2. "Putting the Pieces Back Together: A Group Intervention for Sexually Exploited Adolescents" (Hickle & Roe-Sepowitz, 2014)

   This paper describes a pilot group intervention created for use with domestic minor sex trafficking victims, focusing on … providing education about DMST, reducing shame and addressing stigma, mutual aid, and managing strong emotions … Process examples are given to illustrate this pilot intervention (p. 99).

3. "Comparative Efficacies of Supportive and Cognitive Behavioral Group Therapies for Young Children Who Have Been Sexually Abused and Their Nonoffending Mothers" (Deblinger et al., 2001)

   Forty-four mothers and their respective children participated in either supportive or cognitive behavioral therapy groups with the group format being randomly determined (p. 332).

4. "From Surviving to Thriving: Understanding Reunification Among African American Mothers with Histories of Addiction" (Blakey, 2011)

   Using the multiple embedded case study method, this study illuminates the experiences and feelings of mothers struggling to overcome addiction and highlights the main differences between women who regained custody and those who permanently lost custody of their children. In this study, 50% of the women lost custody and 50% regained custody of their children (p. 91).

5. "Parents' and Children's Perception of Parent-Led Trauma-Focused Cognitive Behavioral Therapy" (Salloum et al., 2015)

   This study explored parent and child experiences of a parent-led, therapist-assisted treatment during Step One of Stepped Care Trauma-Focused Cognitive Behavioral Therapy (TF-CBT). Seventeen parents/guardians and 16 children were interviewed … Participants were interviewed about what they liked and disliked about the treatment as well as what they found to be most and least helpful (p. 12).

6. "Leaving Foster Care—The Influence of Child and Case Characteristics on Foster Care Exit Rates" (Connell et al., 2005)

   This longitudinal study examines characteristics associated with the timing of three potential foster care outcomes—reunification, adoption, and running away from care (i.e., AWOL). Cox regression modeling was used to identify child and case characteristics associated with each outcome for a statewide sample of children … In many cases, the characteristics operated differently depending on exit type (p. 780).

7. "Academic Behavior and Performance Among African American Youth: Associations with Resources for Resilience" (Chesmore et al., 2016)

   Children's resources for resilience were associated with academic outcomes. Among the total sample, greater perceived support from caregivers and behavioral coping by the child were associated with less child-reported school misbehavior and greater teacher-evaluated teaching performance (p. 1).

8. "Motivational Interviewing to Enhance Treatment Initiation in Substance Abusers: An Effectiveness Study" (Carroll et al., 2001)

   Sixty individuals referred for a substance abuse evaluation by a child welfare worker were randomly assigned to either a standard evaluation or an evaluation enhanced by Motivational Interviewing techniques, each delivered in a single session (p. 335).

9. "Predictors of Weapon-Related Behaviors Among African American, Latino, and White Youth" (Shetgiri et al., 2015)

   Emotional distress and substance use were risk factors for all groups. Violence exposure and peer delinquency were risk factors for white and African Americans. Gun availability in the home was associated with weapon involvement for African Americans only (p. 277).

10. "Patterns of Risk and Resilience in African American and Latino Youth" (Ernestus & Prelow, 2015)

    The present study identified subgroups of adolescents with distinctive patterns of risk and protective factors in early adolescence and examined the psychosocial adjustment of these subgroups in middle and late adolescence (p. 954).

11. "Longitudinal Associations Between Experienced Racial Discrimination and Depressive Symptoms in African American Adolescents" (English et al., 2014)

Structural equation modeling revealed that experienced racial discrimination was positively associated with depressive symptoms 1 year later across all waves of measurement ... Findings highlight the role of experienced racial discrimination in the etiology of depressive symptoms for Africans across early adolescence (p. 1190).

12. "Pilot Controlled Trial of Mindfulness Meditation and Education for Dementia Caregivers" (Oken et al., 2010)

The design was a pilot randomized trial to evaluate the effectiveness of a mindfulness meditation intervention adapted from the Mindfulness-Based Cognitive Therapy Program in relation to two comparison groups: an education class based on Powerful Tools for Caregivers serving as an active control group and a respite-only group serving as a pragmatic control (p. 1031).

13. "Outcomes for Adolescent Girls After Long-Term Residential Treatment" (Thomson et al., 2011)

Youth may improve during [residential] treatment, but are these gains sustained upon return to the community? We explore this question by analyzing outcome data collected at three months and one year post-discharge for 49 adolescent girls discharged from long-term programs at a residential treatment center in Massachusetts (p. 251).

See the answers on page 144.

 ACTIVITY 4.2 **Create a Hierarchy of Evidence**

Instructions

1. Write down all of the different research designs that you can remember from research courses you have taken.
2. Prepare to explain each design to a friend, including giving an example of a study that uses that type of design.
3. Order your research designs from highest to lowest (or strongest to weakest) level of evidence and explain why one is higher than the other.

. . . .

TIP   A research design associated with a high level of evidence means that a study using the design produces strong or credible information about the intervention. In other words, based on the study design, we can have confidence in the finding that the intervention was responsible for the outcome, which is symptom reduction.

. . . .

Examples

1. One design uses randomizing. You randomly put people into two groups. You give the intervention to one group. The other group doesn't get the intervention, or they get the intervention that's being used at your agency. (This is a randomized controlled trial or RCT.)
2. Another type of study design is doing only one case. You look at what happens to one person closely. For example, I'm the clinician, I treat my client, and I write about the different ways the intervention helped my client. I don't want to use any instruments because I think they're limiting. (This is a qualitative case study with a single study participant.)
3. I think the case study is a lower level of evidence, because there's only one person in the sample.
4. The study with the randomized groups has a higher level of evidence because they tested it on more than just one person.
5. With the random groups, you can compare the group that got the new intervention with the other group that didn't to see which intervention worked better. This is better evidence than not having anyone to compare to. (Can you think of one more aspect of an RCT that associates it with better evidence?)

Answers are not provided for this activity.

BRIEF LECTURE 4.3

Grading the Level of Evidence

Evidence refers to research findings, as in, "Is there any evidence that the intervention is effective?" Evidence is the information generated from one or more studies on whether a treatment is helpful to those it intends to help. After we locate some studies of interventions that sound relevant to our client's problem areas, we ask, "How good is the evidence?" and, "Which intervention has the best evidence?" To answer these questions, we will need to grade the evidence.

Let's take an example. We have a 14-year-old Latino immigrant client, bicultural and bilingual, who is experiencing depression related to family and peer conflict. Searching a few databases, we find several interventions that have been tested among adolescents and target these problem areas. They are CBT for depression, Interpersonal Therapy for Depressed Adolescents, and Structural Family Therapy. We have gathered a handful of articles published in peer-reviewed journals on each therapy, some of which were studies with samples that included Latinx teens. Now we want to know, "Which is the best therapy from the standpoint of current research findings?" In other words, "Which of these therapies has the best evidence on its effectiveness?"

To answer our question, we will evaluate or grade each study's level of evidence based on the quality of the study design. Did the study's design allow it to produce trustworthy evidence about the intervention's effectiveness? Practitioners use a three-level evidence hierarchy to classify evidence based on the methodological quality of the study design. The top level contains the designs that produce the most reliable or most trustworthy evidence, which is least vulnerable to bias. The lowest level contains the designs that produce the least reliable or least trustworthy evidence, which is most vulnerable to bias. The hierarchy of evidence in Table 4.1 includes study designs relevant to social-behavioral research and is adapted from hierarches used in the medical field (Sackett et al., 2000; Hadorn et al., 1996; Dynamed, n.d.). The designs within each level are also ordered from higher to lower level of evidence.

• •

TIP The study designs are essentially ranked based on their degree of internal validity. Based on your knowledge of internal validity, reason through why each design is where it is.

• •

TABLE 4.1 Hierarchy of Evidence for Social-Behavioral Research

LEVEL A — STRONGEST, MOST RELIABLE EVIDENCE

Represents research results meeting an extensive set of quality criteria, which minimizes bias.

- Evidence from a **systematic review or meta-analysis of RCTs**
- Evidence from **three or more RCTs of higher quality** with similar results
- Evidence from **at least one higher quality RCT** (large sample and most of below characteristics)
    - Large sample of 100 participants or more
    - Participant is blinded to their treatment group
    - Research team is blinded to the participant's treatment group
    - Low dropout rate of less than 15%
    - Intent to treat analysis
    - Multisite study

LEVEL B — MODERATELY STRONG EVIDENCE

Represents research results using some method of scientific investigation but not meeting the quality criteria of Level A.

- Evidence from one **lower quality RCT** (with most of the below characteristics)
    - Small sample of less than 100 participants
    - Participant is not blinded
    - Research team is not blinded
    - High dropout rate of more than 15%
    - No intent to treat analysis
    - Not a multisite study
- Evidence from well-designed **quasi-experimental studies** (e.g., comparison group studies without random assignment)
- Evidence from well-designed **cohort and case-controlled studies**
- Evidence from **pre-post studies** without a comparison group

LEVEL C — WEAKEST EVIDENCE

Represents reports that are not based on scientific analysis.

- Evidence from **case studies and case reports**
- Evidence from **other descriptive and qualitative studies**
- Evidence from **expert opinions** (opinions of authorities or reports of expert committees)

ACTIVITY 4.3 Grade the Evidence

Instructions

For each of the following nine studies, evaluate the level of evidence. The first seven are the studies on interventions from Activity 3.1, with a little more information provided. You can give full grades (A, B, or C) or partial grades (e.g., A– or B+). State your reasoning for the grade you assigned.

1. "Collaborative Care Management of Late-Life Depression in the Primary Care Setting: A Randomized Controlled Trial" (Unützer et al., 2002)

   - Patients were randomly assigned to the IMPACT intervention (n = 906) or to usual care (n = 895) (p. 2836).
   - [The setting was] eighteen primary care clinics from 8 health care organizations in 5 states (p. 2836).
   - Survey response rates were 90% at 3 months, 87% at 6 months, and 83% at 12 months (p. 2839).
   - Interviewers were blind to study assignment at the baseline interview and follow-up interviews at 3, 6, and 12 months (p. 2839).
   - For each dependent [or outcome] variable, we conducted an intention-to-treat analysis (p. 2839).

   Sample Answer. **Grade A**. This is a higher quality RCT, given the large sample of more than 100 participants and use of multiple study sites, blinding, and intent-to-treat analysis, even though the nonresponse or dropout rate was close to 15% at 6-month follow-up and greater than 15% at 12-month follow-up.

2. "Putting the Pieces Back Together: A Group Intervention for Sexually Exploited Adolescents" (Hickle & Roe-Sepowitz, 2014)

   - This paper describes a pilot group intervention created for use with domestic minor sex trafficking (DMST) victims, focusing on ... providing education about DMST, reducing shame and addressing stigma, mutual aid, and managing strong emotions ... Process examples are given to illustrate this pilot intervention (p. 99).
   - The clinical direction of the residential program identified 10 current clients who had sex-traded or been sex-trafficked [to receive the pilot intervention] (p. 103).

- During one group, we sought to address shame associated with having a pimp ... a 14-year old Native American girl, disclosed that ... she had a female pimp who offered her a place to stay (in exchange for sex work) ... "I did it because I was being really sexual ... and someone told me I could make money rather than just do it for free" (p. 108).

3. "Comparative Efficacies of Supportive and Cognitive Behavioral Group Therapies for Young Children Who Have Been Sexually Abused and Their Nonoffending Mothers" (Deblinger et al., 2001)

- Forty-four mothers and their respective children participated in either supportive or cognitive behavioral therapy groups with the group format being randomly determined (p. 332).
- The mothers who participated in cognitive behavioral groups reported greater reductions at post-test in (a) their intrusive thoughts and (b) their negative parental emotional reactions regarding the sexual abuse (p. 332).
- There were 67 mothers and their children between the ages of 2 and 8 who volunteered for the project ... 4 (6%) never returned for assignment, 5 (8%) left after one session, and 4 (6%) left after two sessions [leaving 54 mothers and children, or a dropout rate of 19.4%] (p. 333).
- Out of the 54, nine (17%) failed to complete posttest and 3-month follow-up evaluations and one (2%) completed only a posttest [leaving 44 mothers and children, or a dropout of 18.5%] (p. 334).

4. "Parents' and Children's Perception of Parent-Led Trauma-Focused Cognitive Behavioral Therapy" (Salloum et al., 2015)

- This study explored parent and child experiences of a parent-led, therapist assisted treatment during Step One of Stepped Care Trauma-Focused Cognitive Behavioral Therapy (TF-CBT) (p. 12).
- Seventeen parents/guardians and 16 children were interviewed ... about what they liked and disliked about the treatment as well as what they found to be most and least helpful (p. 12).
- In terms of treatment components, children indicated that the relaxation exercises were the most liked/helpful component (62.5%) (p. 12).

5. "Motivational Interviewing to Enhance Treatment Initiation in Substance Abusers: An Effectiveness Study" (Carroll et al., 2001)

- Sixty individuals referred for a substance abuse evaluation by a child welfare worker were randomly assigned to either a standard evaluation or an evaluation enhanced by Motivational Interviewing (MI) techniques, each delivered in a single session (p. 335).

- To minimize attrition ... the entire study process (informed consent, random assignment, delivery of standard or MI enhanced evaluation) was completed within a single 2-hour sequence (p. 336).
- Four clinicians conducted the standard evaluation and four other clinicians conducted the enhanced evaluation, with the latter completing one day of training in MI (p. 336).
- "The primary outcome measures were the rates of participants who attended one or three subsequent drug abuse treatment sessions after the evaluation" (p. 337).
- The article does not state whether participants were blinded to their group assignment (i.e., whether they were told they were about to receive the "enhanced" evaluation or not).

6. "Pilot Controlled Trial of Mindfulness Meditation and Education for Dementia Caregivers" (Oken et al., 2010)

- The design was a pilot randomized trial to evaluate the effectiveness of a mindfulness meditation intervention adapted from the Mindfulness-Based Cognitive Therapy Program in relation to two comparison groups: an education class ... serving as an active control group and a respite-only group serving as a pragmatic control (p. 1031).
- Subjects were assessed prior to randomization and again after completing classes at 8 weeks (p. 1031).
- There were 31 caregivers randomized and 28 completers.
- The study was designed to help optimize the clinical trial design for a planned larger study (p. 1032).
- Two researchers in the lab were unblinded to the assigned group, but all the outcome assessments were done by the blinded research assistants (p. 1034).

7. "Outcomes for Adolescent Girls After Long-Term Residential Treatment" (Thomson et al., 2011)

- Youth may improve during [residential] treatment, but are these gains sustained upon return to the community? We explore this question by analyzing outcome data collected at three months and one year post-discharge for 49 adolescent girls discharged from long-term programs at a residential treatment center in Massachusetts (p. 251).
- Qualitative data reveals the range of post-discharge challenges experienced by adolescents and their families (p. 251).

- Quantitative data shows a 77% reduction in restrictive level of care placements comparing the year before admission to the year after discharge (p. 251).

8. "Treatment for School Refusal Among Children and Adolescents: A Systematic Review and Meta-Analysis" (Maynard et al., 2018)

   - The authors examine the effects of psychosocial treatments that could be implemented by school or mental health professionals.
   - Studies must have used a pre-post RCT or quasi-experimental design and used statistical controls or reported baseline data on outcomes. A comprehensive search process was used to find eight studies (6 using a randomized design, 2 using a quasi-experimental design) including 435 participants assessing the effects of psychosocial treatments on anxiety and attendance outcomes.
   - Data was quantitatively synthesized using meta-analytic methods.
   - Evidence indicates that improvements in school attendance but not in anxiety occur for children and adolescents with school refusal who receive psychosocial treatment.

9. "Promoting Father Involvement in Early Home Visiting Services for Vulnerable Families: Findings from a Pilot Study of 'Dads Matter'" (Guterman et al., 2018)

   - This paper describes the design, development, and pilot testing of the Dads Matter enhancement to standard perinatal home visiting services. Dads Matter is a manualized intervention package designed to incorporate fathers into home visiting services.
   - Twelve families received standard home visiting services and completed baseline and four-month post-tests by the home visitor staff.
   - After this, the staff was trained in conducting Dads Matter and 12 additional families received standard services enhanced with Dads Matter and completed baseline and four-month post-tests.
   - Outcome measures indicated positive trends in the quality of the mother-father relationship, perceived stress reported by both parents, fathers' involvement with the child, maltreatment indicators, and fathers' verbalizations toward the infant.

See the answers on page 147.

⌘   ## Case Paper Task 4.1

Evaluate the Evidence in the Three EBPs You Are Considering for Your Client and Write the *Identification & Justification of Level of Evidence* Section

Instructions: Below are examples of the *Identification & Justification of Level of Evidence* section for the first of three EBPs from Laura's and Eddie's case papers. You can see other examples in the full case papers in Appendix B (p. 311) and Appendix C (p. 323).

Case Paper Instructions:

Review of EBP #1 (6–7 paragraphs, 9 points)

This section is based on your review of two empirical research articles and other information found online, in print, and through interviews.

Identification & Justification of Level of Evidence: For each article, identify the level of evidence (grade A, B, or C) using the definitions on p. 136 and justify the level by briefly describing the research design. Include the study's main finding. (*1–2 paragraphs, 2 points*)

Laura's Example

Needs Strengthening

> #### Review of EBP #1: Cognitive Behavioral Therapy for Adolescents
> #### Identification and Justification of Level of Evidence
> I reviewed a study with 107 adolescents comparing CBT with other therapies. CBT had the best outcomes. Many adolescents dropped out before starting treatment, and more dropped out after starting treatment. This is a grade "A" study, because CBT was more effective than several other therapies. I reviewed another study with 80 youth in outpatient treatment who received CBT-A treatment. The youth had positive results like another older study. This is a grade "B" study, because outcomes were as good as an older study.

In what ways is the above grading of the level of evidence incorrect? Do you get a full quick picture of the study designs and results?

Well-Written

As you read the below example, reflect on whether the justification of the level of evidence is clearer and the details provided helpful. Notice that the results of a third study (not required for the assignment), a meta-analysis, is introduced at the end.

> #### Review of EBP #1: Cognitive Behavioral Therapy for Adolescents
> #### Identification and Justification of Level of Evidence
> The levels of evidence are Grade "A–" and Grade "B" for the two CBT-A studies I reviewed. The "A–" study was an RCT (Brent et al., 1999). It had a sample size of 107 adolescents and compared CBT with systemic behavioral family therapy

(continued)

and nondirective supportive therapy; CBT had superior outcomes in the acute phase of depression. Dropout was within an acceptable level, given that 12% of those eligible did not agree to be randomized and 14% dropped out or did not start treatment. The "B" study (Weersing et al., 2006) compared the outcomes of 80 youth recruited from an outpatient clinic for adolescents with depression with the outcomes from a gold standard clinical trial considered to be the benchmark for CBT-A. In my view, this is a quasi-experimental design, even though the researchers recruited youth with similar characteristics as the benchmark study conducted years earlier. Without randomization, the two groups are not guaranteed to be similar. Findings showed that improvements in depression were similar between the sample of 80 youth and the benchmark study sample. A third study was a Grade "A" meta-analysis of 11 RCTs that confirms the general effectiveness of CBT-A (Klein et al., 2007).

Eddie's Example

Well-Written

As you read the below example, notice the additional level of detail provided. Also, are the justifications of the levels of evidence stronger than in the above example? Which writing style do you prefer?

Review of EBP #1: Prolonged Exposure Therapy
Identification & Justification of Level of Evidence

I reviewed two PET studies with Grade "B+" level of evidence. First, in a single-blind RCT, PET was compared with three other cognitive behavioral treatments in 118 civilian participants with chronic PTSD in Australia (Bryant et al., 2008). Treatment conditions consisted of eight weeks of Imaginal Exposure (IE), In Vivo Exposure (IVE), combined IE/IVE, or IE/IVE with cognitive restructuring (i.e., PET). The sample consisted of White (92%) and Asian (8%) males and females. Findings included fewer patients with PTSD (31%) in the PET group at 6-month follow-up than the other groups (63%–75%). Those in the PET condition also had lower PTSD and depressive symptoms after treatment (Bryant et al., 2008). This is a "B+" study, given the high dropout rate (24%), blinding of only outcome assessors to participants' treatment conditions, and lack of multisite study (Rich, 2005).

Second, a double-blind RCT with 200 patients with PTSD recruited via outpatient clinics, including rape crisis centers in Seattle and Cleveland, private providers, and public media ads, detected no differential effect of 10-week PET versus medication (sertraline) on interviewer-rated loss of PTSD diagnosis and self-reported PTSD, depression, and anxiety symptoms and functioning (Zoellner et al., 2019). Also, participants given their treatment of choice showed stronger symptom improvements. This is a "B+" and not an "A" study because although the sample was greater than 100 participants, there was an extremely high dropout rate (34%), and it was not a multisite study (Rich, 2005).

ANSWERS

Discussion 4.1 Answers **Is There Such a Thing as "Good" Versus "Bad" Evidence?**

How Students Answered

1. **What makes "good" evidence?**

   a. Good evidence is when you know you can use the intervention with your clients because they've studied it with people like your clients, such as with Asian immigrants or LGBTQ.

   b. Good evidence is when they've tested the intervention in the community and not just in hospitals or medical centers.

   c. The evidence is good if the samples were big and there were repeated studies.

   d. The evidence is useful if the researchers show us ways to tweak or change their intervention to meet different clients' needs.

2. **Can there be "stronger" or "weaker" evidence related to how a study is designed (i.e., without considering who was sampled)?**

   a. The evidence is stronger if the researchers can be sure that the intervention caused the symptom reduction. It is weaker if they're not sure because other factors may have caused a drop in symptoms.

   b. Stronger evidence is when you can trust the results of the study. For example, a randomized controlled trial (RCT) is the best study. You can be sure that the intervention actually worked, because there was a control group that didn't get the intervention, and those people didn't show any improvements.

   c. The evidence isn't as strong if you don't have a comparison group. For example, you give an intervention to your sample, and you find out they reduced their symptoms before versus after, but you didn't compare them with other people.

   d. The evidence is weaker for qualitative studies, which usually have a small sample size. We're not as sure about the results because there isn't a comparison group. [Evidence is also weaker] when no instruments are used before and after the intervention.

e. Longitudinal studies or studies with multiple data collection points would have stronger evidence, because we can be sure that the individuals improved in their outcomes across time.

3. **Have you heard of *levels of evidence or a hierarchy* of evidence? What might this mean?**

a. This is a way of judging what's good evidence and bad evidence, based on the research design.

b. Hierarchy of evidence is about good studies versus bad studies. Good studies use randomization and control groups and use big samples. Bad studies don't use randomization and use small samples. And then there's everything in between.

c. It should also be based on who was studied, but this depends on the people you're working with and wanting the intervention for. For example, if I'm working with Spanish-speaking immigrants, good evidence comes from studies that included Spanish speakers in the samples.

Activity 4.1 Answers Identify Study Designs from Titles and Abstracts

1. **Identify the study design: If interventional, is it an RCT, comparison study, or pre-post study? If observational, is it exploratory, descriptive, or explanatory, and is it a cohort, case control, or case study/ case report? [Letters a–m correspond to abstracts 1–13, respectively.]**

a. This is an **RCT**, an **interventional study**. Like most studies using randomized assignment, the title will say "randomized controlled trial."

b. This is an **interventional** study. It is **preexperimental** because there is neither control in the assignment of participants nor pre- and posttests. It is a pilot study to examine the impact of an intervention. On the other hand, it could also be viewed as **a case study**, an **observational study** aiming to **describe** the reactions of a group of sex-trafficking victims to a pilot intervention.

c. This is an **RCT**, an **interventional study,** since random assignment to groups is stated in the abstract. Two active interventions are being compared, as opposed to one active intervention being compared to no intervention, which is what "treatment as usual" often is.

d. This is a **case study**, an **observational study** aiming to **describe** the experiences of two groups of mothers qualitatively. It could also be viewed as a case control study, since two groups of women are compared. However, the researchers do not state that they are carefully "controlling" the groups, matching cases (those who lost custody) with controls (those who regained custody). Also, a case control study would look back into time to see what predicts or increase the odds of "losing custody." This study is not retrospective but simply describes two groups of women, looking at their different outcomes (experiences and feelings).

e. This is an **interventional** study. It is **preexperimental** because there is no control in the assignment of participants. It may be a pilot study to refine an intervention to be used in a future controlled or uncontrolled trial. On the other hand, it could be viewed as **a case report**, an **observational study** aiming to **describe** what parents and children liked and found helpful qualitatively.

f. This is an **explanatory observational** study, with the aim of explaining why three different outcomes occur—what are the specific factors that lead to each outcome?

· ·

TIP Sophisticated analytical (or statistical) modeling techniques are frequently used in explanatory studies—to show the strength of the linkages.

· ·

g. This is an **explanatory observational** study, with the aim of understanding how positive academic outcomes are "caused by" resilience resources. Because no sophisticated quantitative modeling technique was mentioned in the abstract, it is likely that none was used. It is also possible to view this study as descriptive, but the word *association* and focus on specific, limited variables gives it away as explanatory.

· ·

TIP Whether the authors imply a certain aim, descriptive or explanatory, is important. But whether you see it as descriptive or explanatory, based on your knowledge of the literature and your own reasoning, is more important.

· ·

h. This is an **RCT**, an **interventional study**, since random assignment is stated. The "standard evaluation" is another way of saying "treatment as usual."

i.   This is an **explanatory observational** study, aiming to explain why and how weapons-related behaviors occur. While predictors are not causes, the study is still trying to explain a phenomenon, rather than just describe it.

j.   This is a **descriptive observational** study, aiming to reveal different patterns in early adolescence and linking these with outcomes in later adolescence. Note how the authors are not (yet) trying to explain or predict or associate anything.

k.   This is an **explanatory observational** study, aiming to explain depression as a result of racial discrimination.

l.   This is an **RCT**, an **interventional study** aiming to compare two active interventions with a control group.

m.   This is a **cohort** study, an **observational study** with no manipulation but only observation of a naturally occurring group of girls who received a certain service. The abstract hints that it is **exploring** a new topic. It is also possible to view the study as interventional, with only posttests given at 3 months and 1 year post-discharge.

2. **Pick out the seven studies that provide you with information on the effectiveness of an intervention (i.e., these studies address clinical outcomes).**

    1, 2, 3, 5, 8, 12, 13

3. **Optional. Pick one study that is not about the effectiveness of an intervention and explain how it could support the development of a new intervention.**

    The findings of study #6 (p. 132) by Connell et al. (2005) on the case characteristics of foster children who run away from care could inform a preventative intervention to reduce AWOL rates by addressing the risk factors and issues identified in the cases.

    The findings of study #7 (p. 132) by Chesmore et al. (2016) on African American youths' behavioral coping methods could inform a coping intervention that aims to build resilience, reduce school misbehaviors, and improve academic performance.

Activity 4.3 Answers   **Grade the Evidence**

For each of the seven studies on interventions from Activity 4.1, evaluate the level of evidence. A little more information is provided for each study than what was given in Activity 4.1. You can give full grades (A, B, or C) or partial grades (e.g., A- or B+). State your reasoning for the grade you assigned.

1. "Collaborative Care Management of Late-Life Depression in the Primary Care Setting: A Randomized Controlled Trial" (Unützer et al., 2002)

   Grade A. This is a higher quality RCT, given the large sample of more than 100 participants and use of multiple study sites, blinding, and intent-to-treat analysis, even though the nonresponse or dropout rate was close to 15% at 6-month follow-up and greater than 15% at 12-month follow-up.

2. "Putting the Pieces Back Together: A Group Intervention for Sexually Exploited Adolescents" (Hickle & Roe-Sepowitz, 2014)

   Grade C. This is, in essence, a case study that describes the adolescents' experiences and reactions to a group intervention. It is wholly qualitative. While it is framed as an interventional study aiming to evaluate a pilot intervention, it does not meet the criteria for a strong preexperimental study, since there is neither a comparison group nor pre- and posttests. If it met these criteria, with some quantitative results, we would give it a grade of "B-."

3. "Comparative Efficacies of Supportive and Cognitive Behavioral Group Therapies for Young Children Who Have Been Sexually Abused and Their Nonoffending Mothers" (Deblinger et al., 2001)

   Grade B. This is a lower quality RCT, given the small sample of less than 100 and overall dropout rate far above 15%. Also, it is not a multisite study. We could read further to see if the study used intent-to-treat analysis and blinding. However, even if it used these methods, its grade would not increase to an "A."

4. "Parents' and Children's Perception of Parent-Led Trauma-Focused Cognitive Behavioral Therapy" (Salloum et al., 2015)

   Grade C. This is in essence a case study that describes the parent-child dyads' experiences of an intervention. It is wholly qualitative. While it is framed as an interventional study, aiming to explore an intervention, it does not meet the criteria for a strong preexperimental study, since it uses neither a comparison group nor pre- and posttests.

5. "Motivational Interviewing to Enhance Treatment Initiation in Substance Abusers: An Effectiveness Study" (Carroll et al., 2001)

   Grade B. This is a lower quality RCT, given the small sample of fewer than 100 and being a single-site study, even though there was no attrition (or dropout), given that the study design ensured this. Note that blinding of the research team was not an issue, given that the team did not assess the outcomes. Given that it is an RCT and has some elements of a well-designed RCT, we may choose to assign it a grade of "B+." Its grade would be lower, such as a "B" or "B–," if it has been a quasi-experimental study, which did not use random assignment.

6. "Pilot Controlled Trial of Mindfulness Meditation and Education for Dementia Caregivers" (Oken et al., 2010)

   Grade B. This is a lower quality RCT, given the small sample of less than 100 and being a single-site study. This is clearly an experimental design, rather than quasi-experimental, given the use of random assignment to have a control group and use of pre- and posttests. Even with the use of blinding, an element of a higher quality RCT, the study remains overall a lower quality RCT. If random assignment had not been used but the study had a comparison group, its grade would be lower, such as "B–."

7. "Outcomes for Adolescent Girls After Long-Term Residential Treatment" (Thomson et al., 2011)

   Grade B. This study is preexperimental. There is no comparison group, but the design includes pre-and posttests. If there is a comparison group, it becomes quasi-experimental. If there is a control group, formed by random assignment, the study becomes experimental. A better grade for this study is "B–," since it does not use a comparison group.

8. "Treatment for School Refusal Among Children and Adolescents: A Systematic Review and Meta-Analysis" (Maynard et al., 2018)

   Grade A. This is a systematic review and meta-analysis that includes RCTs with similar findings. It would be advisable to read the article in detail to check that one or more of the included RCTs were of higher quality to ensure this grade.

9. "Promoting Father Involvement in Early Home Visiting Services for Vulnerable Families: Findings from a Pilot Study of 'Dads Matter'" (Guterman et al., 2018)

   Grade B. This study uses a quasi-experimental design, including pre-post tests and a comparison group. With 24 families, the sample is small. If it had used a randomized design, this study could receive a "B+," but as it is, a "B–" is justifiable, given its small sample size.

REFERENCES

Review of Study Designs

Bettmann, J. E., & Jasperson, R. A. (2009). Adolescents in residential and inpatient treatment: A review of the outcome literature. *Child and Youth Care Forum, 38*(4), 161–183. http://doi.org/10.1007/s10566-009-9073-y

Blakey, J. M. (2011). From surviving to thriving: Understanding reunification among African American mothers with histories of addiction. *Children and Youth Services Review, 34*(1), 91–102. doi:10.1016/j.childyouth.2011.09.006

Carroll, K. M., Bryce, L., Sheehan, J., & Hyland, N. (2001). Motivational Interviewing to enhance treatment initiation in substance abusers: An effectiveness study. *The American Journal on Addictions, 10*(4), 335–339. http://www.ncbi.nlm.nih.gov/pmc/articles/PMC3680596/pdf/nihms466091.pdf

Chesmore, A. A., Winston, W., & Brady, S. S. (2016). Academic behavior and performance among African American youth: Associations with resources for resilience. *Urban Review: Issues and Ideas in Public Education, 48*(1), 1–14.

Cohen, J. A., Mannarino, A. P., Knudsen, K., (2005). Treating sexually abused children: 1 year follow-up of a randomized controlled trial. *Child Abuse and Neglect, 29*(2), 135–145.

Connell, C. M., Katz, K. H., Saunders, L., & Tebes, J. K. (2005). Leaving foster care—The influence of child and case characteristics on foster care exit rates. *Children and Youth Services Review, 28*(7), 780–798. doi: 10.1016/j.childyouth.2005.08.007

Deblinger, E., Stauffer, L. B., Steer, R. A. (2001). Comparative efficacies of supportive and cognitive behavioral group therapies for young children who have been sexually abused and their nonoffending mothers. *Child Maltreatment, 6*(4), 332–343.

de Vibe, M., Bjorndal, A., Fattah, S., Dyrdal, G. M., Halland, E., & Tanner-Smith, E. E. (2017). Mindfulness-based stress reduction (MBSR) for improving health, quality of life and social functioning in adults: A systematic review and meta-analysis. *Campbell Systematic Reviews 13*(1), 1–264. https://onlinelibrary.wiley.com/doi/10.4073/csr.2017.11

English, D., Lambert, S. F., & Ialongo, N. S., (2014). Longitudinal associations between experienced racial discrimination and depressive symptoms in African American adolescents. *Developmental Psychology, 50*(4), 1190–1196.

Ernestus, S., & Prelow, H. M. (2015). Patterns of risk and resilience in African American and Latino youth. *Journal of Community Psychology, 43*(8), 954–972.

Guterman, N. B., Bellamy, J. & Banman, A. (2018). Promoting father involvement in early home visiting services for vulnerable families: Findings from a pilot study of "Dads Matter." *Child Abuse & Neglect, 76,* 261–272.

Hickle, K. E., & Roe-Sepowitz, D. E. (2014). Putting the pieces back together: A group intervention for sexually exploited adolescent girls. *Social Work with Groups, 37*(2), 99–113. http://doi.org/10.1080/01609513.2013.823838

Kabat-Zinn J. (1990). *Full catastrophe living: Using the wisdom of your body and mind to face stress, pain, and illness.* Bantam.

Latzman, N. E., Casanueva, C., Brinton, J. & Forman-Hoffman, V.L. (2019). Effectiveness of interventions to promote well-being among children exposed to intimate partner violence: A systematic review. *Campbell Systematic Reviews, 15*(3), e1049. https://onlinelibrary.wiley.com/doi/full/10.1002/cl2.1049

Maynard, B. R., Heyne, D., Brendel, K. E., Bulanda, J. J., Thompson, A. M., & Pigott, T. D. (2018). Treatment for school refusal among children and adolescents. *Research on Social Work Practice, 28*(1), 56–67.

Oken, B. S., Fonareva, I., Haas, M., Wahbeh, H., Lane, J. B., Zajdel, D., & Amen, A. (2010). Pilot controlled trial of mindfulness meditation and education for dementia caregivers. *Journal of Alternative and Complementary Medicine 16*(10), 1031-1038.

Salloum, A., Dorsey, C. S., Swaidan, V. R., Storch, E. A. (2015). Parents' and children's perception of parent-led Trauma-Focused Cognitive Behavioral Therapy. *Child Abuse and Neglect, 40*(2), 12–23.

Shetgiri, R., Boots, D.P., Lin, H. & Cheng, T.L. (2015). Predictors of weapon-related behaviors among African American, Latino, and White youth. *Journal of Pediatrics, 171,* 277–282.

Thomson, S. T., Hirschberg, D., & Qiao, J. (2011). Outcomes for Adolescent girls after long-term residential treatment. *Residential Treatment for Children & Youth, 28*(3), 251–267.

Unützer, J., Katon, W., Callahan, C. M., Williams, J. W., Hunkeler, E., Harpole, L. H., Hoffing, M., Della Penna, R., Noel, P. H., Lin, E. H. B., Arean, P. A., Hegel, M. T., Tang, L., Belin, T. R., Oishi, S. M., & Langston, C. (2002). Collaborative care management of late-life depression in the primary care setting: A randomized controlled trial. *Journal of the American Medical Association, 288*(22), 2836–2845.

Grading the Level of Evidence

Dynamed Website. *Levels of Evidence.* www.dynamed.com & https://connect.ebsco.com/s/article/DynaMed-Levels-of-Evidence?language=en_US

Hadorn, D. C., Baker, D., Hodges, J. S., & Hicks, N. (1996). Rating the quality of evidence for clinical practice guidelines. *Journal of Clinical Epidemiology, 49*(7), 749–754.

Sackett, D. L., Straus, S. E., Richardson, W. S., Rosenberg, W., & Haynes, R. B. (2000). *Evidence-based medicine: How to practice and teach EBM (2nd ed.).* Churchill Livingstone. (Sharen E. Strauss is first author of the current 5th edition of this classic originally authored by David L. Sackett.)

RESOURCES

Understanding Research Quality: Internal and External Validity

Trochim, W. K. (2020, March 10). *Research methods knowledge base: Internal validity.* Conjointly.

This webpage provides a definition and useful diagram illustrating internal validity.

https://conjointly.com/kb/internal-validity

Cuncic, A. (2020, September 17). *Understanding internal and external validity: How these concepts are applied in research.* Verywell Mind.

This web article provides good descriptions of both types of validities and factors that improve them.

https://www.verywellmind.com/internal-and-external-validity-4584479

Ohlund, B., & Yu, C. (n.d.). *Threats to validity of research design.* Portland State University.

This webpage covers factors that jeopardize internal and external validity.

https://web.pdx.edu/~stipakb/download/PA555/ResearchDesign.html

Bhandari, P. (2020, June 19). *Understanding external validity*. Scribbr.

This webpage discusses external validity in depth, including different types of external validity, threats, and the trade-off between external and internal validity.

https://www.scribbr.com/methodology/external-validity

Review of Study Designs

Trochim, W. K. (2020, March 10). *Research methods knowledge base: Types of designs*. Conjointly.

The webpage provides clear explanations and diagrams of different types of designs, including experimental and quasi-experimental designs.

https://conjointly.com/kb/research-design-types

Mitchell, O. (2015, October 2). Experimental research design. *The Encyclopedia of Crime and Punishment*. Wiley Online Library.

This free-access article provides fine explanations of experimental designs, including a focus on why causal inference is important in the area of criminology research. It provides excellent examples of studies to illustrate a variety of research approaches and give a broad overview of research in the applied social sciences.

https://onlinelibrary.wiley.com/doi/full/10.1002/9781118519639.wbecpx113

Institute for Work & Health. (2016). *Observational vs. experimental studies*.

This website defines observational studies (cohort and case control) versus experimental studies (RCTs) and the strengths and weaknesses of each.

https://www.iwh.on.ca/what-researchers-mean-by/observational-vs-experimental-studies

Lu, C. Y. (2009). Observational studies: A review of study designs, challenges and strategies to reduce confounding. *The International Journal of Clinical Practice, 63*(5), 691–697.

This free article provides a more advanced discussion of observational study designs and their applicability to clinical practice in light of RCTs being impractical or unethical.

https://onlinelibrary.wiley.com/doi/pdf/10.1111/j.1742-1241.2009.02056.x

Mann, C. J. (2003). Observational research methods. Research design II: cohort, cross sectional, and case-control studies. *Emergency Medicine, 20*(1), 54–60.

This free article provides an advanced, detailed discussion of observational methods, including how to run each type of study. It includes a thoughtful checklist of key requirements in any study design (see Box 1, p. 54).

https://emj.bmj.com/content/20/1/54

Grading the Level of Evidence

University of Southern California. (2020, December 1). *Research guides: Social work: Evidence-based practice resources: Hierarchy of social work evidence.*

This website displays a detailed and clear pyramid diagram of the hierarchy of evidence and provides links to resources for obtaining evidence from the top levels (which are synthesis and summative reports) and about sample evidence-based programs.

https://libguides.usc.edu/socialwork/socialworkEBP

Dang, D., & Dearholt, S. (2017). *Johns Hopkins nursing evidence-based practice: Model and guidelines.* 3rd ed. Sigma Theta Tau International.

Free Model and Toolkit PDFs may be downloaded after you register your information as a student or faculty member on the website below. The tools include question development, research (hierarchy of evidence) appraisal, action planning, and more.

https://www.hopkinsmedicine.org/evidence-based-practice/ijhn_2017_ebp.html

Haussler, S., & Dang, D. (2009). Johns Hopkins nursing evidence-based practice: Model and guidelines. 2nd ed. Sigma Theta Tau International.

Free comprehensive guide (over 250 pages) covering a spectrum of topics related to EBP decision-making, such as posing a practice or search question when working with an interprofessional EBP team, research designs and concepts, and creating a supportive EBP environment.

https://www.academia.edu/20998026/Johns_Hopkins_Nursing_Evidence_Based_Practice_Model_and_Guidelines

Virginia Commonwealth University Health Library. (2020, September 22). *Nursing evidence based practice resources.*

This webpage provides *Johns Hopkins Nursing EBP Forms and Tools*, including an easy-to-understand "Evidence Level and Quality Guide" and a "Question Development Tool – PICO." The latter, PICO, is a step-by-step process for developing and answering EBP questions, with which to begin a search for current evidence on a specific health problem. Note that PICO is focused on locating research for a specific condition (so that research findings and best practices can be quickly incorporated into patient care), but not for a specific client (which is the focus of the original EBP model).

https://guides.library.vcu.edu/c.php?g=47815&p=6284751

CHAPTER 5

Critiquing EBP for Ethnic Minorities

In this chapter, we will learn to identify the limitations of existing evidence for minority groups. We will also become familiar with several community and culturally based research approaches for producing evidence that can be more relevant and effective for these groups. Overall, this chapter takes a critical view of EBP as the literature stands today and teaches frameworks that can contribute to promoting a science of social work that is less ethnocentric and less participatory in epistemic violence. Given that this chapter is concerned with critiquing research methodologies, it supports the best-evidence component of EBP. This chapter is concerned with both the best-evidence and clinical expertise components of the EBP model. While it teaches skills for critiquing research, the critique is based on a practitioner's understanding of the intervention and social justice needs of clients and their cultural groups.

BRIEF LECTURE 5.1

Ethnocentrism, Epistemic Violence, and Reductionist Science

A social worker's role today as an expert in the use and choice of EBPs carries many critical responsibilities at a moment in history when mental and behavioral health and social services research is beginning to bloom. The social worker is responsible for deciding what should and should not be implemented, as well as influencing the role, content, and format of future research to build a science of social work. How should the social worker, in this context, uphold the professions' values, including challenging social injustice, respecting diversity and clients' interests, and promoting and restoring social groups and communities?

This brief lecture introduces three facets of current science: ethnocentrism, epistemic violence, and reductionist science. These facets underlie the workings of social work practice–related research and are important for building a critical perspective on the evidence that is produced and what should be produced. Consideration of these facets will help the practitioner answer responsibly the more immediate question, *Which intervention should I choose for a client?* and the broader questions, *What should a science of social work look like?* and, *What do I do to promote it?*

Ethnocentrism

Ethnocentrism means judging other groups from one's own cultural point of view. (*Ethnic* comes from the Greek word *ethnos*, which means "nation" or "people," and is commonly used to refer to *a cultural heritage*.) Other definitions include "believing one's group's ways are superior to others" or "judging other groups as inferior to one's own." These definitions imply that one's own way of life is assumed to be natural or the correct one; there is a lack of respect for other ways of life. Ken Barger (2019), a professor of anthropology, provides a definition that touches on deeper issues:

> Ethnocentrism can be defined as making false assumptions about others' ways based on our own limited experience. The key word is assumptions, because we are not even aware that we are being ethnocentric ... we don't understand what we don't understand.

Barger further explains that because our reality is based on only what we have already experienced, it is normal to assume that it is "natural," given that our ways work for us. As a consequence, we continue in our unawareness rather than becoming aware that we can try to develop more valid understandings about how others experience life.

With these definitions of ethnocentrism as background, how does ethnocentrism manifest in social work–related research? In research, ethnocentrism occurs when a researcher takes the view or behavior of their own culture as normal. If other cultures differ from this, the research views them as abnormal, deviant, or deficient. In the area of mental and behavioral health intervention research, most or nearly all of it is founded on psychological theories developed in the last century mainly in Europe and North America. Dasen (2012), a cross-cultural psychologist, notes also that these theories (and interventions based thereon) have been established empirically with only a very small fraction of humanity. As he puts it, they come from the Western "minority" world rather than the "majority world" in which most human populations live (p. 55). He points to the implications of this state of affairs:

> As such, we cannot hold this against these sciences; because after all, each one of us is born and raised in a particular group, of which we learn the rules and the tricks, and which gives us our identity. It only becomes a problem when we compare these rules and tricks to those of others, and believe that our own are better, if not the only valid ones, and when we try to set them up as models and impose them on others. (p. 55)

Dasen's description and warning about ethnocentrism in science lead to important questions. *What does it mean to impose models on others in research? How can we avoid this if most existing evidence is based on Western theories and models?* Two approaches to research, *etic* and *emic*, respectively, provide an answer to these questions. Etic research takes existing methods and models from one culture's experiences and understandings and tests their validity in different cultural contexts. Whether quantitative or qualitative, etic research is ethnocentric, because it attempts to generalize one's theories and interventions to other groups. (An example is taking an assessment instrument based on the DSM-5 criteria and symptoms of schizophrenia, translating the instrument to Nepalese, and administering it to Nepalese people living in Kathmandu, the capital, to see if and how much it detects schizophrenia.) Emic research (also known as "indigenous psychology") is the study of phenomena as understood in and from the viewpoint of other cultural contexts. An emic approach aims to avoid ethnocentrism. (An example is asking the Nepalese people in Kathmandu how they think about problems or conditions affecting the mind and emotions, what conditions exist in their culture, how they define those, and developing and using instruments for one or more conditions they consider similar to schizophrenia.)

John Berry, a psychologist known for his work on acculturation strategies, with Dasen (1974) proposed a cross-cultural psychology that combined emic and etic approaches, rather than considering them as mutually exclusive. They proposed (a) testing existing theories elsewhere, (b) documenting diversity and discovering new phenomena, and (c) comparing the former and the latter to arrive at a more universal psychology.

Reflection Questions

1. Is arriving at a universal psychology possible? Is it desirable, considering the ethical values of social work? Please explain your answers.
2. How might etic research contribute to disparities in the use of mental health services by racial/ethnic minority populations? (*Tip.* Think about the how etic research may be impacting what is known about levels and types of illnesses and the interventions that are made available.)
3. Can ethnocentrism really be avoided through emic research? What could you do as a researcher to minimize ethnocentrism in a study that you conduct?
4. Are we imposing Western models less when we use the DSM-5-based schizophrenia instrument with Cambodian refugees who have lived in the U.S. for 25 years and are semifluent in English versus with recent arrivals?

Epistemic Violence

Epistemic violence (or epistemological violence) refers to the production of knowledge and, specifically, how power relationships condition its production; it is violating the way that people know themselves. (*Epistemic* means "of or related to *knowledge* or *knowing*," coming from the Greek word *episteme*.) Spivak (1988), a postcolonial theorist concerned with the lasting impact of colonization, associates epistemic violence with colonialism and imperialism. According to Spivak, the West assumes an epistemic privilege and obscures the claims and sources of knowledge of others; the West claims knowledge of others by itself; it becomes the subject, and the true subjects are hidden. Through epistemic violence, the voices of a group are marginalized, and the group is left out of the writing of its own history. Such violence also involves the West imposing a false universal value system on those of the lowest level of the hierarchy, who are referred to as "the subaltern" by Spivak. Instead of their values being accepted as valid or internally consistent, their practices are described as strange, harmful, or counterproductive to their own progress.

What Is the Relationship of Epistemic Violence to Ethnocentrism and Science?

It is first important to understand that ethnocentrism engenders epistemic violence, as violence results when an ethnic judgment is imposed on another group who will necessarily fail that judgment. In ethnocentrism, the "other" will necessarily fail because the otherness of the "other" is *reduced* to what the self knows. For instance, if I am a Christian, the "other" is a heathen. If I am modern and civilized, the "other" is undeveloped, savage, barbarous, and uncivilized. The other is the opposite of who I am. I am good; the other is bad. I already know. As another example, consider the "third world." The third world actually includes many countries, but all of their differences are erased when we know them as "premodern," "traditional," and "underdeveloped." Any sign of difference is enough to condemn and reduce them to what I know as the other. In terms of science, the reduction takes place when my knowledge of the other tells me what the other is about. I have no need to find out or learn about the other. I have no need to do research, except to gather data on what I already know. Ethnocentric research, then, is only studying our reduction of the other and what we know. As such, it is an act of epistemic violence.

ACTIVITY   View Jhally et al.'s (2012) 40-minute video, "Edward Said on Orientalism," posted by Palestine Diary (https://www.youtube.com/watch?v=fVC8EYd_Z_g). This video discusses the relationship between power and knowledge in the construction of the European view of the Islamic Arab world.

Reflection Questions

1. Can you think of an example of ethnocentrism? Be sure to describe the epistemic violence that occurs (i.e., name what one group knows and imposes on the other group and how the other group's difference is reduced).
2. Is epistemic violence derived from ethnocentric or emic research that harmful? What could be some of its consequences?

Reductionist Science

Let's now turn to the whole modern scientific endeavor and its relationship to epistemic violence. We will review the claims of contemporary science and an argument that debunks these claims made by Vandana Shiva (1988), a scholar and activist in the alternative globalization movement. Let's begin with the claims. Modern science has claimed to be a means of discovering the true properties of nature and of finding truth. It is contended that through the use of the "scientific method," researchers can generate "objective," "neutral," and "universal" knowledge that is independent of values. With this objective and neutral knowledge about nature and human organisms, including humans, science professes that it can improve human welfare. Modern science has also tried to prove itself to be superior to other ways of knowing, and some view it as the only legitimate way of knowing.

Let's now review how Shiva (1988) discredits these claims to reveal the violent nature of contemporary science. Overall, Shiva rejects modern science as a description of reality unprejudiced by values. Instead, she argues that it is reductionist and inseparably linked with a capitalist logic and that its claim of being independent of values is itself a response to values based on capitalist interests. The result of a reductionist science is the suppression and falsification of facts and an epistemic violence against the poor and against science itself, which should be a search for truth. Shiva's (1988) argument is based on four grounds.

1. ***There is no single scientific method.*** There is no single "scientific method," as claimed. In practice, there is no single procedure or set of rules underlying every study to ensure that it is scientific. Shiva notes that modern scientific knowledge itself has been built through numerous methodologies. She quotes Paul Feyerabend:

   > The idea of a universal and stable method that is an unchanging measure of adequacy and even the idea of a universal and stable rationality is as unrealistic as the idea of a universal and stable measuring instrument that measures any magnitude, no matter what the circumstances. Scientists revise their standards, their procedures, their criteria of rationality as they move along and perhaps entirely replace their theories and their instruments as they move along and enter new domains of research. (p. 234)

   Other philosophers of science, such as Thomas Kuhn (2012) and Michael Polanyi (2015), also argued that modern science does not follow a well-defined and stable scientific method.

2. ***Science is not a discovery of facts.*** Science is not fact. Shiva argues that if scientific knowledge is assumed to be true and factual knowledge of reality, then, citing the argument of David Bohm, Newtonian theory was only true until about 1900. After that time, Newtonian theory suddenly became false, when relativity and quantum theories became the truth(p. 234). In this sense, science is the most favored opinion of the things being observed at any time.

3. ***Scientific knowledge as a purely factual description of nature is ecologically unfounded.*** *Ecology* means "the totality or pattern of relations between organisms and their environment" (Merriam-Webster, n.d.). Shiva explains that what is observed in a scientific study is entirely related, from an ecological standpoint, to the context from which it is observed. And the choice of context is value-laden and driven by capitalist priorities. She writes:

   > Ecology perceives relationships between different elements of an ecosystem. What properties of a particular element or resource are picked up for study or for understanding nature depends on the relationships that are taken as the context defining the properties. In other words, the context is determined by the priorities and values guiding the perception of nature. Selection of the context is a value-determined process and the selection in turn, determines what properties are seen in nature. There is nothing like a neutral fact about nature, independent of the values shaped by human cognitive and economic activity. Properties perceived in nature depend on how you look at them, and how you look depends on the economic interest you have ... Looking does not create properties, but it definitely creates conditions for their perception. Economic values of a particular type generate perceptions and uses of nature that reinforce these values. The value of profit maximization, for example, determines a particular way of looking at nature. (p. 234–235)

4. ***Contemporary science is reductionist and value-laden. It is one approach to looking and thinking, and it is a political one.*** To show the reductionist nature of modern science, Shiva discusses the ontological and epistemological assumptions of reductionism. (*Ontology* is a field of study concerned with the nature of being and the kinds of things that have existence.)

   > The ontological assumptions of reductionism are: (a) that a system is reducible to its parts; and (b) that all systems are made up of the same basic constituents which are discrete and atomistic; and (c) that all systems have the same basic processes which are mechanical. ...

The epistemological assumptions of reductionism are: (a) that knowledge of the parts of a system gives knowledge of the whole system; (b) that 'experts' and 'specialists' are the only legitimate knowledge seekers and knowledge-justifiers. (p. 235)

According to Shiva, the reductionist method is useful in the fields of logic, mathematics, and mechanics, but "it fails singularly to lead to a perception of reality (truth) in the case of living organisms, including man, in which the whole is not merely the sum of the parts, if only because the parts are so cohesively interrelated that isolating any part distorts perception of the whole" (p. 236). She concludes that there is "no warrant for the claim that the reductionist method is a 'scientific method,' much less the sole scientific method" (p. 236). Reductionist science should only be considered as one approach, or one way of looking and thinking.

To argue the value-laden nature of reductionist science, Shiva discusses controlled experiments, a main element of a reductionist methodology. She argues that it is the context, which is the value framework, that determines the properties or outcomes that are perceived in controlled experiments. And it is such properties or findings that are perceived that lead to a particular set of beliefs about that which is studied (i.e., nature or human beings). Furthermore, the method of controlled experiments involves three exclusions: "(i) ontological, in that other properties are not taken note of; (ii) epistemic, in that other ways of perceiving and knowing are not recognized; and (iii) sociological, in that the non-expert is deprived of the right both of access to knowledge and of judging the claims of knowledge" (p. 236). Shiva concludes:

All this is the stuff of politics, not science. Picking one group of people (the specialists), who adopt one way of knowing the physical world (the reductionist) to find one set of properties in nature (the reductionist/mechanistic), is a political, not a scientific, act. It is this act that is claimed to be the "scientific method." (p. 236)

Reflection Questions

1. Do you agree with Shiva's argument that modern science is reductionist, politically motivated, and capitalistically motivated? Explain your answer.

2. Contrary to the claim of modern science that people will benefit from scientific knowledge, is it possible that the poor and those belonging to minority groups are actually its worst victims? How does this happen? Explain your answer.

DISCUSSION 5.1 Is the PHQ-9 Valid for All Cultural Groups?

The objective of this discussion is to gain awareness of ethnocentrism in clinical research. To do so, we will learn to assess and critique the validity of the nine-item Patient Health Questionnaire Depression Module (PHQ-9; Kroenke et al., 2001) for minority populations. The PHQ-9 is a self-report diagnostic assessment tool that also quantifies the severity of depression. Its items come directly from the nine symptoms of depression of the *Diagnostic and Statistical Manual of Mental Disorders* (DSM-5; American Psychiatric Association, 2013). This discussion provides a quick activity, describes the PHQ-9, and reviews and critiques, as an example, study findings on the validity of the PHQ-9 for Chinese American immigrants. There are eight interspersed discussion questions.

Quick Activity

This exercise relates to your experience with depression. If you are not having symptoms currently, do this exercise on the past, when you were experiencing depressive symptoms, or on someone you know well who has talked with you about their depression. Answer the following two questions, keeping in mind that your symptoms can be, but do not have to be, those from the DSM-5 or any depression instrument. Then you will learn about the PHQ-9 and answer two more questions.

a. Considering the past couple of weeks, would you describe yourself as having no depressive symptoms or mild, moderate, or severe symptoms?
b. If you are having symptoms, jot down a few that have been bothering you the most.

PHQ-9: Items and Scoring

The PHQ-9 begins with, "Over the last two weeks, how often have you been bothered by any of the following problems?" There are four response options: *0 (not at all), 1 (several days), 2 (more than half the days),* or *3 (nearly every day).* The items are:

1. Little interest or pleasure in doing things.
2. Feeling down, depressed, or hopeless.
3. Trouble falling or staying asleep or sleeping too much.
4. Feeling tired or having little energy.
5. Poor appetite or overeating.
6. Feeling bad about yourself or that you are a failure or have let yourself or your family down.

7. Trouble concentrating on things, such as reading the newspaper or watching the television.

8. Moving or speaking so slowly that other people could have noticed. Or the opposite; being so fidgety or restless that you have been moving around a lot more than usual.

9. Thoughts that you would be better off dead or of hurting yourself in some way.

The PHQ-9 closes with, "If you checked off any problem on this questionnaire so far, how difficult have these problems made it for you to do your work, take care of things at home, or get along with other people?" The response options are: *Not difficult at all, Somewhat difficult, Very difficult,* or *Extremely difficult.*

The PHQ-9 total score ranges from 0 to 27, given the maximum of three points for each item. To give a depression diagnosis with the PHQ-9, both of the following must be met:

- At least one of the core symptoms of depression, Item *1 (little interest or pleasure)* or Item *2 (down, depressed, or hopeless)* must be endorsed as *2 (more than half the days)* or higher.
- The final question on functional impairment must be answered as at least *Somewhat Difficult.*

Total scores indicate the diagnosis and depression severity, as follows:

- 0–10 points: Mild or minimal depressive symptoms
- 10–14 points: Moderate depression symptoms (minor depression, or chronic depression if symptoms present for at least two years)
- 15–19 points: Moderately severe major depression
- 20–29 points: Severe major depression.

The MacArthur Initiative on Depression & Primary Care (2009) provides a "Depression Management Tool Kit" that explains the PHQ-9 and provides treatment recommendations. It is available at: https://www.depression-primarycare.org/clinicians/toolkits/materials/forms/phq9/

Discussion Questions

1. Would you expect the PHQ-9 to detect depression effectively in different cultural, gender, or other diversity groups? How about for individuals not fluent in English? For which diversity groups might it tend to not be effective, and why?

2. Imagine a client who is not fluent in English, for whom the PHQ-9 items are translated. Which of the nine items might be difficult to understand, and why?

3. How might the PHQ-9 represent the Western culture-based experience and expression of depression? How would you describe a Western conception of depression? What types of symptoms may be present in the expression of depressive distress in other cultures that are absent from the Western one?

See how students answered on page 201.

Validity Problems with the PHQ-9 Among Chinese Immigrants

Researchers have concluded in several studies that the PHQ-9 is a reliable and valid instrument for assessing depression among Chinese American immigrants in the primary care setting (Chen et al., 2006; Huang et al., 2006; Yeung et al., 2008). Yet, they drew these conclusions without taking into consideration the contradictory evidence presented in their own research. (As background, these validation studies used a version of the PHQ-9 that was translated to Chinese, and the study samples consisted predominantly of low-income immigrants whose primary language was Chinese.) The points that do not support the instrument's validity for Chinese immigrants were the findings of unusual differences between Chinese and other groups in rates of depression and how certain items are answered, along with the use of study designs that promoted biased findings. If these findings were taken into consideration, the PHQ-9's validity for Chinese immigrants would be questionable. Let's review four validity issues related to study design and findings.

1. ***Using an instrument based on a Western construct of depression to demonstrate criterion validity neglects cultural difference.*** Criterion validity is the extent to which an instrument is related to an expected outcome. In the case of validating the PHQ-9 for use in another cultural group, the research objective is to show that PHQ-9 outcomes (or results) match

culturally based *criteria*, which are the outcomes on a test that comes from and accurately represents that culture's conception of depression. In other words, the researcher needs to choose a criterion or standard from that culture with which to compare PHQ-9 results. The researcher can conclude that the PHQ-9 demonstrates criterion validity if it effectively detects depression when the culturally based criterion test detects depression.

The use of a Chinese culture-based criterion did not occur in the studies being discussed (Chen et al., 2006; Huang et al., 2006; Yeung et al., 2008). In one case, the researchers chose as their criterion an instrument that is also Western and DSM-based (Yeung et al., 2008). They followed a commonly used procedure for validating self-report instruments, which is comparing PHQ-9 results with results from individual clinical interviews, using a structured clinical interview guide. They used the Structured Clinical Interview for DSM-IV (SCID). The SCID, along with the Composite International Diagnostic Interview (CIDI), are the commonly used criteria or "gold" standard for scale validation research. In another case, the researchers did not make comparisons with a criterion instrument at all (Chen et al., 2006; Huang et al., 2006). To conclude, by not using Chinese culture-based criteria, the researchers did not consider how Chinese people may view and experience depression differently. In essence, with their research design, they only found out that a shorter DSM-based instrument (PHQ-9) works similarly to a longer DSM-based instrument (SCID). Given this, their conclusion of validity was based on an unmentioned assumption that the Western construct of depression applies to Chinese immigrants. This is an example of ethnocentrism and epistemic violence.

Discussion Questions

4. What are the consequences of assuming that the PHQ-9 works well for a culturally different population and using it in practice? For example, you use the PHQ-9 as the screening tool for routing clients who are immigrants and refugees from Myanmar into depression treatment.

See how students answered on page 203.

2. ***Excluding patients with mild depression falsely enhances reliability and validity indicators and excludes those who most need to be included.*** Yeung et al. (2008) reported strong internal consistency reliability (α = 0.91) and criterion validity, as shown by a sensitivity of 0.81 and specificity of 0.98, but these estimates were likely biased upward due to the exclusion of patients who scored less than 15 points on the PHQ-9. (Below are notes explaining the concepts of *reliability* and *sensitivity and specificity*.) In other words, the researchers examined criterion validity (using the SCID) but only included patients with moderately severe and severe depression according to the PHQ-9. If all patients had been included, the sensitivity and specificity indicators would likely be much lower. With this consideration, a more accurate study conclusion would be, "The instrument is reliable and valid only for patients with severe depression." Additionally, the authors' finding, as is, is not so useful, because one expects individuals with severe depression to easily endorse many items (on any depression questionnaire) and end up with a high total score. These individuals are not hard to detect. They easily score high on both the PHQ-9 and the SCID. A more useful finding would be whether the PHQ-9 is valid for those with mild and moderate depression symptoms, because these individuals are the ones who escape detection for various reasons and need timely linkage to treatment the most.

Note on Internal Consistency Reliability. Internal consistency reliability, represented by alpha or α, is a statistical indicator of construct validity. It refers to a scale's items holding together as a homogeneous set, or as measuring the same construct. A simplified explanation is that how people with depression answer the items moves together numerically; their responses will correlate. When developing a new scale, the data analyst aims for high internal consistency. The analyst tests the available items and removes those that do not fit. A reliability indicator greater than 0.90 means strong reliability, 0.80–0.90 means good reliability, 0.70–0.80 means fair to so-so reliability, while less than 0.70 indicates weak reliability and at the borderline of acceptable. (These strength interpretations also apply for correlations and other coefficients that range from 0.0 to 1.0.)

Note on Sensitivity and Specificity. Specificity and sensitivity are characteristics of the instrument. They describe how well the instrument detects what it is supposed to detect. The sensitivity of a depression test is the probability that it will indicate "depressed" out of all those who have depression. (A sensitivity of 0.95 means 95% of those with depression will "test positive" for depression and 5% will "test negative" using the instrument.) The specificity of a depression test is the probability that it will indicate "not depressed" out of all those who do not have depression. (A specificity of 0.90 specificity means 90% of those without depression will "test negative" for depression and 10% will "test positive.") Greater than 0.90, for both indicators, is generally considered very strong. However, what is considered a strong or acceptable sensitivity rate depends on the illness. Imagine the consequences of a test with low sensitivity for an illness with grave consequences if not detected and treated immediately.

Discussion Questions

5. Why would the sensitivity and specificity indicators likely be lower if the researchers had included patients who had mild or moderate depression? In other words, what are some reasons why patients in the mild to low moderate range are harder to detect as having depression?

See how students answered on page 204.

---

3. ***The finding of a lower rate of depression in Chinese men should be considered an indicator of poor validity.*** One of the primary care studies (Huang et al., 2006) compared Chinese Americans, 97% of whom were monolingual non-English-speaking, with African Americans, Latinos, and non-Hispanic whites. They found that Chinese American men had very low rates of depression compared with all other groups. In contrast, Chinese American women's rates were very similar to those other racial/ethnic groups. For example, 11.8% of Chinese men, compared with 18.1% of Chinese women, scored 10 (moderate depression) or higher, and only 4.8% of Chinese American men, compared with 9.6% of Chinese American women, scored 10–14 (moderate depression). The authors did not question why Chinese men in the mild to moderate severity range may not endorse items strongly. Rather, they assume it to be less depression and rather possible issues with scale validity. The article's discussion states:

> The results of this analysis demonstrate that the PHQ-9 total score functions fundamentally the same in subjects from four of the largest

racial/ethnic groups in the United States. The similar mean scores and factor structure of the PHQ-9 in the different groups—even while the vast majority of Chinese Americans and Latinos in the analysis completed the PHQ-9 in a language other than English—suggests that it can be used without adjustment in diverse populations. These findings also support the idea that the DSM-IV criteria for major depression are common to individuals of all cultures. (p. 550)

To support their conclusion, the authors further note that their findings of lower rates among Chinese men versus Chinese women are consistent with prior studies. They also mention the existence of epidemiological studies showing acculturated Chinese American women as having a much higher likelihood of lifetime depressive episodes than Chinese American men.

Discussion Questions

6. Would you assume that fewer Chinese immigrant men experience depression (i.e., would you believe the study findings)? Or would you question why the PHQ-9 is not capturing this group, especially those in the milder range? Explain your answers.

7. What would you explore to find out why Chinese immigrant men show a much lower rate of depression?

See how students answered on page 205.

Note on the "Immigrant Paradox" and the importance of culturally sensitive assessment. The question of whether to believe the results that are reported for immigrant populations is pertinent to a phenomenon called the "Immigrant Paradox," the paradoxical association between immigration status and psychiatric disorders. While one might expect that the life difficulties associated with immigration and acculturation would lead to poorer health and mental health, findings show that this is not always true. Some researchers, especially epidemiologists, have instead found that those who are foreign-born with lower levels of acculturation have better health and mental health. Smaller community-based studies, however, sometimes find very high rates for Asian Americans in the immigrant (or first-generation) population. To explain the paradox, some scholars propose examining cultural differences in the expression of distress rather than continuing to assume a health-protective effect of being foreign-born. (See John et al.'s [2012] article for a discussion of the immigrant paradox among Asian Americans, with their caution that this paradox oversimplifies complex patterns and masks negative outcomes among underserved subgroups. See also findings from the National Latino and Asian American Study [Takeuchi et al., 2007], which revealed complex and subtle differences in prevalence rates based on gender, social class, acculturation level, generational status, and time in the U.S., all of which require untangling.)

4. ***Findings of differences in item functioning between Chinese and other groups indicate differences in meaning or poor understandability and suggest a different construct of depression.*** In the same study wherein a lower rate of depression was observed for Chinese men, the researchers found differences in item functioning for three items—sleep, appetite, and psychomotor disturbances (Huang et al., 2006). (To find differential item functioning, the data for individual items are analyzed to determine if one subgroup endorsed an item more often or differently than another, while controlling for the level of depression. In other words, how Chinese versus Latinx patients with the same level of depression severity answered each item is compared in order to determine if the item was answered differently between the two groups.) Chinese patients endorsed psychomotor agitation at a rate more than double the other groups, endorsed appetite disturbances at a rate less than half the other groups, and had significantly higher mean scores in sleep disturbances. (Latinx Americans showed differential item functioning for sleep disturbances, low energy, and low self-esteem, with significantly lower mean scores on these items compared to Whites and Chinese Americans.)

In discussing these findings, the researchers write, "Although there may be some differences in the expression of individual symptoms across racial/ethnic groups, these differences are relatively minor. In our analysis, there was consistency in the core features of depression across racial/ethnic groups ... This is illustrated by the fact that between all four groups there was no significant difference in mean scores of the individual item of depressed mood" (p. 551). This statement reveals their assumption that the DSM-5-based depression construct is valid for those of Chinese culture–based on four groups having a similar mean score on one single item. The authors did not question the implications of having three items that are endorsed differently, although they note that higher endorsement of psychomotor agitation and sleep disturbance may indicate Asians' higher likeliness of expressing somatic symptoms.

In psychometrics, differential item functioning could indicate poor understandability or different meanings for different groups. Having three items that function differently suggests the need to examine those items and the effectiveness of the entire instrument. Content (or items) corresponding to a culturally different construct may be missing from the instrument. Also, differential item functioning suggests that the diagnostic cutoff score may be different for different groups (e.g., a score of 12 rather than 15 may be a more valid cutoff or threshold score for Chinese American men). To achieve stronger sensitivity and specificity, psychometricians can calculate new cutoff scores. For example, studies of the PHQ-9 in China (Chen et al., 2009) and Hong Kong (Lai et al., 2010) found lower optimal cutoff scores for the PHQ-9, including a cutoff of only 4 points for men in the Hong Kong study. Such lower cutoff scores imply that Chinese respondents endorsed fewer items overall or interpreted items differently, scoring them lower compared to the primarily White samples in previous research, from which the original cutoffs were determined.

Discussion Questions

8. Would you agree that the PHQ-9 studies reviewed have answered the question, "How many Chinese patients can be detected for depression with the PHQ-9?" rather than, "How well does the PHQ-9 detect depression among Chinese immigrants?" Explain your answer.

See how students answered on page 206.

> ## DISCUSSION 5.2 Is IMPACT as Useful for Minority Populations as Suggested?

The objective of this discussion is to continue to build your ability to critique the applicability and quality of research findings for minority populations. We learned in Discussion 5.1 that the evidence on the validity of the PHQ-9 has limitations for minority groups due to study design choices and using a mainstream illness construct of depression. This discussion illustrates the same issues with an EBP with grade A evidence and a high level of dissemination. We will learn about

Improving Mood-Promoting Access to Collaborative Treatment (IMPACT), a program for treating depression in older adults in the primary care setting, and assess and critique the relevance of the evidence for African American and Latino American older adults (Unützer et al., 2002; Hunkeler et al., 2006). The researchers of IMPACT report that it is effective for these minority populations—and that IMPACT erases disparities in the use of services (Areán et al., 2005).

Evidence-based interventions that provide mental and behavioral health screening and treatment in the health care setting are called "integrated care" programs. Integrated care programs are quickly spreading across the U.S. based on growing evidence of their effectiveness, including for racial and ethnic minority populations, and fairly high level of readiness for dissemination. Administrators and policy makers view integrated care as attractive because it promises to improve access and linkage to mental health care, reduce costs of medical help–seeking related to psychological rather than physical problems, and support compliance with medical treatment plans, among other reasons. As an EBP decision-maker, you have the responsibility of evaluating whether IMPACT will be as effective an EBP as its researchers claim for your minority clientele, and in what ways it may or may not be effective. This discussion describes IMPACT and presents two sets of discussion questions to hone your skills for critiquing research.

The IMPACT Study: Background and Recruitment

IMPACT was tested in a multisite RCT, with 1,801 patients age 60 years or older with major depression and/or dysthymic disorder; the study took place in 18 primary care clinics belonging to eight health care organizations in five states (Unützer et al., 2002). Patients recruited into the study were randomly assigned to the IMPACT intervention (n = 906) or usual care (n = 895) in their own primary care clinics. The sample consisted of non-Latino White (77%, 1,388), Black (12%, 222), Latino (8%, 138, primarily of Mexican origin), and other ethnicities (3%, 53). Intervention patients had up to 12 months of care by a depression care manager supervised by a psychiatrist and a primary care expert. Usual care patients could use any primary care or specialty mental care services available to them in usual care. Usual care patients and their primary care doctors received a notification that the patient met study criteria for depression. They could use all treatments available in usual care, including antidepressants, counseling by the doctor, and referral to specialty mental health care. The study assessed health outcomes across 12 months, with assessments made at baseline (before treatment) and at 3, 6, and 12 months. The health outcomes assessed included depression level using the Hopkins Symptom Checklist (HSCL-20), use of depression treatments (medications or psychotherapy), satisfaction with care, functional impairment, and quality of life.

Recruitment of Participants into the Trial

Patients were recruited in two ways. The researchers were (a) approaching English-speaking patients systematically either by telephone or in-person with a two-item depression screener, the PHQ-2, consisting of the first two items of the PHQ-9 on loss of interest or pleasure and depressed mood (Kroenke et al., 2003), and (b) receiving referrals from primary care practitioners, other clinic staff, or patients themselves who saw an announcement in the clinic. Summarized below are the participation counts for each recruitment phase, and Figure 5.1, the article's "Flowchart of Participants in the Trial," contains the same numbers (Unützer et al., 2002, p. 2837–2838).

a. **Out of the 32,908 patients approached:**
   - 16% (5,246) refused to be screened (with the PHQ-2), or participated in the screening but refused further participation;
   - 5% (1,791) had incomplete initial screens;
   - 71% (23,233) were not eligible because they did not endorse one of the two core symptoms of depression (67%) or because of logistics such as transportation or telephone access (4%);
   - **Leaving only 8% (2,638) to complete the eligibility interview using the SCID** in a 30- to 60-minute structured interview to identify major depression or dysthymic disorder.
     - **But only 41% (1,085) of this group of 2,638 were eligible after excluding** those who did not have major depression or dysthymia or had current drinking problems, had history of bipolar disorder or psychosis, were already receiving treatment with a psychiatrist, had severe cognitive impairment, or were at acute risk for suicide.
       - **And only 84% (907) of this group of 1,085 were still eligible after excluding** those with incomplete SCID or who refused participation.

b. **Out of the 2,190 patients referred to the study:**
   - 14% (308) refused to be screened (with the PHQ-2), or participated in the screening but refused further participation;
   - 3% (54) had incomplete initial screens;
   - 9% (202) were not eligible because they did not endorse one of the two core symptoms of depression, or they were younger than 60

years old or would not be using the clinic's services for the coming 12 months;

- **Leaving 74% (1,626) to complete the eligibility interview using the SCID**
  - **But only 63% (1,017) of this group of 1,626 were eligible after excluding** those who did not have major depression or dysthymia or had current drinking problems, had history of bipolar disorder or psychosis, were already receiving treatment with a psychiatrist, had severe cognitive impairment, or were at acute risk for suicide.
    - **And only 88% (894) of this group were still eligible after excluding** those with incomplete SCID or refused participation.

Through these two methods, 1,801 (907 + 894) patients were recruited into the study and randomized into intervention and usual care groups.

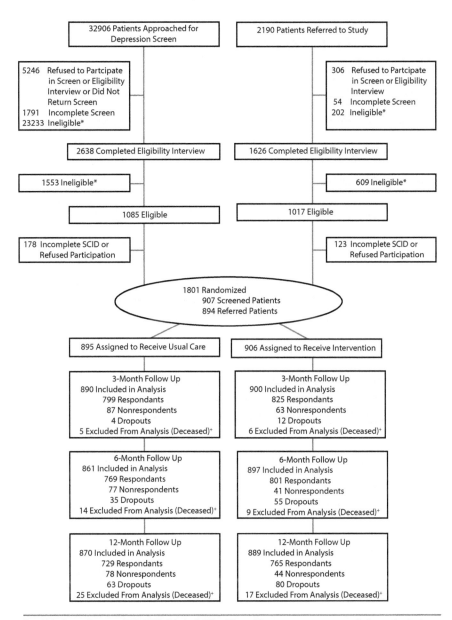

Asterisk indicates that most (90%-95%) of the ineligible subjects did not meet screen or research diagnostic criteria for depression. Dagger indicates that cumulative number of participants who were deceased and who were therefore excluded from analysis: analyses included all other patients after multiple imputation of unit-level missing data. SCID indicates structured clincial interview for *Diagnostic and Statistical Manual of Mental Disorders*, Fourth Edition.

FIGURE 5.1 Flowchart of Participants in the Trial

Discussion Questions, Part I: Who Was Left Out of the Study?

1. Among those who were approached, 21% of 32,908 patients either refused to be screened, participated in the screening but refused further participation, or left the screening instrument incomplete. Do you consider this percentage to be large? What are possible reasons that these patients did not agree or were unable to participate? What might be the intervention needs and problem conceptualizations of these patients who were left out of the study?

2. Among those who were referred (most by their physician), 17% of 2,190 patients either refused the initial screen or further participation, or they left the screen incomplete. Do you consider this percentage to be large? What are possible reasons that these patients did not agree or were unable to participate? What might be the intervention needs and problem conceptualizations of these patients who were left out of the study?

3. Many patients did not endorse any item on the PHQ-2. These were 67% of those approached and close to 9% of those referred. Does this seem high? Is it possible that the two screening items (anhedonia and depressed mood) may leave out a lot of people who have mild depression?

4. Is it possible that more Black and Latino patients would tend to refuse participation—and thus be left out of the study?

See how students answered on page 206.

Description of the Intervention

Intervention participants view a 20-minute educational video and receive a booklet on depression in older adults. Next, they have an initial visit with a depression care manager, along with nurses and psychologists trained for the study, who work as a team with a supervising psychiatrist and primary care physician. During the initial patient visit, the care manager conducts a clinical and psychosocial history, reviews the educational materials with the patient, and discusses the treatment options available, which are either antidepressant medications or a brief psychotherapy, Problem Solving Treatment in Primary Care (PST-PC), which is a 6- to 8-week brief, structured psychotherapy and grade A EBP (Areán et al., 2008). Based on the patient's preferences, the care manager works with the patient's regular primary care physician to establish a treatment plan. For patients who are already taking antidepressants but are still depressed, the recommendation is to increase the dose or add PST-PC to the antidepressant treatment. The care manager is the one to provide PST-PC when it is part of the treatment. Care managers also encourage patients to schedule pleasant life events and provide referrals to additional health or social services as needed. The care manager meets weekly with the supervisory team to discuss new cases and cases needing treatment plan adjustments. They follow patients for up to 12 months, using the PHQ-9 as a monitoring tool.

During the acute treatment phase, the care manager makes in-person or telephone contacts at least every two weeks. For patients who recover (with at least 50% reduction in the PHQ-9 score and having fewer than 3 of 9 symptoms of major depression), the care manager develops a relapse prevention plan and follows up with the patient once per month. Patients who do not respond to initial treatment are discussed with the supervisory team, and a Step 2 treatment plan is developed that either augments the antidepressant medication, switches to a different one, or switches from medications to PST-PC or vice versa. The psychiatrist sees patients who present diagnostic challenges or have persistent depression. If the patient does not respond after 10 weeks of Step 2 treatment, other options are considered, such as further medication changes, psychotherapy, hospitalization, or electroconvulsive therapy.

For patients who chose PST-PC, it teaches them how to solve their own "here and now" problems that contribute to their depression (Areán et al., 2008). It usually involves 6–10 sessions, depending on patient needs. The first session is 1 hour, because PST techniques are explained to the patient and a first problem is identified and a plan for solving it is developed. The remaining sessions are 30 minutes, with each session focused on reviewing how problem-solving went in between sessions and planning how to solve another problem. PST-PC was found to be as effective as antidepressants for treating major depression in primary care patients. The premise of the intervention is that life problems trigger or worsen depression; once depressed, problems become more difficult to solve; and building problem-solving skills will make a patient less vulnerable to depression and provide control over their problems and a sense of self-efficacy. Having fewer problems, a sense of ability and control, and increased hope will lead to improved mood. The goal of PST-PC is for patients to learn problem-solving skills that can be used to address depression in the future.

Outcomes for Blacks, Latinos, and Whites
Using the same IMPACT dataset, another group of researchers compared Blacks (n = 222), Latinos (n = 138), and non-Latino Whites (n = 1,388) on depression

severity, quality of life, and mental health services use (Areán et al., 2005). In this study, the researchers referred to participants who received the IMPACT intervention as Collaborative Care (CC) participants.

Depression severity was measured with the 20-item Hopkins Symptom Checklist (HSCL-20), with a decrease of 50% or more in the total score being a successful treatment response. The study's principle findings at 12 months for intervention vs. usual care participants included:

- Greater rates of use of any antidepressants
    - Blacks: 62% vs. 46%

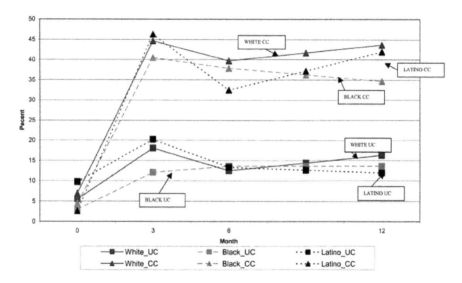

FIGURE 5.2 Use of Counseling or Psychotherapy

- Latinos: 68% vs. 44%
- Whites: 66% vs. 50%

Example of how to read the statistics. At the end of the study (at 12 months), 62% of Black patients who received the IMPACT intervention were using an antidepressant compared to 46% of Black patients who received usual care.

- Greater rates of use of psychotherapy (based on psychotherapy or specialty mental health visits)
    - Blacks: 35% vs. 14%
    - Latinos: 42% vs. 12%

- o   Whites: 44% vs. 16%
- Greater satisfaction with mental health services based on answering "excellent" or "very good" on a questionnaire
  - o   Blacks: 72% vs. 42%
  - o   Latinos: 71% vs. 50%
  - o   Whites: 76% vs. 49%
- Lower depression severity (HSCL-20, score range of 0–4)
  - o   Blacks: 1.4 vs. 0.9
  - o   Latinos: 1.4 vs. 1.0
  - o   Whites: 1.4 vs. 1.0
- Less health-related functional impairment (Sheehan Disability Scale, score range of 0–10)
  - o   Blacks: 4.7 vs. 3.7
  - o   Latinos: 4.7 vs. 3.9
  - o   Whites: 4.5 vs. 3.6

Based on these findings, the authors concluded, "Collaborative care is significantly more effective than usual care for depressed older adults, regardless of their ethnicity. Intervention effects in ethnic minority participants were similar to those observed in whites" (p. 381). Figure 5.2 below, "Use of Counseling or Psychotherapy," is copied from the article (p. 388).

Note on IMPACT effects for low-income participants. In another study using the same IMPACT dataset, another group of researchers reported that a majority of IMPACT participants were of lower income status, with 18% living below the poverty level, 15% living below 30% of the area median income but above poverty, and 24% living between 30%–50% of the area median income (Areán et al., 2007). The researchers found that at 12 months, intervention patients in all economic brackets had greater rates than usual care patients on all of the outcome measures.

Would you adopt this intervention?

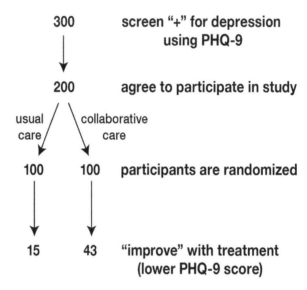

| 300 | screen "+" for depression using PHQ-9 |

200   agree to participate in study

usual care / collaborative care

100   100   participants are randomized

15   43   "improve" with treatment (lower PHQ-9 score)

FIGURE 5.3 Hypothetical Flowchart of an RCT Comparing Collaborative Care for Depression with Treatment as Usual

---

Discussion Questions, Part II: Does IMPACT Erase Disparities for Black and Latino Older Adults?

1. Does IMPACT erase disparities for Latinos and African Americans?
2. What is not shown or is left out of a diagram like Figure 5.2? What questions does this diagram raise (that could be studied in the future)? (Think about the sample, choice of treatments, the setting, and other aspects of the study design.)
3. Look at how much the various rates improved. Are the results good enough for you to decide on implementing IMPACT in your primary care clinic?
4. What ethical obligations may not be met if you implemented IMPACT in your health center?
5. Would you expect IMPACT and PST-PC to be effective with Latino immigrants? Can its evidence be generalized to Latino immigrants whose primary language is Spanish?
6. Should we use IMPACT with Blacks and Latinos, based on the finding that IMPACT is more effective compared with "care as usual"?

See how students answered on page 209.

DISCUSSION 5.3 Evaluate a Hypothetical Study: Would You Adopt this EBP for a Minority Group?

You are the director of a public primary care clinic located in San Francisco. The majority of your patients are low-income Chinese American adults who are immigrants with low proficiency in English. You want to implement an EBP for depression developed and tested in English speakers, which you would have translated. The EBP's flowchart is below (see Figure 5.3). It is an integrated care intervention very similar to IMPACT, in which patients will have the option of medications and/or psychotherapy. The psychotherapy is Problem Solving Therapy with behavioral activation, but it is offered in an 8-week support group format rather than as an individual therapy.

Your task is to decide whether you will adopt this EBP for your clinic. This discussion includes two sets of questions. In between the two sets of questions is a brief presentation on obstacles to mental health care and help-seeking behaviors among Chinese Americans. Begin your decision-making by analyzing the flowchart.

Discussion Questions, Part I: Evaluating the Flowchart and Making a Decision

1. How many people dropped out? Is the dropout too large?
2. How many people improved? Is the number of people who improved large enough?
3. Who is left out of the study? What is being missed?
4. What is your decision? Will you adopt it? Justify your decision.

See how students answered on page 213.

Obstacles to Mental Health Treatment and Help-Seeking Behaviors in the Chinese Immigrant Community

Chinese American immigrants underutilize mental health services more than any other racial/ethnic group in the U.S. (Abe-Kim et al., 2007). Some of the obstacles to obtaining mental health care include having little knowledge of mental illness and available treatments; facing very strong stigma of mental illness within one's family and the Chinese community; doing everything imaginable to avoid loss of face; not understanding how to navigate the health care system, including not having the English skills to do so; and believing in and interpreting problems as one's fate (Hong et al., 1995; Kung, 2004). Stemming from these obstacles, immigrants' help-seeking behaviors include delaying treatment until their condition has become very severe and seeking help in primary care and community organizations rather than in specialty mental health services.

In the case of depression, a conceptualization of depression that integrates somatic, interpersonal, and psychological components is likely related to help-seeking in the primary care setting (Yeung et al., 2004). Although the somatic component of depression is not a phenomenon exclusive to Chinese immigrants, it has been a focus of investigation because it is viewed as a point of linkage to mental health care for this community. In a primary care study, Chinese immigrants' explanatory models of illness intertwined psychological, somatic, and interpersonal causes and symptoms; patients explained their depression in terms of physical complaints but attributed their cause to stress and psychological problems stemming from interpersonal difficulties (Yeung et al., 2004). Patients with lower acculturation to U.S. society especially endorsed stronger levels of somatic symptoms and did not acknowledge depressed mood unless they were probed. Supporting a multicomponent conception of depression, women in a community study also presented explanations of depression that were either more somatic or psychological, but all contained interpersonal triggers and consequences (Ying, 1990).

The prevalence of somatic symptoms in the conceptualization of depression, factors such as stigma and loss of face, and the underutilization of mental health services make primary care an important setting for depression care in Chinese immigrants. This may be especially so for Chinese Americans with lower acculturation and education, who tend to place more emphasis on somatic complaints (Mak & Zane, 2004; Parker et al., 2005). Epidemiological findings have also supported a relationship between acculturation and somatic expressions of distress. A large-scale community survey found that depression overlapped significantly with somatization, anxiety, and neurasthenia, a DSM-IV culture-bound syndrome combining somatic, anxiety, and depression symptoms (Zheng et al., 1997) considered to be a predecessor of depression in Chinese societies (Parker et al., 2005). Primary care is also viewed as an important setting for depression care, given that a focus on somatic symptoms tends to occur in a mild stage of depression (Chen et al., 2003), when an individual may not yet recognize their problem as psychological and seeks medical care. In light of these findings, clinical researchers have begun to develop primary care interventions based on a Chinese explanatory model of depression (Yeung et al., 2008).

Discussion Questions, Part II: Making a Final Decision

1. What is your decision now? Will you adopt the EBP? Justify your decision.

See how students answered on page 216

BRIEF LECTURE 5.2

Community Science, Community-Based Participatory Research, and Emic Research

Given the epistemic violence associated with contemporary science and its reductionist character, social workers need a new science consisting of methodologies and approaches more suited for advancing the field's values and ethical standards. Three existing scientific approaches—community science, community-based participatory research (CBPR), and emic research—present methods that may be useful for this endeavor. These approaches, whether by being based in the community, addressing ethnocentrism, or attempting to incorporate contextual considerations, contain ideas that may be useful for enhancing the benefits of an EBP for a client or for building a science of social work that is motivated by social justice. This brief lecture presents selected content on each area.

Community Science

Community science was born out of the new field of community psychology, which was founded at a conference in Swamscott, Massachusetts in 1965 (Tebes, 2016). The new community psychologists, responding to the limitations of psychology in solving social problems, wanted to move to a focus beyond the individual, conventional science, the medical model, and psychological interventions. They set out to orient their work toward contextual and community-based understandings and social action (Kelly, 1971, 2003). They also questioned the role of research in addressing social problems and social justice and whether "science" was relevant to their aims (Kloos, 2005). They wanted a "community science." Barton's (1968) description of mainstream social science research at that time provides a background to the community psychologists' call to action.

> For the last thirty years, empirical social research has been dominated by the sample survey. But as usually practiced, using random sampling of individuals, the survey is a sociological meatgrinder, tearing the individual from his social context and guaranteeing that nobody in the study interacts with anyone else in it. It is like a biologist putting his experimental animals through a hamburger machine and looking at every hundredth cell through a microscope; anatomy and physiology get lost, structure and function disappear, and one is left with cell biology ... If our aim is to understand people's behavior rather than simply to record it, we want to know about primary groups, neighborhoods, organizations, social circles,

and communities; about interaction, communication, role expectations, and social control. (p. 1)

Since 1965, the role of community science continues to be discussed. A central tenet that has emerged is the use of methods and theories consistent with the view that human behavior occurs within complex processes shaped by multiple contexts (Shinn & Rapkin, 2000; Luke, 2005). Other areas of discussion have included epistemic conventions, foci of interests, methodologies, and standards for judging its work to distinguish itself from other human science fields (Luke, 2005). With this introduction on community science, let's review some of the emphases and directions that have been proposed by this field. (*Tip*. As you read the below ideas, think about which approaches reduce or avoid epistemic violence and support social justice.)

- **Social justice and empowerment:** A community science should address oppression and liberation, empowerment, processes of social change, and careful description of community phenomena, (Rappaport et al., 1975).
- **Community psychology values as a goal:** Evaluate the appropriateness of methods for community-based research and the usefulness of findings by their consistency with the field's values (Rappaport, 2005).
- **Make room for other ways of knowing and new methodologies:** When science is narrowly defined and practiced, epistemologies will be obscured (Rappaport, 2000).
- **Research on the community context and outcomes at both individual and community levels:** Community science aims to enhance theoretical and practical understanding of human behavior in community contexts. It aims to promote competence, resilience, and well-being, and prevent problem behaviors and other harmful outcomes, in individuals and communities (Tebes, 2005).
- **Cultural factors and context:** Community psychologists advocate meaningful consideration of context and cultural factors (Luke, 2005).
- **Many levels of analysis rather than person-centered models:** Organize a science that is community-centered and focused on community-level outcomes and conduct research across levels of analysis rather than only person-centered models (Wandersman, 2003).
- **Methodological 'multiplism':** Community research should be grounded in specific contexts by using methods that systematically represent different perspectives in order to best approximate "truth" and take context seriously. Internal validity and hypothesis testing (in experimental and quasi-experimental designs) as a way of seeking knowledge should not

be the main concern of community-based research, as they limit what can be learned (Tebes, 2005).

- **Use of multiple methodologies and documenting process:** Use discourse analysis, narrative practice, and systematic historical studies to document the process of community research and action (Hess, 2005). Apply narrative analysis and investigative journalism, as well as literature (Rappaport, 2000).

- **Ecological validity, indigenous knowledge, and creative application of conventional evidence in practice:** Focus on identifying, disseminating, and implementing effective programs and include indigenously developed programs, but take the conventional science and apply them to complex settings to document promising practices and applications implemented by practitioners (Miller & Shinn, 2005).

One final community science proposal deserves mention for its relevance to the EBP model. Green (2001) proposed a process of planning for the most appropriate evidence-based interventions for a setting and population. He suggested the development of procedures and theories for achieving the appropriate fit between possible best evidence-based practices and a population's circumstances. Here is his framework:

a. Define best practice as a process rather than a packaged intervention, which professionals from any community can pull off the shelf and apply;

b. Emphasize control by practitioner, patient, client, community, or population, such that they are not passive recipients of scientific information and can exercise their rights and responsibilities in choosing among different options;

c. Emphasize local evaluation and self-monitoring, with local users having the capacity to monitor the implementation and evaluation of the intervention;

d. Conduct research on the tailoring process, including matching information from the research literature with information and evidence about local people and the characteristics of their communities.

Community psychology celebrated its 50th anniversary in 2015. Even though community psychologists have had good intentions for creating a different science, some have argued that they did not live up to the original call to action. Luke (2005) observed that the study methods used by community scientists, in his survey of empirical studies published in the *American Journal of Community Psychology*, had been restricted to a narrow range of statistical tools not well-suited to contextual data. He found that analytic tools more useful for contextual analysis (e.g., multilevel modeling, geographic information systems, social network analysis, and cluster analysis) had been little employed compared with traditional methods (e.g., regression, factory analysis, and ANOVA). Kloos (2005) suggested that the field needed to "heed signs of concern about community psychology's continued relevance in public discourse regarding the analysis of and responses to social problems" and called for a renewal of the field's commitment to social justice and the practice of research that addresses community-based issues (p. 259).

Reflection Questions

1. Is the emphasis on quantitative research designs and data analysis tools, as discussed in the above paragraph, dangerous because they imply a reductionist science?

2. Why are nonconventional research approaches and sources of knowledge (e.g., narrative analysis, investigative journalism, literature, discourse analysis, historical studies) not systematically used in health sciences and intervention research? How might they be useful for developing or evaluating practices or selecting an EBP for a client?

Community-Based Participatory Research

Community-based participatory research (CBPR) takes place in community settings and involves community members in the design and implementation of research projects. It is a partnership approach to research that involves community members, organization representatives, and researchers in all aspects of the research process, with all parties contributing expertise and sharing decision-making and ownership. It was developed in the early 1900s in response to social and political shifts and the critique of colleges and universities for not being sufficiently responsive to the needs of their surrounding communities. Three models of knowledge development influenced the theory and practices associated with CBPR—the Popular Education movement, Action Research, and Participatory Research.

In the Popular Education movement, people were viewed as having the ability to generate their own knowledge, independent of outside experts. This movement had its origins in the Settlement House movement led by Jane Addams in Chicago in the early 20th century; the Highlander Folk School, founded by Myles Horton in 1932 as an adult education model focused on community-generated needs and addressing poverty and inequality in the American South; and Paulo Freire's work in Brazil in the 1940s, wherein he emphasized the power of education as a political tool for raising the consciousness of oppressed people both locally and globally.

Action Research is a set of research methodologies for pursuing action and research simultaneously. It generates research about a social system at the same time as attempts to change that system. Action research uses a cyclical process, alternating between action and critical reflection and continuously refining methods, data, and interpretations in light of the understandings developed in the earlier cycles. This approach was labeled by Kurt Lewin in 1948 and popularized in the 1950s, when it was geared toward increasing worker productivity and satisfaction by creating democratic relationships in the labor structure. Today, CBPR proponents criticize Action Research, because it places little emphasis on active community participation and challenging existing power structures.

Participatory Research is an approach to social research that emerged from the social and political upheaval of the 1960s and 1970s. It is conducted through a process of sequential reflection and action carried out *with* and *by* local people rather than *on* them. It involves not only inquiry but also action, in that people not only discuss problems but also think about possible solutions and actions, including influencing decision-making processes, that need to be taken. The location of power for the research process lies in the local people rather than outside experts, and local knowledge and perspectives are acknowledged. Participatory Research as a methodology reflects postmodern and critical theoretical thinking about the conduct of research. It challenges mainstream positivist science and its assumptions about the purpose of research, the possibility of objectivity, the ideal relationships between researchers and research participants, ethical issues related to data collection, the ownership of research results, the reporting of research findings, and research epistemology. It is also based on a critique of conventional methodologies as reproducing social inequalities based on domination of those with lower social status, including the Western domination of less developed nations and regions.

The characteristics of CBPR include the following (Horowitz et al., 2009):

a.   Community members and researchers contributing equally in all phases;
b.   Shared decision-making and ownership, with findings and knowledge benefiting all partners;
c.   Bidirectional, mutual learning process;
d.   Balance of rigorous research and community action;
e.   Acknowledging strengths, resources, assets, and skills of local people and organizations;
f.   Recognition of community as a unit with an identity;
g.   Focus on multiple determinants;
h.   Commitment to long-term research relationships;
i.   Local capacity building, systems building, sustainability, and empowerment.

CBPR offers the following benefits:

- Allows scholarship and community action to go hand-in-hand, rather than either-or, with power and control shifted away from the researchers.
- Gives voice especially to marginalized, disenfranchised, or silenced communities and individuals.
- Enhances researchers' ability to understand community problems, address community priorities, and develop culturally sensitive research approaches.
- Addresses issues that would not be thoroughly and appropriately addressed using only academic expertise.
- Facilitates the development of practice-based or practice-informed research.
- Brings rigor to applied research studies that are part of social change projects.

Reflection Questions

1. Does using a CBPR approach reduce or eliminate epistemic violence because community members contribute equally to the definition, execution, and ownership of the study? That is, does introducing community partners address the problem of excluding other ways of knowing?

2. Does using a CBPR approach protect against the dangers of reductionist science and the influences of a capitalist logic? That is, will the study's findings be objective, neutral facts that are value-free?

3. Do you see the CBPR approach as incorporating or omitting the contextual emphasis of community science? When would you use CBPR versus a Community Science approach?

⭐ **ACTIVITY** Complete Activity 5.1 now.

Emic Research

Emic is defined as "of, relating to, or involving analysis of cultural phenomena from the perspective of one who participates in the culture being studied (Merriam-Webster, n.d.). Emic research focuses on the norms, values, motives, and customs of the members of the culture as they interpret and understand it themselves. In emic research, the researcher attempts to examine the behaviors and meanings of a culture through the eyes of that culture, to learn how they perceive and categorize their world. Used commonly in anthropology, the researcher investigates how the local people think—what are their explanations, meanings, and logic for their values, practices, and experiences? Linguist Kenneth Pike in 1954 coined the terms *emic* and *etic* research, deriving them from the linguistic terms *phonemic* and *phonetic*, and proposed these as a methodological solution for describing human social behavior. Some researchers use "emic" to refer to insider or subjective accounts and "etic" to refer to outsider or objective accounts.

An emic perspective is one of the principle concepts that guide qualitative research generally, because it is the basis of understanding how people perceive their world. An emic approach is important in health and mental health research because of the need for treatment methods to be congruent with people's culturally based conceptions of illness—so that the treatments can be meaningful and acceptable. Anthropologists and health researchers commonly use Kleinman's (1980) explanatory model of illness interview, a semistructured interview guide consisting of nine questions, to elicit a patient's view of illness, with the objective of improving care. Two questions about relationships were added by a psychologist investigating conceptualizations of depression among Chinese women in the U.S. (Ying, 1990). The questions are below (Kleinman, 1980, p. 106), with Ying's (1990) questions 8 and 9 added for eliciting models of illness in cultures with a collectivistic orientation.

1. *Conceptualization*: What do you call the problem that you have? What is its name?
2. *Cause*: What do you think caused this problem?
3. *Impact*: How does this illness impact you?
4. *Chief problem*: What is/are the chief problem(s) that your illness brings?
5. *Severity*: How severe is your illness?
6. *Most feared consequence*: In terms of your illness, what do you fear the most?
7. *Course*: Does your illness have a long or short course?

8. *Family relationships*: How do you get along with your family members now?
9. *Non-family relationships*: How do you get along with other people in your life?
10. *Help-seeking*: What kind of treatment do you think you should obtain?
11. *Desired treatment outcome*: What is the most important outcome you hope the treatment will result in?

Kleinman used this interview to explore the low prevalence of depression in Chinese societies. He found that a somatic expression of distress was common because it was a socially acceptable "idiom of distress," given the social and political history and environment, which inhibited psychological expressions. Through this research, he also found that neurasthenia, a more culturally acceptable expression, overlapped significantly with depression.

As *guidelines for ensuring an emic approach* in diagnostic, intervention, and descriptive research in the areas of health and mental health, here are 12 questions grouped into three areas:

1. Careful and thorough consideration and representation of the culture:

    a. Are practices, interventions, or instruments (including outreach methods) originating from the culture systematically explored, considered, and used in the research?

    b. Are the instruments, interventions, and other research materials written in terms that are meaningful and understandable to members of the culture (and written by a small team from the culture and with experience with the targeted population)?

    c. Are observations made or data collected in a way that does not involve imposing the researchers' constructs?

    d. Are differences within the cultural group based on acculturation, immigration, social, and economic factors and gender and age considered when developing and evaluating instruments and interventions?

2. Use of research methods that ensure an emic perspective through the research:

    a. Is a methodology, such as the *explanatory model of illness interview*, used so that the description of the condition, what it means, how one experiences it, and what it is called come from members of the culture?

   b. Are *qualitative interviewing and other qualitative methods* used carefully and sufficiently to arrive at a saturation point (where no more new ideas were arising) for gathering data to develop instruments, interventions, and other materials?

   c. Is there a mechanism for *qualitative investigation of unexpected responses* to instruments or to the intervention, including interviewing of participants who drop out?

   d. Are the *measures used for examining validity based in the culture*, rather than in Western culture, for assessing criterion, discriminant, and convergent validity?

3.   Involvement of partners and research team from the culture:

   a. Are members of the culture involved in developing, adapting, and/or testing the instruments, interventions, and materials that are used in the research?

   b. Are practitioners experienced with serving members of the culture involved in designing the research and overseeing research implementation, including any adjustments that needed to be made?

   c. Are the research assistants who collect data and other members of the research team from the culture or knowledgeable about it?

   d. Is the principal investigator (PI) or the co-PI someone with firsthand knowledge of the culture and language?

As an example of mental health research using an emic approach, Wong, author of this book, et al. (2012) conducted a study on the experience and expression of depression among low-income Chinese immigrants residing in the San Francisco area, with the goal of understanding the construct of depression and developing comprehensive and brief assessment instruments. The study design included developing pilot items by (a) administering Kleinman's (1980) explanatory model of interview to immigrants diagnosed with major depression by Chinese clinicians; (b) interviewing health, mental health, and social services professionals with many years of experience providing care to Chinese immigrants to gain their knowledge of relevant symptoms and symptom expressions, including asking them to evaluate the relevance of items from depression instruments developed in Asia; (c) having a small team of experienced clinicians review and decide on the final items and Chinese expressions to compose the pilot instrument; (d) using as the criterion standard the participant's diagnosis as given by a Chinese community

CRITICAL THINKING

1. Does an emic approach meet your requirements for producing culturally based evidence that is not ethnocentric and avoids epistemic violence?

2. Does an emic approach disregard the importance of contextually based and ecologically sound research of CBPR and community science, respectively?

3. If none of the EBPs you find in the literature for a client are based on an emic research approach, would you downgrade their level of evidence?

4. Would you upgrade the level of evidence of a small qualitative study because it does include emic research elements, which make it more culturally valid?

5. Should social work practitioners develop other domains of external validity to evaluate along with level of evidence? How about "level of ecological validity," "level of contextual validity," "level of community validity," and "level of emic validity"?

professional in routine practice; and (e) using neurasthenia and acculturative stress instruments and the PHQ-9 for purposes of comparison and validation. Study findings included a three-dimensional construct of depression, with 59 items across somatic, psychological, and interpersonal dimensions. Below are examples of items.

Somatic items indicating very severe depression:

- Nausea or throwing up
- Temporary unclear vision
- Throat discomfort or soreness
- Sensitivity to light
- Feeling faint or dizzy

Interpersonal items indicating moderately severe depression:

- You feel you are a burden to your family and society.
- You think you made your family lose face.

- You feel you don't have the kind of respect from work and family that you should have.
- You feel life is meaningless.
- You hide your life difficulties from other people.

Psychological items indicating mild to moderate depression:

- You feel very unhappy.
- You think unpleasant things the whole day and cannot stop.
- You are very nervous.
- Many things make you feel worried.
- Many things make you feel very troubled or bothered.

From the 59-item comprehensive scale, nine items considered to be easy-to-answer and less stigmatizing were drawn to compose a 9-item instrument that paralleled the PHQ-9. The authors also composed other 9-item instruments, including a somatic scale and an interpersonal scale. In comparisons with the PHQ-9, all 9-item scales performed similarly well, but each recognized depression in an overlapping but different group out of the sample of n = 229 Chinese-speaking adult immigrants. The authors proposed that the 9-item somatic scale be used and evaluated for screening in primary care settings. This research group has developed educational videos for the Chinese community, including primary care, using CBPR and emic approaches, which can be viewed at vimeo.com/chinesedepression.

 ACTIVITY 5.1 Evaluate IMPACT Using CBPR Guidelines

In this activity, you will appraise the extent to which the IMPACT study aligns with principles of participatory research. You will use the guidelines for participatory research projects in health promotion developed by Lawrence W. Green, a health behavior scholar. Green's guidelines distinguish the structural elements of CBPR methodology from other research approaches through six domains with 25 questions. Green's 25 questions are copied below. You can see the individualized response options for each question online (http://lgreen.net/guidelines.html) or use the following scale for every question: *0-none, 1-low, 2-moderate, 3-moderate-to-high*, or *4-high/comprehensive/explicit*.

Instructions

1. Answer each of the 25 questions below based on what you know about the IMPACT study. Review the methods section of Unützer's (2002) article if needed. Work with a peer or on your own.
2. Discuss your answers with a peer if you did the first step on your own.
3. Answer this question: Would it have been more fruitful (i.e., eventually more effective) to develop an integrated care intervention for depression in older adults using a CBPR approach (i.e., rather than just taking IMPACT to test on them)?
4. Let's say you still wish to conduct IMPACT as an RCT but incorporate some elements of a CBPR approach. Find at least three elements from Green's list and note how exactly you would incorporate them into your study.

· ·

TIP Consider incorporating elements 1c, 1d, 4a, or 4e from the below list.

· ·

See the answers on page 217.

"Guidelines and Categories for Classifying Participatory Research Projects in Health Promotion" by Lawrence W. Green

1. Participants and the Nature of their Involvement:

   a. Is the community of interest clearly described or defined?

   b. Do members of the defined community participating in the research have concern or experience with the issue?

   c. Are interested members of the defined community provided opportunities to participate in the research process?

   d. Is attention given to barriers to participation, with consideration of those who have been under-represented in the past?

   e. Has attention been given to establishing within the community an understanding of the researcher's commitment to the issue?

   f. Are community participants enabled to contribute their physical and/or intellectual resources to the research process?

2. Origin of the Research Question:

   a. Did the impetus for the research come from the defined community?

    b. Is the effort to research the issue supported by members of the defined community?

3. Purpose of the Research:

    a. Can the research facilitate learning among community participants about individual and collective resources for self-determination?

    b. Can the research facilitate collaboration between community participants and resources external to that community?

    c. Is the purpose of the research to empower the community to address determinants of health?

    d. Does the scope of the research encompass some combination of political, social, and economic determinants of health?

4. Process and Contextual/Methodological Implications:

    a. Does the research process apply the knowledge of community participants in the phases of planning, implementation and evaluation?

    b. For community participants, does the [research] process allow for learning about research methods?

    c. For researchers, does the [research] process allow for learning about the community health issue?

    d. Does the [research] process allow for flexibility or change in research methods and focus, as necessary?

    e. Are procedures in place for appraising experiences during implementation of research?

    f. Are community participants involved in [data] analytic issues: interpretation, synthesis, and verification of conclusions?

5. Opportunities to Address the Issue of Interest:

    a. Is the potential of the defined community for individual and collective learning reflected by the research process?

    b. Is the potential of the defined community for action reflected in the research process [i.e., what is the level of alignment of the research process with potential for action]?

    c.   Does the [research] process reflect a commitment by researchers and community participants to social, individual or cultural actions [based on] the learning acquired through research?

6.   Nature of the Research Outcomes:

    a.   Do community participants benefit from the research outcomes?

    b.   Is there attention to or an explicit agreement for acknowledging and resolving in a fair and open way any differences between researchers and community participants in the interpretation of the results?

    c.   Is there attention to or an explicit agreement between researchers and community participants with respect to ownership of the research data?

    d.   Is there attention to or an explicit agreement between researchers and community participants with respect to the dissemination of research results?

Source: http://lgreen.net/guidelines.html#Guidelines%20and%20Categories%20for%20Classifying%20Participatory%20Research%20Projects%20in%20Health%20Promotion

---

ACTIVITY 5.2   **Design a Study Using an Emic Research Approach**

Design a study that produces evidence that is culturally valid for the racial/ethnic or diversity group of your client. Use the *guidelines for ensuring an emic approach* on page 190 and any other research design ideas that you like.

Example Inspired by the Case of Laura (p. 311)
Research Question
What individual, family, school, and community supports are effective for promoting the healthy psychological, social, and academic adaptation of recently immigrated Mexican adolescent girls in single-parent families?

Research Method
The qualitative study will involve six focus groups with six participants in each, using a bilingual Spanish-English interview guide with open-ended questions. Interview transcripts will be analyzed qualitatively for main concepts and themes, including best supportive practices. Focus group meetings will be held in schools and community centers. The research team will consist of (a) two bilingual social workers who are Mexican American immigrants with extensive experience in working with Mexican immigrant teens and families and (b) two middle-aged immigrant parents

who have raised immigrant teen girls. One social worker and one parent will lead each focus group. All four research team members will analyze the qualitative data.

The sample will include 18 Mexican immigrant women age 20–30 who did and did not have difficulties with adaptation after immigrating to the U.S. at high school age and 18 single parents of such young women. The sample of 36 individuals will participate in focus groups as follows:

- For two focus groups, the participants will be single parents.
- For two groups, the participants will be the young adult women.
- For two groups, the participants will be parent-daughter dyads (i.e., parent and daughter participate together).

The following open-ended interview guide will be used in the focus groups:

1. What are the challenges and needs of immigrant teen girls in high school and of their parents that should be addressed to support the teen's healthy adaptation and development?
   - *Prompt:* Explore psychological, social, and academic challenges and needs, but the emphasis is on open discussion that allows participants to express their own ideas and meanings.
   - *Prompt:* Explore the relationship of the identified challenges and needs to culture, language, identity development, family adaptation, and acculturation stressors, if these areas are meaningful to the participants.
2. What supports (such as interventions, services, therapies or groups, or other approaches) can be helpful to meeting the needs of the teen girls and their parents?
   - *Prompt:* Explore individual-, family-, school-, and community-level supports.
3. What are the most important considerations or advice you would give to support the design and provision of support services to immigrant teen girls and their single parents?
   - *Prompt:* Explore cultural considerations, including how supports provided can be respectful of culture, immigration, and intergenerational acculturation processes.
4. Do you have other ideas on how to best support immigrant teen girls and their single parents that have not yet been touched upon?

 ACTIVITY 5.3 **Test Your Understanding of the Chapter**

Answer the following true or false questions. Explain your answer.

1. *Ethnocentrism* means the researcher is taking the cultural viewpoint of the population under study.

2. Epistemic violence is when people use the knowledge of the West to justify the political and cultural domination over the non-West, preventing these "others" from their own discourse of knowing, feeling, and awareness of self.

3. Contemporary scientists emphasize a well-defined and stable scientific method and the use of the scientific method to discover true, factual descriptions of nature. But they neglect the fact that their studies are set in contexts, which the scientists themselves have chosen in a value-determined process and which in turn determine what will be observed.

4. The randomized control trial for IMPACT discussed in this chapter is not an example of reductionist science, because the trial included ethnic minorities in its sample.

5. Translating the PHQ-9 to Arabic and administering the instrument to older adults in primary care settings in Egypt to obtain a prevalence rate for depression is an example of etic research.

6. If the PHQ-9 primary care study in Egypt finds a much higher prevalence rate with less sampling dropout compared to U.S. studies, this suggests strong construct validity of the PHQ-9 and that using an emic approach is unnecessary in this case.

7. Study dropout, where high percentages of recruited participants end their participation at different phases, is a concern because the researcher is unable to make observations or draw any study conclusions about them, and they may be very different from those who remained in the study.

8. Community science refers to focusing on community-level outcomes and research methods that can represent different perspectives and consider complex settings, as well as allowing the community members to participate in the design, monitoring, and evaluation of the intervention.

9. A CBPR study must include a qualitative component (i.e., it cannot be only quantitative).

10. Evidence-based practice decision-making has a "best-evidence component" that excludes the consideration of research designed with an emic approach.

11. CBPR, community science, and emic approaches to research can be used to better understand and address disparities in mental health services utilization experienced by minority communities.

12. A social worker's clinical expertise, including the ability to engage with and conduct a careful and comprehensive assessment of the client from a culturally humble standpoint, is just as important as the ability to critique the available research evidence when deciding which EBP to select and offer to the client.

See the answers on page 221.

Case Paper Task 5.1

Evaluate the Samples in the Three EBPs You Are Considering for Your Client and Write the *Populations Studied & Applicability to My Client* Section

Instructions: Below are examples of the *Populations Studied & Applicability to My Client* section for the first of three EBPs from Laura's and Eddie's case papers. You can see other examples in the full case papers in Appendix B (p. 311) and Appendix C (p. 323).

Case Paper Instructions:

Review of EBP #1 (6–7 paragraphs, 9 points)

This section is based on your review of two empirical research articles and other information found online, in print, and through interviews.

Populations Studied & Applicability to My Client: For each study, evaluate whether its sample included people with diversity characteristics like those of your client and whether the findings support the intervention's use in your client's community. (You may also comment generally based on your search for articles whether you came across many studies on your client's diversity group.) (*1 paragraph, 2 points*)

Laura's Example

Needs Strengthening

Populations Studied & Applicability to My Client

Both studies that I reviewed apply to my client, because CBT-A is for depression and my client's main problem is depression. The samples had some Latinx immigrant teens, which is all that can be expected today, because studies do not include a lot of minority groups. Having some already makes the literature useful. It is important that the studies take place in community organizations and not only research hospitals. This is the case for one of the studies, which supports generalizing the evidence to my client.

How would you strengthen the above? Is the reasoning about the generalizability of the evidence correct? Does it include the content requested in the instructions?

Well-Written

As you read the below example, notice the aspects of the sample and focuses of the studies that are brought out. Does it better assess the generalizability of the evidence to the client?

Review of EBP #1: Cognitive Behavioral Therapy for Adolescents

Populations Studied & Applicability to My Client

The direct generalizability of the findings reviewed to my client is moderate. The samples appeared to be more depressed, likely included few or no Latina immigrant teens, and were in inpatient and outpatient psychiatric settings. The grade A– RCT (Brent et al., 1999) reported neither the racial/ethnic background of participants nor the study setting, but participants, referred to as patients, had moderate depression with substantial rates of comorbid anxiety, dysthymic disorder, and disruptive disorders. The grade B study (Weersing et al., 2006) investigated youth in an outpatient setting and included female (77%) and some minority (15%) participants, which is similar to my client's situation. Showing applicability to my client, the meta-analysis of 11 studies included four studies of students and one study of community youths, rather than outpatients and youth in juvenile justice (Klein et al., 2007).

Eddie's Example

Well-Written

As you read the below example, notice the constant commenting on the applicability of each sample characteristic to the client. Notice also the added commentary on the need to treat race-based trauma.

Review of EBP #1: Prolonged Exposure Therapy

Populations Studied & Applicability to My Client

The first RCT (Bryant et al., 2008) is applicable to Eddie in that he is a civilian and suffered sexual trauma (rape), even though the Australian sample did not include Eddie's racial/ethnic group. Another concern about the generalizability of findings to Eddie is that those who dropped out of treatment had significantly higher baseline PTSD scores than those who completed treatment. Eddie has more severe PTSD. The second RCT (Zoellner et al., 2019) has some generalizability to Eddie given that its sample included African Americans (21.5%), male participants (24.5%), and rape victims. After reviewing the literature beyond these two studies, however, most PET male RCT subject populations are normally veterans who have PTSD symptoms as a result of their time served in the military as adults (and not from childhood abuse and rape). Also, the knowledge base of PET with African American trauma clients, including how to treat race-based trauma, is small and uncertain, given that a systematic review included only 38 RCTs, with small numbers of African Americans in their samples (Benuto et al., 2020).

ANSWERS

Discussion 5.1 Answers   **Is the PHQ-9 Valid for All Cultural Groups?**

How Students Answered

1. **Would you expect the PHQ-9 to detect depression effectively in different cultural, gender, or other diversity groups? How about for individuals not fluent in English? For which diversity groups might it tend not to be effective, and why?**

   a. I don't think it would be effective for non-English speakers. Some of the expressions could be hard to understand if they're not translated well, such as "feeling down" or "moving around a lot more than usual."

   b. "Having little pleasure" is a middle class or upper class problem, not lower class. It sounds a little strange to someone whose life as a new immigrant, for example, is focused on going to three different jobs every week.

   c. "Overeating" isn't seen as a problem in all cultures. *Having a lot to eat* and *eating a lot*, for Chinese people in China, don't have the same meaning as in mainstream U.S. culture. Being able to eat a lot is a good thing. It wouldn't have to be associated with depression.

   d. I think that immigrant men especially may not answer positively to some of these symptoms, like feeling hopeless, or the emotional one about feeling down and depressed. They tend to express and feel anger, but there's no question about anger. They may not recognize they're feeling depressed.

   e. If you're more Americanized and know English well, you might be more open about answering some of the questions. If not, due to stigma or just not recognizing the symptoms as problems, you'd downplay them, or you may not believe they're a problem. The instrument wouldn't be effective for a lot of people.

   f. Some people don't feel safe revealing they are depressed. They don't want to be seen as "crazy" or admit to themselves they are going crazy. They may not answer the questionnaire at all. This is the stigma of mental health that exists in many cultures. It's also because they don't know that depression is common and treatable. The PHQ-9 could leave a lot of people out. That's why you have to meet with people, talk to them, get to know them.

g. It's not a matter of race or ethnicity how someone answers these questions. It could be family dynamics too. Some people don't come from expressive families. Or they learned to hold problems in for a long time.

h. I think any instrument like this will not work for a lot of people. We have to be care to not think, "This person's Latinx and an immigrant, so he must be answering the questions like other Latinx immigrants do." You can't capture people's diversity in a questionnaire.

2. **Imagining a client who is not fluent in English for whom the PHQ-9 items are translated. Which of the nine items might be difficult to understand, and why?**

a. Item 3, "trouble falling or staying asleep or sleeping too much," may be hard to understand. The person might think, "Do you have to have all three sleep issues or just one of them? Do I answer 'yes' if I cannot stay asleep but I do fall asleep, and am I oversleeping?"

b. Item 5, "poor appetite or overeating," may be difficult to understand, because they're two different problems in the same item. This may be more the case for people with less education. It's a lot of ideas in the same sentence. You would need someone to give the questionnaire, explaining each item slowly.

c. Item 8, "moving or speaking so slowly that other people could have noticed … or … being so fidgety or restless that you have been moving around a lot more than usual," is too complicated, especially for people who are depressed. They might think, "Who's noticing?" and "How do I know who noticed?" or "What is 'moving around a lot more'?" I know this item refers to psychomotor agitation, but a lot of our clients won't.

d. I think it would be hard for anyone to be sure that any of the symptoms is a problem until the symptom is a big problem. People struggle for a while with "What's going on with me?" and "Is this a problem?" before they acknowledge it's a problem. People deny or minimize symptoms for a long time—sometimes until they're immobilized by the depression.

3. **How might the PHQ-9 represent the Western culture-based experience and expression of depression? How would you describe a Western conception of depression? What types of symptoms may be present in the expression of depressive distress in other cultures that are absent from the Western one?**

   a. Depressed mood and loss of interest are things that happen in one's mind. The PHQ-9 doesn't touch on all the physical complaints people who are depressed are focused on every day. Headaches, abdominal or gastro-intestinal problems, etc.

   b. Other cultures may talk more about somatic problems. Western culture teaches you to give priority to and talk about emotions and feelings, and depression is this very specific thing about having a very low mood. I think there are cultures where people talk about depression in terms of what's happening physically, or both physically and emotionally.

   c. The DSM-5 core symptoms are depressed mood and not feeling pleasure and loss of interest [anhedonia]. This is very "I" focused, or individualistic. You're supposed to talk about what you like, how happy you are, how you do things to promote your own happiness, and express your emotions on everything. It's not like this in all cultures.

   d. There's a big focus on emotions, but nothing about family problems and how bad one is judging themselves for not being a good provider, or how bad one feels for fighting with their spouse, kids, or in-laws. I know that Latinx clients talk a lot about interpersonal problems. They're focused on that rather than "I'm down" or "My happiness needs to be enhanced."

   e. I would think of the impact of Western religions. The problem of guilt is talked about in the DSM, but that kind of guilt related to committing sins doesn't apply to a lot of cultures. "Loss of face" is more important to Asian cultures. That could be a good item on a depression scale.

4. **What are the consequences of assuming that the PHQ-9 works well for a culturally different population and using it in practice? For example, you use the PHQ-9 as the screening tool for routing clients who are refugees from Myanmar into depression treatment.**

f.   It would be hard to know if they truly understand the questions, or if the questions are meaningful to them. If not, then some who needs treatment won't get it.

g.   It's anti–cultural humility and definitely an act of epistemic violence. If I worked somewhere where I had to use the PHQ-9, I would start with "What do you need help with? What are you experiencing?" and later, "Here's a U.S. instrument; want to learn about it and see if it's useful for understanding your experience?"

h.   I imagine the refugees could be suffering from trauma, loss, resettlement issues, social isolation, and more. Using a depression instrument and isolating depression as one of the person's potential problems and needs is narrow and limiting.

i.   We already assume that the PHQ-9 is valid for different populations. Going along with precedent, without questioning and advocacy for more inclusive and culturally respectful approaches, shows our own lack of integrity and disrespect for the dignity and worth of our clients.

5.   **Why would the sensitivity and specificity indicators likely be lower if the researchers had included patients who had mild or moderate depression? In other words, what are some reasons why patients in the mild to low moderate range are harder to detect as having depression?**

j.   I think that when someone has mild depression, they may have some of the symptoms of depression and not others, and symptoms are also fluctuating as far as how strong they are. This makes depression harder to detect.

k.   People aren't completely aware of their symptoms when the depression is mild and something new for them. They're wondering what's happening to them. They think they have physical health problems, or it's work stress. But when the depression is severe and they're unable to function for a while, then they have to answer each question at a high level. You can't escape it, making it easy to detect.

l.   If the researchers included patients with mild depression in their final samples, the sensitivity and specificity indicators would be lower because the samples would be representative of the whole population. It's pointless to say that the instrument is accurate—but only for those who are super depressed.

m. A good instrument would be most useful if it could detect mild depression. Those are the people who need to be routed into care. But from our discussion, it sounds like mild depression isn't expressed in just one way either.

6. **Would you assume that fewer Chinese immigrant men experience depression (i.e., would you believe the study findings)? Or would you question why the PHQ-9 is not capturing this group, especially those in the milder range? Explain your answers.**

n. This is a good example of epistemic violence. You use a scale that doesn't apply to them, and then the findings are presented like the truth. We're not supposed to question the findings after it's declared in writing that the scale is valid and reliable for all the groups included in the study.

o. I would definitely question why the PHQ-9 isn't recognizing depression at the mild level. There is a lot of stigma in the Chinese community. They may have the symptom but not see it as a "problem" but rather a part of life for immigrants. They may be experiencing anger and irritation, which bothers them a lot, rather than low mood and unhappiness. There are lots of reasons for them to answer the questions like the mainstream population.

p. I definitely don't believe the findings. I would ask some mental health professionals who work with Chinese immigrant men to tell me whether the depression rate is really so low and why DSM depression symptoms don't apply.

q. It seems that those with mild depression are hard to detect, and maybe even more so for Chinese immigrant men. Assuming the findings are true leads us to exclude them from care rather than help them to gain access.

7. **What would you explore to find out why Chinese immigrant men show a much lower rate of depression?**

r. I would ask people who know, such as clinicians who work with this population or immigrant men who have experienced depression, what they experience and express in a mild stage of depression. I've heard that anger and being out of control of one's thinking are common expressions related to depression for Chinese men. There are also somatic complaints. If what's on the scale isn't meaningful to them, then what is? We need a different scale.

s.   I would ask the men in the study why they answered the three problematic questions like they did. I would have Chinese mental health clinicians interview and assess them in an open-ended format and at length to see what problems they are experiencing, and whether depression is one of these.

t.   I would hold a focus group with Chinese immigrant men and women to explore the instrument's items and lower rate [of depression]. This focus group may give the answer or tell me what I should explore.

8. **Would you agree that the PHQ-9 studies reviewed have answered the question, "How many Chinese patients can be detected for depression with the PHQ-9?" rather than, "How well does the PHQ-9 detect depression among Chinese immigrants?" Explain your answer.**

u.   Yes, I agree. The studies reviewed are etic studies, where a construct is forced upon the audience. As findings, we observe only what was asked in the scale, neither more nor less.

v.   I also agree. To answer how well the PHQ-9 detects depression in this population would require comparing the PHQ-9 with a more culturally based assessment method, which was not done in these studies. We would need to start by asking, "What is depression for this group?" and, "How well does the PHQ-9 capture or overlap with this?"

Discussion 5.2 Answers   Is IMPACT as Useful for Minority Populations as Suggested?

How Students Answered

Discussion Questions, Part I: Who Was Left Out of the Study?

1. **Among patients who were approached, 21% of 32,908 either refused to be screened, participated in the screening but refused further participation, or left the screen incomplete. Do you consider this percentage to be large? What are possible reasons that these patients did not agree or were unable to participate? What might be the intervention**

needs and problem conceptualizations of these patients who were left out of the study?

    a. Yes, this percentage is large. It's one out of every five people who didn't want anything to do with being screened.

    b. It's possible they were too busy to be bothered, or they knew they didn't have depression. But it's also possible some of them were denying their depression and needing help.

    c. These patients may be the ones who feel more stigma. They don't want to be seen filling out a depression questionnaire. In this sense, they are the ones who most need to be assessed and hooked up with a treatment that works for them.

    d. These could be the ones who somaticize. They think their problem is physical. They don't see their problem as emotional.

    e. It could be [that these represent] the patients who have very severe depression, and their concentration and energy is so bad that they can't even focus to fill out the screen.

2. Among patients who were referred (most were by their physicians), 17% of 2,190 either refused the initial screen or further participation or left the screen incomplete. Do you consider this percentage to be large? What are possible reasons that these patients did not agree or were unable to participate? What might be the intervention needs and problem conceptualizations of these patients who were left out of the study?

    a. This percentage is definitely large, because their doctor thought they had depression. They're referred and then don't participate in the screening and the next step. We should find out why this is happening, because this group probably needs help the most with depression or something else.

    b. These are the patients who are denying their depression. They might be feeling scared to follow through and face up to it.

    c. It's a large percentage, especially assuming this group likely has at least mild depression.

    d. There's no way to know why they refused to be screened. Maybe the ones who self-referred followed through with the screen and the ones referred by a doctor or staff disagreed with the referral and didn't follow through.

e. You could do a study to find out why so many refused to be screened or continue on to the individual clinical interview. You could do a qualitative study on them. You could also find out what needs to changed so that they can be screened in some way or another in the future.

3. **Many patients did not endorse any item on the PHQ-2. These were 67% of those approached and close to 9% of those referred. Does this seem high? Is it possible that the two screening items (anhedonia and depressed mood) may leave out a lot of people who have mild depression?**

a. It doesn't seem that high, because most people don't have depression. It's kind of surprising, actually, that 33% (100% – 67%) endorsed one of the two items. It seems like the instrument screens in too many people. But it's probably good that a lot are screened in, because they go to the next phase of getting a long individual interview with a clinician.

b. I think these percentages are very high. The 9% were referred. I would expect them to [endorse] one of the two screen items. The 67% not screened in may have depression but don't see their problem as loss of pleasure or a mood problem. A lot of people are left out with a two-item screen, even if these are "core" symptoms.

c. Again, there are those who experience their problem as physical and not in this psychological or emotional way. The PHQ-2 would leave out these people.

d. Sometimes, people don't realize their problem is emotional until someone's talked to them about it in that way, especially when it's mild. At first, they don't know what their problem is exactly.

e. Any brief screen would have these problems of leaving out a lot of people. You really have to talk to people and see how they're experiencing their problems.

4. Is it possible that more Black and Latino patients would tend to refuse to participate in screening—and thus be left out of the study?

a. I think that some Latino immigrants may not want to participate because this type of procedure may be new and unusual for them. This would be more the case for non-English speakers, but the people in this study were all English speakers.

b. I think so, because there may be a basic lack of trust in mental health services coming from these populations.

c. It would be good to see the numbers. Were there more Latinx and Black patients who wouldn't do the screen compared with White patients?

d. It's also possible that more Latinx and Black patients welcome the screening, because it's taking place in primary care, right where they are getting medical services. They don't have to go somewhere else. It's less stigmatizing in primary care.

Discussion Questions, Part II: Does IMPACT Erase Disparities for Black and Latino Older Adults?

1. **Does IMPACT erase disparities for Latino and African Americans?**

   a. I don't know if it "erases" disparities, but the intervention does lead to about the same results for Whites, Blacks, and Latinos, and it is helping all of the groups. It's a good thing to see. It doesn't leave us wondering whether it works for minorities; at least they included minorities in the study.

   b. I'm not sure what "erasing disparities" means. If it means there's no longer any difference between Blacks and Whites on how much care they are getting, for example, then I'd say it erases it a little bit but not completely for Blacks. The findings showed a lot more Whites using psychotherapy and meds than Blacks from getting the intervention vs. not getting it. From the numbers, IMPACT was most helpful for Latinos, even more than Whites. So you can say it erases disparities for Latinos.

   c. Overall, I agree it's good to know that an EBP worked for the different racial/ethnic groups, but there are a lot of questions that have to be answered to "erase" disparities. There were only 222 Black older adults and 138 Latino older adults out of a sample of 1,801. It's still a very small minority sample, and we don't know why or how these 360 minority seniors made it into the study and why others didn't.

   d. How well an intervention reduces disparities also depends on how much depression each population has to begin with. Maybe Blacks and Latinos have much higher rates than Whites, and we probably don't even know what their true rates are, with the DSM-based instruments that are used.

e. The results are hopeful, but also a little spooky. We shouldn't think that having this intervention in primary care clinics across the U.S. will solve the depression problem for Black and Latinx seniors. Something about the study doesn't feel right. It feels like forcing one solution on every group.

2. **What is not shown or left out of a diagram like Figure 5.2? What questions does this diagram raise (that could be studied in the future)? (Think about the sample, choice of treatments, setting, and other aspects of the study design.)**

a. We don't see who got into the study and who didn't. For example, were there proportionally more Blacks and Latinx who didn't want to be screened or refused to continue in the study? The graph is only about a small subset of people who were open to getting screened in and treated. All those dropouts in the different phase of the flowchart should be studied too.

b. It sounds like usual care was no care, or no mental health care right there in the clinic, but patients could be referred out to mental health clinics or go to other places. Given that the comparison is IMPACT versus no care, of course IMPACT would lead to better rates of use of medications and therapy. For a future study, I would want to compare IMPACT with other therapies that are also offered in the primary care clinic.

c. PST-PC is a brief therapy that's cost-effective, but I wonder if there are other therapies that are more culturally sensitive or group-based that would have gotten better results. A next step is to compare PST-PC with other therapies.

d. The results look good for primary care, but I would want to make the same treatments (meds and PST) available in community-based and social services organizations to see if even better results could be achieved there.

3. Look at how much the various rates improved. Are the results good enough for you to decide on implementing IMPACT in your primary care clinic?

a.   The treatment, PST-PC, sounds like it was useful, but what numbers mean in real life isn't clear. From the graph, it looks like, at the 3-month point, 40%–45% of intervention participants, for all groups, were using PST-PC, compared to 12%–20% of usual care participants, who must have been getting some kind of counseling or therapy outside the clinic. But this means 55%–60% of intervention participants were not using or did not want PST-PC. They must have chosen meds instead of therapy; it seems like more patients should have chosen therapy, but maybe therapy in general, or that therapy, wasn't attractive to them? A 40%–45% use rate for PST-PC isn't that high.

b.   It's hard to really know what a score of 1.4 on the symptom checklist (HSCL-20) means. It sounds low, given that the range is 0–4, but we don't know what the person's daily life and difficulties really are.

c.   A 1.4 depression score is an average or median score for the whole group. This means many people scored above and below 1.4. In other words, it looks like IMPACT works okay for your average person, but we still need to aim for a program that treats both average and non-average people.

d.   Looking at the satisfaction percentages, around 50% of usual care patients were satisfied, and 71%–76% of intervention patients were satisfied. The difference isn't that much. I'd do a study on the people who weren't satisfied and didn't make use of the meds and therapy.

e.   I'm not sure I would implement IMPACT. I would wait until different therapies and approaches are tested in primary care, just like IMPACT was with a big sample and in many different clinics, before I decided.

4.   **What ethical obligations may not be met if you implemented IMPACT in your health center?**

a.   I worry about being ethnocentric. The instruments, therapies, and even the meds may not be a good cultural fit for some people from the Black and Latinx communities. The *Code of Ethics* says we have responsibility for evaluation and research and to critically examine emerging knowledge (*5.02 Evaluation and Research*). Implementing IMPACT without recognizing its limitations could be contributing to discrimination (*4.02 Discrimination*). We have to ask, "Does IMPACT really help everyone?" or "Does it just look that way and is maintaining the status quo?" What if IMPACT gets implemented everywhere and there are still disparities?

b. We need to provide services that are sensitive to clients' cultures (*1.05 Cultural Awareness and Social Diversity*). This means we have to promote research that is sensitive and diverse and offer a range of services, rather than choosing IMPACT and sticking with only IMPACT.

c. Social workers should promote practices that demonstrate respect for difference and support the expansion of cultural knowledge and resources, and should advocate programs that demonstrate cultural competence (*6.04 Social and Political Action*). I'd like to be more sure that IMPACT is culturally competent before choosing it. It may be fine, but I'd like to see more comparative culturally based research to see how IMPACT fits into a bigger picture first.

5. **Would you expect IMPACT and PST-PC to be effective with Latino immigrants? Can its evidence be generalized to Latino immigrants whose primary language is Spanish?**

a. No. The Latinos in the study were English speakers, which means they were more acculturated to the U.S. than someone who doesn't know English well. The evidence on IMPACT doesn't apply. For the evidence to be generalizable, the sample has to be representative of the client's cultural or language group. The study would need to be replicated with Spanish speakers.

b. Given the small sample size of 138 Latinos, compared to around 1,400 Whites, this study's level of evidence isn't strong enough even for English-speaking Latinos.

c. The whole program, from the educational video to the screening instrument to the PST-PC materials to the training for care managers, would all have to be to be translated and adapted. It's too big of a leap to say that the English materials would be just as effective.

d. I see the whole IMPACT intervention as pretty straightforward. There's no reason that, if carefully translated, it wouldn't be effective for Spanish-speaking immigrants, but it's always good to test to [see if it will] achieve the same results first. Then, any adjustments can be made as part of the testing.

e. There's a chance that a lot more Latino immigrants don't complete the screen or drop out. There needs to be a different strategy for getting them into treatment. Otherwise, you put IMPACT into place, but no one participates.

f. A lot of first-generation immigrants are dealing with trauma. I'm not sure that the Latinos in the study represented a big range of Latino backgrounds either, since most were Mexican. The evidence isn't generalizable. You have to study Latinos specifically, a lot of them, to find the best interventions for that group. The IMPACT study should not have excluded Spanish speakers but rather made a point of recruiting them and translating all of their materials.

6. **Should we use IMPACT with Blacks and Latinos based on the finding that IMPACT is more effective compared with "care as usual"?**

a. The study was big, with a big sample size and many study sites, but it basically found that IMPACT is better than not having a specific program in place. It's good to know that IMPACT has benefits and does no harm, but it really needs to be compared to other integrated care and non–integrated care interventions.

b. IMPACT was effective to the extent of the outcome rates that were shown, but maybe any intervention could do that well? It's not even a question of whether it's good enough for Blacks and Latinos.

c. From the point of view that there aren't many interventions developed with minority populations in mind, and we see that this one works at all, it might be an argument to try it.

Discussion 5.3 Answers   Evaluate a Hypothetical Study: Would You Adopt This EBP for a Minority Group?

How Students Answered

Discussion Questions, Part I: Evaluating the
Flowchart and Making Your Decision

1. **How many people dropped out? Is the dropout rate too large?**

    a. 100 people who screened in as having depressive symptoms dropped out; they didn't want to participate. That means 33% dropped out (100 out of 300). That's a lot of people.

    b. The dropout is very large, but that sounds like about what happened in the IMPACT study too. Maybe this is just what's expected?

    c. We have to figure out why so many people discontinue.

2. **How many people improved? Is the number of people who improved large enough?**

    a. 43% (43 out of 100) got better with treatment. It doesn't sound large. I think I'd want 75%–80% to improve if I give them a treatment.

    b. Therapy is a people science. One therapy isn't going to work for everyone. 43% sounds good to me. The problem has to be attacked from different directions, with different psychotherapies and types of services anyway.

    c. Maybe this community has a lot of ongoing stressors and not that many people will recover, and a low rate like 43% is pretty good. Plus, it's about the result that the IMPACT study got for use of medications and therapy.

    d. When you compare 43% of intervention participants improving with 15% of usual care participants, the difference is only 28%. This just says the intervention is good for something, but not that much. I'm assuming that usual care means no intervention is given in the clinic, but if the patient has complaints, the doctor refers them out to get mental health care. I'd evaluate other therapies and compare them with this one.

3. **Who is left out of the study? What is being missed?**

    a. The people who need help the most may be the ones being left out of the study. There's the 33% who for some unknown reason didn't agree to participate. They screened in as having depressive symptoms. They need help, but they're gone, possibly because we're not offering the form of help they need.

    b. These could be the ones who work three jobs, have a lot of denial or feel stigma, or don't know what depression is and don't think they have anything.

c. A lot of Asian immigrants think that these problems are just how immigrant life is, and they have to endure. They don't know there's treatment and that it's not normal. They also feel bad letting their family and friends know they have failed—that's how they're thinking about it. They're depressed because they can't keep a job for long, and they blame themselves.

d. The PHQ-9 might have missed a lot of people, too, such as those who have more somatic symptoms, or don't understand all the questions, or endorse the answers very low even though their depression is more severe. This means there are people not even on the flowchart who were left out.

e. It'd be great to know how many who have depression are actually not detected with the PHQ-9. Chinese clinicians with a lot of experience should be the ones to assess the immigrants, based on their experience and not only based on the DSM-5. The results of their assessment could be compared with the PHQ-9 results.

f. There's an ethnocentrism issue. If how Chinese people experience and express depression is different from Whites [i.e., a different construct], then using the PHQ-9 and a European-based intervention is ethnocentric. If we use these, we assume they apply. We can find out how well they perform, but there's never an opening to what other symptoms and experiences there are that should have been considered. We'll never know who wasn't reached, true levels of depression, and culture-based interventions that could be more effective. We'd never even know the true levels of disparities.

4. **What is your decision? Will you adopt it? Justify your decision.**

    a. Because it's a randomized trial, we can be pretty sure that the intervention is responsible for the lowered symptoms. We have a treatment that definitely works. I'd adopt it.

    b. Even though the study has internal validity because it's randomized, I wouldn't adopt it, because 28% more people getting better isn't a lot.

    c. I wouldn't adopt it, because the evidence can't be generalized to Chinese speakers. The intervention was developed and provided in English. The study sample of English speakers isn't representative of people who speak only or mostly Chinese. The intervention needs to be translated, maybe modified, and then evaluated for Chinese immigrants before I would adopt it.

d. I wouldn't adopt it, because I'd want to test and compare with other interventions first. I wonder, "Wouldn't any reasonable intervention that's tested get this rate of people improving?" I'm not convinced that the therapy used, the support group, is that helpful.

e. I wouldn't either. A lot of people are left out, such as the 33% who dropped out and all those who may have depression but didn't get screened in with the PHQ-9. That's a lot of people who need care who aren't going to get it under this model.

f. I would adopt it, because from my experience in the Asian community, immigrants would much rather go to a support group than individual therapy. The support group normalizes what they're going through as immigrants and is less stigmatizing to attend. I see it as culturally sensitive, and this RCT shows it has good results.

Discussion Questions, Part II: Making a Final Decision

1. **What is your decision now? Will you adopt it? If yes, are there steps you would take to ensure effectiveness?**

    a. I still hesitate, but the research findings argue for how important it is for Chinese immigrants to have integrated care treatments. Primary care sounds like the way to reach this population. I would adopt it for sure. The results are good enough to work with.

    b. I would adopt it too. I'd make sure the EBP is carefully translated and that a team of clinicians and social workers fluent in Chinese makes the educational and intervention materials meaningful and accessible.

    c. I would also make sure the depression questionnaire we use for monitoring and tracking outcomes is understandable and relevant to the symptoms patients are having. I see no reason why we can't have a couple of blank items to write in the somatic or other symptoms that each patient is dealing with and check to see whether those are improving over time.

    d. Even though there's a need, I still wouldn't adopt it. Everything that was said earlier, about the evidence not being applicable to Chinese speakers, about the intervention and assessment questionnaires not being culturally relevant, and the results showing that not that many people were helped, it's still all true. We can wait for the dissemination and implementation researchers to take it a bit further before we use it.

e. I think we should be our own researchers. Otherwise, we may have to wait 10 or 20 years or forever. I would start with one team, like one care manager, one psychiatrist, and one expert physician first. They'd work with a few primary care physicians. We can prepare the intervention in Chinese and evaluate it ourselves before expanding to the whole clinic.

Activity 5.1 Answers   **Evaluate IMPACT Using CBPR Guidelines**

How Students Answered

1. **Answer each of the 25 questions based on what you know about the IMPACT study. There is no right answer. Most answers will be low, because IMPACT was an RCT.**

    1. **Participants and the Nature of their Involvement:**

    a. 1 – There is only a general description of the participants.

    b. 1 – The participants, both intervention and control, would have at least a little bit of knowledge about their community's mental health and services needs.

    c. 0 – No, the defined community do not participate in the research process.

    d. 0 – There is no attention to offsetting barriers to participation or finding out why so many patients were not interested or dropped out.

    e. 0 – There is no attention to establishing an understanding of the researcher's commitment to the issue.

    f. 0 – Community participants are not enabled to contribute to the research process.

    2. **Origin of the Research Question:**

    a. 0 – No, the issue was posed by the researchers alone.

b. N/A – It's not known whether the participants or primary care providers and administrators support the research.

3. **Purpose of the Research:**

a. 0 – No, there is no provision for a learning process.

b. 0 – No, there's nothing set up for participants and primary care providers to collaborate with external resources.

c. 1 – There's no empowerment objective in the study. It just makes available a treatment (meds and/or therapy) that wasn't available before. You could argue that Problem Solving Therapy helps the individual change something in their own life, but not at the level of addressing determinants of health in the community.

d. 0 – There is no consideration of combined political, social, and economic determinants of health. This is a person-centered intervention made available to improve only health services, which is a determinant of health.

4. **Process and Contextual/Methodological Implications:**

a. 0 – There is no use of community knowledge at any phase of research.

b. 0 – There is no opportunity for community participants for learning about research.

c. 1 – There is low opportunity for the researchers to learn about the community issue. They only learn if their intervention works and for what proportion of the sample.

d. 0 – It's a predetermined method, since it's an RCT. No flexibility is described.

e. 0 – No procedures for appraising experiences during implementation are described.

f. 0 – Participants are not involved in data analysis and interpretation.

5. **Opportunities to Address the Issue of Interest:**

a. 0 – The research process isn't explicitly aligned with the potential for learning by the defined community, whether participants or the medical providers.

b. 0 – The research process is not aligned with potential for action by the defined community.

c. Unknown – No commitment to social actions based on learning through the research is discussed in the article. It's unknown whether the clinics that were the study sites would be adopting IMPACT if the findings are positive.

6. **Nature of the Research Outcomes:**

a. 2 – There is about equal benefit for researchers/external bodies and the community, given that IMPACT will be implemented in clinics in the future and will help some people.

b. 0 – Nothing is foreseen about resolving any differences between researchers and community participants in the interpretation of the results.

c. 0 – Ownership of the research data definitely belongs to the researchers.

d. 0 – Dissemination of research results is in the hands of the researchers. The participants should know, when they give consent to participate, that their data is being collected, but that is all.

2. **Would it have been more fruitful (i.e., eventually more effective) to develop an integrated care intervention for depression in older adults using a CBPR approach (i.e., rather than just taking IMPACT to test on them)?**

a. Yes, it would likely be more effective, because the community would have a lot of ideas on what type of interventions should be developed and tested. They may also know why some patients don't want any treatment and aren't answering the screening questionnaires, so that something can be done to reach these people who aren't getting care. It's a little too late when you take an intervention like meds and PST and offer people only this, even if it looks like it works fine for a good number of people. This is the epistemic violence issue; we're assuming what we know is best. Plus, it's the medical model and insurance industry driving this—the use of meds and brief behavioral and cognitive therapies.

b. Yes, I think that community professionals and community members could give a lot of input and be allowed to lead in how to identify or create the best intervention or interventions for their own community. They could be told about IMPACT and consider it, but if only IMPACT is ever used and we don't explore other approaches to depression treatment for older adults, we wouldn't ever know how limiting IMPACT is, such as who it isn't reaching and what those people need. A problem with evidence-based practice is that it can limit knowledge about diversity.

3. **Let's say you still wish to conduct IMPACT as an RCT but incorporate some elements of a CBPR approach. Find at least three elements from Green's list and note how exactly you would incorporate them into your study.**

Here are sample answers for incorporating 1c, 1d, 4a, and 4e.

1c. I would let interested members of the community participate in the research process by: (a) forming an advisory board of patients who can let us know how to improve recruitment, interpret what the findings mean (whether they're actually good or not), give ideas for what other interventions should be tested when results are interpreted, and give ideas for changes in how IMPACT is implemented in the future, with quality improvements for the patients, and (b) forming a couple of focus groups, one for intervention participants and one for control group participants, to ask them how their services are going for them and what small or big changes could be introduced to get them and others better care for depression.

1d. To offset barriers for those who were underrepresented in the past studies, I would try to interview a few patients who left their screening instrument blank and a few of each who dropped out in the other phases and ask them why! I would make sure I interview a handful from each racial/ethnic group, low-income and higher income, who had lower and higher total screening scores, etc.

4a. To apply knowledge of community participants in planning, implementation, and evaluation, I would ask them for input on (a) what other outcomes are important to them and should be included in the study, such as whether there's anything beyond symptom levels and how many are using psychotherapy, which are important and we're missing altogether; (b) whether the instruments have the right content, such as whether the

Hopkins Symptom Checklist is appropriate for evaluating depression outcomes; and (c) what we did well in the study and what's missing both in the intervention and the research that can be done in the next study.

4e. As a procedure to appraise experiences during implementation, I would interview a few care managers, a few doctors, the psychiatrist, and a good number of patients to find out what's going well and what's not. I'd especially be sure to interview both patients who dropped out after a couple of sessions and those who made it to the end.

Activity 5.3 Answers   **Test Your Understanding of the Chapter**

Answers: 1. False, 2. True, 3. True, 4. False, 5. True, 6. False, 7. True, 8. True, 9. False, 10. False, 11. True, 12. True.

REFERENCES

Ethnocentrism, Epistemic Violence, and Reductionist Science

Dasen, P. R. (2012). Emics and etics in cross-cultural psychology: Towards a convergence in the study of cognitive styles. In T. M. S. Tchombe, A. B. Nsamenang, H. Keller, & M. Fülöp (Eds.), *Cross-cultural psychology: An Africentric perspective* (pp. 55–73). Design House.

Berry, J. W., & Dasen, P. (Eds.) (1974). *Culture and cognition: Readings in cross-cultural psychology.* Methuen.

Barger, K. (2019), *Ethnocentrism: What is it? Why are people ethnocentric? What is the problem? What can we do about it?* Indiana University Indianapolis. https://anthkb.sitehost.iu.edu/ethnocen.htm

Kuhn, T. (2012). *The structure of scientific revolutions (50th anniversary edition).* University of Chicago Press. (First published 1962)

Merriam-Webster. (n.d.). Merriam-Webster.com dictionary. Retrieved January 10, 2021 from https://www.merriam-webster.com/

Polanyi, M. (2012). *Personal knowledge: Towards a post-critical philosophy.* University of Chicago Press. (First published in 1958)

Shiva, V. (1988). Reductionist science as epistemological violence. In Nandy, A. (Ed.), *Science, hegemony and violence: A Requiem for modernity* (pp. 232–256). Oxford University Press.

Spivak, G. C. (1988). *Can the subaltern speak?* Macmillan.

Jhally, S., Talreja, S., Said, E., Smith, J., McCarthy, S., Greene, V., Monahan, T. Watson, N., & Soar, M. (2012). Edward Said on Orientalism [Video]. Youtube. https://www.youtube.com/watch?v=fVC8EYd_Z_g

PHQ-9 and IMPACT (Discussions 5.1, 5.2, 5.3)

Abe-Kim, J., Takeuchi, D. T., Hong, S., Zane, N., Sue, S., Spencer, M. S., Appel, H., Nicdao, E., & Alegría, M. (2007). Use of mental health-related services among immigrant and US-born Asian Americans: Results of the National Latino and Asian American Study. *American Journal of Public Health*, 97(1), 91–98.

American Psychiatric Association. (2013). *Diagnostic and statistical manual of mental disorders* (5th ed.).

Areán, P., Ayalon, L., Hunkeler, E., Lin, E. H. B., Tang, L., Harpole, L., Hendrie, H., Williams, J. W., Jr., & Unützer, J. (2005). Improving depression care for older, minority patients in primary care. *Medical Care*, 43(4), 381–390.

Areán, P. A., Gum, A. M., Tang, L., & Unützer, J. (2007). Service use and outcomes among elderly persons with low incomes being treated for depression. *Psychiatric Services*, 58(8), 1057–1064.

Areán, P., Hegel, M., Vannoy, S., Fan, M., & Unüzter, J. (2008). Effectiveness of problem-solving therapy for older, primary care patients with depression: Results from the IMPACT Project. *The Gerontologist*, 48(3), 311–323.

Chen. S., Chiu, H., Xu, B., Ma Y., Jin, T., Wu, M. & Conwell, Y. (2009). Reliability and validity of the PHQ-9 for screening late-life depression in Chinese primary care. *International Journal of Geriatric Psychiatry*, 25, 1127–1133.

Chen, T. M., Huang, F. Y., Chang, C., & Chung, H. (2006). Using the PHQ-9 for depression screening and treatment monitoring for Chinese Americans in primary care. *Psychiatric Services*, 57(7), 976–981.

Green, L. W. (2001). From research to "best practices" in other settings and populations. *American Journal of Health Behavior*, 25(3), 165–178.

Hong, G. K., Lee, B. S., & Lorenzo M. K. (1995). Somatization in Chinese American clients: Implications for psychotherapeutic services. *Journal of Contemporary Psychotherapy*, *25*(2), 105–118.

Huang, R. Y., Chung, H., Kroenke, K., Delucchi, K. L., & Spitzer, R. L. (2006). Using the Patient Health Questionniare-9 to measure depression among racially and ethnically diverse primary care patients. *Journal of General and Internal Medicine*, *21*(6), 547–552.

Hunkeler, E., Katon, W., Tang, L., Williams, J. W., Jr., Kroenke, K., Lin, E. H. B., Harpole, L. H., Areán, P., Levine, S., Grypma, L. M., Hargreaves, W. A., & Unützer, J. (2006). Long term outcomes from the IMPACT randomised trial for depressed elderly patients in primary care. *British Medical Journal (Clinical Research Edition)*, *332*(7536), 259–263.

John, D. A., de Castro, A. B., Martin, D. P., Duran, B., & Takeuchi, D. T. (2012). Does an immigrant health paradox exist among Asian Americans? Associations of nativity and occupational class with self-rated health and mental disorders. *Social Science & Medicine*, *75*(12), 2085–2098.

Kroenke, K., Spitzer, R. L., & Williams, J. B. (2001). The PHQ-9: Validity of a brief depression severity measure. *Journal of General Internal Medicine*, *16*(9), 606–613.

Kroenke, K., Spitzer, R. L., & Williams, J. B. (2003). The Patient Health Questionnaire-2: Validity of a two-item depression screener. *Medical Care*, *41*(11), 1284–1294.

Kung, W. (2004). Cultural and practical barriers to seeking mental health treatment for Chinese Americans. *Journal of Community Psychology*, *32*(1), 24–37.

Lai, B. P. Y., Tang, A. K. L., Lee, D. T. S., Yip, A. S. K., & Chung, T. K. H. (2010). Detecting postnatal depression in Chinese men: A comparison of three instruments. *Psychiatry Research*, *180*(2–3), 80–85.

Mak, W., & Zane, N. (2004). The phenomenon of somatization among community Chinese Americans. *Social Psychiatry and Psychiatric Epidemiology*, *39*(12), 967–975.

Parker, G., Chan, B., Tully, L., & Eisenbruch, M. (2005). Depression in the Chinese: The impact of acculturation. *Psychological Medicine*, *35*(10), 1475–1483.

Takeuchi, D. T., Zane, N., Hong, S., Chae, D. H., Gong, F., Gee, G. C., Walton, E., Sue, S., & Alegría M. (2007). Immigration-related factors and mental disorders among Asian Americans. *American Journal of Public Health*, *97*(1), 84–90.

Unützer, J., Katon, W., Callahan, C. M., Williams, J. W., Jr., Hunkeler, E., Harpole, L., Hoffing, M., Della Penna, R. D., Noël, P. H., Lin, E. H. B., Areán, P. A., Hegel, M. T., Tang, L., Beline, T. R., Oishi, S., Langston, C., & IMPACT Investigators. (2002). Collaborative

Care management of late-life depression in the primary care setting: A randomized controlled trial. *Journal of the American Medical Association, 288*(22), 2836–2845.

Wong, R., Wu, R., Guo, C., Lam, J. K., & Snowden, L. R. (2012). Culturally sensitive depression assessment for Chinese American immigrants: Development of a comprehensive measure and a screening scale using an item response approach. *Asian American Journal of Psychology, 3*(4), 230–253.

Yeung, A., Chang, D., Gresham, R. L., Nierenberg, A. A., & Fava, M. (2004). Illness beliefs of depressed Chinese American patients in primary care. *Journal of Nervous and Mental Disease, 192*(4), 324–327.

Yeung, A., Fung, F., Yu, S., Vorono, S., Ly, M., Wu, S., & Fava, M. (2008). Validation of the Patient Health Questionnaire-9 for depression screening among Chinese Americans. *Comparative Psychiatry, 49*(2), 211–217.

Ying, Y.-W. (1990). Explanatory models of major depression and implications for help-seeking among immigrant Chinese-American women. *Culture, Medicine and Psychiatry, 14*(3), 393–408.

Zheng, Y.-P., Lin, K. M., Takeuchi, D., Kurasaki, K. S., Wang, Y., & Cheung, F. (1997). An epidemiological study of neurasthenia in Chinese-Americans in Los Angeles. *Comprehensive Psychiatry, 38*(5), 249–259.

Community Science, CBPR, and Emic Research

Barton, A. (1968). Bringing society back in: Survey research and macro-methodology. *American Behavioral Scientist (pre-1986), 12*(2), 1–9.

Green, L. (n.d.). *Guidelines and categories for classifying participatory research projects in health.* Retrieved January 10, 2021 from http://lgreen.net/guidelines.html

Hess, J. Z. (2005). Scientists in the swamp: Narrowing the language-practice gap in community psychology. *American Journal of Community Psychology, 35*(3–4), 239–252.

Horowitz, C. R., Robinson, M., & Seifer, S. (2009). Community-based participatory research from the margin to the mainstream: are researchers prepared?. *Circulation, 119*(19), 2633–2642.

Kelly, J.G. (1971). Qualities for the community psychologist. *American Psychologist. 26*(10), 897–903.

Kelly, J. G. (2003). Science and community psychology: Social norms for pluralistic inquiry. *American Journal of Community Psychology, 32*(3–4), 2130217.

Kleinman, A. (1980). *Patients and healers in the context of culture.* University of California Press.

Kloos, B. (2005). Community science: Creating an alternative place to stand? *American Journal of Community Psychology, 35*(3–4), 259–267.

Luke, D. A. (2005). Getting the big picture in community science: Methods that capture context. *American Journal of Community Psychology, 35*(3–4), 185–200.

Merriam-Webster. (n.d.). Merriam-Webster.com dictionary. Retrieved January 10, 2021 from https://www.merriam-webster.com/

Miller, R. L., & Shinn, M. (2005). Learning from Communities: Overcoming Difficulties in Dissemination of Prevention and Promotion Efforts. *American Journal of Community Psychology, 35*, 169–183.

Rappaport, J. (2000). Community narratives: Tales of terror and joy. *American Journal of Community Psychology, 28*(1), 1–24.

Rappaport, J. (2005). Community psychology is (thank God) more than science. *American Journal of Community Psychology, 35*(3–4), 231–238.

Rappaport, J., Davidson, W. S., Wilson, M. N., & Mitchell, A. (1975). Alternatives to blaming the victim of the environment: Our places to stand have not moved the earth. *American Psychologist, 40*, 525–528.

Shinn, M., & Rapkin, B. D. (2000). Cross-level research without cross-ups in community psychology. In J. Rappaport & E. Seidman (Eds.), *Handbook of community psychology,* pp. 669–695. Kluwer Academic Publishers.

Tebes, J. K. (2005). Community science, philosophy of science, and the practice of research. *American Journal of Community Psychology, 35*(3–4), 213–230.

Tebes, J. K. (2016). Reflections on the future of community psychology from the generations after Swampscott: A commentary and introduction to the special issue. *American Journal of Community Psychology, 58*(3–4), 229–238.

Wandersman, A. (2003), Community science: Bridging the gap between science and practice with community-centered models. *American Journal of Community Psychology, 31*(3–4), 227–242.

RESOURCES

Ethnocentrism, Epistemic Violence, and Reductionist Science

Minh-ha, T. T. (1989). *Woman, Native, other: Writing postcoloniality and feminism.* Indiana University Press. Read "The Story Began Long Ago," pp. 1–2.

Young, R. (1990). *White mythologies: Writing history and the West.* Routledge. Read Chapter 1, "White Mythologies," pp. 1–20.

Young, R. J. C. (2001). Subjectivity and history: Derrida in Algeria. In *Postcolonialism: An historical introduction* (pp. 412–428). Blackwell Publishers. Read Part 1, "White Mythologies Revisited," pp. 412–416.

PHQ-9 and IMPACT (Discussions 5.1, 5.2, 5.3)

Chiu, C. F. B., & Chin, W. Y. (2018). Systematic review and Meta-analysis on the Patient Health Questionnaire-9 (PHQ-9) for depression screening in Chinese primary care patients. *Open Access Text.*

> This review article, based on four studies of the PHQ-9 among Chinese in the U.S. and Taiwan, concludes that the PHQ-9 is a sensitive screening tool in primary care settings.

> https://www.oatext.com/systematic-review-and-meta-analysis-on-the-patient-health-questionnare-9-phq-9-for-depression-screening-in-chinese-primary-care-patients.php#gsc.tab=0

University of Washington. (2020). IMPACT: Improving mood – promoting access to collaborative treatment. *Advancing Integrated Mental Health Solutions (AIMS) Center.*

> The webpage provides a history of the IMPACT collaborative care treatment for older adults and its findings.

> http://aims.uw.edu/impact-improving-mood-promoting-access-collaborative-treatment

Community Science, CBPR, and Emic Research

Bassett, A. M. (2011). Multicultural clinical interactions: The importance of the Explanatory Model (EM) concept in understanding the cultural dimensions of clinical practice. In D. Scott, J. McCarron, M. Mandere, R. Warwick, & S. Appiah, Eds., *Creative Connections,*

Exploring and Discovering Relationships. Nottingham: Nottingham Trent University, pp. 6–12. http://irep.ntu.ac.uk/id/eprint/3185/

This article explores the Explanatory Model of illness concept with the clinical case of a Hmong child with a seizure disorder.

Stoecker, R. (2005). *Research methods for community change: A project-based approach.* Sage Publications.

This book presents an applied research strategy that benefits community practitioners and academic researchers mutually. The text includes a four-step model on how to implement a community-based project and demonstrates how to render academic research relevant, rigorous, and action-oriented in pursuit of social justice objectives.

Strand, K. J., Marullo, S., Cutforth, N., Stoecker, R., & Donohue, P. (2003). *Community based research and higher education: Principles and practices.* Jossey-Bass.

This book introduces the use of community-based research in higher education. It presents a research model that engages community members with students and faculty and combines classroom learning with social action to empower community groups and prepare students for civic engagement.

Community-Campus Partnerships for Health for the Robert Wood Johnson Clinical Scholars Program. (n.d.). *Community-based participatory research (CBPR) resources.*

This document contains references on journal articles and books, as well as organizations and websites, related to CBPR.

https://www.ccphealth.org/wp-content/uploads/2017/10/rwjcsp-cbpr-resources.pdf

Community-Campus Partnerships for Health. (2006). *Developing and sustaining CBPR partnerships: A skill-building curriculum.*

This organization provides a curriculum for community-institutional partnerships with learning units on the basics of CBPR, partnership development, securing funding, disseminating results, and sustainability. Registration as a member is required to access the curricular materials.

https://www.ccphealth.org/cbpr-curriculum/

Build the Wheel. (n.d.). *Home page.*

This website is a space for people to share curricula and resources relevant to CBPR.

http://www.buildthewheel.org

University of Kansas. (n.d.). *Community tool box.*

> This website provides tools and learning resources on community-building skills for promoting healthy communities.

> http://ctb.ku.edu/en/default.aspx

Prevention Institute. (n.d.). *Prevention institute videos.*

> The Prevention Institute supports the prevention rather than treatment of disease and injury. These videos share their work to make communities safer and healthier using community-based approaches.

> https://www.preventioninstitute.org/resources/multimedia

Open Society Institute. (2008). *Visualizing information for advocacy: An introduction to information design.*

> This manual on information design supports advocacy and research for nongovernmental organizations.

> http://www.schrockguide.net/uploads/3/9/2/2/392267/infodesign.pdf

Credits

Fig. 5.1: Jürgen Unützer, et al., Flowchart of Participants in the Trial, from "Collaborative Care Management of Late-Life Depression in the Primary Care Setting: A Randomized Controlled Trial," *JAMA*, vol. 288, vol. 22. Copyright © 2002 by American Medical Association.

Fig. 5.2: Patricia A. Areán, et al., "Improving Depression Care for Older, Minority Patients in Primary Care"," *Medical Care*, vol. 43, no. 4. Copyright © 2005 by Lippincott Williams & Wilkins Inc.

CHAPTER 6

Role of Clinical Expertise
Fidelity, Dissemination, and Fit for the Client

T his chapter focuses on the clinical expertise component of the EBP model. We will learn how to apply our own and our colleagues' expertise to evaluate the suitability of an intervention reported in the literature for a client. Specifically, we will discuss the role of clinical expertise in the EBP model, the importance of fidelity (how closely your intervention matches the original EBP) and an EBP's level of dissemination, and using input from expert colleagues to assist with decision-making. The chapter also introduces dissemination and implementation research, which promise to ensure the relevance and spread of EBPs to real practice in the future.

BRIEF LECTURE 6.1

Role of Clinical Expertise in EBP

Some social work scholars discuss EBP as a way of reducing the profession's reliance on authority, which means moving away from making decisions based on practice wisdom, precedent, and the direction of colleagues. However, the EBP model explicitly gives a key role to the practitioner. The practitioner should engage with the existing research, applying their own and colleagues' practice-based knowledge to evaluate not only the quality of the evidence but also the interventions' suitability and potential effectiveness for their client. With this model, the ways in which science will come to be applied and have influence is in the hands of social workers.

To place the work of clinicians into context, it is important to note that even if clinical expertise were not part of a decision-making model, the social work practitioner nevertheless has a critical research role assigned by NASW and CSWE in light of the changing times. These times are marked by a growing intervention research literature that is purported by other professions and health care systems to have more and more relevance to social work. In this context, the social worker must engage with the evidence, whether accepting or rejecting it (such as to reduce harm to clients), and they must engage with the pressures placed on the profession due to its existence. Hence, the EBP model, as a working model that supports practice and assigns the role of clinical expert to the social worker, deserves first to be understood and then tested before its value to the work and values of the profession can be assessed.

What, then, is the role of clinical expertise and the practitioner in EBP? The EBP process relies heavily on practitioner flexibility, critical thinking, the application of research knowledge and skills, and close engagement with clients and colleagues, with all of these elements based on attention to social work values and responsibilities. This attention to the ethical standards and principles of social work is particularly important to ensure that "authority" is not handed over to the evidence (or science), but rather to client-centered factors and interests through the application of clinical expertise.

The following eight specific facets of the practitioner's role were gathered from students' reasoning about their future professional role within today's science landscape and the EBP model. The facets range from client assessment to evaluation of the chosen EBP.

1. **Comprehensive and multifaceted assessment** of the client, which depends on a strong client-worker alliance and is the basis for evaluating whether an EBP could be a good fit.
2. **Making decisions on which among many interventions reported in the literature may best address a client's unique problems and goals, cultural background, and preferences**, while balancing these concerns with the EBPs' levels of evidence.
3. **Consultation with expert colleagues to assist in choosing an intervention**, especially when one is not knowledgeable about the available EBPs or a client's diversity background or problem area.

4. Information-gathering and consultation to **decide whether training materials and resources are available and sufficient** and the amount and type of training and supervision that is required for one to provide an EBP competently (or to decide when to refer out to someone who is competent).

5. Providing information to a client as part of the **informed consent process on treatment options and their possible benefits and risks,** including the state of the evidence, its applicability to the client, and one's background for providing it.

6. **Modifying an EBP, if needed**, so it will have the best chance of being effective for the client's problems and needs, and conducting a meaningful and culturally sensitive treatment evaluation.

While the above aspects of EBP are concerned with working with clients and colleagues, there are two additional aspects of a practitioner's role related to accessing and analyzing the research evidence, which were discussed in previous chapters. These are:

7. **Formulating a search question** that can be answered empirically, defining search terms, and conducting a search that considers a variety of EBP resources to find interventions to consider for a client.

8. **Critical evaluation of the level of evidence and its generalizability** (or applicability) to the client's diversity or cultural group.

Reflection Questions

1. Which of the first six facets above relate to the practitioner's relationship with the client? Which relate to the practitioner's relationship with the research evidence? Which relate to applying clinical expertise, one's own and that of colleagues?

    . . . .

    TIP The task is to align each facet with one of the three EBP components. There may not be a neat one-on-one correspondence.

    . . . .

2. Do you agree with the above definition of a social worker's role in EBP? Does it ensure that benefits will be accrued to clients while protecting them from harm? Does implementing the EBP process in social work, compared to other fields like psychology and medicine, require a different or broader role for the clinical expert?

DISCUSSION 6.1 How Important Is It to Conduct an Intervention Exactly as It Was Conducted in the Research Study?

Jot down at least several ideas for each question below. Provide an explanation for your answers.

1. How important is it to conduct an intervention exactly as it was conducted in the study?
2. What are the ethical implications of using an EBP when it is not possible to obtain proper training and supervision and/or the intervention manual used in the study? Cite the *Code of Ethics* values and standards relevant to your answer.
3. Is it acceptable to modify an EBP or use it differently from how it was used in the research to meet a client's needs and characteristics? Cite the *Code of Ethics'* values and principles that support your position.
4. If you provide the intervention differently from how it is described in the EBP manual (i.e., you modify it), what is the likelihood of achieving the same positive outcomes reported in the study? Is it higher or lower than if you follow the manual exactly?

....

NOTE   Social work practitioners need to be aware of and deal with three concerns in EBP decision-making. First, most but not all intervention studies will have an intervention manual that describes, session by session, the intervention's objectives, procedures, and steps, which are to be followed by the clinician. You may have heard of the term *manualized*, as in, "Is that a manualized intervention?" Clinical trials, due to their structured experimental or quasi-experimental nature, should have manuals. The clinicians were trained with and must adhere to the intervention protocol laid out in the manual. Second, some EBPs are completely structured and rigid, while others allow for and rely on the practitioner's flexibility and expertise. Finally, not all EBP manuals are made available to the public by their authors. This is a question of level of dissemination, which is discussed later in this chapter.

....

See how students answered on page 248.

BRIEF LECTURE 6.2

Considering Fidelity and Dissemination

The main goal of EBP decision-making is to identify an intervention with the best chances of being helpful to a client. Once the practitioner identifies the

EBP, they can obtain training and supervision to provide the EBP, if needed, or refer out to someone who is specialized. In either case, whoever is to conduct the EBP should be competent. (Of course, the practitioner may also choose an EBP that they can more easily learn to provide rather than choosing one that is outside of their expertise.) This train of thought assumes that it is important to provide an EBP as it was delivered in the original study. Delivering the EBP as intended, in clinical research, is called *fidelity*, which means faithfulness or exactness. In the implementation of EBPs in the real world, *fidelity to treatment*, or *intervention fidelity*, means providing an intervention exactly or as close as possible to how it was provided in the original research and described in the manualized practice document. The EBP should be provided in the same way to achieve the same results. If a practitioner modifies the EBP (too much), it is no longer "evidence-based," as it is not what was researched.

To achieve fidelity and narrow one's choices of available EBPs for a client, you might ask, "Can I adequately learn this EBP to provide it with fidelity (as well as modify it competently if needed)?" The answer depends on one's training and practice background and whether the EBP's authors and promoters have made available learning materials and resources to the public. This issue of availability, in health research lingo, is called *level of dissemination*, or *readiness for dissemination*. Readiness for dissemination describes how easily an intervention can be implemented with fidelity in real-world practice settings using available training materials and implementation resources. It describes the quality and availability of these materials and services.

In support of EBP decision-making, the practitioner must assess readiness for dissemination and one's own need for training and supervision for each EBP being considered for a client. Information about the availability of resources will help answer the questions "How ready is the EBP for dissemination?" and "Can I learn it?" On a practical level, the practitioner will need to locate available resources, which may include books, training manuals and guides, videos, workshops and courses, certification programs, and supervision. These may be provided by the EBP's researchers or disseminators or by independent specialists. The practitioner will also need to obtain the original treatment protocol, when possible, from the researchers or organization that is disseminating the EBP.

⭐ ACTIVITY 6.1 Assessing Level of Dissemination

In this activity, you will practice assessing level of dissemination by finding resources for learning how to conduct two EBPs: Trauma-Focused Cognitive

Behavioral Therapy (TF-CBT) and Improving Mood-Promoting Access to Collaborative Treatment (IMPACT).

TF-CBT

Trauma-Focused CBT is a widely disseminated mental health intervention for children and youth. It is described in the following systematic review.

- Cary, C. E., & McMillen, J. C. (2012). The data behind the dissemination: A systematic review of trauma-focused cognitive behavioral therapy for use with children and youth. *Children and Youth Services Review, 34*(4), 748–757.

TF-CBT is a highly structured parent-child intervention consisting of 90-minute weekly sessions (12–20 sessions) for children and adolescents who have had single, multiple, and complex trauma experiences. It treats PTSD, depression, and a broad array of emotional and behavioral difficulties. Based on the client's readiness, the clinician moves the client through the following eight components: psychoeducation and parenting skills, relaxation, affective expression and regulation, cognitive coping, trauma narrative development and processing, in vivo gradual exposure, conjoint parent/child sessions, and enhancing safety/ future development.

Instructions

You are an MSW student starting your second year of study. You intern in a high school wellness center. Your supervisor is a licensed clinical social worker who is new in the city's mental health department and splits their time between the school and a community center for children, youth, and families. You took an 8-week academic course on CBT for depression last year and are starting to practice it with two clients. Your supervisor is providing you with supervision on CBT but, like you, has not been trained in TF-CBT. He has, however, 5 years of experience providing other therapies and working with youth and trauma. You are interested in learning and using TF-CBT with your clients.

1. Find the resources available for learning TF-CBT, the amount of training and time required, associated costs, and supervision needs. Find out if you can obtain the training and treatment manuals used in the original study. As you search, pay attention to any resources specific to using TF-CBT with different diversity and minority groups. Note what you find.
2. Consult with someone who is trained and experienced in TF-CBT. Tell them about your background and ask for guidance on the amount of

training and supervision you would need to begin providing TF-CBT to student clients. Jot down their advice.

3. Assess and describe the level of dissemination of TF-CBT. Is what's available enough for you to learn to conduct TF-CBT with competence and fidelity?

• •

TIP Start with the systematic review referenced above, which provides information on dissemination, and search the web.

• •

IMPACT & PST

IMPACT is a collaborative treatment model for depression in older adults. It is described in the following two articles.

- Unützer, J., Katon, W., Callahan, C. M., Williams, J. R., Jr., Hunkeler, E., Harpole, L., Hoffing, M., Della Penna, R. D., Noël, P. H., Lin, E. H. B., Areán, P. A., Hegel, M. T., Tang, L., Beline, T. R., Oishi, S., Langston, C., & IMPACT Investigators. (2002). Collaborative care management of late-life depression in the primary care setting: A randomized controlled trial. *Journal of the American Medical Association, 288*(22), 2836–2845.
- Areán, P., Ayalon, L., Hunkeler, E., Tang, L., Harpole, L., Hendrie, H., Williams, J. W., Jr., Unützer, J., & IMPACT Investigators. (2005). Improving depression care for older, minority patients in primary care. *Medical Care, 43*(4), 381–390.

IMPACT uses an integrated care approach, with depression treatment integrated into primary care services. The treatment team consists of a depression clinical specialist, primary care physician, and psychiatrist. IMPACT is a widely recognized EBP that is slowly being disseminated in the U.S. IMPACT was tested in a multisite randomized controlled study with 1,801 older adult patients with major depression and/or dysthymia in 18 primary care clinics in five states. Intervention group participants received a psychoeducation session and, if they decided to enter treatment, chose either an antidepressant medication or Problem-Solving Treatment, a six- to eight-session structured psychotherapy for depression that includes behavioral activation. When symptom reduction does not occur in this first step, there is change of medications or a switch from medications to PST, or vice versa. If symptom reduction still does not occur in this second step, additional treatments are considered for a third step. Evidence of effectiveness includes that 45% of intervention patients had a 50% or greater reduction in depressive symptoms from baseline, compared with 19% of usual care patients, after 12 months. Also, intervention patients compared to usual care patients had greater rates of depression treatment, more satisfaction with depression care, lower depression severity, less functional impairment, and greater quality of life.

Instructions

You are a clinical social worker working in a primary care clinic that serves low-income patients. The health organization to which your clinic belongs is considering the adoption of IMPACT for older adults who present with depression, particularly because it is an EBP known for its high level of dissemination. You agree to be part of a team to provide feedback to administrators based on evaluating the availability and quality of resources for implementing IMPACT. You are tasked with assessing the level of dissemination of PST, which you and two fellow clinical social workers will be learning and providing should IMPACT be implemented. You are told that the University of Washington has strong resources for implementing IMPACT, and another university has resources for PST specifically. You and your colleagues are very experienced in providing Cognitive Behavioral Therapy and Motivational Interviewing but do not know PST at all.

1. Find the available resources for learning PST, the amount of training and time required, and associated costs. Find out if you can obtain the training and treatment manuals used in the original study. As you search, pay attention to any resources specific to using PST with different diversity and minority groups. Note what you find.
2. Consult with someone who is trained and experienced in PST. Tell them about your background and ask for guidance on the amount of training and supervision you would need to provide PST. Jot down their advice.

Assess and describe the level of dissemination of PST. Is there everything needed for an agency to implement PST? And for you and your colleagues to learn PST?

See the answers on page 252.

BRIEF LECTURE 6.3

Dissemination and Implementation Research

This book teaches EBP as a process for the individual practitioner who is making decisions for specific clients, but EBPs may also be adopted by an agency or a group of agencies within a system of care. In this case, "readiness for dissemination" takes on a broader meaning for health care administrators and researchers, as they must ensure successful uptake involving many practitioners, cost-effectiveness, and a public health benefit. To support EBP decision-making at the organizational level, two emerging interrelated areas of health services research, *dissemination and implementation research* (or "D&I" research), are starting to provide the impetus and knowledge base for successful implementation of EBPs. These areas, a growing priority for major health-related funders, are actually subareas or activities within a *translational research* process, which moves scientific findings along a path from the laboratory to real-world practice. Although these areas of research concern an individual practitioner's decision-making less directly, awareness of these areas is important given social workers' important role in promoting or slowing the uptake of new EBPs within their agencies. This brief lecture explains dissemination and implementation research and discusses where they situate on the translational research spectrum.

• •

NOTE   Dissemination research is not the same as an intervention's *level of dissemination*, discussed above, which is concerned only with the availability of resources for learning the intervention.

• •

Dissemination Research

Dissemination is defined as "an active approach of spreading evidence-based interventions to the target audience via determined channels using planned strategies" (Rabin et al., 2008, p. 118). Dissemination research is the systematic study of processes and factors that lead to the widespread use of EBPs by target audiences. Its objective is to identify methods that advance the uptake and utilization of EBPs. Dissemination research supports external validity, as it examines whether an EBP's outcomes will hold over different settings and clients and providers, and the factors and methods that support this. Dissemination research examines the process of spreading knowledge and information.

Dissemination research as a process involves many steps. First, an intervention is tested in *efficacy trials* in controlled, experimental conditions, where highly trained and supervised professionals administer the intervention. Such efficacy trials aim to demonstrate internal validity, the ability to infer or conclude strongly that the intervention "caused" the observed positive outcomes. (In other words, does the intervention do what it was intended to do?) Once there is enough evidence of efficacy with consistent beneficial effects across multiple trials, the intervention is tested in effectiveness trials. *Effectiveness trials* take place in real practice settings, with real-world professionals administering the intervention. Generally, the settings have broad access to the populations of interest, such as schools, community-based organizations, and community health clinics. Such effectiveness trials aim to build evidence of external validity, that evidence of the intervention's efficacy can be generalized to different real-service settings and populations of clients. (In other words, how well does it do in the real world?) Once there is enough and consistent evidence of effectiveness in increasingly realistic conditions, including outcomes that last beyond the immediate postintervention evaluation, the intervention can be studied specifically for its readiness for dissemination.

Researchers will examine a broad range of factors to show an EBP's readiness for dissemination. They want evidence, for example, on cost-effectiveness, practical and significant benefits for individual clients, benefits for public health, superiority over interventions that were displaced, and lasting effects beyond a few months. They also explore resource and buy-in issues, such as physical space requirements, staffing and monetary resources, administrative and community buy-in, and the role of a healthy mission within an agency. Regarding actual treatment and training needs within an agency, they may examine whether the agency has a system for planning and monitoring client recruitment, resources for providing treatment training, technical assistance resources, treatment monitoring and evaluation tools, and cost tracking and analysis tools.

The Society for Prevention Research defined the following standards of evidence, which differentiate nicely how an intervention moves from being efficacious to effective, and finally to being ready for dissemination (Flay et al., 2005, p. 151).

> An efficacious intervention will have been tested in at least two rigorous trials that (1) involved defined samples from defined populations; (2) used psychometrically sound measures and data collection procedures; (3) analyzed their data with rigorous statistical approaches; (4) showed consistent positive effects (without serious iatrogenic effects); and (5) reported at least one significant long-term follow-up. [Note the experimental and quantitative emphasis, which support internal validity.]
>
> An effective intervention under these Standards will not only meet all standards for efficacious interventions, but also will have (1) manuals, appropriate training, and technical support available to allow third parties to adopt and implement the intervention; (2) been evaluated under real-world conditions in studies that included sound measurement of the level of implementation and engagement of the target audience (in both the intervention and control conditions); (3) indicated the practical importance of intervention outcome effects; and (4) clearly demonstrated to whom intervention findings can be generalized. [Note the real-world focus, which supports external validity.]

An intervention recognized as ready for broad dissemination under these Standards will not only meet all standards for efficacious and effective interventions, but will also provide (1) evidence of the ability to "go to scale"; (2) clear cost information; and (3) monitoring and evaluation tools so that adopting agencies can monitor or evaluate how well the intervention works in their settings. [Note the emphasis on readiness for the intervention to be put out in the real world.]

Below are two examples of specific dissemination studies.

- Lochman, J. E., Boxmeyer, C. L., Powell, N. P., Qu, L., Wells, K., & Windle, M. (2012). Coping Power dissemination study: Intervention and special education effects on academic outcomes. *Behavioral Disorders, 37*(3), 192–205.

  "This study examines whether a school-based preventive intervention for children with aggressive behavior affects children's academic outcomes when it is implemented by school counselors in a dissemination field trial" (p. 192). The Coping Power program focuses on teaching social and emotional skills, rather than intervening around academic performance, to help children make academic gains, which were measured by improvements in social and academic skills and language arts and mathematics grades. The researchers concluded that intervention effects (i.e., positive outcomes) were not as strong and broad for children who had counselors prepared with only a basic Coping Power training compared to children who had counselors prepared with an intensive one. Also, there were no significant differences in outcomes between students in and not in special education. (Note how this study was an effectiveness trial trying to determine if the intervention would be effective for different subpopulations and, at the same time, what level of training is required for successful dissemination.)

- Rebchook, G. M., Kegeles, S. M., & Huebner, D. (2006). Translating research into practice: The dissemination and initial implementation of an evidence-based HIV prevention program. *AIDS Education and Prevention, 18*(4), 119–136.

  The authors note that many HIV prevention interventions have been developed and evaluated, yet these programs make only small contributions to HIV prevention efforts, because they are not widely put into practice. In light of this, the authors explored how one such EBP for young MSM, the Mpowerment Project (MP), is being scaled up in the

U.S. Their research had three objectives: (a) describing their longitudinal study that was underway, especially issues of translating research on MP into practice; (b) presenting detailed data from 69 CBOs that are implementing MP, including characteristics of the agencies, communities, and target populations; and (c) presenting baseline data on how the agencies are implementing MP, including which intervention components they chose to implement, modify, or delete, and the implications of these adaptations. (Note that [c] is more of an implementation research question than a dissemination one.)

• •

TIP   While dissemination research serves a higher level audience, it is also useful for practitioners working with individual clients. Note how Lochman et al.'s study warns us that to use Coping Power effectively, we would need intensive training, while Rebchook et al.'s article may have useful information to help us modify Mpowerment for our client. With this in mind, in our literature search, we can look out for EBPs that have been the object of dissemination research. Let's see how this applies for implementation research.

• •

Implementation Research

Implementation is defined as "the process of putting to use or integrating evidence-based interventions within a setting" (Rabin et al., 2008, p. 118). Implementation science is an emerging field within health care that facilitates the spread of medical and psychosocial EBPs into practice settings. It is defined as "the scientific study of methods to promote the systematic uptake of research findings and other EBPs into routine practice, and, hence, to improve the quality and effectiveness of health services" (Eccles & Mittman, 2006, p. 1). The field strives to close the research-to-practice gap, to ensure that research investments have a public health impact. It was developed as researchers realized that EBPs often failed to be implemented, were not sustained in usual care, or took many years before being incorporated into usual care. For these reasons, implementation became an issue for research, and researchers set out to obtain and apply evidence about implementation, rather than allowing administrators and professionals to rely on anecdotal evidence to support their implementation of new EBPs. Implementation science is also viewed as a means for addressing health disparities among minority populations, especially for understanding the reasons for the low usage of services and treatments by minority groups and for testing implementation strategies that reduce disparities (Chinman et al., 2017).

Implementation researchers assess the processes and factors associated with successful integration of EBPs within particular settings. Specifically, they assess whether the core components of the EBP were faithfully provided in the real-world setting (i.e., the degree of fidelity of the EBP with the original study) and also work on the adaptation of EBPs to local contexts (Rabin et al., 2008). In pursuit of their goals and similar to dissemination researchers, implementation researchers view a "pipeline" approach, whereby an intervention moves from efficacy trials to effectiveness trials to application in practice. In their studies, blockages to implementation appearing in less controlled settings are detected and addressed. Blockages can include lack of knowledge, lack of skills and resources, and poor alignment of research evidence with the organization's priorities. Implementation research is thus also about how to address blockages to uptake. Below is an article that provides an example of an implementation science research agenda for a specific area of practice, school mental health.

- Owens, J. S., Lyon, A. R., Brandt, N. E., Warner, C. M., Nadeem, E., Spiel, C., & Wagner, M. (2014). Implementation science in school mental health: Key constructs in a developing research agenda. *School Mental Health*, 6(2), 99–111. http://doi.org/10.1007/s12310-013-9115-3

  "First, we provide an overview of important contextual issues to be considered when addressing research questions pertinent to the implementation of mental health interventions in schools. Next, we critically review three core implementation components: (a) professional development and coaching for school professionals regarding evidence-based practices (EBPs); (b) the integrity of EBPs implemented in schools; and (c) EBP sustainment under typical school conditions" (p. 99). For each area, the authors articulated research questions that are important for future research and the research methods that can be used to address the questions.

Implementation studies generally use mixed-methods designs to identify blockages or factors that impact the uptake of an EBP across multiple levels, including client, provider, clinic, and organization (Bauer et al., 2015). Researchers work with health care system leaders, program developers, and clients to understand the critical factors, conditions, and practical steps to ensure that an EBP will be carried out successfully in a typical service setting. An implementation strategy for an EBP may include identifying who will be responsible for specific activities, with clear definitions of each person's responsibilities, policies, procedures, and resources and training to ensure successful implementation. These strategies also involve ongoing evaluation and adjustments to increase effectiveness. Below is an example of implementation research. It is an effectiveness study in which the researchers examine implementation-related factors.

- Palinkas, L. A., Ell, K., Hansen, M., Cabassa, L., & Wells, A. (2011). Sustainability of collaborative care interventions in primary care settings. *Journal of Social Work, 11*(1), 99–117.

"We assessed patient and provider barriers and facilitators to sustainability of a collaborative depression care model for depression treatment in predominantly Hispanic diabetes patients in safety net care clinics" (p. 99). The researchers gathered interview and focus group data on the implementation and sustainability of the intervention from patients and providers at two community clinics participating in a randomized controlled effectiveness trial of the Multifaceted Depression and Diabetes Program, a culturally adapted care model. They found barriers that included patient concerns about the use of medication and provider concerns about the use of psychotherapy, increased workload for clinicians, delays in receiving outcomes data, and lack of resources to sustain the program. Facilitators were improved clinical outcomes, quality of care received, access, and satisfaction for patients. For providers, they were increased awareness and reduced anxiety, and for the clinic, it was reduced cost of care. Based on these findings, the researchers recommended changes in communication patterns among physicians and depression care providers, treatment consistent with patient preferences, routine monitoring of patient depression symptoms and treatment adherence and satisfaction, and increased resources such as stable funding, qualified staff, and technologies to facilitate provider access to treatment guidelines.

TIP   There are two ways to differentiate dissemination research and implementation research, which overlap. A first way is to think of dissemination research as a precursor of implementation research. Dissemination comes first, because we want to first know whether the EBP is worth using in a widespread manner, as in, "Does it apply to different populations?" "Is it cost-effective?" "What kind of agencies and communities is it suited for?" and "Does the EBP actually have lasting effects?" Implementation research follows, because we would pursue its actual implementation or use only after we know that the EBP is worth disseminating. A second way is to think of dissemination research as covering the study of everything (context, costs, resources, long-term effectiveness, public health benefit), while implementation research focuses narrowly on putting the EBP itself into practice, as in, "What concerns are clients having with it?" "Who needs to work with whom better in the clinic to make the EBP work?" "What do we do so that providers can conduct the intervention better?" and "What is happening such that clients are not choosing this EBP?" and "Why are the clinicians not wanting to offer it?"

A Spectrum of Translational Research

According to the Harvard Clinical and Translational Science Center, dissemination and implementation research is part of a spectrum of activities where scientific findings can lead to improvements in human health (see https://catalyst.harvard.edu/pathfinder). This Center defines a four-part (T1 to T4) "clinical and translational research spectrum," in which each part incorporates the findings, insights, and implications from the previous part. While the definition originates from medical science, it is also useful for conceptualizing the translation of mental and behavioral health research, especially the important role of dissemination and implementation research. Here are the four parts:

- **T1: Translation to Humans** of basic science findings using research approaches, including:
  - Phase 1 Clinical Trials, which answer the question, "Is the treatment safe in human beings?" using very small samples.
- **T2: Translation to Patients** using research approaches, including:
  - Phase 2 Clinical Trials, which answer the question, "Does the treatment work?" in small groups of patients who are given the same treatment;
  - Phase 3 Clinical Trials, which answer the question, "Is it better than what is already available?" generally through large, randomized samples across multiple study sites.
- **T3: Translation to Practice** using research approaches, including:
  - Phase 4 Clinical Trials, which answer the question, "What else do we need to know?" by examining the longer term impact of treatments that are generally already available to the public, including safety and rare side effects, impact on quality of life, and cost-effectiveness;
  - Health Services Research, including dissemination and implementation research;
  - Clinical Outcomes Research, which aims to optimize an intervention's end results and benefits to the patient and society by focusing not only on the intervention but also associated services and resources, enforcement of policies and regulations that impact use and response, geographical accessibility, convenience and timeliness, and patient preferences.
- **T4: Translation to Population Health** using research approaches, including:
  - Population-Based Outcome Studies, which investigate the health outcomes of groups of individuals (e.g., residents of a particular neighborhood, a racial/ethnic or SES group, or a whole population of a nation) to improve health and address health disparities;

      o   Social Determinants of Health Research, which examines the impact of the intervention and social factors such as personal characteristics (e.g., race, ethnicity, culture, gender identity, sexual preference), economic resources (e.g., education, employment, housing, income), environmental resources (e.g., transportation systems, access to healthy foods), and adverse experiences (e.g., trauma, interpersonal violence, bereavement).

••

NOTE   Observational studies are also a part of T2 and T3. Studies using a community-based participatory research (CBPR) method, which was discussed in Chapter 5, are also a part of T2, T3, and T4.

••

⌘   Case Paper Task 6.1

Gather Input from Clinical Experts on the Three EBPs You Are Considering for Your Client and Write the *Evaluation of Experts* Section

Instructions: Integrate clinical expertise into your decision-making by consulting with an expert who knows about each EBP and your client's population group. This could be your clinical supervisor and/or other mental health professionals at your agency. Provide a thorough description of your client and ask for their assessment of the suitability of the intervention. Ask also if they would make any adaptations to the EBP!

Below are examples of the *Evaluation of Experts* section for the first of three EBPs from Laura's and Eddie's case papers. You can see other examples in the full case papers in Appendix B (p. 311) and Appendix C (p. 323).

Case Paper Instructions:

Review of EBP #1 (6–7 paragraphs, 9 points)

This section is based on your review of two empirical research articles and other information found online, in print, and through interviews.

Evaluation of Experts: State whether the intervention is appropriate for your client based on a discussion with your supervisor or another experienced clinician, and also, if you wish, on your own experience and evaluation. State how it would or would not be appropriate and useful for your client, including modifications to the intervention, if any, that you would make for your client. (*1 paragraph, 2 points*)

Laura's Example

Needs Strengthening

Review of EBP #1: Cognitive Behavioral Therapy for Adolescents
Evaluation of Experts

My supervisor has not used CBT-A before but has extensive experience working in family counseling with Latinx teenagers and parents. She said that brief cognitive therapies are suitable for our clients at our school site because they fit within the 8-week maximum number of sessions. She also commented that cognitive behavioral therapies have some utility for everyone.

How would you strengthen the above? Has the supervisor considered closely who the client is and how the therapy can be helpful? Is it a useful contribution of clinical expertise?

Well-Written

As you read the below example, reflect on whether the expertise provided is useful to decision-making.

Review of EBP #1: Cognitive Behavioral Therapy for Adolescents
Evaluation of Experts

My internship supervisor, who is an LCSW, holds a school social work credential, and has practiced CBT with children for over 10 years, informed me that CBT-A would be effective in the school setting. He believes that CBT-A can be especially useful in assisting the client in building self-esteem through a cognitive behavioral lens, including in helping the client to understand interpersonal problems via awareness of her own thoughts and feelings. Although MCC does not typically have students remain in treatment past eight sessions, this specific client may require the longer period of assistance that is required for the typical CBT-A for depression (D. Pratt, Personal Communication, November 8, 2019).

Eddie's Example

Well-Written

As you read the below example, notice the clinical social worker's recommendation to combine PET with CBT and his reasoning. This would be a modification to PET and CBT (i.e., not following the protocols and manuals strictly).

Review of EBP #1: Prolonged Exposure Therapy
Evaluation of Experts

A Licensed Clinical Social Worker (LCSW) at the Veterans Administration (VA) with whom I consulted supports using PET because my client has shown the desire to use modalities that are more experiential than intellectual or cognitive in approach. This clinician has been using PET with clients with PTSD for many years. The clinician also recommends that PET may be a good therapy alongside Cognitive Behavioral Therapy (CBT) so that the client can have a safe space to face and process his traumas directly, but in a moderated fashion, at a pace that the client is able to handle without it being the sole focus of his therapy, given that exposure alone can be daunting and lead to dropout (J. Worth, personal communication, January 4, 2020).

⌘   ## Case Paper Task 6.2

....

Assess Your Ability to Learn the Three EBPs You Are Considering for Your Client and Write the *Feasibility of Learning & Applying Intervention Correctly* Section

Instructions: Find information about books, resources, manuals, and trainings available for you to learn the EBPs and become competent enough to provide them to your client (i.e., the availability is the EBP's level of dissemination). You can also consult with clinicians who are experts in the specific EBPs to gain their advice on whether and how you can provide the interventions with fidelity. This assessment is an aspect of your clinical expertise (i.e., awareness of your own competence).

Below are examples of the *Feasibility of Learning and Applying Intervention Correctly* section for the first of three EBPs from Laura's and Eddie's case papers. You can see other examples in the full case papers in Appendix B (p. 311) and Appendix C (p. 323).

Case Paper Instructions:

Review of EBP #1 (6–7 paragraphs, 9 points)

This section is based on your review of two empirical research articles and other information found online, in print, and through interviews.

Evaluation of Feasibility & Applying Intervention Correctly: State the probability that you can learn the intervention and apply it correctly and effectively. To do this, gather information on the amount of materials (e.g., manuals, books, and videos) and trainings made available to the public to evaluate whether it is feasible for you to learn to conduct the intervention. If you wish, you can also comment on the intervention's overall level of readiness for dissemination and implementation. (*1 paragraph, 2 points*)

Laura's Example

Needs Strengthening

Review of EBP #1: Cognitive Behavioral Therapy for Adolescents
Evaluation of Feasibility

CBT is used by many counselors at my school-based clinic. All of them would support me with it when I start to use it with my client. My supervisor told me that we have many workbooks and manuals that I can follow week by week. Since this is a good therapy for my client, I can do my best to give it a try without specific training.

How would you strengthen the above? Does it cover the requested content? Is an ethical question raised?

Well-Written

As you read the below example, consider whether the assessment is better justified given the available learning resources and plan. Would you agree that skipping the online training would be acceptable?

Review of EBP #1: Cognitive Behavioral Therapy for Adolescents

Evaluation of Feasibility

CBT is commonly used at MCC and in MCC's school-based clinics. I have had a 10-week academic course on CBT for depression in adults and have practiced CBT with adults in my previous internship. I can obtain a 21-hour online training on CBT with children and adolescents (Feeling Good Institute, n.d.). However, with the CBT-A manuals that have been provided to me by MCC, I feel confident in implementing the intervention with fairly high fidelity given close guidance from my supervisor and additional consultation from other clinicians at MCC.

Eddie's Example

Well-Written

As you read, ask yourself if enough content on level of dissemination is provided? Is mentioning the VA because the writer had completed a previous internship there sufficient? Would it be helpful to know the length of time and cost to become trained or with what background one could self-train?

Review of EBP #1: Prolonged Exposure Therapy

Feasibility of Learning and Applying Intervention Correctly

PET is offered at the VA as a regular part of their PTSD treatment offerings. The client is not a veteran, but my Field Instructor (FI) is trained in PET. It is important to note that whether or not PET is ultimately chosen, a culturally sensitive approach by a licensed therapist that is well-informed of race-based trauma (as well as PET) will provide the best possibilities of success (Williams et al., 2014). Overall, the feasibility of learning and applying this intervention effectively by a licensed therapist is high. I am not a licensed therapist, but my supervisor is well-versed in PET and may let me shadow him in PET sessions with the client's permission. My internship time at TCC is limited, with three months remaining, so instead of patient-splitting, I will transition this client to my supervisor sooner rather than later, especially if PET is chosen.

ANSWERS

Discussion 6.1 Answers **How Important Is It to Conduct an Intervention Exactly as It Was Conducted in the Research Study?**

How Students Answered

1. **How important is it to conduct an intervention exactly as it was conducted in the study?**

    a. It's very important. We want to use the exact intervention that was given in the study. Otherwise, our service wouldn't be based on the evidence. The evidence isn't on an intervention we tweaked.

    b. I think the intervention is still evidence-based even if we change it a bit. For example, my client can't make it in every week like people in the study, or she misses every other appointment. She could also have a substance use problem along with depression, and the people in the study didn't. I'll have to do what it takes to make the intervention useful for her.

    c. It's important, but I think it would be impossible to conduct it exactly the same way. I'd have to get the intervention manual that was used in the study and try to follow it as closely as possible.

    d. I think it's important to *not* conduct it in the same way, because my client is not the average client who was in the study. We have to use our judgment. Otherwise, the intervention may not be effective anyway.

    e. We should try to provide it the same way as much as possible, but we need to deviate if the client has different problems and viewpoints. The *Code of Ethics* says social workers should "demonstrate competence in the provision of services that are sensitive to clients' cultures and to differences among people and cultural groups" (1.05b). I'm responsible for using the EBP in a culturally sensitive manner.

    f. We have to reach a balancing point. We should try to provide the intervention in the spirit of how it was defined, but not get carried away so that it's not addressing what the client needs. We have to keep in mind that we're there to help the client—and not get carried away with the research. That's our job as social workers.

2. **What are the ethical implications of using an EBP when it is not possible to obtain proper training and supervision and/or the intervention manual used in the study? Cite the Code of Ethics values and standards relevant to your answer.**

    a. If we can't get trained in it, then we shouldn't use it. There's an ethical value called "competence" that says social workers should only practice within what they know and have been trained in. We can tell the client about the EBPs we found and refer them to someone who's trained. The *Code of Ethics* says that we should refer out to other professionals when "specialized knowledge or expertise is needed to serve clients fully" (1.16).

    b. The *Code of Ethics* says social workers have a responsibility for "provid[ing] services ... only within the boundaries of their education, training, license, certification, consultation, supervised experience, or other relevant professional experience" (1.04). This means we need to be trained in it.

    c. If my supervisor has 20 years of CBT experience, it would be okay for him to get the manual from the study and give any CBT treatment. As a student, I would take a course and get supervision before I start any therapy that's new for me.

    d. The *Code of Ethics* also says, "[For] an emerging area of practice, social workers should exercise careful judgment and take responsible steps (including appropriate education, research, training, consultation, and supervision) to ensure the competence of their work and to protect clients from harm." This means it's okay if we get training and support, and we are responsible for deciding if we are prepared enough. The "emerging" part means we really *should* use supervision and consultation and be very careful about what we're doing.

    e. We should consult with experts on every step—how much training I need given my background, how much supervision I should get—to make sure we're going to do it right. The *Code of Ethics* says that social workers should "keep themselves informed about colleagues' areas of expertise and competencies" and "seek advice and counsel ... when such advice and counsel is in the best interest of clients" (2.05).

    f. Another ethical consideration is informed consent. When it isn't possible to get the perfect training and the manual, we should let our clients know. The *Code of Ethics* says we should "inform clients of the purpose of the services, risks related to the services, limits to services ... reasonable alternatives" (1.03a). This is the key, to discuss everything—how I might change parts of the intervention, risks if the intervention doesn't help them, the different evidenced-based and non-evidence-based choices open to them, etc.

g. Whether or not you need to get and follow the manual depends on the intervention. Some EBPs are very specific, such as you have to teach the teens one topic in week one, another topic in week two, all with given activities and teaching materials. For these, you need the manual. Other EBPs are more general, such as you give problem-solving treatment for 10 weeks and you have to include behavioral activation. For these, you may not need the manual, although it's always helpful.

h. I would talk to someone who's an expert in the EBP and ask them what's the minimum training and what kind of supervision I need to start providing a new EBP.

i. I would definitely get the treating manuals for the EBPs I found in the literature. How else would I know what exactly was tested?

3. **Is it acceptable to modify an EBP or use it differently from how it was used in the research to meet a client's needs and characteristics? Cite the Code of Ethics values and principles that support your position.**

a. It's definitely acceptable, because we have a primary commitment to promoting our clients' well-being (1.01), and that could mean not using whatever we find blindly, even if it is well researched and supposed to be effective for my client's background. There is a lot of leeway and responsibility for social workers to make the best decision for the client.

b. We have the responsibility to modify it to account for cultural differences. The *Code* says that we have to provide services "sensitive to clients' cultures" (1.05b). For example, I might integrate more family-oriented goals and activities rather than individually focused work, or I might alter an outcome scale so it includes items that are meaningful to my client's background and their goals.

c. I would find several different EBPs that have good evidence and that fit my client, then choose the one that requires the least modification.

d. If I have to modify it a lot, I'm not sure I could still say that I'm pro-viding the intervention that was studied. We have to be deliberate and clear about what we're doing and the responsibilities and risks we're taking toward our client. I might still use it if there's nothing else, but I wouldn't say I gave the intervention in the article.

e. If I modify it a lot, I should monitor that it is helping the client in the ways that the client wants. One of our responsibilities is evaluation. The *Code of Ethics* states that social workers should monitor and evaluate our practice interventions (5.02). We should do this anyway, *whether or not* we modify the EBP.

f. I see it as an informed consent issue (1.03). I'd let the client know that I'll be adapting an intervention that has research evidence—and that the intervention hasn't been studied with people who are like them or have the same exact goals—[and ask,] "Is this okay with you?" I'd also give a couple of different options of EBPs, so they can choose.

g. There's no clear answer. As social workers, we have to consider the intervention, how it was designed, whom it was researched on, if it fits the client's needs, and then we make a decision. It's not an exact science. That's why we have a code of ethics to guide our thinking.

h. It's a matter of "self-determination" (1.02). Let the client decide. A social worker helps clients to "identify and clarify their goals" (1.02), which is telling them different therapy options for their goals, and how an EBP may or may not fit what they are looking for. For example, "Here's an EBP that has been found to be useful for the kind of prob-lem you have, but we're limited to 6 sessions, and the EBP researched was for 10 sessions. We can change it a bit. Do you want to try it?"

i. I would tell the client that the intervention is evidence-based and how much evidence it has or how new it is but that it doesn't have that much evidence for her ethnic group and that I want to adapt it to address her goals and background. The *Code of Ethics* reminds us that we "should not participate in, condone, or be associated with dishonesty, fraud, or deception" (4.05). Clients should know about the research and what agencies are doing. They should not be kept in the dark, especially because they are dependent on us.

4. **If you provide the intervention differently from how it is described in the EBP manual (i.e., you modify it), what is the likelihood of achieving**

the same positive outcomes reported in the study? Is it higher or lower than if you follow the manual exactly?

a. If I modify the intervention, there should be a lower chance of having the positive results observed in the study. This is because the study results are based on the researchers' manualized intervention, and they don't apply to my modified version.

b. I would expect a higher likelihood of having positive results, because I'm changing the intervention so that it works better for my client. I'm doing this to make sure I get at least as good of results as in the study.

c. I think we have to remember that study outcomes are reported for the average participant, not for every single one of them. We don't know how well the original EBP will work, and we don't know how well our modified EBP will work either.

d. I agree that it's all a moving target. Our job is to be very clear about what we are modifying and for what reason. We should monitor the outcomes that we are targeting for that client. We can give before, during, and after tests to make sure we're going in the right direction. We can compare later whether we did better than the study results. This is the clinical expertise part—taking leadership and monitoring and evaluating the client's response to the intervention.

e. We might get a worse outcome if we modify the intervention, but if we don't modify it when it really looks like we need to, that's irresponsible and unethical toward our client.

Activity 6.1 Answers **Assessing Level of Dissemination**

TF-CBT

1. Find the resources available for learning TF-CBT, the amount of training and time required, associated costs, and supervision needs. Find out if you can obtain the training and treatment manuals used in the original study. As you search, pay attention to any resources specific to using TF-CBT with different diversity and minority groups.

    • *Overview:* Cohen et al.'s (2017) version of TF-CBT is the most well-known and is the branded version. It is manualized, has an online course based on it, and has a certification program that includes and begins with taking the online course.

- o Note that there are other manualized child-focused trauma treatments using many of the same intervention components as this one, and they have also been evaluated in clinical trials and disseminated.

- *Treatment Manual:* Cohen, Judith A., Mannarino, Anthony P., & Deblinger, E. (2017). *Treating trauma and traumatic grief in children and adolescents* (2nd Ed.). Guilford Press. ($45)

  - o The course offered by the Medical University of South Carolina (MUSC), described below, is based on this manual.

- *Edited Book:* Cohen, Judith A., Mannarino, Anthony P., & Deblinger, E. (2016). *Trauma-Focused CBT for children and adolescents: Treatment applications.* Guilford Press. ($28)

  - o According to the book description, the book shows how assessment and treatment can be tailored to serve different client needs while maintaining overall fidelity to the TF-CBT model.

  - o According to the book description, the book presents applications for Latino and Native American children and tailoring TF-CBT to varying developmental levels and cultural backgrounds.

- *Online course based on the treatment manual:* TF-CBT Web 2.0: A Course for Trauma-Focused Cognitive Behavioral Therapy, Medical University of South Carolina (MUSC), $35, 11 modules with video demonstrations, https://tfcbt2.musc.edu.

  - o A part of the "Foundations Module," introduces cultural considerations.

  - o Each module takes approximately one hour.

  - o Each module has a pre- and posttest. There is also an overall final evaluation.

  - o Email from MUSC: "A therapist does not have to have official certification in TFCBT to use it in session. We certainly hope that lots of clinicians, not just those who hope to pursue official certification, will use the information presented in TFCBTWeb2.0 to inform their clinical practice—that is its purpose!" (From tfcbt@ musc.edu to Rose Wong on 10/30/2018)

- "Trauma-Focused Cognitive Behavioral Therapy: National Therapist Certification Program" (www.tfcbt.org)

  - o This program provides certification for people who have at least a master's degree in mental health. ($250)

  ○ *Requirements for Certification*: (a) completing MUSC online training; (b) either a live two-day training by a treatment developer or an approved national trainer, or a live training of at least six months in an approved TF-CBT Learning Collaborative; (c) participation in a follow-up consultation or supervision on a twice-a-month basis for at least 6 months or a once-a-month basis for at least 12 months by approved consultants/supervisors, or active participation in at least nine cluster/consultation calls in an approved TF-CBT Learning Collaborative; (d) completion of three treatment cases, with at least two of these including active participation of caretakers/designated third parties; (e) use of at least one standardized instrument to assess TF-CBT treatment progress in each of the three cases; and (f) taking and passing the certification program knowledge-based test.

  ○ Working with diverse populations: There is a free *TF-CBT LGBTQ Implementation Manual* and resources (tips for parents and educators) for helping military children with traumatic grief. See respectively https://tfcbt.org/tf-cbt-lgbtq-implementation-manual and https://tfcbt.org/resources.

2. Consult with someone who is trained and experienced in TF-CBT. Tell them about your background and ask for guidance on the amount of training and supervision you would need to begin providing TF-CBT to students.

  ● I consulted with a child clinical social worker in the mental health department who has TF-CBT certification. She said that if I did the MUSC online course and studied the treatment manual, given my CBT background, I could start providing TF-CBT while I am an intern. She said it is important to have a TF-CBT-certified supervisor while I am an intern and, in addition, for me to be taking the steps to gain certification.

  ● She emphasized that to provide TF-CBT to a child or teen from a minority cultural group, such as Latinx, LGBTQ, or others, it is very important to consult with a TF-CBT-trained clinician who has experience with that group.

3. Assess and describe the level of dissemination of TF-CBT. Is what's available enough for you to learn to conduct the TF-CBT with competence and fidelity?

- TF-CBT is well disseminated, according to the systematic review and the child clinical social worker I consulted with. I agree with this based on browsing the two books and the online course description.
- The online course, the treatment manual, and the additional edited book are sufficient for a basic self-study training in TF-CBT. With this self-training and weekly to biweekly supervision with someone who is certified and has at least several years of TF-CBT practice experience, I would have the competence for providing TF-CBT as an intern. If I had not had a structured 10-week academic course on CBT and some CBT practice experience, this would not be the case.
- To conduct TF-CBT with the highest fidelity, I would obtain the certification. Through certification, I can gain more precise training from "approved trainers" in exactly how TF-CBT was used in the evaluation studies. I could obtain the required consultation or supervision for certification while I begin to treat clients with local supervision.

IMPACT & PST

1. Find the available resources for learning PST, the amount of training and time required, and associated costs. Find out if you can obtain the training and treatment manuals used in the original study. As you search, pay attention to any resources specific to using PST with different diversity and minority groups.

- *Overview:* There is one main resource: National Network of PST Clinicians, Trainers, & Researchers at the University of California, San Francisco (UCSF) Medical Center (https://pstnetwork.ucsf.edu/welcome). This resource directs you to the IMPACT website (www.impact-uw.org), which redirects you to the University of Washington AIMS Center, which notes that free IMPACT training, which would include PST, is no longer available. (See https://aims.uw.edu/impact-improving-mood-promoting-access-collaborative-treatment.)
- *Introductory Training and Certification:* You can earn a certificate of attendance by completing Introductory-Level Training consisting of a one-day in-person workshop and participating in a personalized workshop. (See https://pstnetwork.ucsf.edu/training/individual-supervision.)
  - ○ The workshop includes overview, demonstration video, adapting PST to special populations, question-and-answer sessions, individual practice of one of the eight sessions of PST, and

        explanation/preparation of the case-based training component with audiotape review.

- *Master in PST Certification:* You earn this next level by completing the Introductory Level Training and then submitting at least three audio-taped cases with real clients for implementation review (with 30-minute feedback per tape by the trainer, 9 hours total), after which a monthly toll-free PST technical assistance call is available. (See https://pstnetwork.ucsf.edu/training/individual-supervision.)

- *PST Tele-group Training for Groups of 1–10 Clinicians: 8 Weeks of Group, Simulated Practice Case Role Plays (16 hours total):* Before using PST with actual clients (for the audiotape review and full certification), your group will complete simulated practice cases for 8 weeks, covering each of the eight sessions of PST, led by two PST trainers. This is for organizations, but the cost is not provided on the website. (See https://pstnetwork.ucsf.edu/training/group-role-play.)

- *Abundant Free Training Materials:* There are free manuals, PST worksheets, and excellent online training videos with demonstrations. Some of these are available in Chinese, Spanish, Hebrew, and French. (See https://pstnetwork.ucsf.edu/materials.)

- *Specialized PST and Diverse Populations:* There is specialized PST for case management, cognitive impairment, diabetes management, geriatric work, severe mental illness, and Parkinson's Disease. The trainers also have experience with PST in low-income populations and clients who speak English, Spanish, and Chinese.

2. Consult with someone who is trained and experienced in PST. Tell them about your background and ask for guidance on the amount of training and supervision you would need to provide PST.

- I consulted with a clinical social worker certified in PST who worked as a behavioralist in an integrated mental health program in a public health clinic. In her evaluation, my colleagues and I can train ourselves in PST by using the online manuals and videos provided by UCSF. She suggested that we (a) create our own group training (35–40 hours, 8 hours a week) using the materials, including reading the manuals, watching and discussing the several demonstration cases, and practicing each of the sessions of PST as group exercises (essentially replicating the group training program); (b) afterward, hire a PST-certified trainer to review and coach each of us individually based on one audio-recorded case with an actual client (these reviews could be shared so the whole group learns); and (c) have the certified trainer return in 4–6 weeks to review and coach again based on audio-recorded cases by a few of us.

- She said that we can self-train in PST only because we are proficient in CBT, which is a related and very structured therapy like PST. Also, PST shares CBT tools. She said that our MI expertise will help with PST application indirectly, because we know the process of helping people to direct their thinking toward specific goals and motivations. She commented that a master's student could also learn PST but may need twice the training time and 2–3 times the consultation time, especially if they have not had any CBT training.

- Regarding our need to provide PST to low-income patients in primary care, the clinical social worker suggested that we hire a trainer who has worked with this population in our same context, so that the trainer has familiarity with the types of problems, obstacles, and health care and support needs and contexts faced by this population.

- When asked about any cautions for using PST with low-income primary care patients, she suggested that the offer of individual therapy (PST) can lead some patients to not sign up or drop out, especially with immigrant groups. She suggested offering group PST by language group and calling the group a "health care" or "wellness" group. She also suggested phone-PST and home visits to best reach more of those in need.

3. Assess and describe the level of dissemination of PST. Is there everything needed for an agency to implement PST? And for you and your colleagues to learn PST?
    - PST is well disseminated, given all of the materials provided by the PST Network, including the possibility of hiring trainers and obtaining certification. However, it seems that PST may now be less well disseminated, given that the University of Washington no longer provides free IMPACT and PST training.
    - The online materials are sufficient for self-study in PST for someone who has expertise in CBT. With self-training and consultation with a certified trainer who has experience with low-income primary care patients, my colleagues and I can become competent in providing PST.
    - To conduct PST with the highest fidelity, we will obtain PST certification.

REFERENCES

Dissemination and Implementation Research

Bauer, M. S., Damschroder, L., Hagedorn, H., Smith, J., & Kilbourne, A. M. (2015). An introduction to implementation science for the non-specialist. *BMC Psychology, 3*(32), 1–12. http://doi.org/10.1186/s40359-015-0089-9

Chinman, M., Woodward, E. N., Curran, G. M., & Hausmann, L. (2017). Harnessing implementation science to increase the impact of health equity research. *Medical Care, 55*(Suppl 9 2), S16–S23.

Cohen, J. A., & Mannarino, A. P. (2017). Evidence based intervention: Trauma-focused cognitive behavioral therapy for children and families. In D. M. Teti (Ed.), *Child maltreatment solutions network. Parenting and family processes in child maltreatment and intervention* (p. 91–105). Springer International Publishing AG.

Eccles, M. P., & Mittman, B. S. (2006). Welcome to implementation science. *Implementation Science, 1*, 1.

Flay, B. R., Biglan, A., Boruch, R. F., Castro, F. G., Gottfredson, D., Kellam, S., Mościcki, E. K., Schinke, S., Valentine, J. C., & Ji, P. (2005). Standards of evidence: Criteria for efficacy, effectiveness and dissemination. *Prevention Science, 6*(3), 151–175.

Rabin, B. A., Brownson, R. C., Haire-Joshu, D., Kreuter, M. W., & Weaver, N. L. (2008). A glossary for dissemination and implementation research in health. *Journal of Public Health Management Practice, 14*(2), 117–123.

RESOURCES

Role of Clinical Expertise in EBP

Faulkner, M., & Parrish, D. (n.d.). Evidence-based practice is a process. Texas Institute for Child & Family Wellbeing, Steve Hicks School of Social Work, The University of Texas at Austin.

This article provides a fine description of the role of clinical expertise in the process model of evidence-based practice.

https://txicfw.socialwork.utexas.edu/evidence-based-practice-is-a-process/

Ginex, P. K. (2018). Integrate evidence with clinical expertise and patient preferences and values. Oncology Nursing Society, VOICE.

This article provides a brief description of the role of clinical expertise and patient preferences and values in evidence-based nursing.

https://voice.ons.org/news-and-views/integrate-evidence-with-clinical-exper-tise-and-patient-preferences-and-values

Wieten, S. (2018). Expertise in evidence-based medicine: A tale of three models. *Philosophy, Ethics, and Humanities in Medicine, 13*(2), 7 pages.

This open-access article describes how the field of medicine has tried to integrate expertise into evidence-based medicine. It also reviews the incorporation of expertise in other disciplines, such as psychology and sociology.

https://www.ncbi.nlm.nih.gov/pmc/articles/PMC5797352/pdf/13010_2018_Arti-cle_55.pdf

Considering Fidelity and Dissemination

Murphy, S. L., & Gutman, S. A. (2012). Intervention fidelity: A necessary aspect of intervention effectiveness studies. *The American Journal of Occupational Therapy, 66,* 387–88.

The authors emphasize the importance of examining and reporting on intervention fidelity in research.

https://ajot.aota.org/article.aspx?articleid=1851585

Horner, S., Rew, L., & Torres, R. (2006). Enhancing intervention fidelity: A means of strengthening study impact. *Journal of Specialists in Pediatric Nursing, 11*(2), 80–89.

This article reviews the role of intervention fidelity in research since the 1970s and argues for its importance.

https://www.ncbi.nlm.nih.gov/pmc/articles/PMC1474027

United Kingdom National Institute for Health Research. (2019). *How to disseminate your research.*

This webpage provides a brief definition of dissemination and principles and a plan for good dissemination.

https://www.nihr.ac.uk/documents/how-to-disseminate-your-research/19951

Dissemination and Implementation Research

American Psychological Association Society of Clinical Psychology. (n.d.). Dissemination and implementation.

> The website provides an accessible description of dissemination and implementation research, including theories and frameworks with links to readings.

> https://www.div12.org/implementation/overview

National Institutes of Health Office of Disease Prevention. (n.d.). Research priorities: Dissemination & implementation (D&I) research.

> The website provides links to D&I models and resources.

> https://prevention.nih.gov/research-priorities/dissemination-implementation

Estabrooks, P. A., Brownson, R. C., & Pronk, N. P. (2018). Dissemination and implementation science for public health professionals: An overview and call to action. *Preventing Chronic Disease 2018*, 15.

> This article provides a detailed review of the history of dissemination and implementation science.

> https://www.cdc.gov/pcd/issues/2018/18_0525.htm

CHAPTER 7

Choosing the Best Intervention for the Client

This chapter closes the handbook. It covers the practitioner's final step of reasoning through and articulating the choice of the best intervention for a client based on integrating three components of information. In support of this final step, the chapter addresses what it means to adapt or tailor an intervention culturally for a client and how a practitioner can evaluate the effectiveness of the chosen EBP(s) by using a single subject design. The chapter begins with a discussion of students' final questions before they conclude their case projects and their learning about the EBP model.

DISCUSSION 7.1 What Final Questions Do You Have Before Making a Decision?

1. If I find several different EBPs that are a good fit for my client but I don't have the means to learn them, can I just provide the client with the therapy I know?

2. Can I use two different EBPs, such as combining them or using one and then the other, if I think that both will be helpful to my client?

3. What does it mean to culturally adapt or tailor an intervention? How do we decide whether to use these or the original intervention?
4. What does it mean to "provide a rationale" for my choice?

See how students answered on p. 296.

See how students answered on p. 296.

| BRIEF LECTURE 7.1 |

Culturally Adapted Interventions

A practitioner's choice of an intervention for a client will entail careful thought about whether and how to incorporate the client's culturally based values and perspectives into treatment. In this handbook, we have discussed EBPs with the recognition that the large majority of existing EBPs are based on Western psychological frameworks. We have also discussed the need to promote the development and testing of community interventions using emic and community-based research approaches so that we can move toward a science of social work that is inclusive and less oppressive toward ethnic and minority groups. This brief lecture concludes the handbook's coverage of culture and EBP by introducing culturally adapted interventions. Guillermo Bernal et al. (2009) defined cultural adaptation as "the systematic modification of an evidence-based treatment or intervention protocol to consider language, culture, and context in such a way that it is compatible with the client's cultural patterns, meanings, and values" (p. 362). Such culturally adapted EBPs, situating somewhere in between their original, nonadapted counterparts and community (or indigenous) interventions, are also available to practitioners to choose from when implementing the EBP model.

Clinical psychologists began culturally adapting evidence-based interventions in the 1990s to advance research and inform practice with diverse groups. Bernal et al. (2009) described the empirical context of the advent of such adaptations:

> Clinicians have long known that the best treatment is one that is personalized to the needs and context of the individual. Yet with the increased focus on empirical information regarding treatment development, efficacy and effectiveness, the past two decades have been marked by efforts to achieve uniformity in providing care to a broad base of clients. Promoting a systematic approach to treatment is a double-edged sword; on the one hand, greater structure for researchers and practitioners and a call for accountability for treatment and research procedures are attractive ... [within] a scientist-practitioner model to psychological practice or training.

On the other hand, such systematization can potentially increase the risk of adopting a one-size-fits-all approach to interventions and intervention research that is contrary in practice to what the movement intended to promote in spirit (i.e., competent practice). (p. 361)

In this empirical climate, clinical psychologists began to take sides over the validity of evidence-based interventions for diverse ethnic groups. The question at debate was, "Are evidence-based interventions developed within a particular linguistic and cultural context appropriate for groups that do not share the same cultural values or language?" Supporters of adaptation who were part of a movement to diversify psychology argued for the cultural compatibility of interventions (Bernal et al., 2009; Tharp, 1991). They pushed for treatments to be made compatible with a client's culture in order to be more effective, and for manuals and protocols to be systematically adapted for different cultural groups (Sue et al., 1999; Trimble & Mohatt, 2002). They also argued that without adaptation, interventions would be neither culturally sensitive nor ecologically valid (Bernal et al., 1995; Hwang, 2009).

Opponents of adaptation assumed the universality of psychological theories and models and their principles and mechanisms of change (Bernal et al., 2009). They argued that treatment must follow the same set of procedures when applied with any cultural groups and that fidelity is not achievable with culturally adapted treatments. In their view, there were no grounds for modifying well-established evidence-based interventions (Bernal et al., 2009; Tharp, 1991). Additionally, the fact that cultural adaptation was impractical due to its labor-intensiveness supported the more practical route of simply testing the evidence-based interventions across ethnic groups to show their effectiveness.

With the emphasis on empiricism and the uncertain place of culture within psychological practice, clinical psychologists who are supportive of multiculturalism set out to modify and test treatments systematically in line with the scientific method. Today, there are hundreds of culturally adapted interventions, with cognitive behavioral treatments dominating the stage. A search in the *PsychINFO* database on May 12, 2020, for "culturally adapt*" in the title alone yielded 161 titles.

This lecture provides a critical overview of culturally adapted interventions. We will review two frameworks for adapting interventions, with an example of each. We will also review two meta-analytic studies on the current status and state of the evidence for adapted interventions. The intention is for the practitioner to be able to evaluate whether and when such culturally adapted EBPs may be useful for their clients.

Before beginning the overview, let's situate the culturally adapted intervention as one of several ways in which culture can be incorporated when implementing the EBP model. A practitioner incorporates culture by (a) choosing an EBP that was culturally adapted; (b) using the original, nonmodified EBP and incorporating cultural elements as part of the treatment plan or during treatment itself as the need arises; or (c) finding an EBP that was developed based on ethnic health and healing theories using an emic approach in the ethnic community. The latter can be called *community interventions*, *community-based interventions*, or *indigenous* practices or interventions. In the practitioner's consideration of the best-evidence component of the EBP model, they carefully search for interventions based on a search question that considers the client's culture, preferences, and views, including their goals and desired means of treatment. A successful search could include culturally adapted, original, and community interventions. The practitioner then assesses each intervention's quality of evidence, applying internal and external validity considerations, before integrating the information on best evidence into the final decision. Recognizing that evidence-based community interventions are uncommon, the practitioner's role in the clinical expertise component nevertheless includes searching for, considering, and incorporating community interventions and supports that have not been researched into the client's treatment plan. This latter step has external validity and a person-in-environment wellness perspective in mind.

CRITICAL THINKING

1. Will culturally adapted EBPs be more effective than the original versions for clients who are bicultural (e.g., Pakistani American, Jamaican American)?
2. How about for clients who are monocultural (e.g., Nepalese in Nepal)?
3. Considering the three options (a), (b), and (c) in the above paragraph, in what circumstances might you as practitioner favor one of these? How would you decide?
4. Can culturally adapted EBPs contribute to reducing dropout from mental health services by minority ethnic groups compared with the original EBPs?

Conceptual Models for Adapting Interventions
Over the past several decades, clinical scientists have presented many frameworks for the modification of evidence-based interventions, some published and many

not. We will review an early and well recognized framework by Guillermo Bernal et al. (1995) and a more recent, bottom-up adaptation framework by Wei-Chan Hwang (2009).

Ecological Validity and Cultural Sensitivity Framework

Bernal et al. (1995) proposed a theoretically driven adaptation framework focused on ecological validity. To gain ecological validity, the adapted intervention would need to be culturally sensitive, achieved by taking into account the cultural context in which the treatment is delivered and evaluated. The authors based their approach on Urie Bronfenbrenner's (1977) definition of ecological validity, the "degree of congruence between the environment as experienced by the subject and the properties of the environment the investigator assumes it has" (Bernal et al., 1995, p. 70). Similarly, ecological validity in treatment research is the degree to which the experience of the treatment by participants has the properties assumed by the researchers. With this aim, adaptations would focus on the introduction of culturally sensitive and culturally compatible elements that increase the congruence *between* the client's experience of their cultural world within the treatment *and* the treatment properties assumed by the investigator. Bernal et al. (1995) reasoned how to achieve this congruence as follows:

> Clearly, if ecological validity implies that the research environment is experienced by the client as the investigator assumes it is experienced in the treatment condition, then the process of research entails the integration of subject (client) and investigator (therapist) categories or dimensions about the ecological environment and consequently about the experimental or treatment condition. Therefore, research is a process in which the categories by subjects and investigators are part of the scientific process. The inclusion of this shared experience of the research environment is possible when researchers take into consideration the cultural context of a particular group with which the research is conducted. (p. 70)

On an empirical level, the authors viewed their ecological approach as contributing to a study's internal validity. Specifically, ensuring a shared experience between the subject and investigator fulfills a necessary condition of any interventional study—that the outcomes come from the intervention. It makes sense that if the subject and investigator are "not on the same page" during the treatment (i.e., the client is experiencing something different from what the therapist assumes from the treatment), one cannot infer causality between the treatment and observed outcomes, whether positive or negative.

••

NOTE   The argument that ecological validity supports internal validity illustrates a broader concept of external validity that is important for treatment research in minority populations. The ecologically valid intervention not only strengthens external validity, making it possible to generalize the study's findings to the population of interest, but it is actually a necessary condition of internal validity that should not be neglected. This can be understood in terms of the construct validity of the therapeutic framework and the content of the treatment, which should be recognized as requirements for a study's internal validity, rather than for improving external validity. Following from this, research cannot be assumed to be internally valid when Western culture–based treatments are applied to non-Westerners. Instead, internal validity should be addressed, evaluated, and demonstrated.

••

With this framework, Bernal et al. defined cultural context as the starting point for treatment development and adaptation and data analyses in intervention research (Bernal et al., 2009). They proposed that interventions adapted with cultural sensitivity procedures would provide increased ecological validity. To operationalize their framework, they incorporated content to achieve cultural congruence in eight dimensions of treatment: language, persons, metaphors, content, concepts, goals, methods, and context. As an example, the *persons* dimension involves addressing cultural similarities and differences between the client and clinician. *Metaphors* refers to using symbols and concepts shared by the population in question, such as using *dichos*, sayings or idioms, or having objects and symbols of the client's culture in the office or waiting room. The *content* dimension involves incorporating assessment and discussion of cultural knowledge and information about the values, traditions, and customs of the culture to validate the uniqueness of the ethnic group. *Goals* refers to framing goals of treatment within the values, customs, and traditions of the ethnic group. And, the *context* dimension takes into consideration the client's experiences of changing contexts that can increase risk of experiencing acculturative stress problems, disconnect from social supports and networks, and reduced social mobility. The following table shows culturally sensitive elements in the eight dimensions of treatment for developing or adapting clinical research interventions with Hispanics (Bernal et al., 1995, p. 74).

TABLE 7.1 Culturally Sensitive Elements and the Dimensions of Treatment for Clinical Research Interventions with Hispanics

Intervention	Culturally Sensitive Elements
1. Language	Culturally appropriate, culturally syntonic language
2. Persons	Role of ethnic/racial similarities and differences between client and therapist in shaping therapy relationship
3. Metaphors	Symbols and concepts shared with the population; sayings or *dichos* in treatment
4. Content	Cultural knowledge; values, costumes, and traditions; uniqueness of groups (social, economic, historical, political)
5. Concepts	Treatment concepts consonant with culture and context; dependence vs. interdependence vs. independence; emic (within culture, particular) over etic (outside culture, universal)
6. Goals	Transmission of positive and adaptive cultural values; support adaptive values from the culture of origin
7. Methods	Development and/or cultural adaptation of treatment methods. Examples: "modeling," to include culturally consonant traditions (e.g., cuento therapy [therapy based on folk tales]); "cultural reframing" of drug abuse as intergenerational cultural conflicts; use of language (formal and informal); cultural hypothesis testing; use of genograms, "cultural migration dialogue"
8. Context	Consideration of changing contexts in assessment during treatment or intervention; acculturative stress, phase of migration; developmental stage; social supports and relationship to country of origin; economic and social context of intervention

Putting this cultural adaptation framework into practice, Rosselló and Bernal adapted CBT and Interpersonal Psychotherapy (IPT) for Puerto Rican adolescents (Rosselló & Bernal, 1999). These adaptations took into consideration "interpersonal" aspects of Latino culture as cultural aspects of the treatment. For example, for IPT, the author incorporated cultural values such as familism and *respeto* ("respect") in analyzing interpersonal relationships across the 12 sessions of treatment. They applied the same cultural values in the four final sessions of CBT that dealt with people. Their findings, with a sample of adolescents 13–18 years of age with diagnosis of major depressive disorder, dysthymia, or both, showed that the IPT group had positive outcomes on self-concept and social adaptation, but not the CBT group. They reasoned that IPT itself had a greater degree of compatibility with Puerto Rican cultural values of *personalismo* ("personalism," the preference for personal contacts in social situations) and *familismo* ("familism," the tendency to place the interests of the family over the interests of the individual), because IPT addresses these cultural values directly (p. 742). In another RCT evaluating the same therapies with Puerto Rican adolescents with depressive symptoms, both treatments were effective in individual and group formats, but the CBT group showed greater decreases in depressive symptoms and improved self-concept (Rosselló et al., 2008).

CRITICAL THINKING

The following questions are about the ecological validity framework.

1. Does the approach to adaptation result in an intervention that assists you in achieving congruence with the client's view of their problem, means of resolution, and goals of treatment?
2. Can you effectively implement the adapted intervention with Puerto Rican adolescents if you do not know Hispanic/Latinx culture and language?
3. Can the culturally adapted intervention help you to achieve credibility? Will you follow it step-by-step or use it as a road map of possible stopping points?
4. When using the adapted intervention, is it possible that the "properties of the environment" that you assume as the practitioner still do not agree with the "ecology as experienced by the subject" (Bernal et al., 1995, p. 80; i.e., you still end up not having a shared experience)?
5. How could you integrate a cultural humility approach to treatment with this intervention?

Formative Method for Adapting Psychotherapy (FMAP)

Wei-Chin Hwang (2009) developed the Formative Method for Adapting Psychotherapy (FMAP) during the era of empirically supported treatments (ESTs). FMAP is a bottom-up, community-based developmental approach to culturally modifying psychotherapy for ethnic minorities. In addition to responding to the more common top-down, theoretically driven approaches, Hwang's (2009) efforts were stimulated by the little knowledge of the efficacy of ESTs for people from diverse backgrounds (Miranda et al., 2005) and the lack of detailed literature on cultural adaptation models at the time (Bernal et al., 2009). Hwang also provided a practical rationale in support of cultural adaptations of existing evidence-based treatments:

> Since the majority of therapists working with ethnic minority clientele in the U.S. are trained in western psychotherapy ... developing culture-specific treatments that are based on different healing paradigms ... is less practical. Moreover, developing novel ethnic-specific treatments for each culturally different group in the U.S. may be prohibitively costly, time consuming, and lead to training difficulties, especially if treatments are based on different theoretical paradigms. [Also,] implementing an "as is approach" in disseminating ESTs to ethnic minority clients may not fully address the diverse needs of clients. Therefore, culturally adapting ESTs may be the most responsive and cost-effective approach. (p. 2)

As additional support for the need of an adaptation model, Hwang's article (2009) summarizes a number of culturally adapted therapies that have been found to be effective and the growing evidence that treating clients with cultural sensitivity improves the utilization of mental health services.

• •

NOTE   The distinction between ESTs and EBPs for our discussion of culture and EBP is not critical. Hwang and others culturally adapted ESTs, which are equivalent to today's EBPs. ESTs are interventions identified from the treatment literature to address specific problems; they are supported by quantitative science research. The American Psychological Association (APA) started a project in 1993 of identifying and listing ESTs. Some APA members criticized ESTs as privileging empirical data over psychologists' own clinical expertise. The field has since moved toward the more flexible concept of EBPs, which asks clinical psychologists to apply evidence-based treatment guidelines, which are intended to assist their decision-making (see discussion on this topic by Herbert, 2015).

• •

FMAP is used in conjunction with the top-down Psychotherapy Adaptation and Modification Framework (PAMF), a top-down approach also developed by Hwang (2006). Hwang developed PAMF to help practitioners build specific skills and strategies for working with diverse groups. The adaptation includes three tiers: domains, principles, and rationales. Domains identify general topical areas that should be addressed when modifying therapeutic approaches. They include "(a) understanding dynamic issues and cultural complexities, (b) orienting clients to psychotherapy and increasing mental health awareness, (c) understanding cultural beliefs about mental illness, its causes, and what constitutes appropriate treatment, (d) improving the client-therapist relationship, (e) understanding cultural differences in the expression and communication of distress, and (f) addressing cultural issues specific to the population" (p. 3). Within domains are principles and the rationale of each principle. Principles are specific recommendations for adapting a therapy for a specific diversity group. Rationales are explanations of why the adaptations may be effective with the targeted population.

The bottom-up FMAP was designed to generate ideas for therapy modifications and provide support for theoretically based adaptations from the top-down PAMF process, as well as to gain direct recommendations from clients and therapists for improving treatment responsiveness. FMAP involves working closely with consumers to generate, evaluate, and reformulate ideas for adapting an intervention. The FMAP process involves five phases:

I.   Generating knowledge and collaborating with stakeholders;

II. Integrating generated information with theory and empirical and clinical knowledge;

III. Reviewing the initial culturally adapted clinical intervention with stakeholders and revising the culturally adapted intervention;

IV. Testing the culturally adapted intervention;

V.   Finalizing the culturally adapted intervention. (Hwang, 2009, p. 4)

Hwang used FMAP to adapt a 12-week CBT depression intervention for Chinese Americans (CA-CBT; Hwang, 2009). In Phase I, Hwang collected information from Asian-focused mental health agencies, mental health providers, Traditional Chinese Medicine practitioners, Buddhist monks and nuns, and Taoist masters for their expertise in treating Chinese Americans with depression. In Phase II, Hwang wrote the CA-CBT manual by synthesizing the qualitative data from the previous phase together with information from the PAMF phase, theories, EST literature, and his own experiences as a clinical psychologist. In Phase III, he conducted focus groups with therapists in English and Chinese to gain feedback on the draft CBT manual to finalize it for a clinical trial. The finalized manual, "Improving your Mood: A Culturally Responsive and Holistic Approach to Treating Depression in Chinese Americans," with therapist and client manuals, was translated and back-translated in a careful process by a research team, with feedback from 23 individuals, including university students and therapists. In Phase IV, the adapted intervention was tested in a clinical trial using outcome measures on depression symptoms, treatment satisfaction, working alliance, premature dropout, and receipt and enactment of therapy. Phase V involved gaining feedback from therapists and clients who finished the treatment to finalize the manual, which was also reviewed by a community focus group.

The following are selected sample cultural adaptation principles and rationales across six domains from CA-CBT, which was adapted with PMAF and FMAP (Hwang, 2009, Table 1, p. 9–13):

1. Dynamic Issues & Cultural Complexities (4 Principles):

   Principle: "Individualize statements made to client (e.g., rather than say 'Family is really important to Chinese people,' say, 'You seem to really care a lot about your family')." (p. 9)

   Justification: "Helps client feel validated rather than stereotyped." (p. 9)

   Principle: "Learn when to individualize, when to generalize, and when to examine the complexities of cultural issues (e.g., 'Thought records do not work with Asian Americans' vs. 'Thought records work better with more educated and more acculturated Asian Americans')." (p. 9)

   Justification: "Cultural issues may be moderated by other factors such as level of education or level of acculturation." (p. 9)

2. Therapy Orientation (9 Principles):

   Principle: "Educate the client about the course of therapy (e.g., what their experience is going to be like the first few weeks, several weeks thereafter, and in the long run)." (p. 9)

   Justification: "Helps increase comfort and reduce ambiguity by normalizing experiences and providing realistic expectations." (p. 9)

3. Cultural Beliefs (13 Principles):

   Principle: "Reduce the emphasis on cognitions and changing the way a person thinks. Instead focus on helping client think in more effective and healthy ways." (p. 10)

   Justification: "Focusing on changing one's way of thinking is less in line with client goals of solving their problems. Too much emphasis on cognitive biases and changing negative thinking patterns may alienate the client, whereas a positive reframe of helping the client think more effectively and healthily is more congruent with their goals." (p. 10)

   Principle: "It takes more time to work through therapy materials for people who have less prior knowledge or exposure. In addition, Asian American clients have less exposure to therapy and are more likely to be intimidated by large manuals." (p. 10)

   Justification: "If you are using a manualized treatment, reduce the amount of different materials you cover in each session and focus on applying the most relevant materials to the client's situation. Also, try to reduce the bulkiness of the manual ... so that the treatment does not seem too overwhelming." (p. 10)

4. Client-Therapist Relationship (9 Principles):

    Principle: "Join and engage the client by assessing family background and migration history. Clarify the role that family and/or caregivers will have in therapy." (p. 11)

    Justification: "Facilitates building of working alliance and bonding with therapist. Provides important contextual information on experiences of client. Respects privacy and rights of the client but also acknowledges family and caretakers who may have brought the client to treatment." (p. 11)

5. Cultural Differences in Expression & Communication (4 Principles):

    Principle: "Address and differentiate cognitive and affective experiences of clients." (p. 12)

    Justification: "Helps client differentiate their thoughts from their feelings ... especially important for those from more holistic cultural orientations where there is less differentiation between the two. Although clients may veer away from talking about their thoughts and feelings, discussing them in a culturally sensitive manner can improve treatment outcomes." (p. 12)

6. Cultural Issues of Salience (9 Principles):

    Principle: "Address client's individual rights, but also integrate this understanding with the realities of their roles and responsibilities. Discuss how [these] change when others do not act in appropriate ways." (p. 13)

    Justification: "Contextualize one's rights within a social context of one's roles and responsibilities. Helps highlight the importance of meeting one's own needs while at the same time reducing feelings that one is being selfish." (p. 13)

In CA-CBT, clients learn about the principles of healthy living and how to engage in healthy activities and self-care, strengthen internal self, and live in healthier ways and with better plans for the future (Hwang, 2016). The adapted therapy follows the principles of CBT. Each session has clear session goals, continuing psychoeducation, in-session activities, skills development, and the assignment of homework. Sessions 1–5 emphasize specific behavioral options, problem-solving skills, and behavioral activation. Sessions 6–7 work on cognitive and practical mental strengthening. Sessions 8–10 focus on strengthening healthy activities, managing stress by relaxation, and consolidating therapeutic gains. Session 11 focuses on family relationships. Session 12 closes the intervention with a reflection on the journey of therapy.

The therapist uses an exercise called the Climbing the Mountain Exercise in each session (Hwang, 2009). The exercise helps clients focus on the problem situation (e.g., "You are feeling very depressed today") and visualize the goal (e.g., "Feel less depressed") and the worst outcome (e.g., "Feel even more depressed"). Clients across the sessions design and try different actions and behavioral options and assess how they affect feelings and mood. The Climbing the Mountain Exercise assists clients with self-monitoring and remembering a range of possible behavioral options in everyday life.

Each session has different goals to visualize, but the exercise format is consistent (Hwang, 2009). Clients learn to wear a more holistic lens and come to appreciate the yin and yang. *Yin* refers to darkness, and *yang* refers to brightness. Yin-yang is emblematic of a coherent, harmonious view of the world. This system considers depression as but a part of dynamic harmony and not as isolated psychiatric symptoms. As Hwang stated, "The manual redefines cognitive errors, cognitive biases, and irrational thinking in a more positive, holistic, and goal-focused manner" (p. 119).

Hwang et al. (2015) compared the effectiveness of CA-CBT versus a manualized CBT in an RCT with a sample drawn from community clinics. While the CA-CBT group reported a significantly greater decrease of depressive symptoms, the majority of participants ($N = 50$) in both groups were still depressed after the 12-session intervention.

CRITICAL THINKING

1. Can you effectively implement CA-CBT with Chinese Americans if you do not know much about Chinese culture and language?
2. What are the advantages of CA-CBT to you as a practitioner compared with the intervention adapted using the ecological validity framework?
3. Would you consider CA-CBT a cultural technique, as discussed by Sue & Zane (1987), which is distal from the goals of therapy?
4. What cares and considerations would you take if you were to use CA-CBT with Chinese American clients, whether or not you are familiar with Chinese culture?

Current Status of Cultural Adaptation Science

As the number of culturally adapted interventions grew, clinical psychology researchers started examining the designs of the adaptations and whether and why they were effective. We will provide a brief overview of the status of cultural adaptation science based on the findings of these researchers, which are reported in review and meta-analysis articles.

Exploring the design of adapted treatments, Stanley Sue et al. (2009) observed three areas of cultural competence: (a) matching language and ethnic characteristics of therapists and clients; (b) adapting psychotherapies deemed to be culturally congruent, such as storytelling or *cuentos* (e.g., see Malgady et al., 1990, on *cuentos* with Puerto Rican children), Brief Structural Family Therapy (BSFT; see Szapocznik et al., 1984, on BSFT with Hispanic families) and Cognitive Behavioral Therapy (e.g., see Kohn et al., 2002, on CBT with African American women); and (c) incorporating cultural content, including discussions about and dealing with cultural patterns, immigration, minority status, racism, and cultural background experiences. Chu and Leino (2017), in a recent systematic review of 45 studies of adapted evidence-based interventions (published from 1994 to 2014), concluded that the adapted interventions maintained fidelity to the core components of the original interventions, given that the changes focused only on (a) changes in engagement and treatment delivery components (100%); (b) additions to core components to address cultural skills and sociocultural and psychoeducation needs (60%); and (c) modification of core therapeutic components (only 11%). Chu and Leino (2017) summarized the phases and levels of modification in the Cultural Treatment Adaptation Framework (CTAF, p. 49).

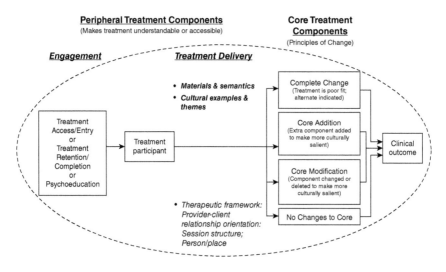

FIGURE 7.1 The Cultural Treatment Adaptation Framework for Cultural Adaptation of Evidence-Based Interventions Components

Regarding when culturally adapted treatments should be applied, Sue et al. cited Lau (2006) and Zavfert (2008), who support the use of cultural adaptations if the problems encountered are influenced by membership in a particular ethnic minority community or if the nonadapted intervention is not effective. Lau (2006) asserts that adapted treatments are warranted only if there is evidence that the particular clinical problem's manifestation within a given ethnic community emerges with its own distinct set of risk and resilience factors or if the client's ethnic group has responded poorly (i.e., not benefited from) the nonadapted interventions. Similar to Lau (2006), Zavfert (2008) proposes that the key cultural factors most relevant to the development and maintenance of a particular problem should first be empirically determined before using an adapted treatment.

Finally, evidence of the benefits of adapted treatments for minority ethnic groups has accumulated slowly. Griner and Smith (2006), in the first meta-analysis of culturally adapted mental health interventions, found a moderate effect size in an analysis of 76 studies. They found that modifications involved adding features rather than replacing components of interventions and categorized the added content into six areas: (a) racial or ethnic match between therapist and client, (b) using the client's preferred language, (c) appropriate location of services, (d) explicit discussion of culture, (e) incorporating cultural values and client's worldview into sessions, (f) collaborating with people from the client's culture (e.g., community healers), and (g) including discussion of spirituality as related to culture. Taking the empirical exploration of effectiveness one step further, Benish et al. (2011) revealed specifically that adapted interventions were efficacious when compared directly with their nonadapted counterparts. They noted that Griner and Smith's earlier (2006) meta-analysis included many early adapted interventions that were evaluated with no comparison to another treatment, or with a supportive condition that was not a therapeutic treatment.

CRITICAL THINKING

1. Do culturally adapted interventions replace the need for identifying, testing, and disseminating community-based and indigenous practices?
2. Do culturally adapted interventions contribute further to or remedy the problem of epistemic violence toward minorities?

ACTIVITY 7.1   Present a Culturally Adapted Intervention

Instructions

1. Working individually or with a peer, you will summarize and critique the study of a culturally adapted intervention and give an 8- to 10-minute oral presentation. The objective of this activity is to become acquainted with currently available adapted interventions, with an eye to using them judiciously. You do not need to create either a handout or presentation slideshow, only your own notes.

2. Browse the article titles of studies of culturally adapted interventions in the Resources section at the end of this chapter. Choose and read one article about a culturally adapted treatment for an ethnic group that you are familiar with. You may also want to find and read a second article, referenced in the article you have chosen, on the same adapted intervention in order to learn more details about how the intervention was modified.

3. Prepare a presentation that addresses the following:

    a. Summarize the basic characteristics of the original nonadapted evidence-based intervention, including theoretical basis (e.g., CBT, Psychodynamic, Structural Family Therapy), number of sessions, topical components/modules, and any other relevant characteristics.

    b. Using Chu and Leino's (2017) Cultural Treatment Adaptation Framework depicted in Figure 7.1, summarize the culturally based adaptations that were made in the areas of Engagement, Treatment Delivery, and Core Treatment Components. If the changes do not fit neatly in these categories, categorize and describe them in your own way.

    c. Provide a critique of the culturally based changes and additions. Will they work? Do they create damaging stereotypes? What care must the practitioner take in order to conduct the intervention sensitively and successfully? How could the authors have done a better job?

    d. Describe the study's sampling procedure and the sample charac- teristics. Provide your analysis of the characteristics of the ethnic population to which the study findings can be generalized. Address

acculturation level, language proficiency, and other relevant characteristics. In other words, the questions are: "Who is the adapted
treatment most suited for based on who was studied?" "Who should
it not be offered to?" and "Does your answer agree with the author's
targeted population (those they intend the modified treatment to
be suited for)?"

e. Describe the study design and its level of evidence. Does the study
have strong or weak internal validity? How does it affect your decision to use it?

f. Give your presentation and ask for feedback and answer questions.

TIP Keep in mind that your peers know little or nothing about the culturally adapted
intervention that you are reviewing. In your presentation, be sure to provide both an overall framework and enough details so that they can grasp the whole picture of the adapted
intervention quickly. For example, it may be too much to explain in detail how four core
components were modified, but you can give an example of two of them and the author's
reasoning behind the modifications. Be sure also to explain the "why," or reasoning behind
your critiques. For example, you may want to introduce an additional core modification. Be
sure to explain its content and why it is important for the targeted diversity group.

BRIEF LECTURE 7.2

Selecting an Outcome Measure

Using an outcome measure to assess the client's progress in treatment is a key
part of the practitioner's work of evaluation. With a carefully selected outcome tool, the practitioner evaluates the effectiveness of the EBP and their own
implementation, as well as contributes to generating practice-based evidence.
The purpose of an outcome measure is to assess whether treatment goals are
met. With client preferences in mind, the choice of a measure would depend
foremost on the client's view of their treatment goals. With the exercise of one's
clinical expertise in mind, the practitioner's role is to carefully choose or design
an outcome tool that is meaningful to the client and reliable for evaluating the
targeted goals.

A starting point for selecting the outcome measure is to consider evidence-based assessment instruments, which are available in the research literature
just like EBPs. Evidence-based scales are commonly used for screening, symptom

tracking, and assistance with diagnosis. They provide research-based cutoff scores that indicate levels of severity. They are generally not diagnostic tools (with the PHQ-9 being an exception). Once evidence-based scales are found, the practitioner can adapt the instruments to make them meaningful and fit with treatment goals. (Note, however, that some researchers will criticize practitioners for introducing any modification to an evidence-based instrument. This is because, once modified, the instrument is no longer an evidence-based instrument, since the modified instrument is no longer the instrument that was studied.) The practitioner will need to decide if their objective is to (a) provide a meaningful instrument or (b) generate outcome scores that can be reliably compared with standardized scores. To satisfy both criteria, a possible solution would be to use the original instrument as is but add a number of items as a separate, self-designed measure. But perhaps minor modifications to enhance understanding by the client would not jeopardize fidelity to the original evidence-based instrument. (Note also that the selection of an instrument may be constrained by the agency's setting, such as being required to use a predetermined instrument to meet reporting requirements for a grant-funded program.)

Process of Selecting an Outcome Measure

The process of selecting an outcome measure consists of the following steps:

1. Find an evidence-based instrument from the literature that has the best fit for your client's goals of treatment and population group and evaluate the findings on the instrument from internal and external validity viewpoints (just like you would for an EBP).

2. Ensure that the instrument is reliable by examining each item and the instrument as a whole by the following criteria:

    a. Fulfills the expectation that it will give the same result each time (assuming the client's state has not changed);

    b. Is easy to use (easy to understand and answerable); and

    c. Provides the same result whether it is administered by the client, you, or a colleague.

3. Ensure that the instrument is valid by making adaptations so that every item is meaningful and the set of items covers the client's conceptualization of their problem. This may involve:

    a. Deleting items that are irrelevant to the client;

     b. Rewording items; or

     c. Adding items.

  4. Decide with the client if the final instrument is appropriate for monitoring your work together. You can do any of the following:

     a. Pilot test the instrument with the client to refine items over a couple of sessions.

     b. Ask colleagues with expertise in the problem area and client group to give input for rewording or adding or deleting items.

     c. Delete relevant items if the instrument is too long to be practical.

     d. Let your client know why you want to not take out items that are irrelevant to them.

Example of Selecting an Outcome Measure

Let's look at an example. Mrs. Ortiz is a 77-year-old who is fluent in Spanish and semifluent in English. She self-identifies as a mother of two sons, a grandmother of three preteen girls, and an immigrant who came from Mexico just after getting married at the age of 27. You, the practitioner, are in your late 20s and immigrated to the U.S. from Columbia at the age of 7. You are fluent in English and near-fluent in Spanish. You are a behaviorist in an urban community health clinic that provides health and integrated mental health services serving a Latinx and Southeast Asian immigrant community.

You provide weekly home visits to Mrs. Ortiz as part of an integrated mental health treatment program for older adults. Mrs. Ortiz's primary care physician assessed her as having a mild major depression and referred her to you for in-home treatment. Mrs. Ortiz is suffering from the loss of her husband 7 months ago, after a 50-year marriage; having to give up a house she and her husband rented for 30 years and move 2 months ago into a studio in an elderly housing community for low-income seniors; self-isolation due to feeling sadness and having few Spanish speakers among the residents; and reduced contact with her sons and granddaughters, who no longer live close enough to visit with any regularity. Her symptoms, all mild-to-moderate, include loss of interest and pleasure in daily activities, sleep disturbance, tiredness and lack of energy, and feelings of sadness and hopelessness about improving her situation. Mrs. Ortiz did not accept the antidepressant offered by the physician but accepted the eight-visit weekly home visit program, which includes behavioral activation and cognitive-behavioral treatment, with biweekly and then monthly follow-ups as needed.

According to Mrs. Ortiz, her problems are feeling sad and lonely; feeling no motivation to socialize, although she normally enjoys this; feeling useless and without purpose due to no longer being a caregiver for her husband and grand-children; feeling resentment toward her sons and their wives for not taking her in; feeling unmotivated and without energy for daily grooming and hygiene; and forgetting to take blood pressure and prediabetes medications. When you and the physician discussed the depression diagnosis with her in the clinic, she neither admitted to having depression nor denied the symptoms that were explained to her as being part of depression. Mrs. Ortiz shows no signs of suicidality or other comorbid psychiatric conditions.

Mrs. Ortiz, with your guidance, formulated the following treatment goals:

1. Increase social activities with other residents from none to 2–3 activities per week;
2. Improve grooming and hygiene from 2–3 days to 4–5 days per week;
3. Take daily medications as scheduled; and
4. Reduce feelings of sadness and loneliness.

She agreed on the final goal only with hesitation. She did not believe that her sadness could go away. After you normalized her situation by explaining that many older adults, when faced with circumstances similar to hers, experience depression and gave hope that learning a few new ways of doing and thinking every day would help her decrease the problems she named, she agreed to include this goal and to try the weekly treatment with you.

In your search for evidence-based instruments, you find two widely used depression screening scales with Spanish versions. They are the PHQ-9 (Kroenke et al., 2001) and the 15-item Short-Form Geriatric Depression Scale (GDS-15; Sheikh & Yesavage, 1986), called *Escala de Depresion Geriatrica (Forma Corta)*. Both are reported to be reliable and valid for Spanish-speaking populations. You also find a Long-Form GDS with 30 items (Yesavage et al., 1983), a Spanish version of the Center for Epidemiologic Studies Depression Scale (CESD-20; Radloff, 1977;), and a Spanish language version of the 21-item Beck Depression Inventory (BDI-S; Bonilla et al., 2004), but you do not consider these, due to their impractical length and the latter's inconclusive evidence on its ability to discriminate between clinical depression and no depression in treatment settings (Roberts et al., 1989).

The GDS-15 is answered on a yes-no response scale. Ten items indicate the presence of depression when answered positively. Five items indicate depression when answered negatively (Items 5, 7, 11, 13, 15) A score greater than 5 points is suggestive of depression. A score greater or equal to 10 points is almost always indicative of depression. The 15 items are as follows, with underlined items discussed below:

Choose the best answer for how you have felt over the past week:

1. Are you basically satisfied with your life?
2. Have you dropped many of your activities and interests?
3. Do you feel that your life is empty?
4. Do you often get bored?
5. Are you in good spirits most of the time?
6. Are you afraid that something bad is going to happen to you?
7. Do you feel happy most of the time?
8. Do you often feel helpless?
9. Do you prefer to stay at home, rather than going out and doing new things?
10. Do you feel you have more problems with memory than most?
11. Do you think it is wonderful to be alive now?
12. Do you feel pretty worthless the way you are now?
13. Do you feel full of energy?
14. Do you feel that your situation is hopeless?
15. Do you think that most people are better off than you are?

You consult with a clinical social worker who has provided depression treatment to immigrant Latinx older adults for many years. She advises you that while the PHQ-9 allows you to monitor the presence and level of DSM depression symptoms, the GDS-15 has been more useful for engaging clients, including helping them to learn a language that allows them to express their experiences. She advises you to try the scale with your client and take time to discuss what each item means in her experience and current life.

You take her advice. Mrs. Ortiz relates well with the 11 underlined items above. She comes to understand the statements in terms of her own specific current problems. These 11 items are meaningful to her, and her total score is 11 points. She does not understand or relate well with the concepts in the remaining four items: Item 4 (boredom), Item 6 (fear of something bad), Item 10 (memory), and Item 11 (wonderful to be alive). She said she has not thought about herself or her life in these ways. Also, she says that she does not know about the memory of other people, although she recognizes that she forgets to take her medications. You explain to Mrs. Ortiz the purpose of using an instrument to monitor her progress in treatment. She agrees that the 11 GDS-15 items would be helpful to talk about again. After the GDS-15, you administer the PHQ-9 items, which she had answered 3 weeks before in the clinic. Mrs. Ortiz acknowledges some of the symptoms but has difficulty in using the 0–3 response scale over a 2-week period. You make some interpretations of answers for her, and the total score is close to the score obtained in the clinic. She agrees with you to not use the PHQ-9 in your work together.

With a shortened GDS-15 of 11 items in hand, you ask Mrs. Ortiz which of the problems she named is the most important to address first in treatment. She answers that she is very worried that she is not able to take care of her grooming and hygiene, which she has never had trouble with before. You remind her about her goal of remembering to take medications and ask if this should be another priority, given the possible negative consequences of not doing so. She agrees that it is very important, especially to not become a burden on her sons. Based on this discussion, she agrees that you will add two more items to the outcome measure. These are "improved grooming and hygiene" and "taking medications as scheduled." While these are treatment goals, they can also be defined as outcomes for monitoring. You could have also incorporated "increase social activities" and "reduce sadness and loneliness," but these are covered in the modified GDS-15. With your outcome tool developed, you are now ready to design your single-subject evaluation.

Reflection Questions

1. What are the disadvantages of using a scale with items answered with only "Yes" or "No" as a monitoring instrument? What do you think about a further modification to the GDS items, such as changing Item 2 to "Have you added back some of your activities and interests, especially socializing?" and changing the response options to *0-Fully, 0.5-Somewhat/Partially,* and *1-Not at All*?

2. Should you have made Mrs. Ortiz's two other goals—feeling useless due to losing her caregiver role and feeling resentment toward her sons and their wives—into outcomes to be monitored and evaluated? Mrs. Ortiz did not see these as goals because she saw no possible solution for them.

3. What do you think about the process of selecting or developing an outcome tool as illustrated by the example of Mrs. Ortiz? What would you change? Is the process client-centered? Does creating and using the outcome measure contribute to practice-based evidence and/or evidence-based practice?

BRIEF LECTURE 7.3

Evaluating Effectiveness: Using Single-Subject Design

Single-subject (or single-case) evaluations support the social worker's duties to evaluate treatment for individual clients and contribute to a science of social work by generating practice-based evidence. A single-subject research design allows the practitioner to evaluate the effectiveness of their chosen EBP for a client. They are evaluations with a sample size of one individual. To address internal validity, single-case designs use repeated measures of an outcome variable across time and across conditions. In other words, the practitioner will observe the client's variations in outcome scores across time to determine whether the client is benefiting from the treatment. Single-case designs can also be used when the practitioner is providing group treatment for evaluating the treatment impact for each participant. They can also be used to study a group, family, or community, in which case the term *single-system* may be used.

Clinical researchers often view single-subject designs as a method for piloting and refining a new intervention before it is evaluated in an RCT or quasi-experimental study, both of which situate high on the hierarchy of evidence compared with the single-case evaluation. This is because a single-case investigation generates low-quality evidence for drawing an inference of causality, with its sample of one. Clinical practitioners, in contrast, view single-subject designs as a method for monitoring and assessing client progress and outcomes. Many practitioners conduct single-case research formally and informally with the objective of monitoring for meaningful changes and outcomes in their clinical work rather than trying to build evidence about the selected EBP. Some therapeutic approaches like CBT rely on single-case evaluation as part of the treatment method for the client to learn the helpfulness of specific homework activities and new behaviors. In this final brief lecture, we will learn about simple and complex single-subject designs so that we can responsibly and skillfully work with our clients while applying EBPs found in the literature.

Introduction to Methodology

Single-subject research relies on time-series designs to evaluate practice effectiveness with a single case or unit. In a baseline or control phase, the practitioner obtains repeated measures of an outcome indicator before an intervention is introduced. In the intervention or experimental phase, the practitioner also obtains repeated measures after the intervention is introduced. Finally, there is a postintervention follow-up phase, during which the practitioner obtains repeated measures to assess short- and medium-term outcomes. The design steps are as follows:

- Select, design, and/or adapt a valid outcome measure.
- Decide on the number and timing of observations in baseline, intervention, and follow-up phases.
- Assess the outcome as designed.
- Display results on a graph, with time on the x-axis and the outcome on the y-axis.
- Draw an inference on whether there is improvement in the person or group and whether the changes depicted are clear or unclear.

Ideally, the practitioner wishes to see if a sustained pattern of improvement begins soon after the onset of the intervention. The assessment of outcomes across time involves determining whether there is (a) a stable pattern of scores during the baseline phase, (b) a sustained improvement trend across the intervention phase, and (c) sustained improvement or at least not a drop back to baseline levels. The more measurement points and the more stability in the trends identified, the easier it is to infer that changes in the outcomes were due to the intervention. That is, it will be more credible to assert the positive impact of the intervention, as opposed to attributing the positive impact to natural healing or statistical regression. Now, let's discuss internal and external validity before embarking on the "how to" of designing an outcome measure and the time-series element of a single-case evaluation.

Internal and External Validity

Identifying stable trends using repeated measures enhances internal validity when the use of a control group is not possible. In a single-case design, the investigator wants to show that positive changes (e.g., a reduction in the client's depression score) coincides with the onset of the intervention. Whatever the results, a single-subject design permits only a reasonably small degree of causal inference, because there is neither a control nor a comparison group (i.e., it is neither an experiment nor a quasi-experiment). Recall that experimental designs provide a higher degree of causal inference, and causal inference typically requires some type of experimental design. In the human services, random sampling is difficult to arrange. We tend to use convenience samples of people who are available to participate. The single-case evaluation conducted by a practitioner with their own client is the perfect convenience sample.

Enhancing a single-case evaluation's external validity is difficult to achieve due to the small sample size and selection bias. Simply stated, a sample of one cannot be considered representative of a population. Recall that whether a study's findings are generalizable depends on whether the study's participants are representative of the population to which you wish to generalize the findings. Nevertheless, if generalizability is of interest, you can pool and analyze the outcomes from 25 single-case evaluations of a particular EBP. For example, you can evaluate the EBP for Mrs. Ortiz and 24 others suffering from depressive distress in the integrated mental health care program. This may give some support to the inference that the selected EBP is effective for the problem area and population group served by the program. To do this, you would replicate the single-case study 25 times, with 25 clients, to build evidence that the EBP is externally valid or generalizable. However, most practitioners are more concerned with helping their individual clients in a meaningful way and improving their programs than building evidence for the purpose of scholarly publications and presentations. To conclude, in EBP decision-making, a single-case design is a useful tool for testing whether an EBP with evidence of effectiveness in larger studies is effective for a specific client or a program's clientele. In conducting a single-case evaluation, you will use your own clinical (and research) expertise to determine whether the EBP with strong evidence of effectiveness from controlled experimental conditions and samples is actually effective for your client in the real-world setting.

Designing a Single-Case Evaluation

Single-case design notation and concepts are similar to the research notation and concepts for experimental and quasi-experimental designs introduced in Chapter 4. The notation consists of the following:

A: Baseline phase in the absence of the intervention.

B: Intervention phase when the intervention is being implemented.

There are three basic designs based on the presence or absence of a baseline phase before and after the intervention phase.

B Design

There is no baseline phase, only an intervention phase. That is, there is no control phase before treatment begins to assess how the client was doing before the intervention started. With this design, the question asked is, "Did the client show improvement in the outcome measure when the intervention was being implemented?" The expected finding is that the intervention was accompanied by improvements in the outcome measure. A graph of this *B* design showing a successful outcome for Mrs. Ortiz would be a downward sloping line connecting the total scores observed across the 8 weeks of the intervention (e.g., her total score decreased steadily from 12–13 points in the first several weeks to 7–9 points in the final several weeks). The pitfall of this design is that alternative explanations for the positive outcomes are not ruled out (i.e., threats to internal validity are not dealt with). Perhaps the client was already making improvements before the intervention started, or another variable beneficial to the client that is occurring simultaneously with the intervention influenced the outcome positively. Introducing baseline observations reduces threats to internal validity.

A-B Design

There is a baseline phase and an intervention phase. Having a baseline phase provides some control to threats to internal validity, because it eliminates the threat of a pretreatment trend. That is, we expect to see the client with a sustained high level of symptoms in the baseline phase, followed by decreasing symptoms during the intervention phase. A pitfall of this design, however, is that it does not eliminate the threat of a concurrent variable that is also contributing to the client's decreases in symptoms. A second B phase—a postintervention assessment of outcomes—addresses this threat. The expected finding is the downward sloping line of the intervention phase being followed by a stabilized level of symptoms, or even an increase in symptoms, due to the client no longer having the help of the intervention. (Recall from Chapter 4 that when it is not possible to have a control or comparison group, another method for controlling threats to validity is to collect many outcome observations across time before and after the intervention.)

A-B-A Design

This is the design that is both feasible to implement and controls for threats to validity as much as possible in a real-world setting. In the A-B-A design, there is a baseline phase, an intervention phase, and another baseline phase. (The final baseline phase can be called a postintervention or follow-up phase, since the intervention is not reintroduced, as in an A-B-A-B design, which is not discussed in this handbook due to its infeasibility with clients in a nonclinical laboratory setting.) This is a withdrawal or experimental removal design, because the intervention is withdrawn or removed, and measurement occurs again. This design allows for some degree of inference because it is able to show that changes in the application of the intervention (i.e., its introduction and then its removal) are associated with changes in outcomes. Let's look at three graphs of hypothetical outcomes for Mrs. Ortiz. All of the designs include three observation points in the first baseline phase, eight observations in the intervention phase (one per week), followed by four more observations in a postintervention follow-up phase.

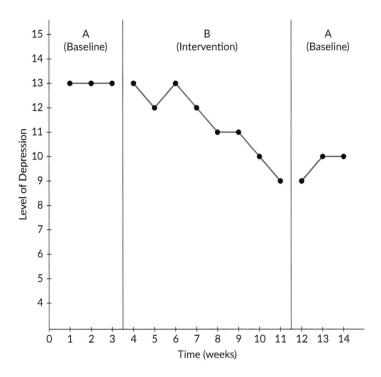

FIGURE 7.2A ABA Design Showing Finding of Intervention Efficacy

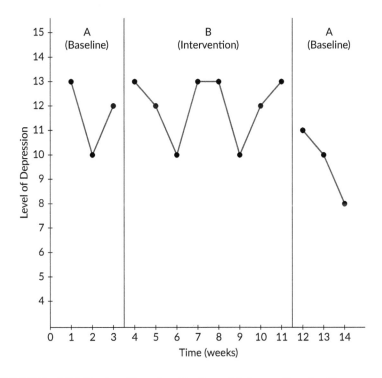

FIGURE 7.2B ABA Design Showing Finding of Intervention Inefficacy

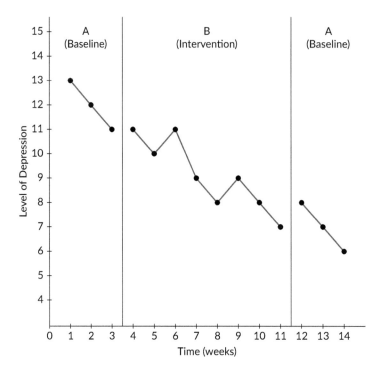

FIGURE 7.2C ABA Design Showing Unclear Finding About the Intervention's Efficacy

Single-case evaluation is a research method available to the practitioner for exercising their clinical expertise in the EBP model in a way that supports their work with clients and generates practice-based evidence on existing EBPs. Single-case evaluation is not a panacea for determining the effectiveness of EBPs that have not been examined sufficiently in implementation research. Rather, the method serves to ensure that EBPs are not doing harm to clients, contributes to practice-based knowledge and a science of social work, and allows the practitioner to responsibly monitor and evaluate the treatments offered. (For a more full discussion of single-subject design, see social work professors Allen Rubin and Earl Babbie's (2014) discussion of using both simple and sophisticated single-case designs as part of evidence-based practice.)

ACTIVITY 7.2 **Test Your Understanding of the Chapter**

Answer the following true or false questions. Explain your answer.

1. The cultural adaptation of an evidence-based treatment is accomplished when the practitioner learns about the client's cultural values during treatment and incorporates these as points for close discussion and intervention throughout the treatment.

2. Opponents of the cultural adaptation of treatments assume the universality of psychological theories and models and argue that the same set of procedures must be followed in work with every cultural group.

3. Ensuring a shared experience between the subject (or study participant) and investigator is important in any treatment study, because otherwise it becomes unclear how the subject benefited from the treatment. An ecologically focused cultural adaptation approach is one way of ensuring the shared experience, which strengthens internal validity.

4. A cultural adaptation to an evidence-based practice could include modifying a therapy's principles of change to make the therapy more culturally salient.

5. There appears to be an ongoing debate among clinical psychology researchers about when and for which groups culturally adapted treatments are warranted. Some researchers argue that it must be shown that the client's ethnic group has responded poorly to the original intervention. Others argue that the ethnic group must be shown to have its own distinct set of risk and resilience factors.

6. The NASW *Code of Ethics* states, in its discussion of the value of *service*, that social workers must use culturally adapted interventions when such exist.

7. In the process of EBP decision-making, a final step of exercising one's clinical expertise can involve selecting an outcome measure and designing a single-subject evaluation, if the practitioner sees this as beneficial to the client and for generating knowledge about the EBP.

8. The EBP decision-making model incorporates a large role for the practitioner in the clinical expertise component. It does not force the practitioner to utilize the EBP that has the highest level of evidence based on internal validity considerations, but rather requires the practitioner to center the decision on the client and the client's community, practice-based knowledge, and the limited state of the evidence base.

See the answers on p. 299.

⌘   **Case Paper Task 7.1**

....

Use the Original EBP Model to Choose the Best Intervention for Your Client and Write the *Best Intervention & Rationale* Section

Instructions

Choose the best intervention or interventions for your client by considering the quality of the evidence (i.e., where the EBPs are located on the hierarchy of evidence), the knowledge of clinical experts about the EBPs (including your assessment of the feasibility of becoming competent for providing them), and the client's background, culture, and preferences. Provide a clear rationale for your choice that integrates and discusses all three components of the EBP decision-making model.

Below are examples of the *Best Intervention & Rationale* section from Laura's and Eddie's case papers.

Case Paper Instructions:

Best Intervention (5–6 paragraphs, 6 points)
Best Intervention & Rationale: Identify the best intervention for your client. Discuss your rationale for choosing it, addressing how you considered and balanced information for each of the three components: (a) best available research, (b) clinical expertise, and (c) patient characteristics, culture, and preferences. Discuss how the other two interventions are less suited based on the three components. If you decide to use more than one intervention or modify an intervention to meet your client's needs and characteristics, describe why and how you would do so. (*4–5 paragraphs, 4 points*)

Laura's Example

Needs Strengthening

Best Treatment and Rationale

The best interventions for Laura are CBT-A and MBSR, because the studies reviewed have the best evidence (i.e., the highest level of evidence). My supervisor said that Laura can use CBT-A to build her self-esteem and gain awareness of relational concerns. She can learn cognitive coping techniques for use in school when she is bullied and depressed, as well as learn to put her core beliefs into perspective. The evidence for IPT-A was weaker, because it is a newer evidence-based practice (i.e., there is not enough accumulated evidence yet). I did not choose IPT-A, even though the studies had evidence that was generalizable to my client, because of its weaker evidence.

My supervisor and others I consulted with said MBSR will be beneficial in providing coping skills, including meditations and relaxation techniques, to the client. MBSR has grade A evidence in a meta-analysis, which will guarantee the success of the treatment for Laura. MBSR and CBT-A can be combined to provide a flexible and adaptable intervention for her. Because I have background in mindfulness practice and have had training in CBT, I can carry out these interventions.

How would you strengthen the above? Is it biased toward one component of the model? Is Laura's view of her problem considered in the decision? Is there a strong justification to apply both CBT-A and MBSR?

Well-Written

As you read the below example, reflect on whether all three components of information are explicitly integrated in making the decision to use IPT-A.

Best Treatment

Best Treatment and Rationale

The best treatment for this client is IPT-A. This treatment fits my client's background, needs, and preferences, which strongly center on relationships. She often experiences depression and anxiety after having interpersonal issues with peers and adults. IPT-A will normalize her interpersonal concerns so that her depressive and anxious symptoms will diminish. Also, the intent of IPT-A is to provide psychoeducation on how to cope with interpersonal concerns and common developmental milestones during adolescence. IPT-A is also suitable because it is intended for mild-to-moderate cases of depression and anxiety, which fits my client's case. Two B+ studies on the hierarchy of evidence indicate that the evidence of IPT-A's efficacy is fairly strong from an internal validity viewpoint. Also, Mufson et al.'s (2004) study demonstrated the external validity of the study for low-SES Latinx teenagers in school settings, like MCC's school-based mental health clinics.

I ruled out CBT-A, even though the evidence is stronger (with the studies I reviewed being A– and B studies), given that the studies included adolescents who were from a clinical or more depressed population, and lower income Latinx adolescents were excluded from the samples. My supervisor evaluated CBT-A as helpful to building my client's self-esteem and understanding interpersonal problems, but IPT-A is a better fit because it is designed specifically to address relational concerns, which is what my client desires help with.

I ruled out MBSR, even though it has grade A evidence from the meta-analytic study (Chi et al., 2018) and B+ evidence from the small RCT (Biegel et al., 2009) and appears to be suited to varying levels of depression severity, including clinical and nonclinical participants, and types of mental health problems. The rule-out was due to the poor generalizability of the evidence to my client on the basis of SES and ethnic background. Also, although my supervisor noted useful aspects of MBSR, especially for building my client's coping strategies, MBSR is not designed specifically to address relational issues, which are, again, my client's top concerns.

Although I am not certified in IPT-A, the manual and support from my supervisor and colleagues at MCC will allow me to provide IPT-A with a strong level of fidelity. At MCC, all therapists use techniques similar to IPT-A to assist clients with normalizing instances of interpersonal issues and life events. We also facilitate therapy groups geared toward individuals dealing with grief and loss and interpersonal struggles. My supervisor has also facilitated culture-based therapy groups that serve minority students' unique needs, including their need for empowerment and ability to relate cross-culturally and intergenerationally. With these resources, it will be possible for me to provide IPT-A with adaptations that can best meet the needs of my client.

Eddie's Example

Well-Written

As you read the below example, notice how case management plays an important role in treatment, how the three therapies are compared and contrasted to bring out their poor fit for Eddie, and how the two EBPs proposed for Eddie are carefully justified.

Best Intervention and Rationale

The best intervention for Eddie in the first stage of intervention is MBCT, to assist with treatment goals related to stabilization in his new living situation. PET for trauma processing may be suited for Eddie in the future after he has achieved stabilization. I will provide my rationale for this choice based on three components of decision-making—best evidence, clinical expertise, and client characteristics, culture, and preferences.

Regarding the best available evidence, MBCT followed by PET has the best (grade A) evidence, according to systematic reviews and meta-analyses, and PET and CPT are interventions considered to have high efficacy and are in use by the U.S. Department of Veterans Affairs et al., 2013). I reviewed B+ PET and B MBCT studies. From an internal validity perspective, all three interventions have a fair amount of credible evidence of effectiveness and situate high on the hierarchy of evidence. However, from an external validity perspective, the generalizability of findings to my client is low. PET appears suited for more severe PTSD, and the available evidence is for veterans with combat trauma. CPT is suited for childhood sexual assault and rape victims, including for severe PTSD, but it has been studied largely with women only. As for MBCT, efficacy for chronic pain and IED is not established. Finally, the samples across studies did not include many participants with Eddie's background, including race, culture, SES, age, health and mental health complexity, and high-crime urban living. Additionally, the high treatment dropout rates in the study are not reassuring, even when those who dropped out are reported as being similar to those who completed treatment. In conclusion, I have strong concerns about the relevance of the available evidence to Eddie's situation.

My rationale for choosing MBCT and PET is based on clinical expertise, through consultations with experts, and Eddie's goals, preferences, and context. The experts evaluated MBCT as the first-stage treatment, with PET being provided and applied cautiously in a later stage. MBCT would support the immediate goal of his stabilization in his new living situation, with concurrent case management activities to link him into a community network and more appropriate longer-term housing. Also, these experts and I concluded that it would be feasible to provide MBCT and PET, by me and my supervisor, respectively. As an MSW intern, I would self-study MBCT and receive close supervision as I work with Eddie.

With regard to the fit of these interventions to Eddie's characteristics, culture, and preferences, along with his treatment goals, MBCT in the short term and PET in the medium term fit well. MBCT fits his short-term goals and suits his cognitive insightfulness. PET suits his interest in cognitive approaches and goal of processing his traumas experientially through imaginal and real-life exposure to relieve the trauma memory. CPT was ruled out for Eddie, given its heavy use of writing and Eddie's preference for experiential learning. My focus on reviewing cognitive behavioral interventions was based on Eddie having all the ingredients necessary for success with such an approach. He can talk about his deeply held negative beliefs about himself and views of others in the safe confines of the therapeutic relationship. And he wants to become more current- and future-oriented, as evidenced by his strongly stated desire, "I want to enjoy my life."

MBCT and PET, together with a strong case management plan, appear to be the best intervention options for this client. Eddie has expressed a strong desire to face his demons, to see them in a different light—no longer whiling away the hours playing violent video games and smoking cannabis to isolate himself from others and from the deep social connection for which he yearns. He wants to be part of society and has a zest for experiencing life, rather than intellectualizing or writing about it. Lastly and most importantly, I talked to Eddie and got his feedback on which treatment sounds like something he would like to pursue. The key for any intervention to be successful is the client's willingness and commitment to be engaged and motivated. The client was the ultimate decider and wanted to give MBCT and PET a try.

Case Paper Task 7.2

Plan How You Will Use the Best Intervention in Treatment and Write the *Evidence-Based Treatment Plan* Section

Instructions

Describe your treatment plan, applying the EBP(s) you have chosen. Discuss the goals and how you will monitor and assess outcomes. If you combine EBPs, describe how they will be sequenced and applied.

Below are examples of the *Evidence-Based Treatment Plan* section from Laura's and Eddie's case papers.

Case Paper Instructions:

Best Intervention (6–7 paragraphs, 6 points)

Evidence-Based Treatment Plan: Describe your treatment plan with the chosen intervention, including length of treatment and specific treatment goals for your client, and method of monitoring and evaluating client progress and outcomes (e.g., client satisfaction scale, symptom scale, or behavioral or other indicators). (*1–2 paragraphs, 2 points*)

Laura's Example

Needs Strengthening

Evidence-Based Treatment Plan

I will begin by using individual MBSR for 4 weeks and then introduce CBT-A with intermittent MBSR for 6 more weeks. The meditation, breathing and relaxation exercises, and coping skills will decrease instances of anger. Cognitive restructuring will decrease depressive symptoms. Cognitive and social skills and social exposure desensitization experiments and exercises will increase her contacts with peers. Following a CBT method, the client will monitor herself, for homework, on a daily basis. She will also complete a depression scale at the start of her weekly sessions with me.

How would you strengthen the above? Is all of the required content covered?

Well-Written

As you read the below, notice the additional details and the focus on relational goals with peers, success in the school environment, and involvement and rebuilding of the relationship with her mother.

Evidence-Based Treatment Plan

IPT-A treatment duration will be 16 weekly sessions. I will use the IPT-A model to provide activities during our sessions that facilitate the expression of feelings, validation of those feelings, and normalization of the occurrences of interpersonal struggles and triumphs. We will also use role-play activities that facilitate and model appropriate social and communication skills for the client. To engage her with peers, I will refer her to a social skills group for students who have similar issues at school. The use of IPT-A principles will most definitely be effective in helping my client cope with challenges in depression, anxiety, and interpersonal difficulties. It will also provide her with communication skills necessary to be successful in a school environment. I will involve the client's mother to gain support and involvement in the client's therapy and case management goals and to process attachment trauma once appropriate to do so. The mother will be invited for dyadic sessions at the start of therapy and every few weeks thereafter.

The treatment goals for my client are to decrease instances of escalation of anger, decrease depressive symptoms, and engage in activities that contribute to building meaningful relationships with others. My client will record instances of anger escalation and positive interactions with others on a daily basis. She will also complete a depression scale at the start of each weekly session and a self-evaluation of social skills development every four weeks.

Eddie's Example

Well-Written

As you read the below example, note how there is no definitive treatment plan for the use of PET, but rather a planned assessment of readiness for trauma-processing needs. Note also the integration of case management into the treatment plan.

Evidence-Based Treatment Plan

MBCT will the first-stage treatment for 8–10 weeks. MBCT will support the goal of stabilization in the new living situation, with concurrent case management activities to link Eddie to community support. Outcomes will be measured by decreases in emotional reactivity; decreases in negative coping, such as cannabis and video games; increases in enjoyable activities; increases in social contacts with children and grandchild; and successful adoption of cognitive coping techniques. Eddie will self-rate each day as part of cognitive-behavioral homework exercises. He will also complete a depression screen at the start of each session with me. During weeks 8–12, I will begin termination and transfer Eddie to my field instructor (FI).

My FI will start by giving the client an overview of PET treatment and learn about his past therapy experiences to evaluate the suitability and intensity of PET for him. My FI will work with him to make a list of people, places, and/or activities that he specifically avoids to restructure his cognitive interpretation of danger and sense of competence. Gradually, the client will confront and feel more comfortable with these situations, and when appropriate, the client will also begin to process through the details of his trauma (Rauch et al., 2012). By confronting the details of the trauma using PET, it is my hope that the client will begin to have less of the unwanted memories than before therapy. The client has frequently articulated, "I can't change the past. I want to enjoy my life." If my FI assesses that Eddie is not ready to use PET, another intervention will be considered to help Eddie realize his goals. If PET is used, Eddie's progress with it will be monitored by PTSD and depression symptom levels and weakened impact of long-held negative core beliefs.

ANSWERS

What Final Questions Do You Have Before Making a Decision?

How Students Answered

1. **If I find several different EBPs that are a good fit for my client but I don't have the means to learn them, can I just provide the client with the therapy I know?**

   a. I don't think so, because the purpose of the EBP model is to consider all the best evidence. If you find an EBP that fits the client's preferences and views, you would work to arrange for the service that is needed. Part of social work values is tapping into our professional relationships and making possible the services that are needed.

   b. If the client isn't in an unsafe or urgent health or mental health situation and the therapy you know can help some of the client's immediate goals, then it would be okay. I think about Sue and Zane's (1987) "gift giving" and "earning credibility." Is the relationship or therapy we are providing actually helpful to the client?

   c. In all cases, we are supposed to work in an honest and trusting way, as well as respect clients' self-determination. We should explain the EBPs we found so the client understands what they are, that they exist, how they can help the client's problems, and how and where to try to get them. We should also explain how the intervention we know could be useful. It's always the client's decision, whether they leave or stay.

   d. Clients are vulnerable in the sense that they feel dependent on us due to their situations. They will rarely say no to what we offer them. But they do vote with their feet—by not showing up again. We have to remember our overall role as social workers, always working with integrity and service in mind. We have a commitment to provide what people really need. We should strive to meet the needs of diverse clients at every moment, rather than, "My agency and I provide this, it's evidence based, and that's it."

2. **Can I use two different EBPs, such as combining them or using one and then the other, if I think that both will be helpful to my client?**

a. This makes sense to me, that we can find two different EBPs to be useful for a client's problems. Or one of the interventions can help with certain goals and the other with other goals. I don't see why we can't, if we have the competence to provide both of them.

b. I think this goes against fidelity, because the interventions were not evaluated in a creative, combined fashion. We would have to evaluate for ourselves very carefully how our combined therapy is going. Thinking further, we should evaluate any EBP we use very carefully anyway, because our client is not the "average client" in any of the studies behind the evidence base.

c. If we use two therapies, we have to be careful that we are using each of them so that the client benefits fully. For example, the client's learning of the CBT process, to learn to do CBT on themselves independently, requires a certain amount of time and repeated work. It can't be cut short and may be compromised if the therapist doesn't go through all the weeks and steps consistently. I would ask, "Is our creative idea really helpful to the client?"

d. Every client has a lot of community support and resource needs. We have to balance a focus on the "right EBP" within the context of our overall role. We are the social work practitioner experts in the EBP model. We should be creative, and our responsibility for the whole person in a person-in-environment focus can't be neglected due to a narrow focus on a therapy. We also ask if the therapy and our overall work is addressing all levels of needs and building the client's strengths and autonomy.

3. **What does it mean to culturally adapt or tailor an intervention? How do we decide whether to use these or the original intervention?**

a. Remembering Sue and Zane's (1987) lesson, it doesn't make sense to culturally adapt an intervention, because culture-specific therapy techniques and knowledge of my client's culture aren't necessarily going to help me. They said that in themselves, knowledge and techniques are very far from the goals of treatment unless they are transformed into concrete strategies, and cultural knowledge is a necessary piece of but is not sufficient for effective treatment. The focus should be on achieving credibility.

   b.   I think that cultural adaptations are important and useful, because to achieve credibility, Sue and Zane (1987) say that the therapist shouldn't ask the client to respond in culturally incompatible ways. A culturally adapted therapy could be helpful for this. I guess whether it is useful depends first on the client's view of the appropriate means of resolution for their problem. I would ask myself, "Does the cultural adaptation of the therapy, and the therapy itself, to begin with, fit with building my credibility with the particular client?"

   c.   Thinking this through, there's no harm in adapting a therapy. The important question is, "Does the adapted therapy, or nonadapted original therapy, for that matter, help us to achieve congruence with the client's thinking on their problem, how to address the problem, and their treatment goals?" This is what enhances our credibility.

   d.   Assuming that an intervention culturally adapted for Japanese culture is the best choice for a Japanese American immigrant can lead to confusing the values of the client with those of their ethnic group. Being treated this way is painful for anyone. The client needs to be treated as an individual, and our work within the EBP model is finding the EBP that meets the client's goals for treatment and supports the way they want to work with us. A good step may be talking openly with the client about the original intervention and the adapted one to find out which, if any, would be useful.

   e.   I don't think we should jump on using culturally adapted interventions just because they were evaluated and shown to be effective. It is not hard to show that any reasonable and thoughtful intervention can be effective; some number of people will improve. The literature is still biased toward proving that mainstream treatments work for everyone, rather than asking the client and experts in their community what ethnic or community-based treatments are available for my client and my client's problem. A client who straddles two cultures often needs support, resources, and opportunities to engage in both communities, so let's not exclude one or the other. From this viewpoint, either the original or culturally adapted therapy could possibly be helpful to the client.

4. **What does it mean to "provide a rationale" for your choice?**

   a.   It means we have to make our decision by integrating information from each of the three EBP components. The first component is best evidence. From critical reading of the research literature, we know which EBPs have the best evidence, and we consider both internal and external validity viewpoints to evaluate the quality of the evidence.

b. The second component is clinical expertise. We are the clinical experts. We've assessed the client very carefully, working with cultural humility and respect. We've gotten additional information from colleagues who know about working with our client's diversity group and have experience with providing the EBP. We can get consultation on the fit of the intervention for our client's specific goals and characteristics. We've also evaluated whether we can learn the EBP, or who else in the community can provide it.

c. The third component is the client's characteristics, culture, and preferences. Our clinical expertise role comes into play here. We have to take into consideration everything we've assessed with our client to decide which EBP has the best fit. Does the EBP meet their health state, diagnosis, view of the problem, and so on? We should always focus on enhancing our credibility, and we should think of the EBP as a tool serving a larger, multilevel treatment plan rather than as a solve-all cure.

d. Providing a rationale means explaining our choice. We would note the information we gathered for each component to form an argument for our choice. We shouldn't leave out any component of information. We may also compare and contrast the EBPs we considered, such as, "I can learn this one but not that one," or "While the level of evidence and internal validity is weak for this EBP, external validity is the strongest."

Activity 7.2   **Test Your Understanding of the Chapter**

Answers: 1. False, 2. True, 3. True, 4. True, 5. True, 6. False, 7. True, 8. True.

REFERENCES

Culturally Adapted Interventions

Benish, S. G., Quintana, S., & Wampold, B. E. (2011). Culturally adapted psychotherapy and the legitimacy of myth: A direct-comparison meta-analysis. *Journal of Counseling Psychology, 58*(3), 279–289.

Bernal, G., Bonilla, J., & Bellido, C. (1995). Ecological validity and cultural sensitivity for outcome research: Issues for the cultural adaptation and development of psychosocial treatments with Hispanics. *Journal of Abnormal Child Psychology, 23*(1), 67–82.

Bernal, G., Jiménez-Chafey, M. I., & Domenech Rodríguez, M. M. (2009). Cultural adaptation of treatments: A resource for considering culture in evidence-based practice. *Professional Psychology: Research and Practice, 40*(4), 361–368. https://doi.org/10.1037/a0016401

Bronfenbrenner, U. (1977). Toward an experimental ecology of human development. *American Psychologist, 32*(7), 513–531.

Chu, J., & Leino, A. (2017). Advancement in the maturing science of cultural adaptations of evidence-based interventions. *Journal of Consulting and Clinical Psychology, 85*(1), 45–57.

Griner D., & Smith, T. B. (2006). Culturally adapted mental health intervention: A meta-analytic review. *Psychotherapy: Theory, Research, Practice & Training, 43*(4), 531–548.

Herbert, J. D. (2015). Empirically Supported Treatments (ESTs) and Empirically Supported Principles Of Change (ESPs). *The Encyclopedia of Clinical Psychology*. Wiley Online Library.

Hwang, W. (2006). The Psychotherapy Adaptation and Modification Framework (PAMF): Application to Asian Americans. *American Psychologist, 61*(7), 702–715.

Hwang, W.-C. (2009). The Formative Method for Adapting Psychotherapy (FMAP): A community-based developmental approach to culturally adapting therapy. *Professional Psychology Research and Practice, 40*(4), 369–377.

Hwang, W.-C. (2016). *Culturally adapting psychotherapy for Asian heritage populations: An evidence-based approach*. Elsevier Academic Press.

Hwang, W.-C., Myers, H. F., Chiu, E., Mak, E., Butner, J. E., Fujimoto, K., Wood, J. J., & Miranda, J. (2015). Culturally adapted cognitive-behavioral therapy for Chinese Americans with depression: A randomized controlled trial. *Psychiatric Services, 66*(10), 1035–1042.

Kohn, L. P., Oden, T., Munoz, R. F., Robinson, A., & Leavitt, D. (2002). Adapted cognitive behavioral group therapy for depressed low-income African American women. *Community Mental Health Journal, 38*(6), 497–504.

Lau, A. S. (2006). Making the case for selective and directed cultural adaptations of evidence-based treatments: Examples from parent training. *Clinical Psychology: Science and Practice, 13*(4), 295–310.

Malgady, R., Rogler, L. H., & Costantino, G. (1990) Culturally sensitive psychotherapy for Puerto Rican children and adolescents: a program of treatment outcome research. *Journal of Consulting and Clinical Psychology, 58*(6), 704–712.

Miranda, J., Bernal, G., Lau, A., Kohn, L., Hwang, W., & La Framboise, T. (2005). State of the science on psychosocial interventions for ethnic minorities. *Annual Review of Clinical Psychology, 1*, 113–142.

Rosselló, J., & Bernal, G. (1999). The efficacy of cognitive-behavioral and interpersonal treatments for depression in Puerto Rican adolescents. *Journal of Consulting and Clinical Psychology, 67*(5), 734–745. https://doi.org/10.1037/0022-006X.67.5.734

Rosselló, J., Bernal, G., & Rivera-Medina, C. (2008). Individual and group CBT and IPT for Puerto Rican adolescents with depressive symptoms. *Cultural Diversity & Ethnic Minority Psychology, 14*(3), 234–245.

Sue, D. W., Bingham, R. P., Porche-Burke, L., & Vasquez, M. (1999). The diversification of psychology: A multicultural revolution. *American Psychologist, 54*(12), 1061–1069.

Sue, S., & Zane, N. (1987). The role of culture and cultural techniques in psychotherapy. *American Psychologist, 42*(1), 37–45.

Sue, S., Zane, N., Nagayama Hall, G. C., & Berger, L. K. (2009). The case for cultural competency in psychotherapeutic interventions. *Annual Review of Psychology, 60*, 525–548.

Szapocznik, J., Santisteban, D., Kurtines, W., Perez-Vidal, A., Hervis, O. (1984). Bicultural effectiveness training (BET): A treatment intervention for enhancing intercultural adjustment. *Hispanic Journal of Behavioral Sciences, 6*(4), 317–344.

Tharp, R. G. (1991). Cultural diversity and treatment of children. *Journal of Consulting and Clinical Psychology, 59*(6), 799–812.

Trimble, J. E., & Mohatt, G. V. (2002). Coda: The virtuous and responsible researcher in another culture. In J. E. Trimble & C. B. Fisher (Eds.), *The Handbook of Ethical Research and Ethnocultural Populations and Communities* (pp. 325–334). SAGE Publishing.

Zavfert C. (2008). Culturally competent treatment of posttraumatic stress disorder in clinical practice: An ideographic, transcultural approach. *Clinical Psychology: Science and Practice, 15*(1), 68–73.

Selecting an Outcome Measure

Bonilla, J., Bernal, G., Santos, A., & Santos, D. (2004). A revised Spanish version of the Beck Depression Inventory: psychometric properties with a Puerto Rican sample of college students. *Journal of Clinical Psychology, 60*(1), 119–130.

Kroenke, K., Spitzer, R. L., & Williams, J. B. (2001). The PHQ-9: Validity of a brief depression severity measure. *Journal of General Internal Medicine, 16*(9), 606–613. https://doi.org/10.1046/j.1525-1497.2001.016009606.x (Spanish version available at: https://elcentro.sonhs.miami.edu/research/measures-library/phq-9/index.html)

Radloff, L. S. (1977). The CES-D Scale: A self-report depression scale for research in the general population. *Applied Psychological Measurement, 1*(3), 385–401. (Spanish version available at: https://elcentro.sonhs.miami.edu/research/measures-library/ces-d/CES-D%20Items_Eng_Spa.pdf)

Roberts, R. E., Vernon, S. W., & Rhoades, H. M. (1989). Effects of language and ethnic status on reliability and validity of the Center for Epidemiologic Studies-Depression Scale with psychiatric patients. *Journal of Nervous and Mental Disorders, 177*(10), 581–592.

Sheikh, J. I., & Yesavage, J. A. (1986). Geriatric Depression Scale (GDS): Recent evidence and development of a shorter version. In T.L. Brink (Ed.), *Clinical gerontology: A Guide to assessment and intervention* (pp. 165–173). NY: The Haworth Press, Inc. (Public domain instrument available at: https://web.stanford.edu/~yesavage/GDS.html)

Yesavage, J. A., Brink, T. L., Rose, T. L., Lum, O., Huang, V., Adey, M. B., & Leirer, V. O. (1983). Development and validation of a geriatric depression screening scale: A preliminary report. *Journal of Psychiatric Research, 17*(1), 37–49.

Evaluating Effectiveness: Using Single-Subject Design

Rubin, A., & Babbie, E. R. (2014). *Research methods for social work.* (8th ed.). Brooks/Cole. (See Chapter 13, Single-case evaluation designs, pp. 320–347.)

RESOURCES

Culturally Adapted Interventions

African American and Caribbean Communities

Berry, K., Day, C., Mulligan, L. D., Seed, T., Degnan, A., & Edge, D. (2018). Culturally adapted Family Intervention (CaFI): Case examples from therapists' perspectives. *The Cognitive Behaviour Therapist, 11*. (Caribbean community in United Kingdom)

Bogart, L. M., Dale, S. K., Daffin, G. K., Patel, K. N., Klein, D. J., Mayer, K. H., & Pantalone, D. W. (2018). Pilot intervention for discrimination-related coping among HIV-positive Black sexual minority men. *Cultural Diversity and Ethnic Minority Psychology, 24*(4), 541–551.

Graves, S. L., Jr., Herndon-Sobalvarro, A., Nichols, K., Aston, C., Ryan, A., Blefari, A., Schutte, K., Schachner, A., Vicoria, L., & Prier, D. (2017). Examining the effectiveness of a culturally adapted social-emotional intervention for African American males in an urban setting. *School Psychology Quarterly, 32*(1), 62–74.

Scott, T. N., Gil-Rivas, V., & Cachelin, F. M. (2019). The need for cultural adaptations to health interventions for African American women: A qualitative analysis. *Cultural Diversity and Ethnic Minority Psychology, 25*(3), 331–341. (Treatment for binge eating disorder)

Smith, G. G., & Celano, M. (2000). Revenge of the mutant cockroach: Culturally adapted storytelling in the treatment of a low-income African American boy. *Cultural Diversity and Ethnic Minority Psychology, 6*(2), 220–227.

Ward, E. C., & Brown, R. L. (2015). A culturally adapted depression intervention for African American adults experiencing depression: Oh Happy Day. *American Journal of Orthopsychiatry, 85*(1), 11–22.

Asian American Communities

Hall, G. C. N., Kim-Mozeleski, J. E., Zane, N. W., Sato, H., Huang, E. R., Tuan, M., & Ibaraki, A. Y. (2019). Cultural adaptations of psychotherapy: Therapists' applications of conceptual models with Asians and Asian Americans. *Asian American Journal of Psychology, 10*(1), 68–78.

Hinton, D. E., & Jalal, B. (2019). Dimensions of culturally sensitive CBT: Application to Southeast Asian populations. *American Journal of Orthopsychiatry, 89*(4), 493–507.

Manne, S. L., Islam, N., Frederick, S., Khan, U., Gaur, S., & Khan, A. (2018). Cultural-ly-adapted behavioral intervention to improve colorectal cancer screening uptake among foreign-born South Asians in new jersey: The desi sehat trial. *Ethnicity & Health 2018*, 1–17.

Rivera, A. M., Zhang, Z., Kim, A., Ahuja, N., Lee, H. Y., & Hahm, H. C. (2019). Mechanisms of action in AWARE: A culturally informed intervention for 15- and 2nd-generation Asian American women. *American Journal of Orthopsychiatry, 89*(4), 475–481.

Soonthornchaiya, R., & Dancy, B. L. (2006). Perceptions of depression among elderly Thai immigrants. *Issues in Mental Health Nursing, 27*(6), 681–698. (Supports future cultural adaptations of interventions)

Latinx American Communities

Cachelin, F. M., Gil-Rivas, V., Palmer, B., Vela, A., Phimphasone, P., de Hernandez, B. U., & Tapp, H. (2019). Randomized controlled trial of a culturally-adapted program for Latinas with binge eating. *Psychological Services, 16*(3), 504–512.

Castro-Olivo, S. M. (2014). Promoting social-emotional learning in adolescent Latino ELLs: A study of the culturally adapted Strong Teens program. *School Psychology Quarterly, 29*(4), 567–577.

Dietz, N. A., Asfar, T., Caban-Martinez, A. J., Ward, K. D., Santiago, K., Ruano-Herreria, E. C., McClure, L. A., & Lee, D. J. (2018). Developing a worksite-based culturally adapted smoking cessation intervention for male Hispanic/Latino construction workers. *Journal of Smoking Cessation.*

Duarté-Vélez, Y., Bernal, G., & Bonilla, K. (2010). Culturally adapted cognitive-behavioral therapy: Integrating sexual, spiritual, and family identities in an evidence-based treatment of a depressed Latino adolescent. *Journal of Clinical Psychology, 66*(8), 895–906.

Gerdes, A. C., Kapke, T. L., Lawton, K. E., Grace, M., & Dieguez Hurtado, G. (2015). Culturally adapting parent training for Latino youth with ADHD: Development and pilot. *Journal of Latina/o Psychology, 3*(2), 71–87. https://doi.org/10.1037/lat0000037

Interian, A., Martinez, I., Rios, L. I., Krejci, J., & Guarnaccia, P. J. (2010). Adaptation of a motivational interviewing intervention to improve antidepressant adherence among Latinos. *Cultural Diversity and Ethnic Minority Psychology, 16*(2), 215–225.

Kopelowicz, A., Zarate, R., Wallace, C. J., Liberman, R. P., Lopez, S. R., & Mintz, J. (2012). The ability of multifamily groups to improve treatment adherence in Mexican Americans with schizophrenia. *Archives of General Psychiatry*, *69*(3), 265–273. https://doi.org/10.1001/archgenpsychiatry.2011.135

Paris, M., Silva, M., Añez-Nava, L., Jaramillo, Y., Kiluk, B. D., Gordon, M. A., Nich, C., Frankforter, T., Devore, K., Ball, S. A., & Carroll, K. M. (2018). Culturally adapted, web-based cognitive behavioral therapy for Spanish-speaking individuals with substance use disorders: A randomized clinical trial. *American Journal of Public Health*, *108*(11), 1535–1542.

Parra, C. R., López, Z. G., Leija, S. G., Maas, M. K., Villa, M., Zamudio, E., Arredondo, M., Yeh, H., & Domenech Rodríguez, M. M. (2018). A culturally adapted intervention for Mexican-origin parents of adolescents: The need to overtly address culture and discrimination in evidence-based practice. *Family Process 58*(2), 334–352.

Shea, M., Cachelin, F. M., Gutierrez, G., Wang, S., & Phimphasone, P. (2016). Mexican American women's perspectives on a culturally adapted cognitive-behavioral therapy guided self-help program for binge eating. *Psychological Services*, *13*(1), 31–41.

Valdez, L. A., Flores, M., Ruiz, J., Oren, E., Carvajal, S., & Garcia, D. O. (2018). Gender and cultural adaptations for diversity: A systematic review of alcohol and substance abuse interventions for Latino males. *Substance Use & Misuse*, *53*(10), 1608–1623.

Wood, J. J., Chiu, A. W., Hwang, W.-C., Jacobs, J., & Ifekwunigwe, M. (2008). Adapting cognitive-behavioral therapy for Mexican American students with anxiety disorders: Recommendations for school psychologists. *School Psychology Quarterly*, *23*(4), 515–532. https://doi.org/10.1037/1045-3830.23.4.515

LGBTQ Communities

Goldbach, J. T., & Holleran Steiker, L. K. (2011). An examination of cultural adaptations performed by LGBT-identified youths to a culturally grounded, evidence-based substance abuse intervention. *Journal of Gay & Lesbian Social Services: The Quarterly Journal of Community & Clinical Practice*, *23*(2), 188–203.

Whitton, S. W., Scott, S. B., Dyar, C., Weitbrecht, E. M., Hutsell, D. W., & Kuryluk, A. D. (2017). Piloting relationship education for female same-sex couples: Results of a small randomized waitlist-control trial. *Journal of Family Psychology*, *31*(7), 878–888.

Middle Eastern Communities

Kananian, S., Ayoughi, S., Farugie, A., Hinton, D., & Stangier, U. (2017). Transdiagnostic culturally adapted CBT with Farsi-speaking refugees: A pilot study. *European Journal of Psychotraumatology*, *8* (Suppl 2), 1–10.

Nygren, T., Brohede, D., Koshnaw, K., Osman, S. S., Johansson, R., & Andersson, G. (2019). Internet-based treatment of depressive symptoms in a Kurdish population: A randomized controlled trial. *Journal of Clinical Psychology, 75*(6), 985–998.

Native American Communities

Hiratsuka, V. Y., Parker, M. E., Sanchez, J., Riley, R., Heath, D., Chomo, J. C., Beltangady, M., & Sarche, M. (2018). Cultural adaptations of evidence-based home-visitation models in tribal communities. *Infant Mental Health Journal, 39*(3), 265–275.

King, J., Trimble, J. E., Morse, G. S., & Thomas, L. R. (2014). North American Indian and Alaska Native spirituality and psychotherapy. In P. S. Richards & A. E. Bergin (Eds.), *Handbook of Psychotherapy and Religious Diversity,* 2nd ed. (pp. 451–472). American Psychological Association.

Kulis, S. S., Tsethlikai, M., Harthun, M. L., Hibbeler, P. K., Ayers, S. L., & Deschine Parkhurst, N. (2020). Parenting in 2 worlds: Effects of a culturally grounded parenting intervention for urban American Indians on participant cultural engagement. *Cultural Diversity and Ethnic Minority Psychology, 26*(4), 437–446. http://dx.doi.org/10.1037/cdp0000315

Pearson, C. R., Kaysen, D., Huh, D., & Bedard-Gilligan, M. (2019). Randomized control trial of culturally adapted cognitive processing therapy for PTSD substance misuse and HIV sexual risk behavior for Native American women. *AIDS and Behavior, 23*(3), 695–706.

Venner, K. L., Greenfield, B. L., Hagler, K. J., Simmons, J., Lupee, D., Homer, E., Yamutewa, Y., & Smith, J. E. (2016). Pilot outcome results of culturally adapted evidence-based substance use disorder treatment with a Southwest Tribe. *Addictive Behaviors Reports, 3,* 21–27.

Reviews & Meta-Analyses

Degnan, A., Baker, S., Edge, D., Nottidge, W., Noke, M., Press, C. J., & Drake, R. J. (2017). The nature and efficacy of culturally-adapted psychosocial interventions for schizophrenia: A systematic review and meta-analysis. *Psychological Medicine, 48*(5), 1–14.

Ennis, N., Shorer, S., Shoval, Z. Y., Freedman, S., Monson, C. M., & Dekel, R. (2020). Treating posttraumatic stress disorder across cultures: A systematic review of cultural adaptations of trauma-focused cognitive behavioral therapies. *Journal of Clinical Psychology, 76*(4), 587–611.

Hall, G. C. N., Ibaraki, A. Y., Huang, E. R., Marti, C. N., & Stice, E. (2016). A meta-analysis of cultural adaptations of psychological interventions. *Behavior Therapy, 47,* 993–1014.

Soto, A., Smith, T. B., Griner, D., Domenech Rodríguez, M., & Bernal, G. (2018). Cultural adaptations and therapist multicultural competence: Two meta-analytic reviews. *Journal of Clinical Psychology: In Session, 74*(11), 1907–1923. http://dx.doi.org/10.1002/jclp.22679

Selecting an Outcome Measure

Therapy Meets Numbers. (n.d.). *How to choose a therapy outcome measure.*

> This article provides brief guidelines on how to choose an outcome measure for a client.

> https://therapymeetsnumbers.com/how-to-choose-a-therapy-outcome-measure

Allied Health Professions (AHP) Outcome Measures UK Working Group. (November 2019). *Key questions to ask when selecting outcome measures: A checklist for allied health professions.*

> An excellent detailed checklist intended to guide professionals in the choice of an outcome measure for evaluation purposes. This checklist is not intended for choosing a measure for an individual client, but it provides a helpful framework.

> https://www.rcslt.org/-/media/docs/selecting-outcome-measures.pdf?la=en&hash=12ECB2CFDA0B2EFB1979E592A383D24E792AB9DD

Evaluating Effectiveness: Using Single-Subject Design

Wambaugh, J., & Schlosser, R. (2014). *Single-subject experimental design: An overview.* Clinical Research Education (CREd) Library.

> This website provides an excellent brief overview with several videos.

> https://academy.pubs.asha.org/2014/12/single-subject-experimental-design-an-overview

Chiang, I.-C. A., Jhangiani, R. S., & Price, P.C. (2015). *Research methods in psychology.* BCcampus Open Textbooks. (Chapter 10: Single-Subject Research Designs)

> This article provides a detailed overview of single-subject designs.

> https://opentextbc.ca/researchmethods/chapter/single-subject-research-designs

Credits

Case Paper Instructions

Objectives

1. Learn to analyze and apply research evidence on mental health interventions to support your provision of appropriate treatment and services for clients from diverse backgrounds.

2. Learn to apply a decision-making model that considers research evidence, clinical expertise, and client characteristics, culture, and preferences, including taking into consideration mental health needs particular to clients from minority, vulnerable, and special needs communities.

Description

For a current or past client, find three different interventions that may be suitable for treating the client, evaluate the interventions using the EBP decision-making model, and choose the best intervention for the client, justifying your decision. The assignment is worth 50 points. The page limit is 10–12 pages, excluding the title and reference pages.

1. **Introduction** *(2–3 paragraphs, 2 points)*

    a. ***Purpose of the Paper.*** State that the purpose is to identify and evaluate the appropriateness and usefulness of three different interventions for a client using an evidence-based practice decision-making model that considers the following: (a) research evidence, (b) clinical expertise, and (c) client characteristics, culture, and preferences. *(2–3 sentences, ½ point)*

    b. ***Identification of the Client, Clinician, and Setting.*** Identify the client, you, your role, and the service setting, including any restrictions on types of interventions that can be considered given service/time limits, insurance, or other factors. *(1 paragraph, 1 point)*

    c. ***Paper Content.*** State the content sections that will be covered in the paper. *(1–2 sentences, ½ point)*

2. **Client Profile** *(2–3 paragraphs, 3 points)*

   a. ***Social and Cultural Background.*** Provide a brief description of your client's sociodemographic and cultural background. *(1 paragraph, 1 point)*

   b. ***Developmental, Psychological, and Environmental Background.*** Provide information on your client's developmental phase, needs, and history; DSM provisional diagnoses; relevant psychological characteristics (e.g., defenses, coping skills, attachment style); strengths (individual, family, and community); and current or past environmental stressors. *(1–2 paragraphs, 2 points)*

3. **Client's Conceptualization** *(3–4 paragraphs, 5 points)*

   a. ***Problem Conceptualization.*** State your client's understanding of their presenting problem, including causes and impact. *(1–2 paragraphs, 2 points)*

   b. ***Treatment Goals and Appropriate Forms of Treatment***. Formulate meaningful and measurable goals for your client and identify form(s) of treatment that would be acceptable and helpful to the client, considering the client's background, preferences, and culture. Address both micro-level (individual and family) and mezzo-level (school, work, and community) goals and interventions, even though the EBPs you review are micro-level interventions. *(2 paragraphs, 3 points)*

4. **Review of EBP #1** *(6–7 paragraphs, 9 points)*

   This section is based on your review of two empirical research articles and other information found online, in print, and through interviews.

   a. ***Description of Intervention.*** Provide information on length of intervention, theoretical foundation, components and activities involved, problem or diagnostic areas or population for which it is suited, and anything else important to give a brief but thorough overview of the intervention. *(1–2 paragraphs, 1 point)*

   b. ***Identification & Justification of Level of Evidence.*** For each article, identify the level of evidence (grade A, B or C) using the definitions on p. 136 and justify the level by briefly describing the research design. Include the study's main finding. *(1–2 paragraphs, 2 points)*

c.   ***Populations Studied & Evaluation of Applicability to My Client.*** For each study, evaluate whether its sample included people with diversity characteristics like those of your client and whether the findings support the intervention's use in your client's community. (You may also comment generally based on your search for articles whether you came across many studies on your client's diversity group.) *(1 paragraph, 2 points)*

d.   ***Evaluation of Experts.*** State whether the intervention is appropriate for your client based on a discussion with your supervisor or another experienced clinician, and also, if you wish, on your own experience and evaluation. State how it would or would not be appropriate and useful for your client, including modifications to the intervention, if any, that you would make for your client. *(1 paragraph, 2 points)*

e.   ***Feasibility of Learning & Applying Intervention Correctly.*** State the probability that you can learn the intervention and apply it correctly and effectively. To do this, gather information on the amount of materials (e.g., manuals, books, and videos) and trainings made available to the public to evaluate whether it is feasible for you to learn to conduct the intervention. If you wish, you can also comment on the intervention's overall level of readiness for dissemination and implementation. *(1 paragraph, 2 points)*

5.   **Review of EBP #2** *(6–7 paragraphs, 9 points)*

Same instructions as for EBP #1.

6.   **Review of EBP #3** *(6–7 paragraphs, 9 points)*

Same instructions as for EBP #1.

7.   **Best Intervention** *(6–7 paragraphs, 6 points)*

a.   ***Best Intervention and Rationale.*** Identify the best intervention for your client. Discuss your rationale for choosing it, addressing how you considered and balanced information for each of the three components: (a) best available research, (b) clinical expertise, and (c) patient characteristics, culture, and preferences. Discuss how the other two interventions are less suited, based on the three components. If you decide to use more than one intervention or modify an intervention to meet your client's needs and characteristics, describe why and how you would do so. *(4–5 paragraphs, 4 points)*

b. ***Evidence-Based Treatment Plan.*** Describe your treatment plan with the chosen intervention, including length of treatment and specific treatment goals for your client and method of monitoring and evaluating client progress and outcomes (e.g., client satisfaction scale, symptom scale, or behavioral or other indicators). *(1–2 paragraphs, 2 points)*

8. **Writing Quality & APA Style** *(7 points)*

a. ***Quality of Writing.*** There should be no punctuation, spelling, subject-verb agreement, and other basic English grammar errors. Please use spell check. Writing should be easy to read, clear, comprehensible, and succinct and nonrepetitive. *(4 points)*

b. ***APA Style.*** Use APA style, including 1" margins, 12-point Times New Roman or Arial font, double-spacing throughout paper, subtitles, proper in-text citations, and correct formatting of title page and references. *(3 points)*

Case Paper on Laura

EBP Decision-Making: Immigrant Adolescent Girl in Sacramento

Introduction

The purpose of this paper is to evaluate three evidence-based interventions to determine which intervention will work best for the presenting client. The interventions evaluated are Cognitive Behavioral Therapy for Adolescents (CBT-A), Mindfulness-Based Stress Reduction (MBSR), and Interpersonal Psychotherapy for Depressed Adolescents (IPT-A). The decision of the best intervention for the client will be based on available research evidence, clinical expertise, and the specific characteristics and needs of the client while encompassing their culture.

My client, Laura (pseudonym), age 15, attends a public high school where I am a school-based counselor. As an MSW student, I intern at Meadowview Community Center (MCC), a community-based social services agency with school-based programs in numerous high schools. My role is to provide mental health interventions, case management, and psychoeducation and to assist in creating environments that support students' academic success. I help monitor students' grades and attendance; contact caregivers and provide resources for families; and work closely with teachers and administrators to provide assistance and consultation for student success. MCC operates on a brief, eight-session therapy model so that the needs of more students can be met throughout the school year. This model is also intended to foster independence for the individual. When additional support is needed, a longer duration of services is permitted, such as ongoing case management for foster youth and homeless youth and families.

This paper will describe the client's cultural and socioeconomic background and views of their presenting problems, goals, preferences, and desired forms of help. As further background, it will include a case conceptualization and identification of appropriate forms of treatment and treatment goals. Next, this paper will describe and assess the three evidence-based interventions. Finally, it will identify the best evidence-based intervention for this unique client and explain how it will be implemented in this particular setting.

Client Profile

Social and Cultural Background

Laura is a 15-year-old Latina female in the 10th grade. She was born and grew up in a small town in rural Mexico and immigrated to the U.S. at the age of 14. She lives in a suburb of Sacramento, California, with her younger brother, age 11, and her mother, age 42. Laura's father migrated to the U.S. when Laura was 3 years old, followed by her mother's migration when Laura was 7 years old. Laura and her brother lived with her maternal grandparents until they joined their mother in the U.S. Before and after coming to the U.S., Laura has been her brother's primary caregiver. Laura has had almost no contact with her father, who remarried and started a new family within 2 years of settling in the U.S. He lives with his new family in Reno, Nevada. Laura is semifluent in English and fluent in Spanish. Laura's mother, who works for two families as a nanny, is the family's single provider.

Developmental, Psychological, and Environmental Background

Acquiring a sense of identity and defining her role in life are important to Laura as an adolescent in Erikson's psychosocial stage of identity vs. role confusion. Laura is trying to experience and define her sense of self and her future, but she requires supportive resources and grounding at home and school for this to occur. She has struggled with developing trusting relationships with those outside her home, especially peers, teachers, and administrators. From an attachment perspective, Laura's working model of relationships is one of mistrust and insecure-anxious avoidance due to the separations from her father and mother as a young child, her grandparents' inattentiveness, and her current lack of emotional and social support. She copes by acting out and keeping to herself. She has exhibited defiant behaviors in the classroom and begun to engage in physical fights as a result of being bullied and being unable to manage her anger. She exhibits some symptoms of depression and anxiety, but not enough to indicate major depression or generalized anxiety. Her provisional DSM-5 diagnosis is Mood Disorder, Not Otherwise Specified.

Laura's individual strengths include her excellent insight and cognitive and emotional awareness, desire to grow, and openness to receiving therapy and other interventions. Laura's home environment is also an important strength.

Laura's mother is very supportive of Laura, although the mother works two jobs, with only most Sundays off. Laura has a close relationship with her younger brother, and the family has relatives in the San Francisco Bay Area. The school setting, however, is an environmental stressor. Laura's being bullied, acting out, avoidance and lack of friendships, and having no mental health and academic counselors until recently contribute to a very stressful and unsupportive environment. Laura has struggled academically due to the unfriendly classroom environments, with negative attitudes from peers and teachers. Also, because she does not live near the school, she must take the bus to her school. She has expressed that she feels isolated in her neighborhood. She does not feel connected to the school because she must leave immediately after school to get home to care for her younger brother.

Client's Conceptualization

Problem Conceptualization

Laura reports that she has problems controlling her anger, especially with other students, teachers, and administrators. She says she feels anxious when there are any possible interactions and confrontations with others. She also reports that she is sad and lonely, has problems trusting peers and adults, and does not feel connected to school or to her mother. Laura would like to work on managing her anger and to learn how to develop trusting relationships, including making friends and being closer to her mother. She would like individual therapy to vent about her experiences, explore the reasons for these problems, and come up with possible solutions. She is open to involving and learning to talk with her mother. She also expressed interest in academic counseling and planning for college. She recognizes that addressing the separation traumas that occurred will be helpful to her, but she is not ready to connect with her father.

Treatment Goals and Appropriate Forms of Treatment

The treatment goals are to decrease instances of anger escalation, decrease symptoms of depression, establish meaningful relationships with others, and build the relationship with her mother, including processing the attachment traumas. The treatment outcomes will be measured by recording all instances in which the client has had altercations with others as a result of anger, client's report of number and severity of depression symptoms at each session, and client's record-keeping of positive social interactions with peers and adults. Individual and family psychotherapy will be beneficial in treating the client on the micro level. Also, gaining the support and involvement of the client's mother on the client's goals and planned interventions and building an active alliance with the family will be an important component of treatment. At the mezzo level, the intervention is to provide case management that ensures linkages and supportive resources that promote academic success and personal and social development.

Review of EBP #1: Cognitive Behavioral Therapy for Adolescents

Description of Intervention

Cognitive Behavioral Therapy for Adolescents (CBT-A) is an adaptation of Aaron Beck's cognitive behavioral therapy for adults but modified for the psychological development of adolescents. It can be applied for depression, anxiety, and adjustment issues. In CBT, the client learns to become aware of their automatic thoughts that occur in stressful situations and the relationship of thoughts, emotions, and behaviors. By questioning the validity of the automatic thoughts, as well as the inaccurate core beliefs underlying the everyday thoughts, the client can reduce the associated negative emotional states and behaviors. The role of the cognitive behavioral therapist for adolescents is to use examples given by the client that help explain the cognitive behavioral model. Also, CBT-A focuses on helping the client to gain independence and nurture trusting relationships with others by developing problem-solving and healthy coping skills. In the adolescent model for cognitive behavioral therapy, the clients are not expected to do extensive homework, such as logging automatic thoughts. However, the therapist uses the 12–16 sessions to develop skills in recognizing thoughts and affects.

Identification & Justification of Level of Evidence

The levels of evidence are grade A– and grade B for the two CBT-A studies I reviewed. The A– study was an RCT (Brent et al., 1999). It had a sample size of 107 adolescents and compared CBT with systemic behavioral family therapy and nondirective supportive therapy; CBT had superior outcomes in the acute phase of depression. Dropout was within an acceptable level, given that 12% of those eligible did not agree to be randomized and 14% dropped out or did not start treatment. The B study (Weersing et al., 2006) compared the outcomes of 80 youth recruited from an outpatient clinic for adolescents with depression with the outcomes from a gold-standard clinical trial considered to be the benchmark for CBT-A. In my view, this is a quasi-experimental design, even though the researchers recruited youth with similar characteristics as the benchmark study conducted years earlier. Without randomization, the two groups are not guaranteed to be similar. Findings showed that improvements in depression were similar between the sample of 80 youth and the benchmark study sample. A third study was a grade A meta-analysis of 11 RCTs that confirms the general effectiveness of CBT-A (Klein et al., 2007).

Populations Studied & Evaluation of Applicability to My Client

The direct generalizability of the findings reviewed to my client is moderate. The samples appeared to be more depressed, likely included few or no Latina immigrant teens, and were in inpatient and outpatient psychiatric settings. The grade A– RCT (Brent et al., 1999) neither reported the racial/ethnic background of participants nor the study setting, but participants, referred to as patients, had moderate depression with substantial rates of comorbid anxiety, dysthymic disorder, and disruptive disorders. The grade B study (Weersing et al., 2006) investigated youth in an outpatient setting and included female (77%) and some minority (15%) participants, which is similar to my client's situation. Showing applicability to my client, the meta-analysis of 11 studies included four studies of students and one study of community youths rather than outpatients and youth in juvenile justice (Klein et al., 2007).

Evaluation of Experts

My internship supervisor, who is an LCSW, holds a school social work credential, and has practiced CBT with children for over 10 years, informed me that CBT-A would be effective in the school setting. He believes that CBT-A can be especially useful in assisting the client in building self-esteem through a cognitive behavioral lens, including in helping the client to understand interpersonal problems via awareness of her own thoughts and feelings. Although MCC does not typically have students remain in treatment past eight sessions, this specific client may require the longer period of assistance that is required for the typical CBT-A for depression (D. Pratt, Personal Communication, November 8, 2019).

Feasibility of Learning & Applying Intervention Correctly

CBT is commonly used at MCC and in MCC's school-based clinics. I have had a 10-week academic course on CBT for depression in adults and have practiced CBT with adults in my previous internship. I can obtain a 21-hour online training on CBT with children and adolescents (Feeling Good Institute, n.d.). However, with the CBT-A manuals that have been provided to me by MCC, I feel confident in implementing the intervention with fairly high fidelity given close guidance from my supervisor and additional consultation from other clinicians at MCC.

Review of EBP #2: Mindfulness-Based Stress Reduction

Description of Intervention

Mindfulness-Based Stress Reduction (MBSR) is psychoeducation-based intervention that is geared toward adolescents and adults to help reduce stress and anxiety and depression symptoms for individuals who have chronic illness or have experienced stressful life events. This program focuses on the principle of mindfulness training, which seeks to help the client become aware of their thoughts, emotions, and bodily sensations in the moment in order to cope with everyday stressors affecting them physically, emotionally, and in particular interpersonal situations. Therapists use three experiential forms of treatment: mindfulness meditation, yoga, and body scanning. Mindfulness mediation focuses on breathing and noticing one's daily activities, such as walking. Gentle yoga uses simple body postures that calm the brain while improving concentration. Body scanning helps the client to understand their body's reaction to stress by noticing their body's sensations when focusing on each part of the body. The goal is to assist the client in understanding their own thoughts and emotions while using techniques learned in mindfulness training to adjust how they react to negative thoughts, feelings, and situations. MSRB takes place in ten sessions within a group setting.

Identification & Justification of Level of Evidence

I reviewed a grade A systematic review and meta-analysis (Chi et al., 2018) and a grade B+ RCT (Biegel et al., 2009). The systematic review and meta-analysis included 18 RCTs, with samples totaling 2,042 participants ranging in age from 12 to 25 years. In the meta-analysis, MBSR showed moderate effects in reducing depression symptoms. The B+ RCT, with a sample of 102 teens with heterogeneous mental illness diagnoses recruited from an outpatient psychiatric facility, found that the MBSR group experienced higher diagnostic improvement (including reduced symptoms of anxiety, depression, and somatic distress, and increased self-esteem and sleep quality) and significant increases in global assessment of functioning relative to controls, as rated by blinded outcome assessors (Biegel et al., 2009). However, this study had a 22% dropout rate in the MBSR group and was not multisite, although it used intent-to-treat analysis.

Populations Studied & Evaluation of Applicability to My Client

A review of the populations studied indicate that the evidence is moderately generalizable to my client, especially because of the diversity of levels of severity and diagnoses among participants and the inclusion of youth not from a psychiatric setting. The systematic review (Chi et al., 2018) included studies with clinical and nonclinical samples, and the samples included adolescents and young adults who were diagnosed as depressed using any diagnostic criterion (e.g., DSM-5 or a depression rating scale). This inclusion of nonclinical samples means that youth not reaching the level of clinical diagnosis were included. The B+ study included participants who had mood disorders (49%), anxiety disorders (30.4%), and other disorders (24.5%) (Biegel et al., 2009). A majority also had parent-child relational problems and/or problems related to abuse or neglect. However, poor generalizability may exist at the level of SES and racial/ethnic match. The systematic review did not report such data (Chi et al., 2018), while the other study reported that its sample was predominantly female (73.5%), included Latinx teens (28.4%), and had a mean age of 15.4 years (Biegel et al., 2009). There may still be a cultural barrier that hinders the effectiveness of this treatment for a bicultural adolescent Latina of low economic status.

Evaluation of Experts

According to my supervisor, MBSR could be very useful in providing focus to my client and decreasing her anxiety with interpersonal concerns. Although this treatment is usually given in a group setting, a therapist can use the elements, such as body scanning and mindfulness meditation, in individual sessions. My supervisor suggested that the therapist focus on providing education on these skills so the client can build her coping strategies. She also noted that MBSR can be implemented in schools successfully in individual and group work (D. Pratt, personal communication, November 8, 2019).

Feasibility of Learning & Applying Intervention Correctly

MBSR is commonly used by MCC counselors at our school-based clinics. I have practiced mindfulness techniques individually and in groups for 5 years, although I have not been trained in the manualized MBSR protocol. MBSR manuals and books, available to me at MCC, provide extensive tools for learning and carrying out this therapy. To become a licensed MBSR instructor, you are required to take rigorous training courses and attend teacher retreats. This may not be feasible for the typical therapist. I feel confident in implementing the intervention with fairly high fidelity with self-study and close guidance from my supervisor and additional consultation from other clinicians at MCC.

Review of EBP 3: Interpersonal Psychotherapy
for Depressed Adolescents

Interpersonal Psychotherapy for Depressed Adolescents (IPT-A) assists adolescents with mild-to-moderate depression in dealing with interpersonal struggles (Mufson et al., 2004). It is an adaptation of Interpersonal Psychotherapy for adults, which focuses on improving relationships by increasing social and communication skills. It is a time-limited (12–16 sessions) individual treatment for teens ages 12–18. The focus of IPT-A is on how relationship issues are related to depressive symptoms. Adolescents are taught to be aware of the impact of interpersonal conflict on mood changes. The therapist helps the clients identify the most common sources of depressive symptoms stemming from relationships, including grief, role transitions and disputes, and lack of interpersonal interactions. The therapy also seeks to normalize stressful events in an adolescent's life, such as the loss of a friend or relative, conflict regarding independence from caregivers, single-parent families, peer pressure, and romantic relationships. This therapy is intended as a short-term intervention and not for severely depressed, suicidal, homicidal, bipolar, or psychotic adolescents. It is also not intended for adolescents who have severe learning disabilities or are abusing substances.

Identification & Justification of Level of Evidence
I reviewed two grade B+ RCTs (Mufson et al., 2004; Gunlicks-Stoessel et al., 2019). First, a 16-week RCT was conducted in five school-based mental health clinics in New York City with 65 teens, including 76% Hispanic, who were referred for a mental health intake. Those receiving IPT-A compared with treatment as usual showed greater depression symptom reduction and improved social and overall functioning (Mufson et al., 2004). Second, in another 16-week RCT, 40 adolescents (10% Latinx) were randomized to three treatment strategies that began with IPT-A and augmented at week 4 for those who did not respond sufficiently. Augmented treatments included the addition of an antidepressant (fluoxetine) or four additional IPT-A sessions. IPT-A was found to reduce attachment anxiety and avoidance significantly across the 16 weeks of treatment. Higher avoidance in relationships at baseline predicted greater reductions in depression, indicating the possible stronger benefits of IPT-A for teens with a high level of avoidant attachment.

Populations Studied & Evaluation of Applicability to My Client

The two studies reviewed have moderately strong generalizability to my client. Mufson et al.'s (2004) study has strong direct applicability. It included Hispanic (76%), single-parent homes (74%), families on public assistance (29%), and parents with a mean education level less than high school. Participants had a wide range of depressive disorder diagnoses, including adjustment disorder with depressive symptoms. Also like my client, the majority had not received previous mental health treatment. Most importantly, the study setting was in five school-based mental health clinics (like MCC). Additionally, Reyes-Portillo et al., (2017), analyzing the Latinx intent-to-treat sample (N=50) from Mufson et al.'s (2004) study, observed improvements in relationships with peers and family using IPC. Gunlicks-Stoessel et al.'s (2019) study has less applicability to my client. The study required participants to have a depressive disorder and significant symptoms of depression and impairment in general functioning, which my client does not have. However, its finding regarding the effectiveness of IPT-A for teens with avoidant attachment is of interest to my client, given the losses and neglect she experienced.

Evaluation of Experts

My supervisor believes that IPT-A could be the most useful of the three interventions for my client, as much of her interpersonal struggles have left her depressed. She stated that IPT-A could be specifically helpful for this client to understand the reality of the interpersonal situations she faces and how they developed. The work with my client would include developing coping skills and understanding specific instances of interpersonal distress. Additionally, my supervisor believed that IPT-A would be useful in naming feelings and receiving validation from the dynamic feelings resulting from interpersonal situations (D. Pratt, personal communication, November 20, 2019).

Feasibility of Learning and Applying Intervention Correctly

My supervisor and another clinician at MCC who has worked with me believed that it would be feasible for me to learn to provide IPT-A correctly and effectively. The IPT-A manual is available at MCC, and even though IPT-A has not been specifically implemented at my work setting, my colleagues and supervisors at MCC all use techniques similar to IPT-A extensively. The manual is easy to follow, detailed, and provides case vignettes and scripts for the therapist to follow. Therapists are also allowed to make adaptations when they cannot provide the intervention in the standard number of sessions. In addition, the manual provides information for dealing with common adolescent issues and crises during the intervention and provides tools for assessing progress. There is also an intervention website helpful for additional training resources (California Evidence-Based Clearinghouse, 2018). To become certified in IPT-A, however, is unfeasible, due to the training being very rigorous and time-consuming (see Interpersonal Therapy Institute, n.d.).

Best Intervention

Best Intervention and Rationale

The best treatment for this client is IPT-A. This treatment fits my client's background, needs, and preferences, which strongly center on relationships. She often experiences depression and anxiety after having interpersonal issues with peers and adults. IPT-A will normalize her interpersonal concerns so that her depressive and anxious symptoms will diminish. Also, the intent of IPT-A is to provide psychoeducation on how to cope with interpersonal concerns and common developmental milestones during adolescence. IPT-A is also suitable because it is intended for mild-to-moderate cases of depression and anxiety, which is my client's case. Two B+ studies on the hierarchy of evidence indicate that the evidence of IPT-A's efficacy is fairly strong from an internal validity viewpoint. Also, Mufson et al.'s (2004) study demonstrated the external validity of the study for low SES Latinx teenagers in school settings, like MCC's school-based mental health clinics.

I ruled out CBT-A, even though the evidence is stronger (with the studies I reviewed being A– and B studies), given that the studies included adolescents who were from a clinical or more depressed population, and lower income Latinx adolescents were excluded from the samples. My supervisor evaluated CBT-A as helpful to building my client's self-esteem and understanding interpersonal problems, but IPT-A is a better fit because it is designed specifically to address relational concerns, which is what my client desires help with.

I ruled out MBSR, even though it has grade A evidence from the meta-analytic study (Chi et al., 2018) and B+ evidence from the small RCT (Biegel et al., 2009) and appears to be suited to varying levels of depression severity, including clinical and nonclinical participants, and types of mental health problems. The rule-out was due to the poor generalizability of the evidence to my client on the basis of SES and ethnic background. Also, although my supervisor noted useful aspects of MBSR, especially for building my client's coping strategies, MBSR is not designed specifically to address relational issues, which are again my client's top concerns.

Although I am not certified in IPT-A, the manual and support from my supervisor and colleagues at MCC will allow me to provide IPT-A with a strong level of fidelity. At MCC, all therapists use techniques similar to IPT-A to assist clients with normalizing instances of interpersonal issues and life events. We also facilitate therapy groups geared toward individuals dealing with grief and loss and interpersonal struggles. My supervisor has also facilitated culture-based therapy groups that serve minority students' unique needs, including their need for empowerment and ability to relate cross-culturally and intergenerationally. With these resources, it will be possible for me to provide IPT-A with adaptations that can best meet the needs of my client.

Evidence-Based Treatment Plan

IPT-A treatment duration will be 16 weekly sessions. I will use the IPT-A model to provide activities during our sessions that facilitate the expression of feelings, validation of those feelings, and normalization of the occurrences of interpersonal struggles and triumphs. We will also use role-play activities that facilitate and model appropriate social and communication skills for the client. To engage her with peers, I will refer her to a social skills group for students who have similar issues at school. The use of IPT-A principles will most definitely be effective in helping my client cope with challenges in depression, anxiety, and interpersonal difficulties. It will also provide her with the communication skills necessary to be successful in a school environment. I will involve the client's mother to gain support and involvement on the client's therapy and case management goals and to process attachment trauma once appropriate to do so. The mother will be invited for dyadic sessions at the start of therapy and every few weeks thereafter.

The treatment goals for my client are to decrease instances of escalation of anger, decrease depressive symptoms, and engage in activities that contribute to building meaningful relationships with others. My client will record instances of anger escalation and positive interactions with others on a daily basis. She will also complete a depression scale at the start of each weekly session and a self-evaluation of social skills development every 4 weeks.

References

Biegel, G. M., Brown, K. W., Shapiro, S. L., & Schubert, C. M. (2009). Mindfulness-based stress reduction treatment for the treatment of adolescent psychiatric outpatients: A randomized clinical trial. *Journal of Consulting and Clinical Psychology, 77*(5), 855–866.

Brent, D. A., Kolko, D., Birmaher, B., Baugher, M., Roth, C., Iyengar, S., & Johnson, B. A. (1999). A clinical trial for adolescent depression: Predictors of additional treatment in the acute and follow-up phases of the trial. *Journal of American Academy of Child and Adolescent Psychiatry, 38*(3), 263–270. https://doi.org/10.1001/archpsyc.1997.01830210125017

California Evidence-based Clearinghouse (2018). *Interpersonal psychotherapy for depressed adolescents* (IPT-A). https://www.cebc4cw.org/program/interpersonal-psychotherapy-for-depressed-adolescents/detailed

Chi, X., Bo, A., Liu, T., Zhang, P., & Chi, I. (2018). Effects of mindfulness-based stress reduction on depression in adolescents and young adults: A systematic review and meta-analysis. *Frontiers in Psychology, 9.* https://doi.org.10.3389/fpsyg.2018.01034

Feeling Good Institute (n.d.). *Comprehensive Live Online CBT Training for therapist working with children and adolescents.* http://www.feelinggoodinstitute.com/comprehensive-12-week-course-cbt-with-children-and-adolescents-for-therapists

Gunlicks-Stoessel, M., Westervelt, A., Reigstad, K., Mufson, L., & Lee, S. (2019). The role of attachment style in interpersonal psychotherapy for depressed adolescents. *Psychotherapy Research, 29*(1), 78–85. https://doi.org.10.1080/10503307.2017.1315465

Interpersonal Therapy Institute (n.d.). *IPT training courses and consultation on-line and on-site.* https://iptinstitute.com

Klein, J. B., Jacobs, R. H., & Reinecke, M. A. (2007). Cognitive-behavioral therapy for adolescent depression: A meta-analytic investigation of changes in effect size estimates. *Journal of the American Academy of Child and Adolescent Psychiatry.* 46(11), 1403–1413. https://doi.org/10.1097/chi.0b013e3180592aaa.

Mufson, L., Dorta, K. P., Wickramaratne, P., Nomura, Y., Olfson, M., & Weissman, M. M. (2004). A randomized effectiveness clinic trial of interpersonal therapy for depression adolescents. *Archives of General Psychiatry, 61*(6), 577–584. https://o-doi.org.pacificatclassic.pacific.edu/10.1001/archpsyc.61.6.577

Reyes-Portillo, J. A., McGlinchey, E. L., Yanes-Lukin, P. K., Turner, J. B., & Mufson, L. (2017). Mediators of interpersonal psychotherapy for depressed adolescents on outcomes in Latinos: The role of peer and family interpersonal functioning. *Journal of Latina/o Psychology, 5*(4), 248–260. https://doi.org/10.1037/lat0000096

Weersing, V. R., Iyengar, S., Kolko, D. J., Birmaher, B., & Brent, D. A. (2006). Effectiveness of cognitive-behavioral therapy for adolescent depression: A benchmarking investigation. *Behavior Therapy, 37*(1), 36–48. https://doi.org/ 10.1016/j.beth.2005.03.003

APPENDIX C

Case Paper on Eddie

EBP Decision-Making: African American Man in Los Angeles

Introduction

The purpose of this paper is to identify and evaluate the usefulness and appropriateness of three different evidence-based practices (EBPs) for a therapy client using a decision-making model that considers research evidence, clinical expertise, and client characteristics, culture, and preferences. The client's profile, background, and treatment goals will be discussed, and then three EBPs will be reviewed, concluding with the rationale for the intervention with the best fit for the client and a proposed treatment plan using that EBP.

The client, whom I will call "Eddie," is a 39-year-old heterosexual African American male who lives in a single-room occupancy (SRO) apartment in a low-income, high-crime neighborhood in downtown Los Angeles. Eddie self-referred to Mission Community Clinic (MCC) to address his experiences of severe emotional dysregulation and explosive behaviors. MCC provides services to low income and homeless residents of Los Angeles. As a mental health intern at MCC, I conduct intakes, provide therapy under supervision, refer clients to the onsite case manager for housing referrals, and generally advocate for clients. The three EBPs that I will consider for Eddie are Prolonged Exposure Therapy (PET), Cognitive Processing Therapy (CPT), and Mindfulness-Based Cognitive Therapy (MBCT).

Client Profile

Social and Cultural Background

Eddie was born and raised in Columbia, Mississippi and moved to Los Angeles 6 months ago. Eddie suffered severe physical abuse by his mother and grew up in extreme poverty (e.g., his family lived for several years in a van when he was a child). When he was 9 years old, a worker raped him while he was admitted to a psychiatric hospital. Without a high school education, he worked in construction until he was severely injured on the job at age 22. Eddie holds dear to him and uses as his lens of the world the strong traditional Southern morals and values instilled by his physically abusive mother. He also maintains strong Southern cultural norms and mores from the region where he grew up. Eddie has four children and one grandchild, all residing in Mississippi. Currently, Eddie does not have the capacity to work due to his severe chronic pain and his sometimes debilitating mental health diagnoses. His chronic pain causes him to readily assert chronic suicidal ideation with no plan.

Developmental, Psychological, and Environmental Background

Eddie is diagnosed with Major Depressive Disorder (single episode, unspecified), Bipolar Disorder, Post-Traumatic Stress Disorder (chronic), and Intermittent Explosive Disorder (IED). Living in a new city, especially a high-crime, drug-use neighborhood, has exacerbated his various symptoms and behaviors. While these symptoms and behaviors were present before his move, he was more easily able to keep his emotions in check because he was not living in a congested urban area with neighbors on the other side of his walls. Eddie's difficulties with impulse control and behaving violently toward others led to two prison terms. Eddie copes by isolating and keeping himself out of harm's way when he is feeling agitated, for his own and others' safety and to avoid returning to prison. He is highly cognizant that he needs to avoid triggering situations. Eddie's early history, including extreme poverty, physical abuse, and rape, led to core beliefs of worthlessness and being unlovable, and to stronger and stronger anger over time as adulthood life stressors impacted him. Eddie's strengths include his overriding good insight and vigilance that have kept him out of jail for the last 5 years, his traditional Southern morals and values, and a strong focus on his children. Also, his children's mother's family maintain a positive view of Eddie, even though their mother does not, which allows him to build strong bonds with his children and provides him with a reason for living.

Client's Conceptualization

Problem Conceptualization

Eddie sought therapy at MCC to address his feelings of severe emotional dysregulation and explosive behaviors, especially in situations where he feels stressed and attacked. He also wants to address his use of video games and smoking cannabis as his sole coping strategies after recently relocating to an urban high-crime neighborhood from rural Mississippi. His goals are to address the negative symptoms of his PTSD by learning healthier and varied coping skills to feel less angry, to talk about his past traumas, and to continue to foster healthier relationships and strengthen the emotional bonds with his children and grandchild after being estranged for years. Eddie declared, "I want to enjoy my life." He is interested in exploring Los Angeles, increasing his social activities, and reducing his isolation in his small SRO. He is open to different types of therapies and activity groups.

Treatment Goals and Appropriate Forms of Treatment

Individual and group therapy and social groups would be appropriate types of intervention for achieving the following treatment goals defined with Eddie that support promoting his ability to regulate his emotions and behaviors in the short and long term:

a. Learn strategies for managing anxiety and regulating emotions and behaviors, such as practicing mindfulness and breathing exercises, visiting serene places, and avoiding potentially triggering situations like certain bus lines;

b. Learn healthy coping skills to replace smoking cannabis and playing video games;

c. Join and participate in community support networks that affirm him and promote his ability to manage anxiety and regulate emotions;

d. Increase social activities (see sf.freecheap.com), including leaving his tense neighborhood, visiting scenic areas of Los Angeles, creating new hobbies, and participating in the photography group therapy at MCC;

e. Increase positive social contacts with children and grandchild;

f. Process past life experiences with a therapist, especially processing traumas so he can view them in their proper place; and

g. Learn to challenge long-held negative core beliefs and assumptions that are maladaptive and no longer serve him.

Review of EBP #1: Prolonged Exposure Therapy

Description of Intervention

Prolonged Exposure Therapy (PET) is based on emotional processing theory (EPT; Foa & Kozak, 1986). According to EPT, it is the avoidance of processing the trauma memory and not the trauma memory itself that prevents the emotional processing of trauma and symptomatic relief from PTSD. EPT posits that two dysfunctional beliefs may be created: (a) the world is completely dangerous (e.g., "It is dangerous to be alone") and (b) one's self is totally incompetent (e.g., "I can't handle any stress" and "My PTSD symptoms mean that I am going crazy") (p. 62). Most PTSD survivors correct these mistaken beliefs through daily activities, but those who systematically avoid trauma-related thoughts and activities do not get the chance to challenge and correct these erroneous beliefs, leaving the trauma memory undisturbed. Due to systematic avoidance, the habituation achieved by challenging erroneous beliefs through repeated and prolonged exposure to traumatic events does not occur. In these cases, EPT asserts that effective psychological intervention is required to remedy the two inaccurate conclusions of the world—its overwhelming danger and the inability to cope with that danger (Foa, 2011).

Following the EPT hypothesis, PET involves systematic confrontation of the trauma memories by having patients repeatedly retell the trauma (Foa, 2011). PET consists of 10–12 90-minute sessions and four main modules: psychoeducation, breathing retraining, imaginal exposure, and in vivo exposure. The imaginal exposure component consists of repeating, reconsidering, and recounting the initial trauma aloud. The in vivo ("real life") component is repeated exposure to the trauma activators. These two activities are immediately followed by a discussion of the revisiting experience, known as the processing phase. By concurrently disconfirming the erroneous beliefs that underlie PTSD, the memory is restructured.

Identification & Justification of Level of Evidence

I reviewed two PET studies with grade B+ level of evidence. First, in a single-blind RCT, PET was compared with three other cognitive behavioral treatments in 118 civilian participants with chronic PTSD in Australia (Bryant et al., 2008). Treatment conditions consisted of 8 weeks of imaginal exposure (IE), in vivo exposure (IVE), combined IE/IVE, or IE/IVE with cognitive restructuring (i.e., PET). The sample consisted of White (92%) and Asian (8%) males and females. Findings included fewer patients with PTSD (31%) in the PET group at 6-month follow-up than the other groups (63%–75%). Those in the PET condition also had lower PTSD and depressive symptoms after treatment (Bryant et al., 2008). This is a B+ study given the high dropout rate (24%), blinding of only outcome assessors to participants' treatment conditions, and not being a multisite study (Rich, 2005).

Second, a double-blind RCT with 200 patients with PTSD recruited via outpatient clinics, including rape crisis centers in Seattle and Cleveland; private providers; and public media ads detected no differential effect of 10-week PET versus medication (sertraline) on interviewer-rated loss of PTSD diagnosis and self-reported PTSD, depression, and anxiety symptoms and functioning (Zoellner et al., 2019). Also, participants given their treatment of choice showed stronger symptom improvements. This is a B+ and not an A study, because although the sample was greater than 100 participants, there was an extremely high dropout rate (34%), and it was not a multisite study (Rich, 2005).

Populations Studied & Evaluation of Applicability to My Client

The first RCT (Bryant et al., 2008) is applicable to Eddie in that he is a civilian and suffered sexual trauma (rape), even though the Australian sample did not include Eddie's racial/ethnic group. Another concern about the generalizability of findings to Eddie is that those who dropped out of treatment had significantly higher baseline PTSD scores than those who completed treatment. Eddie has more severe PTSD. The second RCT (Zoellner et al., 2019) has some generalizability to Eddie, given that its sample included African Americans (21.5%), male participants (24.5%), and rape victims. After reviewing the literature beyond these two studies, however, most PET male RCT subject populations are normally veterans who have PTSD symptoms as a result of their time served in the military as adults (and not from childhood abuse and rape). Also, the knowledge base of PET with African American trauma clients, including how to treat race-based trauma, is small and uncertain, given that a systematic review included only 38 RCTS with small numbers of African Americans in their samples (Benuto et al., 2020).

Evaluation of Experts

A licensed clinical social worker (LCSW) at the Veterans Administration (VA) with whom I consulted supports using PET because my client has shown the desire to use modalities that are more experiential than intellectual or cognitive in approach. This clinician has been using PET with clients with PTSD for many years. The clinician also recommends that PET may be a good therapy alongside Cognitive Behavioral Therapy (CBT) so that the client can have a safe space to face and process his traumas directly but in a moderated fashion, at a pace that the client is able to handle without it being the sole focus of his therapy, given that exposure alone can be daunting and lead to dropout (J. Worth, personal communication, January 4, 2020).

Feasibility of Learning and Applying Intervention Correctly

PET is offered at the VA as a regular part of their PTSD treatment offerings. The client is not a veteran, but my field instructor (FI) is trained in PET. It is important to note that whether or not PET is ultimately chosen, a culturally-sensitive approach by a licensed therapist that is well-informed on race-based trauma (as well as PET) will provide the best possibilities of success (Williams et al., 2014). Overall, the feasibility of learning and applying this intervention effectively is high by a licensed therapist. I am not a licensed therapist, but my supervisor is well-versed in PET and may let me shadow him in PET sessions with the client's permission. My internship time at MCC is limited, with 3 months remaining, so instead of patient-splitting, I will transition this client to my supervisor sooner rather than later, especially if PET is chosen.

Review of EBP #2: Cognitive Processing Therapy for PTSD

Description of Intervention

Cognitive Processing Therapy (CPT), developed to treat PTSD for rape, is a recognized EBP including for individuals with cooccurring conditions and personality disorders (National Center for PTSD, U.S. Department of Veterans Affairs, n.d.). It is a type of CBT, and like PET, it is based on an information-processing formulation of PTSD that emphasizes how information is encoded, stored in memory, and recalled. It differs from traditional cognitive therapy, however, in that rape is not assumed to elicit already existing distorted and dysfunctional thinking patterns or danger schemata (Resick & Schnicke, 1992). Instead, the PTSD symptoms of intrusion, avoidance, and arousal are viewed as being caused by conflicts, called "stuck points" between the new information from the rape and prior schemata on self-esteem, competence, or intimacy, which have impeded recovery. CPT also considers negative conflicting schemata imposed by others (e.g., blaming of the victim), avoidant coping styles, and cases where the rape is outside of the person's experiences and beliefs altogether. CPT, like PET and unlike traditional cognitive theory, also encourages the expression of emotions, including the overwhelming ones that tend to be avoided after trauma.

CPT consists of twelve 1.5-hour sessions and has four parts: 1) educating the client about PTSD and how CPT treatment works; 2) becoming aware of thoughts and feelings associated with the trauma; 3) learning cognitive skills to challenge false interpretations and feelings (i.e., cognitive restructuring); and 4) focusing on thoughts and feelings about oneself, others, and the world, and then focusing on the areas of safety, trust, power and control, self-esteem, and future intimacy goals (Paunovic, 2001). Cognitive restructuring occurs through Socratic questioning. Using worksheets when stuck points arise, clients ask themselves challenge questions: 1) "Is there evidence for the stuck point?"; 2) "Is there evidence against the stuck point?"; and 3) "Is the stuck point not including all the information?" Finally, the client creates a new belief by answering, "What can I tell myself in the future?" The mechanics of CPT involve writing and analyzing narratives to change faulty thinking patterns (Resick & Schnicke, 1992).

Identification & Justification of Level of Evidence

I reviewed two CPT studies with grade B level of evidence. First, a quasi-experimental study of sexual assault survivors, with 19 who received a 12-session group CPT intervention, compared with 20 who remained on a wait list and received no treatment, showed that CPT participants improved significantly from pre- to posttreatment on PTSD and depression instruments and maintained their gains for 6 months (Resick & Schnicke, 1992). This is a B study, given that it is a pre-post quasi-experimental study with a small sample, using a (nonrandomized) comparison group and with small (10%) dropout (Rich, 2005). Second, an RCT of 71 female childhood sexual abuse survivors randomly assigned to CPT adapted for rape victims (involving 17 weeks of manual-based group and individual therapy) versus minimal attention (i.e., no treatment) given to a wait-listed control group found CPT to significantly lower PTSD, depression, and dissociation scores (Chard et al., 2005). This is a B rather than A study, even though it is an RCT, due to the small sample size (under 100) and high dropout rate of 18% in the treatment group. It could be considered B+ evidence, since it is an RCT (i.e., experimental) rather than quasi-experimental. (In my view, the strength of the evidence in both studies is weakened because CPT was compared with no treatment. A stronger design would be to compare with no treatment and another treatment.)

Populations Studied & Evaluation of Applicability to My Client

The sample in Resick and Schnicke's (1992) study matched my client's characteristics very partially. Participants were younger (mean age of 30.6 years) and more educated (mean of 14.3 years) than my client. Participants in the intervention and comparison groups were all women and mostly White, with only two African American women in each group. They had experienced 1–3 rapes by strangers and non-strangers, with a mean length of 6.4 years since the last rape, and had no severe competing pathology, which is unlike my client's history and concurrent depression and IED. Like my client, however, they reported significant PTSD symptomatology and were individuals recruited from the community.

The sample in Chard et al.'s (2005) study is relevant to my client, given that participants had experienced multiple traumas. However, even though African Americans (14%) were included, participants were all women and majority

White (81%). After reviewing the literature, little research exists for CPT for black male sexual abuse survivors, but the treatment appears to have strong evidence of effectiveness applicable to his severe PTSD and depressive symptoms related to his childhood physical abuse and rape.

Evaluation of Experts

When I consulted with my supervisor at MCC, he advised that both PET and CPT would be helpful treatment interventions for trauma. However, given that Eddie's preferences for facing his fears head-on (experientially, rather than through writing) and lower education level, he recommended PET for Eddie. Also, PET is more appropriate, given that my supervisor is well-versed in PET and much less so CPT, as provider expertise and familiarity is a major factor when considering which intervention choice can be made available to a client (R. Wheeler, personal communication, January 15, 2020).

Feasibility of Learning and Applying Intervention Correctly

Feasibility for using CPT with this client is fair, though less so at this point than PET. CPT is a commonly used intervention at the VA, but the client is not a veteran and does not have access to these services. I have some background for learning CPT given my recent 8-week academic course on CBT for depression. Additionally, the CPT manual is freely available online (Resick et al., 2008). However, I am not currently trained with CPT and so would not feel comfortable applying it myself presently. Once trained, I would need close supervision in applying CPT. I will seek out opportunities to learn it in-house from the training development lead and clinicians at our sister organization. Once I am trained and a supervisor with expertise in CPT is available, I could reconsider using CPT with Eddie.

Review of EBP #3: Mindfulness-Based Cognitive Therapy

Description of Intervention

Mindfulness-Based Cognitive Therapy (MBCT) is a 2- to 2.5-hour-per-week eight-session manualized psychoeducational and group skills-training program that integrates mindfulness into the treatment of depression (Segal et al., 2013). It is a recognized EBP with grade A evidence for depression relapse, according to systematic reviews and meta-analyses (Galante et al., 2013; Lenz et al., 2016). The research of its efficacy for decreasing chronic pain (de Jong et al., 2016) and dealing with emotional reactivity (Britton et al., 2012) and IED (Osma & Crespo, 2016) are relatively newer. I review MBCT in these areas rather than for depression alone to explore MBCT's efficacy in areas of relevance to Eddie. There is some low-quality evidence that mindfulness meditation is associated with small decreases in pain (Hilton et al., 2017) and incipient evidence of the efficacy of MCBT for treating IED (e.g., Osma & Crespo, 2016).

For the treatment of chronic pain and depression, the MBCT framework considers body awareness as playing an important role in the experience of emotions (de Jong et al., 2016). MBCT views increased body (or interoceptive) awareness as leading to reduced depression and views attention styles toward chronic pain sensations as key to managing pain psychologically. Individuals experiencing depression have lower body awareness, and the ability to accurately perceive one's bodily functions is related to the intensity of emotions. MBCT trains patients in body awareness, as well as awareness of thoughts and emotions. MBCT adapted for chronic pain and depression includes psychoeducation linking chronic pain, negative thoughts and emotions, and depressive behaviors (e.g., withdrawal), along with meditations focused on mindfulness of chronic pain experiences.

For the treatment of emotional regulation, MBCT aims to decrease emotional reactivity when the individual is confronted by stressors that produce negative affect so that a depressive episode is avoided (Britton et al., 2012). Life stress is viewed as leading to negative affect, which activates negative thinking patterns, which in turn escalates negative affect—in a cycle that leads to a depressive episode. MBCT for emotional reactivity is based on increased vulnerability to depression and depression becoming an autonomous process as the individual experiences more and more episodes of depression, such that lower levels of external stress are needed to trigger future depressive episodes (Britton et al., 2012). This is due to cognitive reactivity, which is negative information-processing biases in response to negative emotions. Biologically, the prefrontal cortex is not modulating the limbic system sufficiently, leading to prolonged activation of the amygdala and sympathetic nervous system in response to stressors. MBCT fosters a nonjudgmental attitude toward one's internal and external experiences.

Identification & Justification of Level of Evidence

I reviewed two MBCT studies with grade B level of evidence. First, de Jong et al.'s (2016) RCT of 31 patients with persistent chronic pain and active depression recruited from outpatient clinics, in an 8-week group intervention (with 2 hours of mindfulness practice and homework activities per week), showed significant increases in body awareness in the areas of self-regulation and not distancing and significant decreases in depression severity in the MBCT group compared with the treatment as usual (TAU) group. This is a B study due to the small sample size (less than 100), blinding only in the person who generated the random assignment, and very large dropout rates (20% of those screened to enter the study and 27% of those in the MBCT treatment group).

Second, Britton et al.'s (2012) RCT of 52 participants with unipolar depression, in partial or full remission with varying degrees of residual symptoms, in an 8-week MBCT course, found that intervention-group participants had decreased emotional reactivity to social stress in the post-stressor phase of a laboratory-based social stress test, compared with waitlist controls. Waitlist controls also showed an increase in prestressor anxiety, which the MBCT participants did not experience. Improvements in emotional reactivity were also associated with improvements in depressive symptoms. This is a B (perhaps B+, but not an A study, although it is an RCT) study given its sample size of less than 100, having only outcome assessors blinded to participants' group assignments, and moderate dropout rates greater than 15% (22% of those enrolled dropped out before randomization, although only 10% dropped out in the MBCT group).

Populations Studied & Evaluation of Applicability to My Client

De Jong et al.'s (2016) study has relevance to my client's problem area of chronic pain and its possible linkage with his chronic depression. However, the generalizability of their findings to my client is questionable, given that only three of 31 participants were African American, and participants were much older (mean age of 50 years), more educated (mean of 16.3 years), and mostly female (74%). However, the study included individuals with multiple types of chronic pain and disability status (38% of sample), which is more inclusive of my client's characteristics.

Britton et al.'s (2012) study has little direct relevance to my client's IED and its social triggers. This study did not target individuals with IED, but rather individuals with depression-facing emotional reactivity. The laboratory-based social distress test was a public speaking activity where the participant faced a judge sitting next to the participant and other viewers behind a one-way mirror. This experimental condition is far from the types of stressors faced by Eddie (e.g., danger triggers in his living environment). The MBCT sample (mean age of 47 years, 79% female, mean depression length of 5 years) did not share my client's characteristics, and there was no report of the sample's racial/ethnic diversity.

Evaluation of Experts

I consulted with a clinical social worker in our sister organization with expertise in MBCT and working with African Americans with childhood trauma, emotional regulation difficulties, and previous incarcerations. With consideration of Eddie's goals and preferences, she recommended that MBCT be the first-stage intervention, given his immediate need of stabilization in a new, stressful, and triggering living environment. MBCT will support Eddie in building a sense of control in this environment. Cognitive processing should focus first on non-trauma-related needs (e.g., coping with the noise next door and people's disturbances). Mindfulness skills will support cognitive processing and the ability to self-soothe. She emphasized that, along with therapeutic needs, Eddie needs foremost to be connected with a community where he will be affirmed and receive support for keeping emotionally regulated (e.g., joining the local antirecidivism network). She emphasized support groups, recreational groups, and engagement in joyful activities. Case management is also needed to move him out of the SRO to a housing community that supports his short- and long-term goals, affirms his strengths, and provides opportunity for his contribution to the community. Only when there is stability in his living situation and an established therapeutic alliance with a longer term therapist (not an intern about to leave) should trauma-processing therapies like PET or CPT be considered. The client needs first to be in control of his story and be able to deal with the daily struggles involving disturbances by others. Also, the decision to engage in trauma-processing should consider whether Eddie has been a collaborator in long-term therapy and trauma-focused processing before. A final piece of advice was to consider Acceptance and Commitment Therapy, related to CBT (M. Lewis, personal communication, January 30, 2020).

Feasibility of Learning and Applying Intervention Correctly

Given my 8-week academic course in CBT, my own regular practice of and training in mindfulness for over 10 years individually and in group settings, the availability of a free 25-hour online MBCT course (Universiteit Leiden, n.d.), and the availability of the clinical social worker with whom I consulted to provide support along with my supervisor, it is feasible that I can learn and provide the intervention with a fair level of fidelity. There are also numerous books on MBCT (Crane, 2017; Segal et al., 2013) for self-training.

Best Interviention

Best Intervention and Rationale

The best intervention for Eddie in the first stage of intervention is MBCT to assist with treatment goals related to stabilization in his new living situation. PET for trauma-processing may be suited for Eddie in the future after he has achieved stabilization. I will provide my rationale for this choice based on three components of decision-making—best evidence, clinical expertise, and client characteristics, culture, and preferences.

Regarding the best available evidence, MBCT followed by PET has the best (grade A) evidence, according to systematic reviews and meta-analyses, and PET and CPT are interventions considered to have high efficacy and are in use by the U.S. Department of Veterans Affairs (Laska, et al., 2013). I reviewed B+ PET and B MBCT studies. From an internal validity perspective, all three interventions have a fair amount of credible evidence of effectiveness and situate high in the hierarchy of evidence. However, from an external validity perspective, the generalizability of findings to my client is low. PET appears suited for more severe PTSD, and the available evidence is for veterans with combat trauma. CPT is suited for childhood sexual assault and rape victims, including for severe PTSD, but it has been studied largely with women only. As for MBCT, efficacity for chronic pain and IED is not established. Finally, the samples across studies did not include many participants with Eddie's background, including race, culture, SES, age, health and mental health complexity, and high-crime urban living. Additionally, the high treatment dropout rates in all the studies are not reassuring, even when those who dropped out are reported as being similar to those who completed treatment. In conclusion, I have strong concerns about the relevance of the available evidence to Eddie's situation.

My rationale for choosing MBCT and PET is based on clinical expertise, through consultations with experts, and Eddie's goals, preferences, and context. The experts evaluated MBCT as the first-stage treatment, with PET being provided and applied cautiously at a later stage. MBCT would support the immediate goal of his stabilization in his new living situation, with concurrent case management activities to link him into a community network and more appropriate longer term housing. Also, these experts and I concluded that it would be feasible to provide MBCT and PET, by me and my supervisor, respectively. As an MSW intern, I would self-study MBCT and receive close supervision as I work with Eddie.

With regard to the fit of these interventions to Eddie's characteristics, culture, and preferences, along with his treatment goals, MBCT in the short term and PET in the medium term fit well. MBCT fits his short-term goals and suits his cognitive insightfulness. PET suits his interest in cognitive approaches and goal of processing his traumas experientially through imaginal and real-life exposure to relieve the trauma memory. CPT was ruled out for Eddie, given its heavy use of writing and Eddie's preference for experiential learning. My focus on reviewing cognitive behavioral interventions was based on Eddie having all the ingredients necessary for success with such an approach. He can talk about his deeply held negative beliefs about himself and views of others in the safe confines of the therapeutic relationship. And he wants to become more current- and future-oriented, as evidenced by his strongly stated desire, "I want to enjoy my life."

MBCT and PET, together with a strong case management plan, appear to be the best intervention options for this client. Eddie has expressed a strong desire to face his demons, to see them in a different light—no longer whiling away the hours playing violent video games and smoking cannabis to isolate himself from others and from the deep social connection for which he yearns. He wants to be part of society and has a zest for experiencing life, rather than intellectualizing or writing about it. Lastly and most importantly, I talked to Eddie and got his feedback on which treatment sounds like something he would like to pursue. The key for any intervention to be successful is the client's willingness and commitment to be engaged and motivated. The client was the ultimate decider and wanted to give MBCT and PET a try.

Evidence-Based Treatment Plan

MBCT will be the first stage treatment, for 8–10 weeks. MBCT will support the goal of stabilization in the new living situation, with concurrent case management activities to link Eddie to community support. Outcomes will be measured by decreases in emotional reactivity; decreases in negative coping, such as cannabis and video games; increases in enjoyable activities increases in social contacts with children and grandchild; and successful adoption of cognitive coping techniques. Eddie will self-rate each day as part of cognitive behavioral homework exercises. He will also complete a depression screen at the start of each session with me. During weeks 8–12, I will begin termination and transfer Eddie to my field instructor.

I will provide MBCT to Eddie for the next 2.5 months, focusing on stabilization in his living environment and regulating emotions and behaviors, while the case manager and I provide linkage to social and community support and longer term housing. Eddie will learn mindfulness, breathing techniques, and cognitive coping methods to help him manage anxiety related to his living environment.

My client will start to see my field instructor (FI), a LCSW competent in PET, for 3–4 months of weekly PET therapy after I leave. Eddie's progress with MBCT will be monitored weekly based on reduction in cannabis use and video games, increase in use of healthy coping methods, increase in social and pleasurable activities, and decrease in intensity of negative emotional reactions to environmental disturbances.

a. Learn strategies for managing anxiety and regulating emotions and behaviors, such as practicing mindfulness and breathing exercises, visiting serene places, and avoiding potentially triggering situations like certain bus lines;

b. Learn healthy coping skills to replace smoking cannabis and playing video games;

c. Join and participate in community support networks that affirm him and promote his ability to manage anxiety and regulate emotions;

d. Increase social activities including leaving his tense neighborhood, visiting scenic areas of Los Angeles, creating new hobbies, and participating in the photography group therapy at MCC;

e. Increase positive social contacts with children and grandchild;

f. Process past life experiences with a therapist, especially processing traumas so he can view them in their proper place; and

g. Learn to challenge long-held negative core beliefs and assumptions that are maladaptive and no longer serve him.

My FI will start by giving the client an overview of PET treatment and learn about his past therapy experiences to evaluate the suitability and intensity of PET to provide. My FI will work with him to make a list of people, places, and/or activities that he specifically avoids in order to restructure his cognitive interpretation of danger and sense of competence. Gradually, the client will confront and feel more comfortable with these situations, and when appropriate, the client will also begin to process through the details of his trauma (Rauch, et al., 2012). It is my hope that in confronting the details of the trauma using PET, the client will begin to have less of the unwanted memories than before therapy. The client has frequently articulated, "I can't change the past. I want to enjoy my life." If my FI assesses that Eddie is not ready to use PET, another intervention will be considered to help Eddie realize his goals. If PET is used, Eddie's progress with will be monitored by PTSD and depression symptom levels and weakened impact of long-held negative core beliefs.

References

Benuto, L. T., Bennett, N. M., & Casas, J. B. (2020). Minority participation in randomized controlled trials for prolonged exposure therapy: A systematic review of the literature. *Journal of Traumatic Stress, 33*(1). https://doi.org/10.1002/jts.22539

Britton, W. B., Shahar, B., Szepsenwol, O., Jacobs, W. J., Britton, W. B., Shahar, B., Szepsenwol, O., & Jacobs, W. J. (2012). Mindfulness-based cognitive therapy improves emotional reactivity to social stress: results from a randomized controlled trial. *Behavior Therapy, 43*(2), 365–380. https://doi.org/10.1016/j.beth.2011.08.006

Bryant, R. A., Moulds, M. L., Guthrie, R. M., Dang, S. T., Mastrodomenico, J., Nixon, R. D. V, Felmingham, K. L., Hopwood, S., & Creamer, M. (2008). A randomized controlled trial of exposure therapy and cognitive restructuring for posttraumatic stress disorder. *Journal of Consulting and Clinical Psychology, 76*(4), 695–703. http://doi.org/10.1037/a0012616

Chard, K. M. (2005). An evaluation of cognitive processing therapy for the treatment of posttraumatic stress disorder related to childhood sexual abuse. *Journal of Consulting and Clinical Psychology, 73*(5), 965–971.

Crane, R. (2017). *Mind-based Cognitive Therapy: Distinctive features (CBT distinctive features)* (2nd ed.). Routledge.

de Jong, M., Lazar, S. W., Hug, K., Mehling, W. E., Hölzel, B. K., Sack, A. T., Peeters, F., Ashih, H., Mischoulon, D., & Gard, T. (2016). Effects of mindfulness-based cognitive therapy on body awareness in patients with chronic pain and comorbid depression. *Frontiers in Psychology, 7*, 967.

Foa, E. (2011). Prolonged exposure therapy: past, present, and future. *Depression and Anxiety, 28*(12), 1043–1047. http://doi.org/10.1002/da.20907

Foa, E., & Kozak, M. (1986). Emotional processing of fear: exposure to corrective information. *Psychological Bulletin, 99*(1), 20–35. http://doi.org/10.1037/0033-2909.99.1.20

Galante, J., Iribarren, S. J., & Pearce, P. F. (2013). Effects of mindfulness-based cognitive therapy on mental disorders: a systematic review and meta-analysis of randomised controlled trials. *Journal of Research in Nursing, 18*(2), 133–155. https://doi.org/10.1177/1744987112466087

Hilton, L., Hempel, S., Ewing, B. A., Apaydin, E., Xenakis, L., Newberry, S., Colaiaco, B., Maher, A. R., Shanman, R. M., Sorbero, M. E., & Maglione, M. A. (2017). Mindfulness meditation for chronic pain: Systematic review and meta-analysis. *Annals of Behavioral Medicine, 51*(2), 199–213. https://doi.org/10.1007/s12160-016-9844-2

Laska, K. M., Smith, T. L., Wislocki, A. P., Minami, T., & Wampold, B. E. (2013). Uniformity of evidence-based treatments in practice? Therapist effects in the delivery of cognitive processing therapy for PTSD. *Journal of Counseling Psychology, 60*(1), 31–41. http://doi.org/10.1037/a0031294

Lenz, A. S., Hall, J., & Bailey Smith, L. (2016). Meta-analysis of group Mindfulness-Based Cognitive Therapy for decreasing symptoms of acute depression. *Journal for Specialists in Group Work, 41*(1), 44–70. https://doi.org/10.1080/01933922.2015.1111488

National Center for PTSD. (n.d.). *Cognitive Processing Therapy for PTSD.* U.S. Department of Veterans Affairs. https://www.ptsd.va.gov/understand_tx/cognitive_processing.asp

Osma, J., & Crespo, E. (2016). Multicomponent cognitive-behavioral therapy for intermittent explosive disorder by videoconferencing: a case study. *Anales de Psicología, 32*(2), 424–432. http://doi.org/10.6018/analesps.32.2.211351

Paunovic, N. (2001). Cognitive-behavior therapy vs exposure therapy in the treatment of PTSD in refugees. *Behaviour Research and Therapy, 39*(10), 1183–1197. http://doi.org/10.1016/S0005-7967(00)00093-0

Rauch, S. a. M., Eftekhari, A., & Ruzek, J. I. (2012). Review of exposure therapy: A gold standard for PTSD treatment. *The Journal of Rehabilitation Research and Development, 49*(5), 679. http://doi.org/10.1682/JRRD.2011.08.0152

Resick, P. A., Monson, C. M., & Chard, K. M. (2008). *Cognitive processing therapy veteran/military version: Therapist's manual.* Department of Veterans' Affairs.

Resick, P. A., & Schnicke, M. K. (1992). Cognitive processing therapy for sexual assault victims. *Journal of Consulting and Clinical Psychology, 60*(5), 748–756. http://doi.org/10.1037/0022-006X.60.5.748

Rich, N. C. (2005). Levels of evidence. *Women's Health Physical Therapy, 29*(2), 19–20. https://doi.org/10.1097/01274882-200529020-00005

Segal, Z.V., Williams, J. M.G., & Teasdale, J.D. (2013). *Mindfulness-based Cognitive Therapy for depression* (2nd ed.). Guilford Press.

Universiteit Leiden (n.d.). *Mindfulness-based cognitive therapy: De-Mystifying Mindfulness.* https://www.coursera.org/lecture/mindfulness/mindfulness-based-cognitive-therapy-CEuxs.

Williams, M., Malcoun, E., Sawyer, B., Davis, D., Nouri, L., & Bruce, S. (2014). Cultural adaptations of prolonged exposure therapy for treatment and prevention of posttraumatic stress disorder in African Americans. *Behavioral Sciences, 4*(2), 102–124. http://doi.org/10.3390/bs4020102

Zoellner, L. A., Roy-Byrne, P. P., Mavissakalian, M., & Feeny, N. C. (2019). Doubly randomized preference trial of prolonged exposure versus sertraline for treatment of PTSD. *The American Journal of Psychiatry, 176*(4), 287–296. https://doi.org/10.1176/appi.ajp.2018.17090995

Index

CPSIA information can be obtained
at www.ICGtesting.com
Printed in the USA
BVHW010244070222
628280BV00007B/362